MW00398903

# *Toxic Relationships*
## Abuse and Its Aftermath

*4ᵗʰ EDITION*

## Sam Vaknin, Ph.D.
The Author is NOT a Mental Health Professional.
The Author is certified in Counselling Techniques by Brainbench.

Editing and Design:
**Lidija Rangelovska**

*A Narcissus Publications Imprint*
*Prague & Skopje 2007*

To get FREE updates of this book JOIN the Narcissism Study List.
To JOIN, visit our Web sites:
http://www.geocities.com/vaksam/narclist.html or
http://www.narcissistic-abuse.com/narclist.html or
http://groups.yahoo.com/group/narcissisticabuse

Visit the Author's Web site:

http://samvak.tripod.com

Narcissistic Personality Disorder Suite 101 Topic:
http://www.suite101.com/welcome.cfm/npd

The Suite 101 Emotional and Verbal Abuse Web Site:
http://www.suite101.com/welcome.cfm/verbal_emotional_abuse

Spousal Abuse and Domestic Violence on Suite 101:
http://www.suite101.com/welcome.cfm/spousal_domestic_abuse


Buy other books about pathological narcissism and relationships with abusive narcissists here:

http://www.narcissistic-abuse.com/thebook.html

Or click HERE for additional information!


Created by:

Lidija Rangelovska, Skopje
REPUBLIC OF MACEDONIA

# C O N T E N T S

## Case Studies

## The Narcissistic Personality Disorder (NPD) Catechism

## The Author

**Online index**

Go here: http://samvak.tripod.com/siteindex.html

# *Toxic Relationships*

## Abuse and Its Aftermath

**Verbal and Emotional Abuse**

# What is Abuse?

Violence in the family often follows other forms of more subtle and long-term abuse: verbal, emotional, psychological sexual, or financial.

It is closely correlated with alcoholism, drug consumption, intimate-partner homicide, teen pregnancy, infant and child mortality, spontaneous abortion, reckless behaviours, suicide, and the onset of mental health disorders.

Most abusers and batterers are males – but a significant minority are women. This being a 'Women's Issue', the problem was swept under the carpet for generations and only recently has it come to public awareness. Yet, even today, society – for instance, through the court and the mental health systems – largely ignores domestic violence and abuse in the family. This induces feelings of shame and guilt in the victims and 'legitimizes' the role of the abuser.

Violence in the family is mostly spousal – one spouse beating, raping, or otherwise physically harming and torturing the other. But children are also and often victims – either directly, or indirectly. Other vulnerable familial groups include the elderly and the disabled.

Abuse and violence cross geographical and cultural boundaries and social and economic strata. It is common among the rich and the poor, the well-educated and the less so, the young and the middle-aged, city dwellers and rural folk. It is a universal phenomenon.

The marked reduction in domestic violence in the last decade and the fact that different societies and cultures have widely disparate rates of intimate partner abuse – give the lie to the assumption that abusive conduct is the inevitable outcome of mental illness. Though the offenders' mental problems do play their part – it would seem that cultural, social, and even historical factors are the determinants of spousal abuse and domestic violence.

Contrary to common opinion, there has been a marked decline in domestic violence in the last decade. Moreover, rates of domestic violence and intimate partner abuse in various societies and cultures – vary widely. It is, therefore, safe to conclude that abusive conduct is not inevitable and is only loosely connected to the prevalence of mental illness (which is stable across ethnic, social, cultural, national, and economic barriers).

There is no denying that the mental problems of some offenders do play a part – but it is smaller than we intuit. Cultural, social, and even historical factors are the decisive determinants of spousal abuse and domestic violence.

### *The United States*

The National Crime Victimization Survey (NCVS) reported 691,710 nonfatal violent victimizations committed by current or former spouses, boyfriends, or girlfriends of the victims during 2001. About 588,490, or 85% of intimate partner violence incidents, involved women. The offender in one fifth of the totality of crimes committed against women was an intimate partner – compared to only 3% of crimes committed against men.

Still, this type of offences against women declined by half between 1993 (1.1 million nonfatal cases) and 2001 (588,490) – from 9.8 to 5 per thousand women. Intimate partner violence against men also declined from 162,870 (1993) to 103,220 (2001) – from 1.6 to 0.9 per 1000 males. Overall, the incidence of such crimes dropped from 5.8 to 3.0 per thousand.

Even so, the price in lost lives was and remains high.

In the year 2000, 1247 women and 440 men were murdered by an intimate partner in the United States – compared to 1357 men and 1600 women in 1976 and around 1300 women in 1993.

This reveals an interesting and worrying trend:

The number overall intimate partner offences against women declined sharply – but not so the number of fatal incidents. These remained more or less the same since 1993!

The cumulative figures are even more chilling:

One in four to one in three women have been assaulted or raped at a given point in her lifetime [Commonwealth Fund survey, 1998].

The Mental Health Journal says:

*"The precise incidence of domestic violence in America is difficult to determine for several reasons: it often goes unreported, even on surveys; there is no nationwide organization that gathers information from local police departments about the*

*number of substantiated reports and calls; and there is disagreement about what should be included in the definition of domestic violence."*

Using a different methodology (counting separately multiple incidents perpetrated on the same woman), a report titled "Extent, Nature and Consequences of Intimate Partner Violence: Findings from the National Violence Against Women Survey", compiled by Patricia Tjaden and Nancy Thoennes for the National Institute of Justice and the Centres for Disease Control and published in 1998, came up with a figure of 5.9 million physical assaults against 1.5 million targets in the USA annually.

According to the Washington State Domestic Violence Fatality Review Project, and Neil Websdale, Understanding Domestic Homicide, Northeastern University Press, 1999 – women in the process of separation or divorce were the targets of half of all intimate partner violent crimes. In Florida the figure is even higher (60%).

Hospital staff are ill-equipped and ill-trained to deal with this pandemic. Only 4% of hospital emergency room admissions of women in the United States were put down to domestic violence. The true figure, according to the FBI, is more like 50%.

Michael R. Rand in "Violence-related Injuries Treated in Hospital Emergency Departments", published by the U.S. Department of Justice, Bureau of Justice Statistics, August 1997 pegs the real number at 37%. Spouses and ex-husbands were responsible for one in three murdered women in the USA.

Two million spouses (mostly women) are threatened with a deadly weapon annually, according to the US Department of Justice. One half of all American homes are affected by domestic violence at least once a year.

And the violence spills over.

One half of wife-batterers also regularly assault and abuse their children, according to M. Straus, R. Gelles, and C. Smith, "Physical Violence in American Families: Risk Factors and Adaptations to Violence in 8,145 Families, 1990" and U.S. Advisory Board on Child Abuse and Neglect, A Nation's Shame: Fatal child abuse and neglect in the United States: Fifth report, Department of Health and Human Services, Administration for Children and Families, 1995.

*"Black females experienced domestic violence at a rate 35% higher than that of white females, and about 22 times the rate of women of other races. Black males experienced domestic violence*

*at a rate about 62% higher than that of white males and about 22 times the rate of men of other races."*

[Rennison, M. and W. Welchans. Intimate Partner Violence. U.S. Department of Justice, Office of Justice Programs, Bureau of Justice Statistics. May 2000, NCJ 178247, Revised 7/14/00]

The young, the poor, minorities, divorced, separated, and singles were most likely to experience domestic violence and abuse.

[Adapted from the "Family Violence" entry I wrote for the Open Site Encyclopaedia]

Abusers exploit, lie, insult, demean, ignore (the "silent treatment"), manipulate, and control.

There are many ways to abuse. To love too much is to abuse. It is tantamount to treating someone as an extension, an object, or an instrument of gratification. To be over-protective, not to respect privacy, to be brutally honest, with a sadistic sense of humour, or consistently tactless – is to abuse.

To expect too much, to denigrate, to ignore – are all modes of abuse. There is physical abuse, verbal abuse, psychological abuse, sexual abuse. The list is long. Most abusers abuse surreptitiously. They are "stealth abusers". You have to actually live with one in order to witness the abuse.

There are three important categories of abuse:

1. *Overt Abuse* – The open and explicit abuse of another person. Threatening, coercing, beating, lying, berating, demeaning, chastising, insulting, humiliating, exploiting, ignoring ("silent treatment"), devaluing, unceremoniously discarding, verbal abuse, physical abuse and sexual abuse are all forms of overt abuse.

2. *Covert or Controlling Abuse* – Abuse is almost entirely about control. It is often a primitive and immature reaction to life circumstances in which the abuser (usually in his childhood) was rendered helpless. It is about re-exerting one's identity, re-establishing predictability, mastering the environment – human and physical.

3. The bulk of abusive behaviours can be traced to this panicky reaction to the remote potential for loss of control. Many abusers are hypochondriacs (and difficult patients) because they are afraid to lose control over their body, its looks and its proper functioning. They are obsessive-compulsive in an effort to subdue their physical habitat and render it

foreseeable. They stalk people and harass them as a means of "being in touch" – another form of control.

To the abuser, nothing exists outside himself. Meaningful others are extensions, internal, assimilated, objects – not external ones. Thus, losing control over a significant other – is equivalent to losing control of a limb, or of one's brain. It is terrifying.

Independent or disobedient people evoke in the abuser the realization that something is wrong with his worldview, that he is not the centre of the world or its cause and that he cannot control what, to him, are internal representations.

To the abuser, losing control means going insane. Because other people are mere elements in the abuser's mind – being unable to manipulate them literally means losing it (his mind). Imagine, if you suddenly were to find out that you cannot manipulate your memories or control your thoughts... Nightmarish!

In his frantic efforts to maintain control or re-assert it, the abuser resorts to a myriad of fiendishly inventive stratagems and mechanisms. Here is a partial list:

### Unpredictability and Uncertainty

The abuser acts unpredictably, capriciously, inconsistently and irrationally. This serves to render others dependent upon the next twist and turn of the abuser, his next inexplicable whim, upon his next outburst, denial, or smile.

The abuser makes sure that HE is the only reliable element in the lives of his nearest and dearest – by shattering the rest of their world through his seemingly insane behaviour. He perpetuates his stable presence in their lives – by destabilizing their own.

TIP

Refuse to accept such behaviour. Demand reasonably predictable and rational actions and reactions. Insist on respect for your boundaries, predilections, preferences, and priorities.

### Disproportional Reactions

One of the favourite tools of manipulation in the abuser's arsenal is the disproportionality of his reactions. He reacts with supreme rage to the slightest slight. Or, he would punish severely for what he perceives to be an offence against him, no matter how minor. Or, he would throw a temper tantrum over any discord or disagreement, however gently and considerately expressed. Or, he would act inordinately attentive, charming and tempting (even over-sexed, if need be).

This ever-shifting code of conduct and the unusually harsh and arbitrarily applied penalties are premeditated. The victims are kept in the dark. Neediness and dependence on the source of "justice" meted and judgement passed – on the abuser – are thus guaranteed.

TIP

Demand a just and proportional treatment. Reject or ignore unjust and capricious behaviour.

If you are up to the inevitable confrontation, react in kind. Let him taste some of his own medicine.

### Dehumanization and Objectification (Abuse)

People have a need to believe in the empathic skills and basic good-heartedness of others. By dehumanizing and objectifying people – the abuser attacks the very foundations of human interaction. This is the "alien" aspect of abusers – they may be excellent imitations of fully formed adults but they are emotionally absent and immature.

Abuse is so horrid, so repulsive, so phantasmagoric – that people recoil in terror. It is then, with their defences absolutely down, that they are the most susceptible and vulnerable to the abuser's control. Physical, psychological, verbal and sexual abuse are all forms of dehumanization and objectification.

TIP

Never show your abuser that you are afraid of him. Do not negotiate with bullies. They are insatiable. Do not succumb to blackmail.

If things get rough – disengage, involve law enforcement officers, friends and colleagues, or threaten him (legally).

Do not keep your abuse a secret. Secrecy is the abuser's weapon.

Never give him a second chance. React with your full arsenal to the first transgression.

### Abuse of Information

From the first moments of an encounter with another person, the abuser is on the prowl. He collects information. The more he knows about his potential victim – the better able he is to coerce, manipulate, charm, extort or convert it "to the cause". The abuser does not hesitate to misuse the information he gleaned, regardless of its intimate nature or the circumstances in which he obtained it. This is a powerful tool in his armoury.

TIP

Be guarded. Don't be too forthcoming in a first or casual meeting. Gather intelligence.

Be yourself. Don't misrepresent your wishes, boundaries, preferences, priorities, and red lines.

Do not behave inconsistently. Do not go back on your word. Be firm and resolute.

### Impossible Situations

The abuser engineers impossible, dangerous, unpredictable, unprecedented, or highly specific situations in which he is sorely needed. The abuser makes sure that his knowledge, his skills, his connections, or his traits are the only ones applicable and the most useful in the situations that he, himself, wrought. The abuser generates his own indispensability.

TIP

Stay away from such quagmires. Scrutinize every offer and suggestion, no matter how innocuous.

Prepare backup plans. Keep others informed of your whereabouts and appraised of your situation.

Be vigilant and doubting. Do not be gullible and suggestible. Better safe than sorry.

### Control by Proxy

If all else fails, the abuser recruits friends, colleagues, mates, family members, the authorities, institutions, neighbours, the media, teachers – in short, third parties – to do his bidding. He uses them to cajole, coerce, threaten, stalk, offer, retreat, tempt, convince, harass, communicate and otherwise manipulate his target. He controls these unaware instruments exactly as he plans to control his ultimate prey. He employs the same mechanisms and devices. And he dumps his props unceremoniously when the job is done.

Another form of control by proxy is to engineer situations in which abuse is inflicted upon another person. Such carefully crafted scenarios of embarrassment and humiliation provoke social sanctions (condemnation, opprobrium, or even physical punishment) against the victim. Society, or a social group become the instruments of the abuser.

TIP

Often the abuser's proxies are unaware of their role. Expose him. Inform them. Demonstrate to them how they are being abused, misused, and plain used by the abuser.

Trap your abuser. Treat him as he treats you. Involve others. Bring it into the open. Nothing like sunshine to disinfest abuse.

### Ambient Abuse

The fostering, propagation and enhancement of an atmosphere of fear, intimidation, instability, unpredictability and irritation. There are no acts of traceable explicit abuse, nor any manipulative settings of control. Yet, the irksome feeling remains, a disagreeable foreboding, a premonition, a bad omen. This is sometimes called "gaslighting".

In the long-term, such an environment erodes the victim's sense of self-worth and self-esteem. Self-confidence is shaken badly. Often, the victim adopts a paranoid or schizoid stance and thus renders himself or herself exposed even more to criticism and judgement. The roles are thus reversed: the victim is considered mentally deranged and the abuser – the suffering soul.

TIP

Run! Get away! Ambient abuse often develops to overt and violent abuse.

You don't owe anyone an explanation – but you owe yourself a life. Bail out.

### Indifference and Decompensation in Pathological Narcissism

The narcissist lacks empathy. Consequently, he is not really interested in the lives, emotions, needs, preferences, and hopes of people around him. Even his nearest and dearest are, to him, mere instruments of gratification. They require his undivided attention only when they "malfunction" – when they become disobedient, independent, or critical. He loses all interest in them if they cannot be "fixed" (for instance, when they are terminally ill or develop a modicum of personal autonomy and independence).

Once he gives up on his erstwhile Sources of Supply, the narcissist proceeds to promptly and peremptorily devalue and discard them. This is often done by simply ignoring them – a facade of indifference that is known as the "silent treatment" and is, at heart, hostile and aggressive. Indifference is, therefore, a form of devaluation. People find the narcissist "cold", "inhuman", "heartless", "clueless", "robotic or machine-like".

Early on in life, the narcissist learns to disguise his socially-unacceptable indifference as benevolence, equanimity, cool-headedness, composure, or superiority. "It is not that I don't care about others" – he shrugs off his critics – "I am simply more level-headed, more resilient, more composed under pressure... They mistake my equanimity for apathy."

The narcissist tries to convince people that he is compassionate. His profound lack of interest in his spouse's life, vocation, interests, hobbies, and whereabouts he cloaks as benevolent altruism. "I give her all the freedom she can wish for!" – he protests – "I don't spy on her, follow her, or nag her with endless questions. I don't bother her. I let her lead her life the way she sees fit and don't interfere in her affairs!" He makes a virtue out of his emotional truancy.

All very commendable but when taken to extremes such benign neglect turns malignant and signifies the voidance of true love and attachment. The narcissist's emotional (and, often, physical) absence from all his relationships is a form of aggression and a defence against his own thoroughly repressed feelings.

In rare moments of self-awareness, the narcissist realizes that without his input – even in the form of feigned emotions – people will abandon him. He then swings from cruel aloofness to maudlin and grandiose gestures intended to demonstrate the "larger than life" nature of his sentiments. This bizarre pendulum only proves the narcissist's inadequacy at maintaining adult relationships. It convinces no one and repels many.

The narcissist's guarded detachment is a sad reaction to his unfortunate formative years. Pathological narcissism is thought to be the result of a prolonged period of severe abuse by primary caregivers, peers, or authority figures. In this sense, pathological narcissism is, therefore, a reaction to trauma. Narcissism IS a form of Post-Traumatic Stress Disorder that got ossified and fixated and mutated into a personality disorder.

All narcissists are traumatized and all of them suffer from a variety of post-traumatic symptoms: abandonment anxiety, reckless behaviours, anxiety and mood disorders, somatoform disorders, and so on. But the presenting signs of narcissism rarely indicate post-trauma. This is because pathological narcissism is an EFFICIENT coping (defence) mechanism. The narcissist presents to the world a facade of invincibility, equanimity, superiority, skilfulness, cool-headedness, invulnerability, and, in short: indifference.

This front is penetrated only in times of great crises that threaten the narcissist's ability to obtain Narcissistic Supply. The narcissist then "falls apart" in a process of disintegration known as decompensation. The dynamic forces which render him paralyzed and fake – his vulnerabilities, weaknesses, and fears – are starkly exposed as his defences crumble and become dysfunctional. The narcissist's extreme dependence on his social milieu for the regulation of his sense of self-worth are painfully and pitifully evident as he is reduced to begging and cajoling.

At such times, the narcissist acts out self-destructively and anti-socially. His mask of superior equanimity is pierced by displays of impotent rage, self-loathing, self-pity, and crass attempts at manipulation of his friends, family, and colleagues. His ostensible benevolence and caring evaporate. He feels caged and threatened and he reacts as any animal would do – by striking back at his perceived tormentors, at his hitherto "nearest" and "dearest".

Return

# The Gradations of Abuse

Is sexual abuse worse than emotional abuse? Is verbal abuse less deleterious than physical abuse (beatings)? Somehow, the professional literature implies that there is a hierarchy with sexual mistreatment at its nadir. It is rare to hear about a Dissociative Identity Disorder ("multiple personality") that is the outcome of constant oral humiliation in early childhood. But it is thought to be a common response to egregious sexual molestation of infants and to other forms of deviance and perversions with minors.

Yet, these distinctions are spurious. One's mental space is as important to one's healthy development and proper adult functioning as one's body. Indeed, the damage in sexual abuse is hardly corporeal. It is the psychological intrusion, coercion, and the demolition of nascent boundaries of the self that inflict the most damage.

Abuse is a form of long-term torture usually inflicted by one's nearest and dearest. It is a grievous violation of trust and it leads to disorientation, fear, depression, and suicidal ideation. It generates aggression in the abused and this overwhelming and all-pervasive emotion metastasizes and transforms into pathological envy, violence, rage, and hatred.

The abused are deformed by the abuser both overtly – many develop mental health disorders and dysfunctional behaviours – and, more perniciously, covertly. The abuser, like some kind of alien life form, invades and colonizes the victim's mind and becomes a permanent presence. Abused and abuser never cease the dialog of hurt, recrimination, and glib denial or rationalization that is an integral part of the act.

In a way, psychological abuse – emotional and verbal – is harder to "erase" and "deprogram". Words resonate and reverberate, pain resurfaces, narcissistic wounds keep opening. The victims proceeds to pay with stunted growth and recurrent failure for his own earlier degradation and objectification.

Social attitudes don't help. While sexual and physical abuse are slowly coming to the open and being recognized as the scourges that they are – psychological abuse is still largely ignored. It is difficult to draw a line between strict discipline and verbal harassment. Abusers find refuge in the general disdain for the weak and the vulnerable which is the result of suppressed collective guilt. The "good intentions" defence is still going strong.

The professional community is no less to blame. Emotional and verbal abuse are perceived and analyzed in "relative" terms – not as the absolute evils that they are. Cultural and moral relativism mean that many aberrant and deplorable behaviour patterns are justified based on bogus cultural "sensitivities" and malignant political correctness.

Some scholars even go as far as blaming the victim for his or her maltreatment (the discipline is known as victimology). Is the abused guilty – even partially – for the abuse? Does the victim emit a "come-on" signal, picked up by would-be abusers? Are certain types of people more prone to abuse than others?

Return

# The Guilt of the Abused

## Pathologizing the Victim

It is telling that precious few psychology and psychopathology textbooks dedicate an entire chapter to abuse and violence. Even the most egregious manifestations – such as child sexual abuse – merit a fleeting mention, usually as a sub-chapter in a larger section dedicated to paraphilias or personality disorders.

Abusive behaviour did not make it into the diagnostic criteria of mental health disorders, nor were its psychodynamic, cultural and social roots explored in depth. As a result of this deficient education and lacking awareness, most law enforcement officers, judges, counselours, guardians, and mediators are worryingly ignorant about the phenomenon.

Only 4% of hospital emergency room admissions of women in the United States are attributed by staff to domestic violence. The true figure, according to the FBI, is more like 50%. One in three murdered women was done in by her spouse, current or former.

The US Department of Justice pegs the number of spouses (mostly women) threatened with a deadly weapon at almost 2 million annually. Domestic violence erupts in a mind-boggling half of all American homes at least once a year. Nor are these isolated, "out of the blue", incidents.

Mistreatment and violence are part of an enduring pattern of maladaptive behaviour within the relationship and are sometimes coupled with substance abuse. Abusers are possessive, pathologically jealous, dependent, and, often, narcissistic. Invariably, both the abuser and his victim seek to conceal the abusive episodes and their aftermath from family, friends, neighbours, or colleagues.

This dismal state of things is an abuser's and stalker's paradise. This is especially true with psychological (verbal and emotional) abuse which leaves no visible marks and renders the victim incapable of coherence.

Still, there is no "typical" offender. Maltreatment crosses racial, cultural, social, and economic lines. This is because, until very recently, abuse has constituted normative, socially-acceptable, and, sometimes, condoned, behaviour. For the bulk of human history, women and children were considered no better than property.

Indeed, well into the 18th century, they still made it into lists of assets and liabilities of the household. Early legislation in America – fashioned after European law, both Anglo-Saxon and Continental – permitted wife battering for the purpose of behaviour modification. The circumference of the stick used, specified the statute, should not exceed that of the husband's thumb.

Inevitably, many victims blame themselves for the dismal state of affairs. The abused party may have low self-esteem, a fluctuating sense of self-worth, primitive defence mechanisms, phobias, mental health problems, a disability, a history of failure, or a tendency to blame herself, or to feel inadequate (autoplastic neurosis).

She may have come from an abusive family or environment – which conditioned her to expect abuse as inevitable and "normal". In extreme and rare cases – the victim is a masochist, possessed of an urge to seek ill-treatment and pain. Gradually, the victims convert these unhealthy emotions and their learned helplessness in the face of persistent "gaslighting" into psychosomatic symptoms, anxiety and panic attacks, depression, or, in extremis, suicidal ideation and gestures.

Therapists, marriage counselours, mediators, court-appointed guardians, police officers, and judges are human. Some of them are social reactionaries, others are narcissists, and a few are themselves spouse abusers. Many things work against the victim facing the justice system and the psychological profession.

Start with denial. Abuse is such a horrid phenomenon that society and its delegates often choose to ignore it or to convert it into a more benign manifestation, typically by pathologizing the situation or the victim – rather than the perpetrator.

A man's home is still his castle and the authorities are loath to intrude.

Most abusers are men and most victims are women. Even the most advanced communities in the world are largely patriarchal. Misogynistic gender stereotypes, superstitions, and prejudices are strong.

Therapists are not immune to these ubiquitous and age-old influences and biases.

They are amenable to the considerable charm, persuasiveness, and manipulativeness of the abuser and to his impressive thespian skills. The abuser offers a plausible rendition of the events and interprets them to his favour. The therapist rarely has a chance to witness an abusive exchange first hand and at close quarters. In contrast, the abused are often on the verge of a nervous breakdown: harassed, unkempt, irritable, impatient, abrasive, and hysterical.

Confronted with this contrast between a polished, self-controlled, and suave abuser and his harried casualties – it is easy to reach the conclusion that the real victim is the abuser, or that both parties abuse each other equally. The prey's acts of self-defence, assertiveness, or insistence on her rights are interpreted as aggression, lability, or a mental health problem.

The profession's propensity to pathologise extends to the wrongdoers as well. Alas, few therapists are equipped to do proper clinical work, including diagnosis.

Abusers are thought by practitioners of psychology to be emotionally disturbed, the twisted outcomes of a history of familial violence and childhood traumas. They are typically diagnosed as suffering from a personality disorder, an inordinately low self-esteem, or co-dependence coupled with an all-devouring fear of abandonment. Consummate abusers use the right vocabulary and feign the appropriate "emotions" and affect and, thus, sway the evaluator's judgement.

But while the victim's "pathology" works against her – especially in custody battles – the culprit's "illness" works for him, as a mitigating circumstance, especially in criminal proceedings.

In his seminal essay, "Understanding the Batterer in Visitation and Custody Disputes", Lundy Bancroft sums up the asymmetry in favour of the offender:

*"Batterers ... adopt the role of a hurt, sensitive man who doesn't understand how things got so bad and just wants to work it all out 'for the good of the children'... Because of the effects of trauma, the victim of battering will often seem hostile, disjointed, and agitated... Evaluators are thus tempted to conclude that the victim is the source of the problems in the relationship."*

There is little the victim can do to "educate" the therapist or "prove" to him who is the guilty party. Mental health professionals are as ego-centred as the next person. They are emotionally invested in opinions they form or in their interpretation of the abusive relationship. They perceive every disagreement as a challenge to their authority and are likely to pathologise such behaviour, labelling it "resistance" (or worse).

In the process of mediation, marital therapy, or evaluation, counselours frequently propose various techniques to ameliorate the abuse or bring it under control. Woe betides the party that dares object or turn these "recommendations" down. Thus, an abuse victim who declines to have any further contact with her batterer – is bound to be chastised by her therapist for obstinately refusing to constructively communicate with her violent spouse.

Better to play ball and adopt the sleek mannerisms of your abuser. Sadly, sometimes the only way to convince your therapist that it is not all in your head and that you are a victim – is by being insincere and by staging a well-calibrated performance, replete with the correct vocabulary. Therapists have Pavlovian reactions to certain phrases and theories and to certain "presenting signs and symptoms" (behaviours during the first few sessions). Learn these – and use them to your advantage. It is your only chance.

## Appendix: Why Good People Ignore Abuse

Why do good people – church-goers, pillars of the community, the salt of the earth – ignore abuse and neglect, even when it is on their doorstep and in their proverbial backyard (for instance, in hospitals, orphanages, shelters, prisons, and the like)?

### Lack of Clear Definition

Perhaps because the word "abuse" is so ill-defined and so open to culture-bound interpretation.

We should distinguish functional abuse from the sadistic variety. The former is calculated to ensure outcomes or to punish transgressors. It is measured, impersonal, efficient, and disinterested.

The latter – the sadistic variety – fulfils the emotional needs of the perpetrator.

This distinction is often blurred. People feel uncertain and, therefore, reluctant to intervene. "The authorities know best" – they lie to themselves.

### Avoiding the Unpleasant

People, good people, tend to avert their eyes from certain institutions which deal with anomalies and pain, death and illness – the unsavoury aspects of life which no one likes to be reminded of.

Like poor relatives, these institutions and events inside them are ignored and shunned.

### The Common Guilt

Moreover, even good people abuse others habitually. Abusive conduct is so widespread that no one is exempt. Ours is a narcissistic – and, therefore, abusive – civilization.

People who find themselves caught up in anomic states – for instance, soldiers in war, nurses in hospitals, managers in corporations, parents or spouses in disintegrating families, or incarcerated inmates – tend to feel helpless and alienated. They experience a partial or total loss of control.

They are rendered vulnerable, powerless, and defenceless by events and circumstances beyond their influence.

Abuse amounts to exerting an absolute and all-pervasive domination of the victim's existence. It is a coping strategy employed by the abuser who wishes to reassert control over his life and, thus, to re-establish his mastery and superiority. By subjugating the victim – he regains his self-confidence and regulate his sense of self-worth.

### Abuse as Catharsis

Even perfectly "normal" and good people (witness the events in the Abu Ghraib prison in Iraq) channel their negative emotions – pent up aggression, humiliation, rage, envy, diffuse hatred – and displace them.

The victims of abuse become symbols of everything that's wrong in the abuser's life and the situation he finds himself caught in. The act of abuse amounts to misplaced and violent venting.

### The Wish to Conform and Belong - The Ethics of Peer Pressure

Many "good people" perpetrate heinous acts – or refrain from criticizing or opposing evil – out of a wish to conform. Abusing others is their way of demonstrating obsequious obeisance to authority, group affiliation, colleagueship, and adherence to the same ethical code of conduct and common values. They bask in the praise that is heaped on them by their superiors, fellow workers, associates, team mates, or collaborators.

Their need to belong is so strong that it overpowers ethical, moral, or legal considerations. They remain silent in the face of neglect, abuse, and atrocities because they feel insecure and they derive their identity almost entirely from the group.

Abuse rarely occurs where it does not have the sanction and blessing of the authorities, whether local or national. A permissive environment is sine qua non. The more abnormal the circumstances, the less normative the milieu, the further the scene of the crime is from public scrutiny – the more is egregious abuse likely to occur. This acquiescence is especially true in totalitarian societies where the use of physical force to discipline or eliminate dissent is an acceptable practice. But, unfortunately, it is also rampant in democratic societies.

Return

# Coping with Your Abuser

How to cope with your abuser?

Sometimes it looks hopeless. Abusers are ruthless, immoral, sadistic, calculated, cunning, persuasive, deceitful – in short, they appear to be invincible. They easily sway the system in their favour.

Here is a list of escalating countermeasures. They represent the distilled experience of thousands of victims of abuse. They may help you cope with abuse and overcome it.

Not included are legal or medical steps. Consult an attorney, an accountant, a therapist, or a psychiatrist, where appropriate.

First, you must decide:

Do you want to stay with him – or terminate the relationship?

To victims of abuse, my advice is unequivocal:

LEAVE NOW. Leave before the effects of abuse – including PTSD (Post-Traumatic Stress Disorder) – become entrenched. Leave before your children begin to pay the price as well.

But, if you insist on staying (always against the best interests of yourself and your nearest and dearest) – here is a survival manual:

**I Want to Stay with Him**

*FIVE DON'T DO'S – How to Avoid the Wrath of the Abuser*

- Never disagree with the abuser or contradict him;
- Never offer him any intimacy;
- Look awed by whatever attribute matters to him (for instance: by his professional achievements or by his good looks, or by his success with women and so on);
- Never remind him of life out there and if you do, connect it somehow to his sense of grandiosity;
- Do not make any comment, which might directly or indirectly impinge on his self-image, omnipotence, judgement, omniscience, skills, capabilities, professional record, or even omnipresence. Bad sentences start with: "I think you overlooked ... made a mistake here ... you don't know ... do you know ... you were not here yesterday so ... you cannot ... you should ... (interpreted as rude imposition, abusers react very badly to perceived restrictions placed on their freedom) ... I (never mention the fact that you are a separate, independent entity, abusers regard others as extensions of their selves)..." You get the gist of it.

*The TEN DO'S – How to Make Your Abuser Dependent on You*
*If You INSIST on Staying with Him*

- Listen attentively to everything the abuser says and agree with it all. Don't believe a word of it but let it slide as if everything is just fine, business as usual.
- Personally offer something absolutely unique to the abuser which he cannot obtain anywhere else. Also be prepared to line up future Sources of Primary Narcissistic Supply for your abuser because you will not be IT for very long, if at all. If you take over the procuring function for the abuser, he becomes that much more dependent on you which makes it a bit tougher for him to pull his haughty stuff – an inevitability, in any case.

- Be endlessly patient and go way out of your way to be accommodating, thus keeping the Narcissistic Supply flowing liberally, and keeping the peace (relatively speaking).
- Be endlessly giving. This one may not be attractive to you, but it is a take it or leave it proposition.
- Be absolutely emotionally and financially independent of the abuser. Take what you need: the excitement and engulfment and refuse to get upset or hurt when the abuser does or says something dumb, rude, or insensitive. Yelling back works really well but should be reserved for special occasions when you fear your abuser may be on the verge of leaving you; the silent treatment is better as an ordinary response, but it must be carried out without any emotional content, more with the air of boredom and "I'll talk to you later, when I am good and ready, and when you are behaving in a more reasonable fashion".
- If your abuser is cerebral narcissist and NOT interested in having much sex – then give yourself ample permission to have "hidden" sex with other people. Your cerebral narcissist will not be indifferent to infidelity so discretion and secrecy is of paramount importance.
- If your abuser is somatic narcissist and you don't mind, join in on endlessly interesting group sex encounters but make sure that you choose properly for your abuser. Somatic narcissists are heedless and very undiscriminating in respect of sexual partners and that can get very problematic (STDs and blackmail come to mind).
- If you are a "fixer", then focus on fixing situations, preferably before they become "situations". Don't for one moment delude yourself that you can FIX the abuser – it simply will not happen. Not because he is being stubborn – he just simply can't be fixed.
- If there is any fixing that can be done, it is to help your abuser become aware of his condition, and this is VERY IMPORTANT, with no negative implications or accusations in the process at all. It is like living with a physically handicapped person and being able to discuss, calmly, unemotionally, what the limitations and benefits of the handicap are and how the two of you can work with these factors, rather than trying to change them.
- FINALLY, and most important of all: KNOW YOURSELF. What are you getting from the relationship? Are you actually a

masochist? A co-dependent perhaps? Why is this relationship attractive and interesting?

Define for yourself what good and beneficial things you believe you are receiving in this relationship.

Define the things that you find harmful TO YOU. Develop strategies to minimize the harm to yourself. Don't expect that you will cognitively be able to reason with the abuser to change who he is. You may have some limited success in getting your abuser to tone down on the really harmful behaviours THAT AFFECT YOU which emanate from the unchangeable WHAT the abuser is. This can only be accomplished in a very trusting, frank and open relationship.

## Insist on Your Boundaries - Resist Abuse

- Refuse to accept abusive behaviour. Demand reasonably predictable and rational actions and reactions. Insist on respect for your boundaries, predilections, preferences, and priorities.
- Demand a just and proportional treatment. Reject or ignore unjust and capricious behaviour.
- If you are up to the inevitable confrontation, react in kind. Let him taste some of his own medicine.
- Never show your abuser that you are afraid of him. Do not negotiate with bullies. They are insatiable. Do not succumb to blackmail.
- If things get rough – disengage, involve law enforcement officers, friends and colleagues, or threaten him (legally).
- Do not keep your abuse a secret. Secrecy is the abuser's weapon.
- Never give him a second chance. React with your full arsenal to the first transgression.
- Be guarded. Don't be too forthcoming in a first or casual meeting. Gather intelligence.
- Be yourself. Don't misrepresent your wishes, boundaries, preferences, priorities, and red lines.
- Do not behave inconsistently. Do not go back on your word. Be firm and resolute.
- Stay away from such quagmires. Scrutinize every offer and suggestion, no matter how innocuous.
- Prepare backup plans. Keep others informed of your whereabouts and appraised of your situation.
- Be vigilant and doubting. Do not be gullible and suggestible. Better safe than sorry.

- Often the abuser's proxies are unaware of their role. Expose him. Inform them. Demonstrate to them how they are being abused, misused, and plain used by the abuser.
- Trap your abuser. Treat him as he treats you. Involve others. Bring it into the open. Nothing like sunshine to disinfest abuse.

### Mirror His Behaviour

Mirror the abuser's actions and repeat his words.

If, for instance, he is having a rage attack – rage back. If he threatens – threaten back and credibly try to use the same language and content. If he leaves the house – leave it as well, disappear on him. If he is suspicious – act suspicious. Be critical, denigrating, humiliating, go down to his level.

### Frighten Him

Identify the vulnerabilities and susceptibilities of the abuser and strike repeated, escalating blows at them.

If an abuser has a secret or something he wishes to conceal – use your knowledge of it to threaten him. Drop cryptic hints that there are mysterious witnesses to the events and recently revealed evidence. Do it cleverly, noncommittally, gradually, in an escalating manner.

Let his imagination do the rest. You don't have to do much except utter a vague reference, make an ominous allusion, delineate a possible turn of events.

Needless to add that all these activities have to be pursued legally, preferably through the good services of law offices and in broad daylight. If done in the wrong way – they might constitute extortion or blackmail, harassment and a host of other criminal offences.

### Lure Him

Offer him continued Narcissistic Supply. You can make an abuser do ANYTHING by offering, withholding, or threatening to withhold Narcissistic Supply (adulation, admiration, attention, sex, awe, subservience, etc.).

### Play on His Fear of Abandonment

If nothing else works, explicitly threaten to abandon him.

You can condition the threat ("If you don't do something or if you do it - I will desert you").

The abuser perceives the following as threats of abandonment, even if they are not meant as such:

- Confrontation, fundamental disagreement, and protracted criticism;
- When completely ignored;
- When you insist on respect for your boundaries, needs, emotions, choices, preferences;
- When you retaliate (for instance, shout back at him).

## I Can't Take It Any Longer – I Have Decided to Leave Him

### Fight Him in Court

Here are a few of the things the abuser finds devastating, especially in a court of law, for instance during a deposition:

- Any statement or fact, which seems to contradict his inflated perception of his grandiose self. Any criticism, disagreement, exposure of fake achievements, belittling of "talents and skills" which the abuser fantasizes that he possesses, any hint that he is subordinated, subjugated, controlled, owned or dependent upon a third party. Any description of the abuser as average and common, indistinguishable from many others. Any hint that the abuser is weak, needy, dependent, deficient, slow, not intelligent, naive, gullible, susceptible, not in the know, manipulated, a victim.
- The abuser is likely to react with rage to all these and, in an effort to re-establish his fantastic grandiosity, he is likely to expose facts and stratagems he had no conscious intention of exposing.
- The abuser reacts with narcissistic rage, hatred, aggression, or violence to an infringement of what he perceives to be his entitlement. Any insinuation, hint, intimation, or direct declaration that the abuser is not special at all, that he is average, common, not even sufficiently idiosyncratic to warrant a fleeting interest will inflame the abuser.
- Tell the abuser that he does not deserve the best treatment, that his needs are not everyone's priority, that he is boring, that his needs can be catered to by an average practitioner (medical doctor, accountant, lawyer, psychiatrist), that he and his motives are transparent and can be easily gauged, that he will do what he is told, that his temper tantrums will not be tolerated, that no special concessions will be made to accommodate his inflated sense of self, that he is subject to court procedures, etc. – and the abuser will lose control.
- Contradict, expose, humiliate, and berate the abuser ("You are not as intelligent as you think you are", "Who is really behind

all this? It takes sophistication which you don't seem to have", "So, you have no formal education", "You are (mistake his age, make him much older) … sorry, you are … old", "What did you do in your life? Did you study? Do you have a degree? Did you ever establish or run a business? Would you define yourself as a success?", "Would your children share your view that you are a good father?", "You were last seen with a Ms. … who is (suppressed grin) a cleaning lady (in demeaning disbelief)".

- Be equipped with absolutely unequivocal, first rate, thoroughly authenticated and vouched for information.

### *If You Have Common Children*

I described in "The Guilt of the Abused - Pathologizing the Victim" how the system is biased and titled against the victim.

Regrettably, mental health professionals and practitioners – marital and couple therapists, counselours – are conditioned, by years of indoctrinating and dogmatic education, to respond favourably to specific verbal cues.

The paradigm is that abuse is rarely one sided – in other words, that it is invariably "triggered" either by the victim or by the mental health problems of the abuser. Another common lie is that all mental health problems can be successfully treated one way (talk therapy) or another (medication).

This shifts the responsibility from the offender to his prey. The abused must have done something to bring about their own maltreatment – or simply were emotionally "unavailable" to help the abuser with his problems. Healing is guaranteed if only the victim were willing to participate in a treatment plan and communicate with the abuser. So goes the orthodoxy.

Refusal to do so – in other words, refusal to risk further abuse – is harshly judged by the therapist. The victim is labelled uncooperative, resistant, or even abusive!

The key is, therefore, feigned acquiescence and collaboration with the therapist's scheme, acceptance of his/her interpretation of the events, and the use of key phrases such as: "I wish to communicate/work with (the abuser)", "trauma", "relationship", "healing process", "inner child", "the good of the children", "the importance of fathering", "significant other" and other psycho-babble. Learn the jargon, use it intelligently and you are bound to win the therapist's sympathy.

Above all – do not be assertive, or aggressive and do not overtly criticize the therapist or disagree with him/her.

I make the therapist sound like yet another potential abuser – because in many cases, he/she becomes one as they inadvertently collude with the abuser, invalidate the abuse experiences, and pathologise the victim.

### Phrases to Use

- "For the children's sake..."
- "I want to maintain constructive communications with my husband/wife..."
- "The children need the ongoing presence of (the other parent)..."
- "I wish to communicate/work with (the abuser) on our issues..."
- "I wish to understand our relationship, help both sides achieve closure and get on with their lives/my life..."
- "Healing process..."

### Things to Do

- Attend every session diligently. Never be late. Try not to cancel or reschedule meetings.
- Pay attention to your attire and makeup. Project a solid, conservative image. Do not make a dishevelled and disjointed appearance.
- Never argue with the counselour or the evaluator or criticize them openly. If you have to disagree with him or her – do so elliptically and dispassionately.
- Agree to participate in a long-term treatment plan.
- Communicate with your abuser politely and reasonably. Do not let yourself get provoked! Do not throw temper tantrums or threaten anyone, not even indirectly! Restrain your hostility. Talk calmly and articulately. Count to ten or take a break, if you must.
- Repeatedly emphasize that the welfare and well-being of your children is uppermost in your mind – over and above any other (selfish) desire or consideration.

### Refuse All Contact

- Be sure to maintain as much contact with your abuser as the courts, counselours, mediators, guardians, or law enforcement officials mandate.
- Do NOT contravene the decisions of the system. Work from the inside to change judgements, evaluations, or rulings – but NEVER rebel against them or ignore them. You will only turn the system against you and your interests.

- But with the exception of the minimum mandated by the courts – decline any and all GRATUITOUS contact with the abuser.
- Do not respond to his pleading, romantic, nostalgic, flattering, or threatening e-mail messages.
- Return all gifts he sends you.
- Refuse him entry to your premises. Do not even respond to the intercom.
- Do not talk to him on the phone. Hang up the minute you hear his voice while making clear to him, in a single, polite but firm, sentence, that you are determined not to talk to him.
- Do not answer his letters.
- Do not visit him on special occasions, or in emergencies.
- Do not respond to questions, requests, or pleas forwarded to you through third parties.
- Disconnect from third parties whom you know are spying on you at his behest.
- Do not discuss him with your children.
- Do not gossip about him.
- Do not ask him for anything, even if you are in dire need.
- When you are forced to meet him, do not discuss your personal affairs – or his.
- Relegate any inevitable contact with him – when and where possible – to professionals: your lawyer, or your accountant.

Return

# The Abuser in Denial

Abusers regularly deny the abuse ever took place – or rationalize their abusive behaviours. Denial is an integral part of the abuser's ability to "look at himself/herself in the mirror".

There are many types of denial. When confronted by his victims, most abusers tend to shift blame or avoid the topic altogether.

## Total Denial

### Outright Denial

Typical retorts by the abuser: "It never happened, or it was not abuse, you are just imagining it, or you want to hurt my (the abuser's) feelings."

### Alloplastic Defence

Common sentences when challenged: "It was your fault, you, or your behaviour, or the circumstances, provoked me into such behaviour."

### Altruistic Defence

Usual convoluted explanations: "I did it for you, in your best interests."

### Transformative Defence

Recurring themes: "What I did to you was not abuse – it was common and accepted behaviour (at the time, or in the context of the prevailing culture or in accordance with social norms), it was not meant as abuse."

Abusers frequently have narcissistic traits. As such, they are more concerned with appearance than with substance. Dependent for Narcissistic Supply on the community – neighbours, colleagues, co-workers, bosses, friends, extended family – they cultivate an unblemished reputation for honesty, industriousness, religiosity, reliability, and conformity.

## Forms of Denial in Public

### Family Honour Stricture

Characteristic admonitions: "We don't do dirty laundry publicly, the family's honour and repute must be preserved, what will the neighbours say?"

### Family Functioning Stricture

Dire and ominous scenarios: "If you snitch and inform the authorities, they will take me (the abusive parent) away and the whole family will disintegrate."

Confronting the abuser with incontrovertible proof of his abusive behaviour is one way of minimizing contact with him. Abusers – like the narcissists that they often are – cannot tolerate criticism or disagreement.

Return

# Avoiding Your Abuser

## Submissive and Conflictive Postures

Abuse is a multifaceted phenomenon. It is a poisonous cocktail of control-freakery, conforming to social and cultural norms, and latent sadism. The abuser seeks to subjugate his victims and "look good" or "save face" in front of family and peers. Many abusers also enjoy inflicting pain on helpless victims.

But, even assuming that you want to stay with your abuser and to maintain the relationship, maltreatment can, to some extent, be avoided.

### The Submissive Posture

Abusers react to the slightest provocation – real or imagined – with disproportionate wrath and, often, violence. It is important, therefore, never to openly and repeatedly disagree with your abuser or contradict him. If you do – your abuser is bound to walk away, but only after he has vilified and harmed you in every way he can.

Abusers feel threatened by real sharing and common decision-making. Never offer your abuser any intimacy – it is a sure way to turn him off and his aggression on. Abusers perceive intimacy as the prelude to manipulation ("What is she getting at? What does she really want? What is her hidden agenda?").

Abusers are narcissistic – so admire and adore them openly. But do not lie or exaggerate – this will be perceived as cunning and will provoke your abuser to feats of paranoia and jealousy. Look awed by whatever matters to him (for instance: by his professional achievements or by his good looks, or even by his success with other women).

The abuser tries to transform his personal space into the exact opposite of his real life. At home, he is the master of a fantasy of perfection and harmony and the undisputed recipient of adulation and obeisance. Any reminder that, in reality, his life is a drab dead end, that he is a failure, or a tyrant, or a swindler, or a wannabe, sometimes hated by his own oppressed family – is likely to be met with unbridled hostility.

Never remind him of life out there and if you do, connect it somehow to his sense of grandiosity. Reassure him of the permanence of your obedient and self-sacrificial love for him. Do not make any comment, which might directly or indirectly impinge on his self-image, omnipotence, judgement, omniscience, skills, capabilities, professional record, or even omnipresence.

Listen attentively to his words and never disagree, or contradict him or offer your point of view. You are there to witness the abuser's train of thought – not to derail it with reminders of your separate existence. Be saintly patient and accommodating and endlessly giving with nothing in return. Never let your energy be depleted or your guard down.

Your abuser is likely to be provoked to extremes by signs of your personal autonomy. Conceal your thoughts and plans, make no overt choices and express no preferences, never mention your emotions, needs, earnings, wages, profits, or trust money. Tell him how much you rely on him to reach the right decisions for both of you. Play dumb – but not too dumb, or it may be provoke his suspicions. It is a thin line between pleasing the abuser and rendering him a raving paranoid.

Never give your abuser cause to doubt or suspect you. Surrender all control to him, deny yourself access to property and funds, don't socialize, drop all your friends and hobbies, quit your job and your studies, and confine yourself to your abode. Your abuser is bound to be virulently jealous and suspect illicit liaisons between you and the least likely persons, your family included. He envies the attention you give to others, even to your common children. Place him on a pedestal and make sure he notices how you ignore, spurn, and neglect everyone else.

To your abuser, you are an object, no matter how ostensibly revered and cherished. Hence the battering. He monopolizes your time and your mind. He makes for you even the minutest choices: what to wear, what to cook for dinner, when to go out and with whom. In extreme cases, he regards even your body as his to share with others, if he sees fit.

It is an onerous existence, consistently tiptoeing on eggshells. Neither is it invariably successful. The submissive posture delays the more egregious manifestations of abuse but cannot prevent them altogether. Choosing to live with an abuser is like opting to share a cage with a predator. No matter how domesticated,

Nature is bound to prevail. You are more likely than not to end up as the abuser's next meal.

Unless, that is, you adopt the Conflictive Posture.

### The Conflictive Posture

Contrary to its name, the conflictive posture is actually about avoiding conflict by minimizing contact and insisting on boundaries. It is about refusal to accept abusive behaviour by demanding reasonably predictable and rational actions and reactions. It is about respect for you and for your predilections, preferences, emotions, needs, and priorities.

A healthy relationship requires justice and proportionality. Reject or ignore unjust and capricious behaviour. Conflicts are inevitable even in the most loving and mature bonds – but the rules of engagement are different in an abusive liaison. There, you must react in kind and let him taste some of his own medicine.

Abusers are predators, attuned to the subtlest emotional cues of their prey. Never show your abuser that you are afraid or that you are less than resolute. The willingness to negotiate is perceived as a weakness by bullies. Violent offenders are insatiable. Do not succumb to blackmail or emotional extortion – once you start compromising, you won't see the end of it.

The abuser creates a "shared psychosis" (folie-a-deux) with his victim, an overwhelming feeling of "the two of us against the whole world". Don't buy into it. Feel free to threaten him (with legal measures), to disengage if things get rough – or to involve law enforcement officers, friends, neighbours, and colleagues.

Here are a few counterintuitive guidelines:

The abused feel ashamed, somehow responsible, guilty, and blameworthy for their maltreatment. The abuser is adept at instilling these erroneous notions in his victims ("Look what you made me do!"). So, above all, do not keep your abuse a secret. Secrecy is the abuser's weapon. Share your story with friends, colleagues, neighbours, social workers, the police, the media, your minister, and anyone else who will listen.

Don't make excuses for him. Don't try to understand him. Do not empathize with him – he, surely, does not empathize with you. He has no mercy on you – you, in return, do not harbour misplaced pity for him. Never give him a second chance. React with your full arsenal to the first transgression. Teach him a lesson he is unlikely to forget. Make him go elsewhere for his sadistic pursuits or to offload his frustrations.

Often the abuser's proxies are unaware of their role. Expose him. Inform them. Demonstrate to them how they are being abused, misused, and plain used by the abuser. Trap your abuser. Treat him as he treats you. Involve others. Bring it into the open. Nothing like sunshine to disinfest abuse.

There are a few techniques which work wonders with abusers. Some psychologists recommend to treat repeat offenders as one would toddlers. The abuser is, indeed, an immature brat – though a dangerous one, endowed as he is with the privileges and capabilities of an adult. Sometimes ignoring his temper tantrums until it is over is a wise policy. But not very often – and, definitely not as a rule.

Return

# How to Spot an Abuser on Your First Date

Is there anything you can do to avoid abusers and narcissists to start with? Are there any warning signs, any identifying marks, rules of thumbs to shield you from the harrowing and traumatic experience of an abusive relationship?

Imagine a first or second date. You can already tell if he is a would-be abuser. Here's how:

Perhaps the first telltale sign is the abuser's alloplastic defences – his tendency to blame every mistake of his, every failure, or mishap on others, or on the world at large. Be tuned: does he assume personal responsibility? Does he admit his faults and miscalculations? Or does he keep blaming you, the cab driver, the waiter, the weather, the government, or fortune for his predicament?

Is he hypersensitive, picks up fights, feels constantly slighted, injured, and insulted? Does he rant incessantly? Does he treat animals and children impatiently or cruelly and does he express negative and aggressive emotions towards the weak, the poor, the needy, the sentimental, and the disabled? Does he confess to having a history of battering or violent offences or behaviour? Is his language vile and infused with expletives, threats, and hostility?

Next thing: is he too eager? Does he push you to marry him having dated you only twice? Is he planning on having children on your first date? Does he immediately cast you in the role of the love of his life? Is he pressing you for exclusivity, instant intimacy, almost rapes you and acts jealous when you as much as cast a glance at another male? Does he inform you that, once you get hitched, you should abandon your studies or resign your job (forgo your personal autonomy)?

Does he respect your boundaries and privacy? Does he ignore your wishes (for instance, by choosing from the menu or selecting a movie without as much as consulting you)? Does he disrespect your boundaries and treats you as an object or an instrument of gratification (materializes on your doorstep unexpectedly or calls you often prior to your date)? Does he go through your personal belongings while waiting for you to get ready?

Does he control the situation and you compulsively? Does he insist to ride in his car, holds on to the car keys, the money, the theatre tickets, and even your bag? Does he disapprove if you are away for too long (for instance when you go to the powder room)? Does he interrogate you when you return ("Have you seen anyone interesting") – or make lewd "jokes" and remarks? Does he hint that, in future, you would need his permission to do things – even as innocuous as meeting a friend or visiting with your family?

Does he act in a patronizing and condescending manner and criticizes you often? Does he emphasize your minutest faults (devalues you) even as he exaggerates your talents, traits, and skills (idealizes you)? Is he wildly unrealistic in his expectations from you, from himself, from the budding relationship, and from life in general?

Does he tell you constantly that you "make him feel" good? Don't be impressed. Next thing, he may tell you that you "make" him feel bad, or that you make him feel violent, or that you "provoke" him. "Look what you made me do!" is an abuser's ubiquitous catchphrase.

Does he find sadistic sex exciting? Does he have fantasies of rape or paedophilia? Is he too forceful with you in and out of the sexual intercourse? Does he like hurting you physically or finds it amusing? Does he abuse you verbally – does he curse you, demeans you, calls you ugly or inappropriately diminutive names, or persistently criticizes you? Does he then switch to being saccharine and "loving", apologizes profusely and buys you gifts?

If you have answered "yes" to any of the above – stay away! He is an abuser.

Then there is the abuser's body language. It comprises an unequivocal series of subtle – but discernible – warning signs. Pay attention to the way your date comports himself – and save yourself a lot of trouble!

Return

# The Abuser's Body Language

Abusers are an elusive breed, hard to spot, harder to pinpoint, impossible to capture. Even an experienced mental health diagnostician with unmitigated access to the record and to the person examined would find it fiendishly difficult to determine with any degree of certainty whether someone is being abusive because he suffers from an impairment, i.e., a mental health disorder.

Some abusive behaviour patterns are a result of the patient's cultural-social context. The offender seeks to conform to cultural and social morals and norms. Additionally, some people become abusive in reaction to severe life crises.

Still, most abusers master the art of deception. People often find themselves involved with a abuser (emotionally, in business, or otherwise) before they have a chance to discover his real nature. When the abuser reveals his true colours, it is usually far too late. His victims are unable to separate from him. They are frustrated by this acquired helplessness and angry that they failed to see through the abuser earlier on.

But abusers do emit subtle, almost subliminal, signals in his body language even in a first or casual encounter. These are:

*"Haughty" body language* – The abuser adopts a physical posture which implies and exudes an air of superiority, seniority, hidden powers, mysteriousness, amused indifference, etc. Though the abuser usually maintains sustained and piercing eye contact, he often refrains from physical proximity (he maintains his personal territory).

The abuser takes part in social interactions – even mere banter – condescendingly, from a position of supremacy and faux "magnanimity and largesse". But even when he feigns gregariousness, he rarely mingles socially and prefers to remain the "observer", or the "lone wolf".

*Entitlement markers* – The abuser immediately asks for "special treatment" of some kind. Not to wait his turn, to have a longer or a shorter therapeutic session, to talk directly to authority figures (and not to their assistants or secretaries), to be granted special payment terms, to enjoy custom tailored arrangements. This tallies well with the abuser's alloplastic defences – his tendency to shift responsibility to others, or to the world at large, for his needs, failures, behaviour, choices, and mishaps ("Look what you made me do!").

The abuser is the one who – vocally and demonstratively – demands the undivided attention of the head waiter in a restaurant, or monopolizes the hostess, or latches on to celebrities in a party. The abuser reacts with rage and indignantly when denied his wishes and if treated the same as others whom he deems inferior. Abusers frequently and embarrassingly "dress down" service providers such as waiters or cab drivers.

*Idealization or devaluation* – The abuser instantly idealizes or devalues his interlocutor. He flatters, adores, admires and applauds the "target" in an embarrassingly exaggerated and profuse manner – or sulks, abuses, and humiliates her.

Abusers are polite only in the presence of a potential would-be victim – a "mate", or a "collaborator". But they are unable to sustain even perfunctory civility and fast deteriorate to barbs and thinly-veiled hostility, to verbal or other violent displays of abuse, rage attacks, or cold detachment.

*The "membership" posture* – The abuser always tries to "belong". Yet, at the very same time, he maintains his stance as an outsider. The abuser seeks to be admired for his ability to integrate and ingratiate himself without investing the efforts commensurate with such an undertaking.

For instance: if the abuser talks to a psychologist, the abuser first states emphatically that he never studied psychology. He then proceeds to make seemingly effortless use of obscure professional terms, thus demonstrating that he mastered the discipline all the same – which is supposed to prove that he is exceptionally intelligent or introspective.

In general, the abuser always prefers show-off to substance. One of the most effective methods of exposing a abuser is by trying to delve deeper. The abuser is shallow, a pond pretending to be an ocean. He likes to think of himself as a Renaissance man, a Jack of all trades, or a genius. Abusers never admit to ignorance or to failure in any field – yet, typically, they are ignorant and losers. It is surprisingly easy to penetrate the gloss and the veneer of the abuser's self-proclaimed omniscience, success, wealth, and omnipotence.

*Bragging and false autobiography* – The abuser brags incessantly. His speech is peppered with "I", "my", "myself", and "mine". He describes himself as intelligent, or rich, or modest, or intuitive, or creative – but always excessively, implausibly, and extraordinarily so.

The abuser's biography sounds unusually rich and complex. His achievements – incommensurate with his age, education, or renown. Yet, his actual condition is evidently and demonstrably incompatible with his claims. Very often, the abuser's lies or fantasies are easily discernible. He always name-drops and appropriates other people's experiences and accomplishments as his own.

*Emotion-free language* – The abuser likes to talk about himself and only about himself. He is not interested in others or what they have to say. He is never reciprocal. He acts disdainful, even angry, if he feels an intrusion on his precious time.

In general, the abuser is very impatient, easily bored, with strong attention deficits – unless and until he is the topic of discussion. One can dissect all aspects of the intimate life of a abuser, providing the discourse is not "emotionally tinted". If asked to relate directly to his emotions, the abuser intellectualizes, rationalizes, speaks about himself in the third person and in a detached "scientific" tone or composes a narrative with a fictitious character in it, suspiciously autobiographical.

Most abusers get enraged when required to delve deeper into their motives, fears, hopes, wishes, and needs. They use violence to cover up their perceived "weakness" and "sentimentality". They distance themselves from their own emotions and from their loved ones by alienating and hurting them.

*Seriousness and sense of intrusion and coercion* – The abuser is dead serious about himself. He may possess a fabulous sense of humour, scathing and cynical, but rarely is he self-deprecating. The abuser regards himself as being on a constant mission, whose importance is cosmic and whose consequences are global.

If a scientist – he is always in the throes of revolutionizing science. If a journalist – he is in the middle of the greatest story ever. If an aspiring businessman – he is on the way to concluding the deal of the century. Woe betide those who doubt his grandiose fantasies and impossible schemes.

This self-misperception is not amenable to light-headedness or self-effacement. The abuser is easily hurt and insulted (narcissistic injury). Even the most innocuous remarks or acts are interpreted by him as belittling, intruding, or coercive slights and demands.

His time is more valuable than others' – therefore, it cannot be wasted on unimportant matters such as social intercourse, family obligations, or household chores. Inevitably, he feels constantly misunderstood.

Any suggested help, advice, or concerned inquiry are immediately cast by the abuser as intentional humiliation, implying that the abuser is in need of help and counsel and, thus, imperfect. Any attempt to set an agenda is, to the abuser, an intimidating act of enslavement. In this sense, the abuser is both schizoid and paranoid and often entertains ideas of reference.

Finally, abusers are sometimes sadistic and have inappropriate affect. In other words, they find the obnoxious, the heinous, and the shocking – funny or even gratifying. They are sexually sadomasochistic or deviant. They like to taunt, to torment, and to hurt people's feelings ("humorously" or with bruising "honesty").

While some abusers are "stable" and "conventional" – others are antisocial and their impulse control is flawed. These are very reckless (self-destructive and self-defeating) and just plain destructive: workaholism, alcoholism, drug abuse, pathological gambling, compulsory shopping, or reckless driving.

Yet, these – the lack of empathy, the aloofness, the disdain, the sense of entitlement, the restricted application of humour, the unequal treatment, the sadism, and the paranoia – do not render the abuser a social misfit. This is because the abuser mistreats only his closest – spouse, children, or (much more rarely) colleagues, friends, neighbours. To the rest of the world, he appears to be a composed, rational, and functioning person. Abusers are very adept at casting a veil of secrecy – often with the active aid of their victims – over their dysfunction and misbehaviour.

Return

# The Path to Abuse

The abuser mistreats only his closest – spouse, children, or (much more rarely) colleagues, friends, and neighbours. To the rest of the world, he appears to be a composed, rational, and functioning person. Abusers are very adept at casting a veil of secrecy – often with the active aid of their victims – over their dysfunction and misbehaviour. This is why the abuser's offending behaviour comes as a shock even to his closest, nearest, and dearest.

In the October 2003 issue of the Journal of General Internal Medicine, Dr. Christina Nicolaidis of the Oregon Health and Science University in Portland, studied 30 women between the ages of 17 and 54, all survivors of attempted homicide by their intimate partners.

Half of them (14) confessed to have been "completely surprised" by the attack. They did not realize how violent their partner can be and the extent of risk they were continuously exposed to. Yet, all of them were the victims of previous episodes of abuse, including the physical sort. They could easily have predicted that an attempt to end the relationship would result in an attack on body and property.

*"If I had talked to some of these women before the attack, I would have counselled them about the domestic violence, but I would not have necessarily felt that their lives were in danger"*, Nicolaidis told Reuters – *"Now I am more careful to warn any woman who has experienced intimate partner violence about the risk to her life, especially around the time that the relationship is ending"*.

Secrecy is a major weapon in the abuser's arsenal. Many batterers maintain a double life and keep it a well-guarded secret. Others show one face – benign, even altruistic – to an admiring world and another - ominous and aggressive - at home. All abusers insist on keeping the abuse confidential, safe from prying eyes and ears.

The victims collaborate in this cruel game through cognitive dissonance and traumatic bonding. They rationalize the abuser's behaviour, attributing it to incompatibility, mental health problems, temporary setbacks or circumstances, a bad relationship, or substance abuse. Many victims feel guilty. They have been convinced by the offender that they are to blame for his misconduct ("You see what you made me do!", "You constantly provoke me!").

Others re-label the abuse and attribute it to the batterer's character idiosyncrasies. It is explained away as the sad outcome of a unique upbringing, childhood abuse, or passing events. Abusive incidents are recast as rarities, an abnormality, few and far between, not as bad as they appear to be, understandable outbursts, justified temper tantrums, childish manifestations, a tolerable price to pay for an otherwise wonderful relationship.

When is a woman's life at risk?

Nicolaidis Reuters: *"Classic risk factors for an attempted homicide by an intimate partner include escalating episodes or severity of violence, threats with or use of weapons, alcohol or drug use, and violence toward children."*

Yet, this list leaves out ambient abuse – the stealth, subtle, underground currents of maltreatment that sometimes go unnoticed even by the victims themselves. Until it is too late.

Return

# Ambient Abuse

Ambient abuse is the stealth, subtle, underground currents of maltreatment that sometimes go unnoticed even by the victims themselves, until it is too late. Ambient abuse penetrates and permeates everything – but is difficult to pinpoint and identify. It is ambiguous, atmospheric, diffuse. Hence its insidious and pernicious effects. It is by far the most dangerous kind of abuse there is.

It is the outcome of fear – fear of violence, fear of the unknown, fear of the unpredictable, the capricious, and the arbitrary. It is perpetrated by dropping subtle hints, by disorienting, by constant – and unnecessary – lying, by persistent doubting and demeaning, and by inspiring an air of unmitigated gloom and doom ("gaslighting").

Ambient abuse, therefore, is the fostering, propagation, and enhancement of an atmosphere of fear, intimidation, instability, unpredictability and irritation. There are no acts of traceable explicit abuse, nor any manipulative settings of control. Yet, the irksome feeling remains, a disagreeable foreboding, a premonition, a bad omen.

In the long-term, such an environment erodes the victim's sense of self-worth and self-esteem. Self-confidence is shaken badly. Often, the victim adopts a paranoid or schizoid stance and thus renders himself or herself exposed even more to criticism and judgement. The roles are thus reversed: the victim considered mentally deranged and the abuser – the suffering soul.

There are five categories of ambient abuse and they are often combined in the conduct of a single abuser:

## Inducing Disorientation

The abuser causes the victim to lose faith in her ability to manage and to cope with the world and its demands. She no longer trusts her senses, her skills, her strengths, her friends, her family, and the predictability and benevolence of her environment.

The abuser subverts the target's focus by disagreeing with her way of perceiving the world, her judgement, the facts of her existence, by criticizing her incessantly – and by offering plausible but specious alternatives. By constantly lying, he blurs the line between reality and nightmare.

By recurrently disapproving of her choices and actions – the abuser shreds the victim's self-confidence and shatters her self-esteem. By reacting disproportionately to the slightest "mistake" – he intimidates her to the point of paralysis.

### Incapacitating

The abuser gradually and surreptitiously takes over functions and chores previously adequately and skilfully performed by the victim. The prey finds itself isolated from the outer world, a hostage to the goodwill – or, more often, ill-will – of her captor. She is crippled by his encroachment and by the inexorable dissolution of her boundaries and ends up totally dependent on her tormentor's whims and desires, plans and stratagems.

Moreover, the abuser engineers impossible, dangerous, unpredictable, unprecedented, or highly specific situations in which he is sorely needed. The abuser makes sure that his knowledge, his skills, his connections, or his traits are the only ones applicable and the most useful in the situations that he, himself, wrought. The abuser generates his own indispensability.

### Shared Psychosis (Folie-a-Deux)

The abuser creates a fantasy world, inhabited by the victim and himself, and besieged by imaginary enemies. He allocates to the abused the role of defending this invented and unreal Universe. She must swear to secrecy, stand by her abuser no matter what, lie, fight, pretend, obfuscate and do whatever else it takes to preserve this oasis of inanity.

Her membership in the abuser's "kingdom" is cast as a privilege and a prize. But it is not to be taken for granted. She has to work hard to earn her continued affiliation. She is constantly being tested and evaluated. Inevitably, this interminable stress reduces the victim's resistance and her ability to "see straight".

### Abuse of Information

From the first moments of an encounter with another person, the abuser is on the prowl. He collects information. The more he knows about his potential victim – the better able he is to coerce, manipulate, charm, extort or convert it "to the cause". The abuser does not hesitate to misuse the information he gleans, regardless of its intimate nature or the circumstances in which he obtained it. This is a powerful tool in his armoury.

### Control by Proxy

If all else fails, the abuser recruits friends, colleagues, mates, family members, the authorities, institutions, neighbours, the media, teachers – in short, third parties – to do his bidding. He uses them to cajole, coerce, threaten, stalk, offer, retreat, tempt, convince, harass, communicate and otherwise manipulate his target. He controls these unaware instruments exactly as he plans to control his ultimate prey. He employs the same mechanisms and devices. And he dumps his props unceremoniously when the job is done.

Another form of control by proxy is to engineer situations in which abuse is inflicted upon another person. Such carefully crafted scenarios of embarrassment and humiliation provoke social sanctions (condemnation, opprobrium, or even physical punishment) against the victim. Society, or a social group become the instruments of the abuser.

Return

# Abuse by Proxy

If all else fails, the abuser recruits friends, colleagues, mates, family members, the authorities, institutions, neighbours, the media, teachers – in short, third parties – to do his bidding. He uses them to cajole, coerce, threaten, stalk, offer, retreat, tempt, convince, harass, communicate and otherwise manipulate his target. He controls these unaware instruments exactly as he plans to control his ultimate prey. He employs the same mechanisms and devices. And he dumps his props unceremoniously when the job is done.

One form of control by proxy is to engineer situations in which abuse is inflicted upon another person. Such carefully crafted scenarios of embarrassment and humiliation provoke social sanctions (condemnation, opprobrium, or even physical punishment) against the victim. Society, or a social group become the instruments of the abuser.

Abusers often use other people to do their dirty work for them. These – sometimes unwitting – accomplices belong to three groups:

### The Abuser's Social Milieu

Some offenders – mainly in patriarchal and misogynist societies – co-opt other family members, friends, and colleagues into aiding and abetting their abusive conduct. In extreme cases, the victim is held "hostage" – isolated and with little or no access to funds or transportation. Often, the couple's children are used as bargaining chips or leverage. Ambient abuse by the abuser's clan, kin, kith, and village or neighbourhood is rampant.

### The Victim's Social Milieu

Even the victim's relatives, friends, and colleagues are amenable to the considerable charm, persuasiveness, and manipulativeness of the abuser and to his impressive thespian skills. The abuser offers a plausible rendition of the events and interprets them to his favour. Others rarely have a chance to witness an abusive exchange first hand and at close quarters. In contrast, the victims are often on the verge of a nervous breakdown: harassed, unkempt, irritable, impatient, abrasive, and hysterical.

Confronted with this contrast between a polished, self-controlled, and suave abuser and his harried casualties – it is easy to reach the conclusion that the real victim is the abuser, or that both parties abuse each other equally. The prey's acts of self-defence, assertiveness, or insistence on her rights are interpreted as aggression, lability, or a mental health problem.

### The System

The abuser perverts the system – therapists, marriage counselours, mediators, court-appointed guardians, police officers, and judges. He uses them to pathologise the victim and to separate her from her sources of emotional sustenance – notably, from her children.

### Forms of Abuse by Proxy

Socially isolating and excluding the victim by discrediting her through a campaign of malicious rumours.

Harassing the victim by using others to stalk her or by charging her with offences she did not commit.

Provoking the victim into aggressive or even antisocial conduct by having others threaten her or her loved ones.

Colluding with others to render the victim dependent on the abuser.

But, by far, her children are the abuser's greatest source of leverage over his abused spouse or mate.

Return

# Leveraging the Children

The abuser often recruits his children to do his bidding. He uses them to tempt, convince, communicate, threaten, and otherwise manipulate his target, the children's other parent or a devoted relative (e.g., grandparents). He controls his – often gullible and unsuspecting – offspring exactly as he plans to control his ultimate prey. He employs the same mechanisms and devices. And he dumps his props unceremoniously when the job is done – which causes tremendous (and, typically, irreversible) emotional hurt.

## Co-Opting

Some offenders – mainly in patriarchal and misogynist societies – co-opt their children into aiding and abetting their abusive conduct. The couple's children are used as bargaining chips or leverage. They are instructed and encouraged by the abuser to shun the victim, criticise and disagree with her, withhold their love or affection, and inflict on her various forms of ambient abuse.

This is especially true with young – and, therefore vulnerable – offspring, particularly if they live with the abuser. They are frequently emotionally blackmailed by him ("If you want daddy to love you, do this or refrain from doing that"). They lack life experience and adult defences against manipulation. They may be dependent on the abuser economically and they always resent the abused for breaking up the family, for being unable to fully cater to their needs (she has to work for a living), and for "cheating" on her ex with a new boyfriend or husband.

## Co-Opting the System

The abuser perverts the system – therapists, marriage counselours, mediators, court-appointed guardians, police officers, and judges. He uses them to pathologise the victim and to separate her from her sources of emotional sustenance – notably, from her children. The abuser seeks custody to pain his ex and punish her.

### Threatening

Abusers are insatiable and vindictive. They always feel deprived and unfairly treated. Some of them are paranoid and sadistic. If they fail to manipulate their common children into abandoning the other parent, they begin treat the kids as enemies. They are not above threatening the children, abducting them, abusing them (sexually, physically, or psychologically), or even outright harming them – in order to get back at the erstwhile partner or in order to make her do something.

Most victims attempt to present to their children a "balanced" picture of the relationship and of the abusive spouse. In a vain attempt to avoid the notorious (and controversial) Parental Alienation Syndrome (PAS), they do not besmirch the abusive parent and, on the contrary, encourage the semblance of a normal, functional, liaison. This is the wrong approach. Not only is it counterproductive – it sometimes proves outright dangerous.

Return

# Tell Your Children the Truth

Children have a right to know the overall state of affairs between their parents. They have a right not to be cheated and deluded into thinking that "everything is basically OK" – or that the separation is reversible. Both parents are under a moral obligation to tell their offspring the truth: the relationship is over for good.

Younger kids tend to believe that they are somehow responsible or guilty for the breakdown of the marriage. They must be disabused of this notion. Both parents would do best to explain to them, in straightforward terms, what led to the dissolution of the bond. If spousal abuse is wholly or partly to blame – it should be brought out to the open and discussed honestly.

In such conversations it is best not to allocate blame. But this does not mean that wrong behaviours should be condoned or whitewashed. The victimized parent should tell the child that abusive conduct is wrong and must be avoided. The child should be taught how to identify the warning signs of impending abuse – sexual, verbal, psychological, and physical.

Moreover, a responsible parent should teach the child how to resist inappropriate and hurtful actions. The child should be brought up to insist on being respected by the other parent, on having him or her observe the child's boundaries and accept the child's needs and emotions, choices, and preferences.

The child should learn to say "no" and to walk away from potentially compromising situations with the abusive parent. The child should be brought up not to feel guilty for protecting himself/herself and for demanding his/her rights.

Remember this: An abusive parent IS DANGEROUS TO THE CHILD.

## Idealization - Devaluation Cycles

Most abusers accord the same treatment to children and adults. They regard both as Sources of Narcissistic Supply, mere instruments of gratification - idealize them at first and then devalue them in favour of alternative, safer and more subservient, sources. Such treatment – being idealized and then dumped and devalued – is traumatic and can have long-lasting emotional effects on the child.

### Jealousy

Some abusers are jealous of their offspring. They envy them for being the centre of attention and care. They treat their own kids as hostile competitors. Where the uninhibited expression of the aggression and hostility aroused by this predicament is illegitimate or impossible – the abuser prefers to stay away. Rather than attack his children, he sometimes immediately disconnects, detaches himself emotionally, becomes cold and uninterested, or directs transformed anger at his mate or at his parents (the more "legitimate" targets).

### Objectification

Sometimes, the child is perceived to be a mere bargaining chip in a drawn out battle with the erstwhile victim of the abuser (read the previous article in this series – Leveraging the Children). This is an extension of the abuser's tendency to dehumanize people and treat them as objects.

Such abusive partners seek to manipulate their former mate by "taking over" and monopolizing their common children. They foster an atmosphere of emotional (and bodily) incest. The abusive parent encourages his kids to idolize him, to adore him, to be awed by him, to admire his deeds and capabilities, to learn to blindly trust and obey him, in short to surrender to his charisma and to become submerged in his folie-de-grandeur.

### Breach of Personal Boundaries and Incest

It is at this stage that the risk of child abuse – up to and including outright incest – is heightened. Many abusers are auto-erotic. They are the preferred objects of their own sexual attentions. Molesting or having intercourse with one's children is as close as one gets to having sex with oneself.

Abusers often perceive sex in terms of annexation. The molested child is "assimilated" and becomes an extension of the offender, a fully controlled and manipulated object. Sex, to the abuser, is the ultimate act of depersonalization and objectification of the other. He actually masturbates with other people's bodies, his children's included.

The abuser's inability to acknowledge and abide by the personal boundaries set by others puts the child at heightened risk of abuse

– verbal, emotional, physical, and, often, sexual. The abuser's possessiveness and panoply of indiscriminate negative emotions – transformations of aggression, such as rage and envy – hinder his ability to act as a "good enough" parent. His propensities for reckless behaviour, substance abuse, and sexual deviance endanger the child's welfare, or even his or her life.

## Conflict

Minors pose little danger of criticizing the abuser or confronting him. They are perfect, malleable and abundant Sources of Narcissistic Supply. The narcissistic parent derives gratification from having incestuous relations with adulating, physically and mentally inferior, inexperienced and dependent "bodies".

Yet, the older the offspring, the more they become critical, even judgemental, of the abusive parent. They are better able to put into context and perspective his actions, to question his motives, to anticipate his moves. As they mature, they often refuse to continue to play the mindless pawns in his chess game. They hold grudges against him for what he has done to them in the past, when they were less capable of resistance. They can gauge his true stature, talents and achievements – which, usually, lag far behind the claims that he makes.

This brings the abusive parent back a full cycle. Again, he perceives his sons/daughters as threats. He quickly becomes disillusioned and devaluing. He loses all interest, becomes emotionally remote, absent and cold, rejects any effort to communicate with him, citing life pressures and the preciousness and scarceness of his time.

He feels burdened, cornered, besieged, suffocated, and claustrophobic. He wants to get away, to abandon his commitments to people who have become totally useless (or even damaging) to him. He does not understand why he has to support them, or to suffer their company and he believes himself to have been deliberately and ruthlessly trapped.

He rebels either passively-aggressively (by refusing to act or by intentionally sabotaging the relationships) or actively (by being overly critical, aggressive, unpleasant, verbally and psychologically abusive and so on). Slowly – to justify his acts to himself – he gets immersed in conspiracy theories with clear paranoid hues.

To his mind, the members of the family conspire against him, seek to belittle or humiliate or subordinate him, do not understand him, or stymie his growth. The abuser usually finally gets what he wants – his kids detach and abandon him to his great sorrow, but also to his great relief.

Return

# The Relief of Being Abandoned

The dissolution of the abuser's marriage or other meaningful (romantic, business, or other) relationships constitutes a major life crisis and a scathing narcissistic injury. To soothe and salve the pain of disillusionment, he administers to his aching soul a mixture of lies, distortions, half-truths and outlandish interpretations of events around him.

All abusers present with rigid and infantile (primitive) defence mechanisms: splitting, projection, Projective Identification, denial, intellectualization, and narcissism. But some abusers go further and decompensate by resorting to self-delusion. Unable to face the dismal failures that they are, they partially withdraws from reality.

## The Masochistic Avoidant Solution

The abuser directs some of this fury inwards, punishing himself for his "failure". This masochistic behaviour has the added "benefit" of forcing the abuser's closest to assume the roles of dismayed spectators or of persecutors and thus, either way, to pay him the attention that he craves.

Self-administered punishment often manifests as self-handicapping masochism – a cop-out. By undermining his work, his relationships, and his efforts, the increasingly fragile abuser avoids additional criticism and censure (negative supply). Self-inflicted failure is the abuser's doing and thus proves that he is the master of his own fate.

Masochistic abusers keep finding themselves in self-defeating circumstances which render success impossible – and *"an objective assessment of their performance improbable"* [Millon, 2000]. They act carelessly, withdraw in mid-effort, are constantly fatigued, bored, or disaffected and thus passive-aggressively sabotage their lives. Their suffering is defiant and by "deciding to abort" they reassert their omnipotence.

The abuser's pronounced and public misery and self-pity are compensatory and *"reinforce (his) self-esteem against overwhelming convictions of worthlessness"* [Millon, 2000]. His tribulations and anguish render him, in his eyes, unique, saintly, virtuous, righteous, resilient, and significant. They are, in other words, self-generated Narcissistic Supply.

Thus, paradoxically, the worst his anguish and unhappiness, the more relieved and elated such an abuser feels! He is "liberated" and "unshackled" by his own self-initiated abandonment, he insists. He never really wanted this commitment, he tells any willing (or buttonholed) listener – and anyhow, the relationship was doomed from the beginning by the egregious excesses and exploits of his wife (or partner or friend or boss).

## The Delusional Narrative Solution

This kind of abuser constructs a narrative in which he figures as the hero – brilliant, perfect, irresistibly handsome, destined for great things, entitled, powerful, wealthy, the centre of attention, etc. The bigger the strain on this delusional charade – the greater the gap between fantasy and reality – the more the delusion coalesces and solidifies.

Finally, if it is sufficiently protracted, it replaces reality and the abuser's reality test deteriorates. He withdraws his bridges and may become schizotypal, catatonic, or schizoid.

## The Antisocial Solution

This type of abuser has a natural affinity with the criminal. His lack of empathy and compassion, his deficient social skills, his disregard for social laws and morals – now erupt and blossom. He becomes a full fledged antisocial (sociopath or psychopath). He ignores the wishes and needs of others, he breaks the law, he violates all rights – natural and legal, he holds people in contempt and disdain, he derides society and its codes, he punishes the ignorant ingrates – that, to his mind, drove him to this state – by acting criminally and by jeopardizing their safety, lives, or property.

## The Paranoid Schizoid Solution

Another class of abuser develop persecutory delusions. He perceives slights and insults where none were intended. He becomes subject to ideas of reference (people are gossiping about him, mocking him, prying into his affairs, cracking his e-mail, etc.). He is convinced that he is the centre of malign and malintentioned attention. People are conspiring to humiliate him, punish him, abscond with his property, delude him, impoverish him, confine him physically or intellectually, censor him, impose on his time, force him to action (or to inaction), frighten him, coerce him, surround and besiege him, change his mind, part with his values, victimize or even murder him, and so on.

Some abusers withdraw completely from a world populated with such minacious and ominous objects (really projections of internal objects and processes). They avoid all social contact, except the most necessary. They refrain from meeting people, falling in love, having sex, talking to others, or even corresponding with them. In short: they become schizoids – not out of social shyness, but out of what they feel to be their choice. "This evil, hopeless world does not deserve me" – goes the inner refrain – "and I shall waste none of my time and resources on it."

## The Paranoid Aggressive (Explosive) Solution

Other abusers who develop persecutory delusions, resort to an aggressive stance, a more violent resolution of their internal conflict. They become verbally, psychologically, situationally (and, more rarely, physically) abusive. They insult, castigate, chastise, berate, demean, and deride their nearest and dearest (often well wishers and loved ones). They explode in unprovoked displays of indignation, righteousness, condemnation, and blame. Theirs is an exegetic Bedlam. They interpret everything – even the most innocuous, inadvertent, and innocent comment – as designed to provoke and humiliate them. They sow fear, revulsion, hate, and malignant envy. They flail against the windmills of reality – a pathetic, forlorn, sight. But often they cause real and lasting damage – fortunately, mainly to themselves.

Return

# How to Cope with Your Paranoid Ex

Your abusive ex is likely to cope with the pain and humiliation of separation by spreading lies, distortions, and half-truths about you and by proffering self-justifying interpretations of the events leading to the break-up. By targeting your closest, nearest, and dearest – your family, your children, boss, colleagues, co-workers, neighbours, and friends – your ex hopes to achieve two equally unrealistic goals:

1. To isolate you socially and force you to come running back to his waiting and "loving" arms.
2. To communicate to you that he still "loves" you, is still interested in you and your affairs and that, no matter what, you are inseparable. He magnanimously is willing to forgive all the "horrible things" you did to him and revive the relationship (which, after all, had its good moments).

How to cope with delusional, paranoid – and, therefore, dangerous – stalkers?

It may be difficult, but turn off your emotions. Abusers prey on other people's empathy, pity, altruism, nostalgia, and tendency to lend a helping hand. Some stalkers "punish" themselves – drink to excess, commit offences and get caught, abuse drugs, have accidents, fall prey to scams – in order to force their victims to pity them and get in touch.

The only viable coping strategy is to ignore your abusive ex. Take all necessary precautions to protect yourself and your family. Alert law enforcement agencies to any misbehaviour, violence, or harassment. File charges and have restraining orders issued. But, otherwise, avoid all gratuitous interactions.

[For additional tips and advice see: Coping with Your Abuser - Refuse All Contact.]

Do not collude or collaborate in your ex's fantasies and delusions. You cannot buy his mercy or his goodwill – he has none. Do not support his notions, even indirectly, that he is brilliant, perfect, irresistibly handsome, destined for great things, entitled, powerful, wealthy, the centre of attention, etc. Abusers act on these misperceptions and try to coerce you into becoming an integral part of their charades.

Abuse is a criminal offence and, by definition, abusers are criminals: they lack empathy and compassion, have deficient social skills, disregard laws, norms, contracts, and morals. You can't negotiate with your abusive ex and you can't strike a bargain with him. You can't reform, cure, or recondition him. He is a threat to you, to your property, and to your dear ones. Treat him as such.

The most dangerous class of abusers is the paranoid-delusional. If your ex is one of these, he is likely to:

1. Believe that you still love him (erotomania). Interpret everything you do or say – even to third parties – as "hidden messages" addressed to him and professing your undying devotion (ideas of reference).
2. Confuse the physical with the emotional (regard sex as "proof" of love and be prone to rape you).
3. Blame the failure of the relationship on you or on others – social workers, your friends, your family, your children.
4. Seek to "remove" the obstacles to a "happy" and long relationship – sometimes by resorting to violence (kidnapping or murdering the sources of frustration).
5. Be very envious of your newfound autonomy and try to sabotage it by reasserting his control over you (for instance, break and enter into your house, leave intrusive messages on your answering machine, follow you around and monitor your home from a stationary car).
6. Harm you (and sometimes himself) in a fit of indignation (and to punish you) if he feels that no renewed relationship is possible.
7. Develop persecutory delusions. Perceive slights and insults where none are intended. Become convinced that he is the centre of a conspiracy to deny him (and you) happiness, to humiliate him, punish him, delude him, impoverish him, confine him physically or intellectually, censor him, impose on his time, force him to action (or to inaction), frighten him, coerce him, surround and besiege him, change his mind, part with his values, victimize or even murder him, and so on.

The paranoid's conduct is unpredictable and there is no "typical scenario". But experience shows that you can minimize the danger to yourself and to your household by taking some simple steps.

Return

# Avoiding Your Paranoid Ex

If at all possible, put as much physical distance as you can between yourself and the stalker. Change address, phone number, email accounts, cell phone number, enlist the kids in a new school, find a new job, get a new credit card, open a new bank account. Do not inform your paranoid ex about your whereabouts and your new life. You may have to make painful sacrifices, such as minimize contact with your family and friends.

Even with all these precautions, your abusive ex is likely to find you, furious that you have fled and evaded him, raging at your newfound existence, suspicious and resentful of your freedom and personal autonomy. Violence is more than likely. Unless deterred, paranoid former spouses tend to be harmful, even lethal.

Be prepared: alert your local law enforcement officers, check out your neighbourhood domestic violence shelter, consider owning a gun for self-defence (or, at the very least, a stun gun or mustard spray). Carry these with you at all times. Keep them close by and accessible even when you are asleep or in the bathroom.

Erotomanic stalking can last many years. Do not let down your guard even if you haven't heard from him. Stalkers leave traces. They tend, for instance, to "scout" the territory before they make their move. A typical stalker invades his or her victim's privacy a few times long before the crucial and injurious encounter.

Is your computer being tampered with? Is someone downloading your e-mail? Has anyone been to your house while you were away? Any signs of breaking and entering, missing things, atypical disorder (or too much order)? Is your post being delivered erratically, some of the envelopes opened and then sealed? Mysterious phone calls abruptly disconnected when you pick up? Your stalker must have dropped by and is monitoring you.

Notice any unusual pattern, any strange event, any weird occurrence. Someone is driving by your house morning and evening? A new "gardener" or maintenance man came by in your absence? Someone is making enquiries about you and your family? Maybe it's time to move on.

Teach your children to avoid your paranoid ex and to report to you immediately any contact he has made with them. Abusive bullies often strike where it hurts most – at one's kids. Explain the danger without being unduly alarming. Make a distinction between adults they can trust – and your abusive former spouse, whom they should avoid.

Ignore your gut reactions and impulses. Sometimes, the stress is so onerous and so infuriating that you feel like striking back at the stalker. Don't do it. Don't play his game. He is better at it than you are and is likely to defeat you. Instead, unleash the full force of the law whenever you get the chance to do so: restraining orders, spells in jail, and frequent visits from the police tend to check the abuser's violent and intrusive conduct.

The other behavioural extreme is equally futile and counterproductive. Do not try to buy peace by appeasing your abuser. Submissiveness and attempts to reason with him only whet the stalker's appetite. He regards both as contemptible weaknesses, vulnerabilities he can exploit. You cannot communicate with a paranoid because he is likely to distort everything you say to support his persecutory delusions, sense of entitlement, and grandiose fantasies. You cannot appeal to his emotions – he has none, at least not positive ones.

Remember: your abusive and paranoid former partner blames it all on you. As far as he is concerned, you recklessly and unscrupulously wrecked a wonderful thing you both had going. He is vengeful, seething, and prone to bouts of uncontrolled and extreme aggression. Don't listen to those who tell you to "take it easy". Hundreds of thousands of women paid with their lives for heeding this advice. Your paranoid stalker is inordinately dangerous – and, more likely than not, he is with you for a long time to come.

How long and how it all ends depends on a few factors.

Return

# The Three Forms of Closure

For her traumatic wounds to heal, the victim of abuse requires closure – one final interaction with her tormentor in which he, hopefully, acknowledges his misbehaviour and even tenders an apology. Fat chance. Few abusers – especially if they are narcissistic – are amenable to such weakling pleasantries. More often, the abused are left to wallow in a poisonous stew of misery, self-pity, and self-recrimination.

Depending on the severity, duration, and nature of the abuse, there are three forms of effective closure:

## Conceptual Closure

This most common variant involves a frank dissection of the abusive relationship. The parties meet to analyze what went wrong, to allocate blame and guilt, to derive lessons, and to part ways cathartically cleansed. In such an exchange, a compassionate offender (quite the oxymoron, admittedly) offers his prey the chance to rid herself of cumulating resentment.

He also disabuses her of the notion that she, in any way, was guilty or responsible for her maltreatment, that it was all her fault, that she deserved to be punished, and that she could have saved the relationship (malignant optimism). With this burden gone, the victim is ready to resume her life and to seek companionship and love elsewhere.

## Retributive Closure

When the abuse has been "gratuitous" (sadistic), repeated, and protracted, conceptual closure is not enough. Retribution is called for, an element of vengeance, of restorative justice and a restored balance. Recuperation hinges on punishing the delinquent and merciless party. The penal intervention of the Law is often therapeutic to the abused.

Regrettably, the victim's understandable emotions often lead to abusive (and illegal) acts. Many of the tormented stalk their erstwhile abusers and take the law into their own hands. Abuse tends to breed abuse all around, in both prey and predator.

**Dissociative Closure**

Absent the other two forms of closure, victims of egregious and prolonged mistreatment tend to repress their painful memories. In extremis, they dissociate. The Dissociative Identity Disorder (DID) – formerly known as "Multiple Personality Disorder" – is thought to be such a reaction. The harrowing experiences are "sliced off", tucked away, and attributed to "another personality".

Sometimes, the victim "assimilates" his or her tormentor, and even openly and consciously identifies with him. This is the narcissistic defence. In his own anguished mind, the victim becomes omnipotent and, therefore, invulnerable. He or she develops a False Self. The True Self is, thus, shielded from further harm and injury.

According to psychodynamic theories of psychopathology, repressed content rendered unconscious is the cause of all manner of mental health disorders. The victim thus pays a hefty price for avoiding and evading his or her predicament.

Return

# How Victims are Affected by Abuse

Repeated abuse has long lasting pernicious and traumatic effects such as panic attacks, hypervigilance, sleep disturbances, flashbacks (intrusive memories), suicidal ideation, and psychosomatic symptoms. The victims experience shame, depression, anxiety, embarrassment, guilt, humiliation, abandonment, and an enhanced sense of vulnerability.

In "Stalking – An Overview of the Problem" [Can J Psychiatry 1998;43:473-476], authors Karen M Abrams and Gail Erlick Robinson write:

*"Sometimes the victim develops an almost fatal resolve that, inevitably, one day she will be murdered. Victims, unable to live a normal life, describe feeling stripped of self-worth and dignity. Personal control and resources, psychosocial development, social support, premorbid personality traits, and the severity of the stress may all influence how the victim experiences and responds to it..."*

Surprisingly, verbal, psychological, and emotional abuse have the same effects as the physical variety [Psychology Today, September/October 2000 issue, pp. 24]. Abuse of all kinds also interferes with the victim's ability to work. Abrams and Robinson wrote this [in "Occupational Effects of Stalking", Can J Psychiatry 2002;47:468-472]:

*"... (B)eing stalked by a former partner may affect a victim's ability to work in 3 ways. First, the stalking behaviours often interfere directly with the ability to get to work (for example, flattening tires or other methods of preventing leaving the home). Second, the workplace may become an unsafe location if the offender decides to appear. Third, the mental health effects of such trauma may result in forgetfulness, fatigue, lowered concentration, and disorganization. These factors may lead to the loss of employment, with accompanying loss of income, security, and status."*

Still, it is hard to generalize. Victims are not a uniform lot. In some cultures, abuse is commonplace and accepted as a legitimate mode of communication, a sign of love and caring, and a boost to the abuser's self-image. In such circumstances, the victim is likely to adopt the norms of society and avoid serious trauma.

Deliberate, cold-blooded, and premeditated torture has worse and longer-lasting effects than abuse meted out by the abuser in rage and loss of self-control. The existence of a loving and accepting social support network is another mitigating factor. Finally, the ability to express negative emotions safely and to cope with them constructively is crucial to healing.

Typically, by the time the abuse reaches critical and all-pervasive proportions, the abuser had already, spider-like, isolated his victim from family, friends, and colleagues. She is catapulted into a nether land, cult-like setting where reality itself dissolves into a continuing nightmare.

When she emerges on the other end of this wormhole, the abused woman (or, more rarely, man) feels helpless, self-doubting, worthless, stupid, and a guilty failure for having botched her relationship and "abandoned" her "family". In an effort to regain perspective and avoid embarrassment, the victim denies the abuse or minimizes it.

No wonder that survivors of abuse tend to be clinically depressed, neglect their health and personal appearance, and succumb to boredom, rage, and impatience. Many end up abusing prescription drugs or drinking or otherwise behaving recklessly.

Some victims even develop Post-Traumatic Stress Disorder (PTSD).

Return

# How Victims are Affected by Abuse

## Post-Traumatic Stress Disorder (PTSD)

Contrary to popular misconceptions, Post-Traumatic Stress Disorder (PTSD) and Acute Stress Disorder (or Reaction) are not typical responses to prolonged abuse. They are the outcomes of sudden exposure to severe or extreme stressors (stressful events). Some victims whose life or body have been directly and unequivocally threatened by an abuser react by developing these syndromes. PTSD is, therefore, typically associated with the aftermath of physical and sexual abuse in both children and adults.

One's (or someone else's) looming death, violation, personal injury, or powerful pain are sufficient to provoke the behaviours, cognitions, and emotions that together are known as PTSD. Even learning about such mishaps may be enough to trigger massive anxiety responses.

The first phase of PTSD involves incapacitating and overwhelming fear. The victim feels like she has been thrust into a nightmare or a horror movie. She is rendered helpless by her own terror. She keeps re-living the experience through recurrent and intrusive visual and auditory hallucinations ("flashbacks") or dreams. In some flashbacks, the victim completely lapses into a dissociative state and physically re-enacts the event while being thoroughly oblivious to her whereabouts.

In an attempt to suppress this constant playback and the attendant exaggerated startle response (jumpiness), the victim tries to avoid all stimuli associated, however indirectly, with the traumatic event. Many develop full-scale phobias (Agoraphobia, Claustrophobia, fear of heights, aversion to specific animals, objects, modes of transportation, neighbourhoods, buildings, occupations, weather, and so on).

Most PTSD victims are especially vulnerable on the anniversaries of their abuse. They try to avoid thoughts, feelings, conversations, activities, situations, or people who remind them of the traumatic occurrence ("triggers").

This constant hypervigilance and arousal, sleep disorders (mainly insomnia), the irritability ("short fuse"), and the inability to concentrate and complete even relatively simple tasks erode the victim's resilience. Utterly fatigued, most patients manifest protracted periods of numbness, automatism, and, in radical cases, near-catatonic posture. Response times to verbal cues increase dramatically. Awareness of the environment decreases, sometimes dangerously so. The victims are described by their nearest and dearest as "zombies", "machines", or "automata".

The victims appear to be sleepwalking, depressed, dysphoric, anhedonic (not interested in anything and find pleasure in nothing). They report feeling detached, emotionally absent, estranged, and alienated. Many victims say that their "life is over" and expect to have no career, family, or otherwise meaningful future.

The victim's family and friends complain that she is no longer capable of showing intimacy, tenderness, compassion, empathy, and of having sex (due to her post-traumatic "frigidity"). Many victims become paranoid, impulsive, reckless, and self-destructive. Others somatize their mental problems and complain of numerous physical ailments. They all feel guilty, shameful, humiliated, desperate, hopeless, and hostile.

PTSD need not appear immediately after the harrowing experience. It can be – and often is – delayed by days or even months. It lasts more than one month (usually much longer). Sufferers of PTSD report subjective distress (the manifestations of PTSD are ego-dystonic). Their functioning in various settings – job performance, grades at school, sociability – deteriorates markedly.

The DSM-IV-TR (Diagnostic and Statistical Manual) criteria for diagnosing PTSD are far too restrictive. PTSD seems to also develop in the wake of verbal and emotional abuse and in the aftermath of drawn out traumatic situations (such as a nasty divorce). Hopefully, the DSM text will be adapted to reflect this sad reality.

Return

# How Victims are Affected by Abuse

## Recovery and Healing

Victims of abuse in all its forms – verbal, emotional, financial, physical, and sexual – are often disorientated. They require not only therapy to heal their emotional wounds, but also practical guidance and topical education. At first, the victim is, naturally, distrustful and even hostile. The therapist or case worker must establish confidence and rapport painstakingly and patiently.

The therapeutic alliance requires constant reassurance that the environment and treatment modalities chosen are safe and supportive. This is not easy to do, partly because of objective factors such as the fact that the records and notes of the therapist are not confidential. The offender can force their disclosure in a court of law simply by filing a civil lawsuit against the survivor!

The first task is to legitimize and validate the victim's fears. This is done by making clear to her that she is not responsible for her abuse or guilty for what happened. Victimization is the abuser's fault – it is not the victim's choice. Victims do not seek abuse – although, admittedly some of them keep finding abusive partners and forming relationships of co-dependence. Facing, reconstructing, and reframing the traumatic experiences is a crucial and indispensable first phase.

The therapist should present the victim with her own ambivalence and the ambiguity of her messages – but this ought to be done gently, non-judgementally, and without condemnation. The more willing and able the abuse survivor is to confront the reality of her mistreatment (and the offender), the stronger she would feel and the less guilty.

Typically, the patient's helplessness decreases together with her self-denial. Her self-esteem as well as her sense of self-worth stabilize. The therapist should emphasize the survivor's strengths and demonstrate how they can save her from a recurrence of the abuse or help her cope with it and with her abuser.

Education is an important tool in this process of recovery. The patient should be made aware of the prevalence and nature of violence against women and stalking, their emotional and physical effects, warning signs and red flags, legal redresses, coping strategies, and safety precautions.

The therapist or social worker should provide the victim with lists of contacts: help organizations, law enforcement agencies, other women in her condition, domestic violence shelters, and victims' support groups both online and in her neighbourhood or city. Knowledge empowers and reduces the victim's sense of isolation and worthlessness.

Helping the survivor regain control of her life is the over-riding goal of the entire therapeutic process. With this aim in mind, she should be encouraged to re-establish contact with family, friends, colleagues, and the community at large. The importance of a tightly-knit social support network cannot be exaggerated.

Ideally, after a period of combined tutoring, talk therapy, and (anti-anxiety or antidepressant) medications, the survivor will self-mobilize and emerge from the experience more resilient and assertive and less gullible and self-deprecating.

Return

# How Victims are Affected by Abuse

## The Conflicts of Therapy

*Disclaimer*

*Statistically, the majority of abuse victims are female and most abusers are male. Still, we should bear in mind that there are male victims and female offenders as well.*

Ideally, after a period of combined tutoring, talk therapy, and (anti-anxiety or antidepressant) medications, the survivor will self-mobilize and emerge from the experience more resilient and assertive and less gullible and self-deprecating.

But therapy is not always a smooth ride.

Victims of abuse are saddled with emotional baggage which often provokes even in the most experienced therapists reactions of helplessness, rage, fear and guilt. Countertransference is common: therapists of both genders identify with the victim and resent her for making them feel impotent and inadequate (for instance, in their role as "social protectors").

Reportedly, to fend off anxiety and a sense of vulnerability ("it could have been me, sitting there!"), female therapists involuntarily blame the "spineless" victim and her poor judgement for causing the abuse. Some female therapists concentrate on the victim's childhood (rather than her harrowing present) or accuse her of overreacting.

Male therapists may assume the mantle of the "chivalrous rescuer", the "knight in the shining armour" - thus, inadvertently upholding the victim's view of herself as immature, helpless, in need of protection, vulnerable, weak, and ignorant. The male therapist may be driven to prove to the victim that not all men are "beasts", that there are "good" specimen (like himself). If his (conscious or unconscious) overtures are rejected, the therapist may identify with the abuser and re-victimize or pathologise his patient.

Many therapists tend to overidentify with the victim and rage at the abuser, at the police, and at "the system". They expect the victim to be equally aggressive even as they broadcast to her how powerless, unjustly treated, and discriminated against she is. If she "fails" to externalize aggression and show assertiveness, they feel betrayed and disappointed.

Most therapists react impatiently to the victim's perceived co-dependence, unclear messages, and on-off relationship with her tormentor. Such rejection by the therapist may lead to a premature termination of the therapy, well before the victim learned how to process anger and cope with her low self-esteem and learned helplessness.

Finally, there is the issue of personal security. Some ex-lovers and ex-spouses are paranoid stalkers and, therefore, dangerous. The therapist may even be required to testify against the offender in a court of law. Therapists are human and fear for their own safety and the security of their loved ones. This affects their ability to help the victim.

This is not to say that therapy invariably fails. On the contrary, most therapeutic alliances succeed to teach the victim to accept and transform her negative emotions into positive energy and to competently draw and implement realistic plans of action while avoiding the pitfalls of the past. Good therapy is empowering and restores the victim's sense of control over her life.

Return

# *Toxic Relationships*

## Abuse and Its Aftermath

**Spousal Abuse and Domestic Violence**

# Danse Macabre

## The Dynamics of Spousal Abuse

It takes two to tango – and an equal number to sustain a long-term abusive relationship. The abuser and the abused form a bond, a dynamic, and a dependence. Expressions such as "folie-a-deux" and the "Stockholm Syndrome" capture facets – two of a myriad – of this danse macabre. It often ends fatally. It is always an excruciatingly painful affair.

Abuse is closely correlated with alcoholism, drug consumption, intimate-partner homicide, teen pregnancy, infant and child mortality, spontaneous abortion, reckless behaviours, suicide, and the onset of mental health disorders. It doesn't help that society refuses to openly and frankly tackle this pernicious phenomenon and the guilt and shame associated with it.

People – overwhelmingly women – remain in an abusive household for a variety of reasons: economic, parental (to protect the children), and psychological. But the objective obstacles facing the battered spouse cannot be overstated.

The abuser treats his spouse as an object, an extension of himself, devoid of a separate existence and denuded of distinct needs. Thus, typically, the couple's assets are on his name – from real estate to medical insurance policies. The victim has no family or friends because her abusive partner or husband frowns on her initial independence and regards it as a threat. By intimidating, cajoling, charming, and making false promises, the abuser isolates his prey from the rest of society and, thus, makes her dependence on him total. She is often also denied the option to study and acquire marketable skills or augment them.

Abandoning the abusive spouse frequently leads to a prolonged period of destitution and peregrination. Custody is usually denied to parents without a permanent address, a job, income security, and, therefore, stability. Thus, the victim stands to lose not only her mate and nest – but also her off-spring. There is the added menace of violent retribution by the abuser or his proxies – coupled with emphatic contrition on his part and a protracted and irresistible "charm offensive".

Gradually, she is convinced to put up with her spouse's cruelty in order to avoid this harrowing predicament.

But there is more to an abusive dyad than mere pecuniary convenience. The abuser – stealthily but unfailingly – exploits the vulnerabilities in the psychological makeup of his victim. The abused party may have low self-esteem, a fluctuating sense of self-worth, primitive defence mechanisms, phobias, mental health problems, a disability, a history of failure, or a tendency to blame herself, or to feel inadequate (autoplastic neurosis). She may have come from an abusive family or environment – which conditioned her to expect abuse as inevitable and "normal". In extreme and rare cases – the victim is a masochist, possessed of an urge to seek ill-treatment and pain.

The abuser may be functional or dysfunctional, a pillar of society, or a peripatetic con-artist, rich or poor, young or old. There is no universally-applicable profile of the "typical abuser". Yet, abusive behaviour often indicates serious underlying psychopathologies. Absent empathy, the abuser perceives the abused spouse only dimly and partly, as one would an inanimate source of frustration. The abuser, in his mind, interacts only with himself and with "introjects" – representations of outside objects, such as his victims.

Return

# Intimacy and Abuse

It is an established fact that abuse – verbal, psychological, emotional, physical, and sexual – co-occurs with intimacy. Most reported offences are between intimate partners and between parents and children. This defies common sense. Emotionally, it should be easier to batter, molest, assault, or humiliate a total stranger. It's as if intimacy CAUSES abuse, incubates and nurtures it.

And, in a way, it does.

Many abusers believe that their abusive conduct fosters, enhances, and cements their intimate relationships. To them, pathological jealousy is proof of love, possessiveness replaces mature bonding, and battering is a form of paying attention to the partner and communicating with her.

Such habitual offenders do not know any better. They were often raised in families, societies, and cultures where abuse is condoned outright – or, at least, not frowned upon. Maltreatment of one's significant others is part of daily life, as inevitable as the weather, a force of nature.

Intimacy is often perceived to include a license to abuse. The abuser treats his nearest, dearest, and closest as mere objects, instruments of gratification, utilities, or extensions of himself. He feels that he "owns" his spouse, girlfriend, lovers, children, parents, siblings, or colleagues. As the owner, he has the right to "damage the goods" or even dispose of them altogether.

Most abusers are scared of real intimacy and deep commitment. They lead a "pretend", confabulated life. Their "love" and "relationships" are gaudy, fake imitations. The abuser seeks to put a distance between himself and those who truly love him, who cherish and value him as a human being, who enjoy his company, and who strive to establish a long-term, meaningful relationship with him.

Abuse, in other words, is a reaction to the perceived threat of looming intimacy, aimed at fending it off, intended to decimate closeness, tenderness, affection, and compassion before they thrive and consume the abuser. Abuse is a panic reaction. The batterer, the molester, are scared out of their wits – they feel entrapped, imprisoned, shackled, and insidiously altered.

Lashing out in blind and violent rage they punish the perceived perpetrators of intimacy. The more obnoxiously they behave, the less the risk of lifelong bondage. The more heinous their acts, the safer they feel. Battering, molesting, raping, berating, taunting – are all forms of reasserting lost control. In the abuser's thwarted mind, abuse equals mastery and continued, painless, emotionally numbed, survival.

Return

# The Mind of the Abuser

To embark on our exploration of the abusive mind, we first need to agree on a taxonomy of abusive behaviours. Methodically observing abuse is the surest way of getting to know the perpetrators.

Abusers appear to be suffering from dissociation (multiple personality). At home, they are intimidating and suffocating monsters – outdoors, they are wonderful, caring, giving, and much-admired pillars of the community. Why this duplicity?

It is only partly premeditated and intended to disguise the abuser's acts. More importantly, it reflects his inner world, where the victims are nothing but two-dimensional representations, objects, devoid of emotions and needs, or mere extensions of his self. Thus, to the abuser's mind, his quarries do not merit humane treatment, nor do they evoke empathy.

Typically, the abuser succeeds to convert the abused into his worldview. The victim – and his victimizers – don't realize that something is wrong with the relationship. This denial is common and all-pervasive. It permeates other spheres of the abuser's life as well. Such people are often narcissists – steeped in grandiose fantasies, divorced from reality, besotted with their False Self, consumed by feelings of omnipotence, omniscience, entitlement, and paranoia.

Contrary to stereotypes, both the abuser and his prey usually suffer from disturbances in the regulation of their sense of self-worth. Low self-esteem and lack of self-confidence render the abuser – and his confabulated self – vulnerable to criticism, disagreement, exposure, and adversity – real or imagined.

Abuse is bred by fear – fear of being mocked or betrayed, emotional insecurity, anxiety, panic, and apprehension. It is a last ditch effort to exert control – for instance, over one's spouse – by "annexing" her, "possessing" her, and "punishing" her for being a separate entity, with her own boundaries, needs, feelings, preferences, and dreams.

In her seminal tome, "The Verbally Abusive Relationship", Patricia Evans lists the various forms of manipulation which together constitute verbal and emotional (psychological) abuse:

Withholding (the silent treatment), countering (refuting or invalidating the spouse's statements or actions), discounting (putting down her emotions, possessions, experiences, hopes, and fears), sadistic and brutal humour, blocking (avoiding a meaningful exchange, diverting the conversation, changing the subject), blaming and accusing, judging and criticizing, undermining and sabotaging, threatening, name calling, forgetting and denying, ordering around, denial, and abusive anger.

To these we can add:

Wounding "honesty", ignoring, smothering, dotting, unrealistic expectations, invasion of privacy, tactlessness, sexual abuse, physical maltreatment, humiliating, shaming, insinuating, lying, exploiting, devaluing and discarding, being unpredictable, reacting disproportionately, dehumanizing, objectifying, abusing confidence and intimate information, engineering impossible situations, control by proxy and ambient abuse.

In his comprehensive essay, "Understanding the Batterer in Custody and Visitation Disputes", Lundy Bancroft observes:

*"Because of the distorted perceptions that the abuser has of rights and responsibilities in relationships, he considers himself to be the victim. Acts of self-defence on the part of the battered woman or the children, or efforts they make to stand up for their rights, he defines as aggression AGAINST him. He is often highly skilled at twisting his descriptions of events to create the convincing impression that he has been victimized. He thus accumulates grievances over the course of the relationship to the same extent that the victim does, which can lead professionals to decide that the members of the couple 'abuse each other' and that the relationship has been 'mutually hurtful'."*

Yet, whatever the form of ill-treatment and cruelty – the structure of the interaction and the roles played by abuser and victim are the same. Identifying these patterns – and how they are influenced by prevailing social and cultural mores, values, and beliefs – is a first and indispensable step towards recognizing abuse, coping with it, and ameliorating its inevitable and excruciatingly agonizing aftermath.

Return

# Condoning Abuse

Statistics show that intimate partner abuse, including domestic violence, has declined by ONE HALF in the last decade in the United States. Jay Silverman and Gail Williamson demonstrated in "Social Ecology and Entitlements Involved in Battering by Heterosexual College Males" [published in Violence and Victims, Volume 12, Number 2, Spring 1997] that abuse is best predicted by two factors: the belief that mistreatment is justified and the succour of peers.

These two facts elucidate the cultural and social roots of abusive behaviour. Abuse is bound to be found in patriarchal, narcissistic, or misogynistic collectives. Many societies exhibit cross sections of these three traits. Thus, most patriarchal groups are also misogynistic, either overtly and ideologically so – or covertly and in denial.

Paradoxically, women's lib initially makes things worse. The first period of social dislocation – when gender roles are redefined – often witnesses a male backlash in the form of last ditch patriarchy and last resort violence, trying to restore the "ancient regime". But as awareness and acceptance of women's equal rights grow, abuse is frowned upon and, consequently, declines.

Alas, four fifths of humanity are far from this utopian state of things. Even in the most prosperous, well-educated, and egalitarian societies of the West there are sizable pockets of ill-treatment that cut across all demographic and social-economic categories.

Women are physically weaker and, despite recent strides, economically deprived or restricted. This makes them ideal victims – dependent, helpless, devalued. Even in the most advanced societies, women are still expected to serve their husbands, maintain the family, surrender their autonomy, and abrogate their choices and preferences if incompatible with the ostensible breadwinner's.

Women are also widely feared. The more primitive, poorer, or less educated the community – the more women are decried as evil temptresses, whores, witches, possessors of mysterious powers, defilers, contaminants, inferior, corporeal (as opposed to spiritual), subversive, disruptive, dangerous, cunning, or lying.

Violence is considered by members of such collectives a legitimate means of communicating wishes, enforcing discipline, coercing into action, punishing, and gaining the approval of kin, kith, and peers. To the abuser, the family is an instrument of gratification – economic, narcissistic, and sexual. It is a mere extension of the offender's inner world, and, thus, devoid of autonomy and independent views, opinions, preferences, needs, choices, emotions, fears, and hopes.

The abuser feels that he is entirely within his rights to impose his species of order in his own impregnable "castle". The other members of the household are objects. He reacts with violent rage to any proof or reminder to the contrary. Moreover, his view of the family is embedded in many legal systems, supported by norms and conventions, and reflected in social arrangements.

But abusive behaviour is frequently the outcome of objective societal and cultural factors.

Abuse and violence are "intergenerationally transmitted". Children who grow up in dysfunctional and violent families – and believe that the aggression was justified – are vastly more likely to become abusive parents and spouses.

Social stresses and anomy and their psychological manifestations foster intimate partner violence and child abuse. War or civil strife, unemployment, social isolation, single parenthood, prolonged or chronic sickness, unsustainably large family, poverty, persistent hunger, marital discord, a new baby, a dying parent, an invalid to be cared for, death of one's nearest and dearest, incarceration, infidelity, substance abuse – have all proven to be contributing factors.

Return

# The Anomaly of Abuse

Is abuse anomalous – or an inevitable part of human nature? If the former – is it the outcome of flawed genetics, nurture (environment and upbringing) – or both? Can it be "cured" – or merely modified, regulated, and accommodated? There are three groups of theories – three schools – regarding abusers and their conduct.

## Abuse as an Emergent Phenomenon

The precipitous drop in intimate partner abuse in the last decade (especially in the West) seems to imply that abusive behaviour is emergent and that its frequency fluctuates under given circumstances. It seems to be embedded in social and cultural contexts and to be a learned or acquired behaviour. People who grew up in an atmosphere of domestic violence, for instance, tend to perpetuate and propagate it by abusing their own spouses and family members.

Social stresses and anomy and their psychological manifestations foster domestic violence and child abuse. War or civil strife, unemployment, social isolation, single parenthood, prolonged or chronic sickness, unsustainably large family, poverty, persistent hunger, marital discord, a new baby, a dying parent, an invalid to be cared for, death of one's nearest and dearest, incarceration, infidelity, substance abuse – have all proven to be contributing factors.

## Hard-Wired Abuse

Abuse cuts across countries, continents, and disparate societies and cultures. It is common among the rich and the poor, the highly educated and the less so, people of all races and creeds. It is a universal phenomenon – and always has been, throughout the ages.

More than half of all abusers do not come from abusive or dysfunctional households where they could have picked up this offensive comportment. Rather, it seems to "run in their blood".

Additionally, abuse is often associated with mental illness, now fashionably thought to be biological-medical in nature.

Hence the hypothesis that abusive ways are not learned – but hereditary. There must be a complex of genes which controls and regulates abuse, goes the current thinking. Turning them off may well end the maltreatment.

## Abuse as a Strategy

Some scholars postulate that all modes of behaviour – abuse included – are results-orientated. The abuser seeks to control and manipulate his victims and develops strategies aimed at securing these results [see "What is Abuse?" for details].

Abuse is, therefore, an adaptive and functional behaviour. Hence the difficulty encountered by both the offender and society in trying to modify and contain his odious demeanour.

Yet, studying the very roots of abuse – social-cultural, genetic-psychological, and as a survival strategy – teaches us how to effectively cope with its perpetrators.

Return

# Reconditioning Your Abuser

Can abusers be "reconditioned"? Can they be "educated" or "persuaded" not to abuse?

As I wrote elsewhere, *"Abuse is a multifaceted phenomenon. It is a poisonous cocktail of control-freakery, conforming to social and cultural norms, and latent sadism. The abuser seeks to subjugate his victims and 'look good' or 'save face' in front of family and peers. Many abusers also enjoy inflicting pain on helpless victims."*

Tackling each of these three elements separately and in conjunction sometimes serves to ameliorate abusive behaviour.

The abuser's need to control his environment is compulsive and motivated by fear of inevitable and painful loss. It has, therefore, emotional roots. The abuser's past experiences – especially in early childhood and adolescence – taught him to expect injurious relationships, arbitrary or capricious treatment, sadistic interactions, unpredictable or inconsistent behaviours, and their culmination – indifferent and sudden abandonment.

About half of all abusers are products of abuse – they have either endured or witnessed it. As there are many forms of past mistreatment – there are a myriad shades of prospective abuse. Some abusers have been treated by Primary Objects (parents or caregivers) as instruments of gratification, objects, or mere extensions. They were loved on condition that they satisfied the wishes, dreams, and (often unrealistic) expectations of the parent. Others were smothered and doted upon, crushed under overweening, spoiling, or overbearing caregivers. Yet others were cruelly beaten, sexually molested, or constantly and publicly humiliated.

Such emotional wounds are not uncommon in therapeutic settings. They can be – and are – effectively treated, though the process is sometimes long and arduous, hampered by the abuser's resistance to authority and narcissism.

Some offenders abuse so as to conform to the norms of their society and culture and, thus, be "accepted" by peers and family. It is easier and more palatable to abuse one's spouse and children in a patriarchal and misogynist society – than in a liberal and egalitarian one. That these factors are overwhelmingly important is evidenced by the precipitous decline in intimate partner violence in the United States in the last two decades. As higher education and mass communications became widespread, liberal and feminist strictures permeated all spheres of life. It was no longer "cool" to batter one's mate.

Some scholars say that the amount of abuse remained constant and that the shift was merely from violent to non-violent (verbal, emotional, and ambient) forms of mistreatment. But this is not supported by the evidence.

Any attempt to recondition the abuser and alter the abusive relationship entails a change of social and cultural milieu. Simple steps like relocating to a different neighbourhood, surrounded by a different ethnic group, acquiring a higher education, and enhancing the family's income – often do more to reduce abuse than years of therapy.

The really intractable abuser is the sadist, who derives pleasure from other people's fears, consternation, pain, and suffering. Barring the administering of numbing medication, little can be done to counter this powerful inducement to hurt others deliberately. Cognitive-Behavioural Therapies and Transactional Treatment Modalities have been known to help. Even sadists are amenable to reason and self-interest. The pending risk of punishment and the fruits of well-observed contracts with evaluators, therapists, and family – sometimes do the job.

But how to get your abuser to see reason in the first place? How to obtain for him the help he needs – without involving law enforcement agencies, the authorities, or the courts? Any attempt to broach the subject of the abuser's mental problems frequently ends in harangues and worse. It is positively dangerous to mention the abuser's shortcomings or imperfections to his face.

Return

# Reforming the Abuser

Preventing or controlling the abuser's behaviour is complex. His family, friends, peers, co-workers, and neighbours – normally, levers of social control and behaviour modification – condone his misbehaviour. The abuser seeks to conform to norms and standards prevalent in his milieu, even if only implicitly. He regards himself as normal, definitely not in need of therapeutic intervention.

Thus, the complaints of a victim are likely to be met with hostility and suspicion by the offender's parents or siblings, for instance. Instead of reining in the abusive conduct, they are likely to pathologise the victim ("She is a nutcase") or label her ("She is a whore or a bitch").

Nor is the victim of abuse likely to fare better in the hands of law enforcement agencies, the courts, counselours, therapists, and guardians ad litem. The propensity of these institutions is to assume that the abused has a hidden agenda – to abscond with her husband's property, or to deny him custody or visitation rights. [Read more about it here]

Abuse remains, therefore, the private preserve of the predator and his prey. It is up to them to write their own rules and to implement them. No outside intervention is forthcoming or effective. Indeed, the delineation of boundaries and reaching an agreement on co-existence are the first important steps towards minimizing abuse in your relationships. Such a compact must include a provision obliging your abuser to seek professional help for his mental health problems.

Personal boundaries are not negotiable, neither can they be determined from the outside. Your abusive bully should have no say in setting them or in upholding them. Only you decide when they have been breached, what constitutes a transgression, what is excusable and what not.

The abuser is constantly on the lookout for a weakening of your resolve. He is repeatedly testing your mettle and resilience. He pounces on any and every vulnerability, uncertainty, or hesitation. Don't give him these chances. Be decisive and know yourself: what do you really feel? What are your wishes and desires in the short and longer terms? What price are you willing to pay and what sacrifices are you ready to make in order to be you? What behaviours will you accept and where does your red line run?

Verbalize your emotions, needs, preferences, and choices without aggression but with assertiveness and determination. Some abusers – the narcissistic ones – are detached from reality. They avoid it actively and live in fantasies of everlasting and unconditional love. They refuse to accept the inevitable consequences of their own actions. It is up to you to correct these cognitive and emotional deficits. You may encounter opposition – even violence – but, in the long-run, facing reality pays.

Play it fair. Make a list – if need be, in writing – of do's and don'ts. Create a "tariff" of sanctions and rewards. Let him know what actions of his – or inaction on his part – will trigger a dissolution of the relationship. Be unambiguous and unequivocal about it. And mean what you say. Again, showing up for counselling must be a cardinal condition.

Yet, even these simple, non-threatening initial steps are likely to provoke your abusive partner. Abusers are narcissistic and possessed of alloplastic defences. More simply put, they feel superior, entitled, above any law and agreement, and innocent. Others – usually the victims – are to blame for the abusive conduct ("See what you made me do?").

How can one negotiate with such a person without incurring his wrath? What is the meaning of contracts "signed" with bullies? How can one motivate the abuser to keep his end of the bargain – for instance, to actually seek therapy and attend the sessions? And how efficacious is psychotherapy or counselling to start with?

Return

# Contracting with Your Abuser

It is useless to confront the abuser head on and to engage in power politics ("You are guilty or wrong, I am the victim and right", "My will should prevail", and so on). It is decidedly counterproductive and unhelpful and could lead to rage attacks and a deepening of the abuser's persecutory delusions, bred by his humiliation in the therapeutic setting. Better, at first, to co-opt the abuser's own prejudices and pathology by catering to his infantile emotional needs and complying with his wishes, complex rules and arbitrary rituals.

Here a practical guide how to drag your abuser into treatment and into a contract of mutual respect and cessation of hostilities (assuming, of course, you want to preserve the relationship):

1.  Tell him that you love him and emphasize the exclusivity of your relationship by refraining, initially and during the therapy, from anxiety-provoking acts. Limiting your autonomy is a temporary sacrifice – under no circumstances make it a permanent feature of your relationship. Demonstrate to the abuser that his distrust of you is misplaced and undeserved and that one of the aims of the treatment regimen is to teach him to control and reduce his pathological and delusional jealousy.

2.  Define areas of your common life that the abuser can safely – and without infringing on your independence – utterly control. Abusers need to feel that they are in charge, sole decision-makers and arbiters.

3.  Ask him to define – preferably in writing – what he expects from you and where he thinks that you, or your "performance" are "deficient". Try to accommodate his reasonable demands and ignore the rest. Do not, at this stage, present a counter-list. This will come later. To move him to attend couple or marital therapy, tell him that you need his help to restore your relationship to its former warmth and intimacy. Admit to faults of your own which you

want "fixed" so as to be a better mate. Appeal to his narcissism and self-image as the omnipotent and omniscient macho. Humour him for a while.

4. Involve your abuser, as much as you can, in your life. Take him to meet your family, ask him to join in with your friends, to visit your workplace, to help maintain your car (a symbol of your independence), to advise you on money matters and career steps. Do not hand over control to him over any of these areas – but get him to feel a part of your life and try to mitigate his envy and insecurity.

5. Encourage him to assume responsibility for the positive things in his life and in your relationship. Compliment the beneficial outcomes of his skills, talents, hard work, and attitude. Gradually, he will let go of his alloplastic defences – his tendency to blame every mistake of his, every failure, or mishap on others, or on the world at large.

6. Make him own up to his feelings by identifying them. Most abusers are divorced from their emotions. They seek to explain their inner turmoil by resorting to outside agents ("Look what you made me do" or "They provoked me"). They are unaware of their anger, envy, or aggression. Mirror your abuser gently and unobtrusively ("How do you feel about it?", "When I am angry I act the same", "Would you be happier if I didn't do it?").

7. Avoid the appearance – or the practice – of manipulating your abuser (except if you want to get rid of him). Abusers are very sensitive to control issues and they feel threatened, exploited, and ill-treated when manipulated. They invariably react with violence.

8. Treat your abuser as you would like him to behave towards you. Personal example is a powerful proselytizer. Don't act out of fear or subservience. Be sincere. Act out of love and conviction. Finally, your conduct is bound to infiltrate the abuser's defences.

9. React forcefully, unambiguously, and instantly to any use of force. Make clear where the boundary of civilized exchange lies. Punish him severely and mercilessly if he crosses it. Make known well in advance the rules of your relationship – rewards and sanctions included. Discipline him for verbal and emotional abuse as well – though less strenuously. Create a hierarchy of transgressions and a penal code to go with it.
[Read these for further guidance: "Coping with Your Abuser", "The Guilt of the Abused - Pathologizing the Victim"]

10. As the therapy continues and progress is evident, try to fray the rigid edges of your sex roles. Most abusers are very much into "me Tarzan, you Jane" gender-casting. Show him his feminine sides and make him proud of them. Gradually introduce him to your masculine traits, or skills – and make him proud of you.

   This, essentially, is what good therapists do in trying to roll back or limit the offender's pathology.

From "Treatment Modalities and Therapies":

*"Most therapists try to co-opt the narcissistic abuser's inflated Ego (False Self) and defences. They compliment the narcissist, challenging him to prove his omnipotence by overcoming his disorder. They appeal to his quest for perfection, brilliance, and eternal love – and his paranoid tendencies – in an attempt to get rid of counterproductive, self-defeating, and dysfunctional behaviour patterns.*

*By stroking the narcissist's grandiosity, they hope to modify or counter cognitive deficits, thinking errors, and the narcissist's victim-stance. They contract with the narcissist to alter his conduct. Some even go to the extent of medicalizing the disorder, attributing it to a hereditary or biochemical origin and thus 'absolving' the narcissist from guilt and responsibility and freeing his mental resources to concentrate on the therapy."*

But is therapy worth the effort? What is the success rate of various treatment modalities in modifying the abuser's conduct, let alone in "healing" or "curing" him?

Return

# Your Abuser in Therapy

Your abuser "agrees" (is forced) to attend therapy. But are the sessions worth the effort? What is the success rate of various treatment modalities in modifying the abuser's conduct, let alone in "healing" or "curing" him? Is psychotherapy the panacea it is often made out to be – or a nostrum, as many victims of abuse claim? And why is it applied only after the fact – and not as a preventive measure?

Courts regularly send offenders to be treated as a condition for reducing their sentences. Yet, most of the programs are laughably short (between 6 to 32 weeks) and involve group therapy – which is useless with abusers who are also narcissists or psychopaths.

Rather than cure him, such workshops seek to "educate" and "reform" the culprit, often by introducing him to the victim's point of view. This is supposed to inculcate in the offender empathy and to rid the habitual batterer of the residues of patriarchal prejudice and control freakery. Abusers are encouraged to examine gender roles in modern society and, by implication, ask themselves if battering one's spouse was proof of virility.

Anger management – made famous by the eponymous film – is a relatively late newcomer, though currently it is all the rage. Offenders are taught to identify the hidden – and real – causes of their rage and learn techniques to control or channel it.

But batters are not a homogeneous lot. Sending all of them to the same type of treatment is bound to end up in recidivism. Neither are judges qualified to decide whether a specific abuser requires treatment or can benefit from it. The variety is so great that it is safe to say that – although they share the same misbehaviour patterns – no two abusers are alike.

In their article, "A Comparison of Impulsive and Instrumental Subgroups of Batterers", Roger Tweed and Donald Dutton of the Department of Psychology of the University of British Columbia, rely on the current typology of offenders which classifies them as:

"...Overcontrolled-dependent, impulsive-borderline (also called 'dysphoric-borderline' – SV) and instrumental-antisocial. The overcontrolled-dependent differ qualitatively from the other two expressive or 'undercontrolled' groups in that their violence is, by definition, less frequent and they exhibit less florid psychopathology. [Holtzworth-Munroe & Stuart 1994, Hamberger & Hastings 1985]... Hamberger & Hastings [1985,1986] factor analyzed the Millon Clinical Multiaxial Inventory for batterers, yielding three factors which they labelled 'schizoid/borderline' (cf. Impulsive), 'narcissistic/antisocial' (instrumental), and 'passive/dependent/compulsive' (overcontrolled)... Men, high only on the impulsive factor, were described as withdrawn, asocial, moody, hypersensitive to perceived slights, volatile and over-reactive, calm and controlled one moment and extremely angry and oppressive the next – a type of 'Jekyll and Hyde' personality. The associated DSM-III diagnosis was Borderline Personality. Men high only on the instrumental factor exhibited narcissistic entitlement and psychopathic manipulativeness. Hesitation by others to respond to their demands produced threats and aggression..."*

But there are other, equally enlightening, typologies (mentioned by the authors). Saunders suggested 13 dimensions of abuser psychology, clustered in three behaviour patterns: Family Only, Emotionally Volatile, and Generally Violent. Consider these disparities: one quarter of his sample – those victimized in childhood – showed no signs of depression or anger! At the other end of the spectrum, one of every six abusers was violent only in the confines of the family and suffered from high levels of dysphoria and rage.

Impulsive batterers abuse only their family members. Their favourite forms of mistreatment are sexual and psychological. They are dysphoric, emotionally labile, asocial, and, usually, substance abusers. Instrumental abusers are violent both at home and outside it – but only when they want to get something done. They are goal-orientated, avoid intimacy, and treat people as objects or instruments of gratification.

Still, as Dutton pointed out in a series of acclaimed studies, the "abusive personality" is characterized by a low level of organization, abandonment anxiety (even when it is denied by the abuser), elevated levels of anger, and trauma symptoms.

Return

# Testing the Abuser

It is clear that each abuser requires individual psychotherapy, tailored to his specific needs – on top of the usual group therapy and marital (or couple) therapy. At the very least, every offender should be required to undergo the following tests to provide a complete picture of his personality and the roots of his unbridled aggression:

1. The Relationship Styles Questionnaire (RSQ)
2. Millon Clinical Multiaxial Inventory-III (MCMI-III)
3. Conflict Tactics Scale (CTS)
4. Multidimensional Anger Inventory (MAI)
5. Borderline Personality Organization Scale (BPO)
6. The Narcissistic Personality Inventory (NPI)

In the court-mandated evaluation phase, you should insist to first find out whether your abuser suffers from mental health disorders. These may well be the – sometimes treatable – roots of his abusive conduct. A qualified mental health diagnostician can determine whether someone suffers from a personality disorder only following lengthy tests and personal interviews.

The predictive power of these tests – often based on literature and scales of traits constructed by scholars – has been hotly disputed. Still, they are far preferable to subjective impressions of the diagnostician which are often amenable to manipulation.

By far the most authoritative and widely used instrument is the *Millon Clinical Multiaxial Inventory-III (MCMI-III)* - a potent test for personality disorders and attendant anxiety and depression. The third edition was formulated in 1996 by Theodore Millon and Roger Davis and includes 175 items. As many abusers show narcissistic traits, it is advisable to universally administer to them the *Narcissistic Personality Inventory (NPI)* as well.

Many abusers have a borderline (primitive) organization of personality. It is, therefore, diagnostically helpful to subject them to the *Borderline Personality Organization Scale (BPO)*. Designed in 1985, it sorts the responses of respondents into 30 relevant scales. It indicates the existence of identity diffusion, primitive defences, and deficient reality testing.

To these one may add the *Personality Diagnostic Questionnaire-IV*, the *Coolidge Axis II Inventory*, the *Personality Assessment Inventory [1992]*, the excellent, literature-based, *Dimensional assessment of Personality Pathology*, and the comprehensive *Schedule of Nonadaptive and Adaptive Personality and Wisconsin Personality Disorders Inventory*.

Having established whether your abuser suffers from a personality impairment, it is mandatory to understand the way he functions in relationships, copes with intimacy, and responds with abuse to triggers.

The *Relationship Styles Questionnaire (RSQ) [1994]* contains 30 self-reported items and identifies distinct attachment styles (secure, fearful, preoccupied, and dismissing). The *Conflict Tactics Scale (CTS) [1979]* is a standardized scale of the frequency and intensity of conflict resolution tactics – especially abusive stratagems – used by members of a dyad (couple).

The *Multidimensional Anger Inventory (MAI) [1986]* assesses the frequency of angry responses, their duration, magnitude, mode of expression, hostile outlook, and anger-provoking triggers.

Yet, even a complete battery of tests, administered by experienced professionals sometimes fails to identify abusers and their personality disorders. Offenders are uncanny in their ability to deceive their evaluators.

Return

# Conning the System

Abusers often succeed in transforming therapists and diagnosticians into four types of collaborators: the adulators, the blissfully ignorant, the self-deceiving, and those deceived by the batterer's conduct or statements.

Abusers co-opt mental health and social welfare workers and compromise them – even when the diagnosis is unequivocal – by flattering them, by emphasizing common traits or a common background, by forming a joint front against the victim of abuse ("shared psychosis"), or by emotionally bribing them. Abusers are master manipulators and exploit the vulnerabilities, traumas, prejudices, and fears of the practitioners to "convert" them to the offender's cause.

## The Adulators

The adulators are fully aware of the nefarious and damaging aspects of the abuser's behaviour but believe that they are more than balanced by his positive traits. In a curious inversion of judgement, they cast the perpetrator as the victim of a smear campaign orchestrated by the abused or attribute the offender's predicament to bigotry.

They mobilize to help the abuser, promote his agenda, shield him from harm, connect him with like-minded people, do his chores for him and, in general, create the conditions and the environment for his ultimate success.

## The Ignorant

As I wrote in "The Guilt of the Abused", it is telling that precious few psychology and psychopathology textbooks dedicate an entire chapter to abuse and violence. Even the most egregious manifestations – such as child sexual abuse – merit a fleeting mention, usually as a sub-chapter in a larger section dedicated to paraphilias or personality disorders.

Abusive behaviour did not make it into the diagnostic criteria of mental health disorders, nor were its psychodynamic, cultural and social roots explored in depth. As a result of this deficient education and lacking awareness, most law enforcement officers, judges, counselours, guardians, and mediators are worryingly ignorant about the phenomenon.

Only 4% of hospital emergency room admissions of women in the United States are attributed by staff to domestic violence. The true figure, according to the FBI, is more like 50%. One in three murdered women was done in by her spouse, current or former.

The blissfully ignorant mental health professionals are simply unaware of the "bad sides" of the abuser – and make sure they remain oblivious to them. They look the other way, or pretend that the abuser's behaviour is normative, or turn a blind eye to his egregious conduct.

Even therapists sometimes deny a painful reality that contravenes their bias. Some of them maintain a generally rosy outlook premised on the alleged inbred benevolence of Mankind. Others simply cannot tolerate dissonance and discord. They prefer to live in a fantastic world where everything is harmonious and smooth and evil is banished. They react with discomfort or even rage to any information to the contrary and block it out instantly.

Once they form an opinion that the accusations against the abusers are overblown, malicious, and false – it becomes immutable. "I have made up my mind", they seem to be broadcasting – "Now don't confuse me with the facts."

**The Self-Deceivers**

The self-deceivers are fully aware of the abuser's transgressions and malice, his indifference, exploitativeness, lack of empathy, and rampant grandiosity – but they prefer to displace the causes, or the effects of such misconduct. They attribute it to externalities ("a rough patch"), or judge it to be temporary. They even go as far as accusing the victim for the offender's lapses, or for defending herself ("she provoked him").

In a feat of cognitive dissonance, they deny any connection between the acts of the abuser and their consequences ("His wife abandoned him because she was promiscuous, not because of anything he did to her"). They are swayed by the batterer's undeniable charm, intelligence, or attractiveness. But the abuser needs not invest resources in converting them to his cause – he does not deceive them. They are self-propelled.

**The Deceived**

The deceived are deliberately taken for a premeditated ride by the abuser. He feeds them false information, manipulates their judgement, proffers plausible scenarios to account for his indiscretions, soils the opposition, charms them, appeals to their reason, or to their emotions, and promises the Moon.

Again, the abuser's incontrovertible powers of persuasion and his impressive personality play a part in this predatory ritual. The deceived are especially hard to deprogram. They are often themselves encumbered with the abuser's traits and find it impossible to admit a mistake, or to atone.

Return

# Working with Professionals

Selecting the right professional is crucial. In the hands of an incompetent service provider, you may end up feeling abused all over again.

Go through the following check list before you settle on a divorce attorney, a financial consultant, a tax planner, a security adviser, or an accountant. Don't be ashamed to demand full disclosure – you have a right to do so. If you are met with impatience, arrogance, or a patronizing attitude – leave. This is not the right choice.

Make additional enquiries. Join online support groups and ask the members for recommendations. Visit directories on the Web – they are usually arranged by city, state, region, and country. Compare notes with others who have had similar experiences. Ask friends, neighbours, and family members to do the same. Scan the media for mentions of experts and mavens. Seek advice and referrals – the more the better.

## Suggested Check List

Is the professional certified in your state/country? Can he himself fully represent you?

Will you be served by the expert himself – or by his staff? Don't end up being represented by someone you never even met! Make the professional's personal services an explicit condition in any written and verbal arrangement you make.

Obtain a complete financial offer, all fees and charges included, before you hire the services. Make sure you are aware of the full monetary implications of your decisions. Finding yourself financially stranded midway through is bad policy. If you can afford it – don't compromise and go for the best. But if you don't have the pecuniary means – don't overshoot.

What is the professional's track record? Does he have a long, varied, and successful experience in cases similar to yours? Don't hesitate to ask him or her for recommendations and referrals, testimonials and media clips.

What are the likely outcomes of the decisions you make, based on the specialist's recommendations? A true pro will never provide you with an iron-clad guarantee but neither will he dodge the question. Your expert should be able to give you a reasonably safe assessment of risks, rewards, potential and probable outcomes, and future developments.

Always enquire about different courses of action and substitute measures. Ask your professional why he prefers one method or approach to another and what is wrong with the alternatives. Don't accept his authority as the sole arbiter. Don't hesitate to argue with him and seek a second opinion if you are still not convinced.

Make the terms of your agreement crystal-clear, get it in writing, and in advance. Don't leave anything to chance or verbal understanding. Cover all grounds: the scope of activities, the fees, the termination clauses. Hiring a consultant is like getting married – you should also contemplate a possible divorce.

Relegate any inevitable contact with your abusive ex – when and where possible – to professionals: your lawyer, or your accountant. Work with professionals to extricate yourself and your loved ones from the quagmire of an abusive relationship.

Return

# Interacting with Your Abuser

Be sure to maintain as much contact with your abuser as the courts, counselours, mediators, guardians, or law enforcement officials mandate. Do NOT contravene the decisions of the system. Work from the inside to change judgements, evaluations, or rulings – but NEVER rebel against them or ignore them. You will only turn the system against you and your interests. But with the exception of the minimum mandated by the courts – decline any and all GRATUITOUS contact with the narcissist.

Remember that many interactions are initiated by your abusive ex in order to trap or intimidate you. Keep referring him to your lawyer regarding legal issues, to your accountant or financial advisor concerning money matters, and to therapists, psychologists, and counselours with regards to everything else (yourself and your common children).

Abusers react badly to such treatment. Yours will try to manipulate you into unintended contact. Do not respond to his pleading, romantic, nostalgic, flattering, or threatening e-mail and snail mail messages. Keep records of such correspondence and make it immediately available to the courts, law enforcement agencies, court-mandated evaluators, guardians ad litem, therapists, marital counselours, child psychologist – and to your good friends. Keep him away by obtaining restraining orders and injunctions aplenty.

Abusers crave secrecy. Expose their misdeeds. Deter abuse by being open about your predicament. Share with like-minded others. It will ease your burden and keep him at bay, at least for awhile.

Your abusive ex-partner will try to dazzle you with attention. Return all gifts he sends you – unopened and unacknowledged. Keep your communications with him to the bare, cold, minimum. Do not be impolite or abusive – it is precisely how he wants you to behave. It may be used against you in a court of law. Keep your cool but be firm.

Do not let him re-enter your life surreptitiously. Stealth and ambient abuse are powerful tools. Refuse him entry to your premises. Do not even respond to the intercom. Do not talk to him on the phone. Hang up the minute you hear his voice while making clear to him, in a single, polite but unambiguous, sentence, that you are determined not to talk to him, that it's over for good.

Do not succumb to your weakness. It is tough living alone. You are bound to miss him horribly at times, selectively recalling only the good moments and the affection in your doomed relationship. Do not "dip" into the poisonous offerings of your abuser. Do not relapse. Be strong. Fill your life with new hobbies, new interests, new friends, new loves, and a new purpose.

Do not visit your abuser on "special occasions", or in emergencies. Do not let him convince you to celebrate an anniversary, a birthday, a successful business transaction, a personal achievement or triumph. Do not let him turn your own memories against you. Do not visit him in the hospital, in jail, a rehab centre, or join him in a memorial service.

Do not ask him for anything, even if you are in dire need. When you are forced to meet him, do not discuss your personal affairs – or his. Your abuser's friendship is fake, his life with you a confabulation, his intentions dishonest and dishonourable. He is the enemy.

Abuse by proxy continues long after the relationship is officially over (at least as far as you are concerned). Do not respond to questions, requests, or pleas forwarded to you through third parties. Disconnect from third parties whom you know are spying on you at his behest. Do not discuss him with your children. Do not gossip about him.

The majority of abusers get the message, however belatedly and reluctantly. Others – more vindictive and obsessed – continue to haunt their quarry for years to come. These are the stalkers.

Return

# Coping with Your Stalker

Most stalkers are what Zona (1993) and Geberth (1992) call "Simple Obsessional" or, as Mullen and Pathe put it (1999) – "Rejected". They stalk their prey as a way of maintaining the dissolved relationship (at least in their diseased minds). They seek to "punish" their quarry for refusing to collaborate in the charade and for resisting their unwanted and ominous attentions.

Such stalkers come from all walks of life and cut across social, racial, gender, and cultural barriers. They usually suffer from one or more (co-morbid) personality disorders. They may have anger management or emotional problems and they usually abuse drugs or alcohol. Stalkers are typically lonely, violent, and intermittently unemployed – but they are rarely full fledged criminals.

Contrary to myths perpetrated by the mass media, studies show that most stalkers are men, have high IQ's, advanced degrees, and are middle aged (Meloy and Gothard, 1995; and Morrison, 2001).

Rejected stalkers are intrusive and inordinately persistent. They recognize no boundaries – personal or legal. They honour to "contracts" and they pursue their target for years. They interpret rejection as a sign of the victim's continued interest and obsession with them. They are, therefore, impossible to get rid of. Many of them are narcissists and, thus, lack empathy, feel omnipotent and immune to the consequences of their actions.

Even so, some stalkers are possessed of an uncanny ability to psychologically penetrate others. Often, this gift is abused and put at the service of their control freakery and sadism. Stalking – and the ability to "mete out justice" makes them feel powerful and vindicated. When arrested, they often act the victim and attribute their actions to self-defence and "righting wrongs".

Stalkers are emotionally labile and present with rigid and infantile (primitive) defence mechanisms: splitting, projection, Projective Identification, denial, intellectualization, and narcissism. They devalue and dehumanize their victims and thus "justify" the harassment or diminish it. From here, it is only one step to violent conduct.

[Return](#)

# The Stalker as Antisocial Bully

Stalkers have narcissistic traits. Many of them suffer from personality disorders. The vindictive stalker is usually a psychopath (has Antisocial Personality Disorder). They all conform to the classic definition of a bully.

Before we proceed to delineate coping strategies, it is helpful to review the characteristics of each of these mental health problems and dysfunctional behaviours.

## The Narcissistic Stalker

The dramatic and erotomaniac stalker is likely to show one or more of these narcissistic traits:

1. Feels grandiose and self-important (e.g., exaggerates accomplishments, talents, skills, contacts, and personality traits to the point of lying, demands to be recognized as superior without commensurate achievements);
2. Is obsessed with fantasies of unlimited success, fame, fearsome power or omnipotence, unequalled brilliance (the cerebral narcissist), bodily beauty or sexual performance (the somatic narcissist), or ideal, everlasting, all-conquering love or passion;
3. Firmly convinced that he or she is unique and, being special, can only be understood by, should only be treated by, or associate with, other special or unique, or high-status people (or institutions);
4. Requires excessive admiration, adulation, attention and affirmation – or, failing that, wishes to be feared and to be notorious (Narcissistic Supply);
5. Feels entitled. Demands automatic and full compliance with his or her unreasonable expectations for special and favourable priority treatment;
6. Is "interpersonally exploitative", i.e., uses others to achieve his or her own ends;

7. Devoid of empathy. Is unable or unwilling to identify with, acknowledge, or accept the feelings, needs, preferences, priorities, and choices of others;
8. Constantly envious of others and seeks to hurt or destroy the objects of his or her frustration. Suffers from persecutory (paranoid) delusions as he or she believes that they feel the same about him or her and are likely to act similarly;
9. Behaves arrogantly and haughtily. Feels superior, omnipotent, omniscient, invincible, immune, "above the law", and omnipresent (magical thinking). Rages when frustrated, contradicted, or confronted by people he or she considers inferior to him or her and unworthy.

[Adapted from "Malignant Self Love - Narcissism Revisited"]

## The Antisocial (Psychopathic) Stalker

APD or AsPD was formerly called "psychopathy" or, more colloquially, "sociopathy". Some scholars, such as David Hare, still distinguish psychopathy from mere antisocial behaviour. The disorder appears in early adolescence but criminal behaviour and substance abuse often abate with age, usually by the fourth or fifth decade of life. It may have a genetic or hereditary determinant and afflicts mainly men. The diagnosis is controversial and regarded by some scholar as scientifically unfounded.

Psychopaths regard other people as objects to be manipulated and instruments of gratification and utility. They have no discernible conscience, are devoid of empathy and find it difficult to perceive other people's nonverbal cues, needs, emotions, and preferences. Consequently, the psychopath rejects other people's rights and his commensurate obligations. He is impulsive, reckless, irresponsible and unable to postpone gratification. He often rationalizes his behaviour showing an utter absence of remorse for hurting or defrauding others.

Their (primitive) defence mechanisms include splitting (they view the world – and people in it – as "all good" or "all evil"), projection (attribute their own shortcomings unto others) and Projective Identification (force others to behave the way they expect them to).

The psychopath fails to comply with social norms. Hence the criminal acts, the deceitfulness and identity theft, the use of aliases, the constant lying, and the conning of even his nearest and dearest for gain or pleasure. Psychopaths are unreliable and do not honour their undertakings, obligations, contracts, and responsibilities. They rarely hold a job for long or repay their debts. They are vindictive, remorseless, ruthless, driven, dangerous, aggressive, violent, irritable, and, sometimes, prone to magical thinking. They seldom plan for the long and medium terms, believing themselves to be immune to the consequences of their own actions.

[Adapted from my Mental Health Dictionary]

## The Stalker as a Bully

Bullies feel inadequate and compensates for it by being violent – verbally, psychologically, or physically. Some bullies suffer from personality and other mental health disorders. They feel entitled to special treatment, seek attention, lack empathy, are rageful and envious, and exploit and then discard their co-workers.

Bullies are insincere, haughty, unreliable, and lack empathy and sensitivity to the emotions, needs, and preferences of others whom they regard and treat as objects or instruments of gratification.

Bullies are ruthless, cold, and have alloplastic defences (and outside locus of control) – they blame others for their failures, defeats, or misfortunes. Bullies have low frustration and tolerance thresholds, get bored and anxious easily, are violently impatient, emotionally labile, unstable, erratic, and untrustworthy. They lack self-discipline, are egotistic, exploitative, rapacious, opportunistic, driven, reckless, and callous.

Bullies are emotionally immature and control freaks. They are consummate liars and deceivingly charming. Bullies dress, talk, and behave normally. Many of them are persuasive, manipulative, or even charismatic. They are socially adept, liked, and often fun to be around and the centre of attention. Only a prolonged and intensive interaction with them – sometimes as a victim – exposes their dysfunctions.

[Based on an entry I have written for the Open Site Encyclopaedia – Workplace Bullying]

Return

# Coping with Various Types of Stalkers

## Summary

## A Typology of Stalkers

Stalkers are not made of one cloth. Some of them are psychopaths, others are schizoids, narcissists, paranoids, or an admixture of these mental health disorders. Stalkers harass their victims because they are lonely, or because it is fun (these are latent sadists), or because they can't help it (clinging or co-dependent behaviour), or for a myriad different reasons.

Clearly, coping techniques suited to one type of stalker may backfire or prove to be futile with another. The only denominator common to all bullying stalkers is their pent-up rage. The stalker is angry at his or her targets and hates them. He perceives his victims as unnecessarily and churlishly frustrating. The aim of stalking is to "educate" the victim and to punish her.

Hence the catch-22 of coping with stalkers:

The standard – and good – advice is to avoid all contact with your stalker, to ignore him, even as you take precautions. But being evaded only inflames the stalker's wrath and enhances his frustration. The more he feels sidelined and stonewalled, the more persistent he becomes, the more intrusive and the more aggressive.

It is essential, therefore, to first identify the type of abuser you are faced with.

## The Erotomaniac

This kind of stalker believes that he is in love with you. To show his keen interest, he keeps calling you, dropping by, writing e-mails, doing unsolicited errands "on your behalf", talking to your friends, co-workers, and family, and, in general, making himself available at all times. The erotomaniac feels free to make for you legal, financial, and emotional decisions and to commit you without your express consent or even knowledge.

The erotomaniac intrudes on your privacy, does not respect your express wishes and personal boundaries and ignores your emotions, needs, and preferences. To him – or her – "love" means enmeshment and clinging coupled with an overpowering separation anxiety (fear of being abandoned). He or she may even force himself (or herself) upon you sexually.

Moreover, no amount of denials, chastising, threats, and even outright hostile actions will convince the erotomaniac that you are not in love with him. He knows better and will make you see the light as well. You are simply unaware of what is good for you, divorced as you are from your emotions. The erotomaniac determinedly sees it as his or her task to bring life and happiness into your dreary existence.

Thus, regardless of overwhelming evidence to the contrary, the erotomaniac is convinced that his or her feelings are reciprocated – in other words, that you are equally in love with him or her. The erotomanic stalker interprets everything you do (or refrain from doing) as coded messages confessing to and conveying your eternal devotion to him and to your "relationship".

Erotomaniacs are socially-inapt, awkward, schizoid, and suffer from a host of mood and anxiety disorders. They may also be people with whom you have been involved romantically (e.g., your former spouse, a former boyfriend, a one night stand) – or otherwise (for instance, colleagues or co-workers). They are driven by their all-consuming loneliness and all-pervasive fantasies.

Consequently, erotomaniacs react badly to any perceived rejection by their victims. They turn on a dime and become dangerously vindictive, out to destroy the source of their mounting frustration – you. When the "relationship" looks hopeless, many erotomaniacs turn to violence in a spree of self-destruction.

### Best Coping Strategy

Ignore the erotomaniac. Do not communicate with him or even acknowledge his existence. The erotomaniac clutches at straws and often suffers from ideas of reference. He tends to blow out of proportion every comment or gesture of his "loved one".

Follow these behaviour tips – the No Contact Policy:
- With the exception of the minimum mandated by the courts – decline any and all GRATUITOUS contact with your stalker;

- Do not respond to his pleading, romantic, nostalgic, flattering, or threatening e-mail messages;
- Return all gifts he sends you;
- Refuse him entry to your premises. Do not even respond to the intercom;
- Do not talk to him on the phone. Hang up the minute you hear his voice while making clear to him, in a single, polite but firm, sentence, that you are determined not to talk to him;
- Do not answer his letters;
- Do not visit him on special occasions, or in emergencies;
- Do not respond to questions, requests, or pleas forwarded to you through third parties;
- Disconnect from third parties whom you know are spying on you at his behest;
- Do not discuss him with your children;
- Do not gossip about him;
- Do not ask him for anything, even if you are in dire need;
- When you are forced to meet him, do not discuss your personal affairs – or his;
- Relegate any inevitable contact with him – when and where possible – to professionals: your lawyer, or your accountant.

## The Narcissist

Feels entitled to your time, attention, admiration, and resources. Interprets every rejection as an act of aggression which leads to a narcissistic injury. Reacts with sustained rage and vindictiveness. Can turn violent because he feels omnipotent and immune to the consequences of his actions.

### *Best Coping Strategy*

Make clear that you want no further contact with him and that this decision is not personal. Be firm. Do not hesitate to inform him that you hold him responsible for his stalking, bullying, and harassment and that you will take all necessary steps to protect yourself. Narcissists are cowards and easily intimidated. Luckily, they never get emotionally attached to their prey and so can move on with ease.

### *Other Coping Strategies*

#### *I. Frighten Him*

Narcissists live in a state of constant rage, repressed aggression, envy and hatred. They firmly believe that everyone else is precisely like them. As a result, they are paranoid, suspicious, scared, labile, and unpredictable. Frightening the narcissist is a powerful behaviour modification tool. If sufficiently deterred - the narcissist promptly disengages, gives up everything he fought for and sometimes makes amends.

To act effectively, one has to identify the vulnerabilities and susceptibilities of the narcissist and strike repeated, escalating blows at them - until the narcissist lets go and vanishes.

Example: If a narcissist has a secret - one should use this fact to threaten him. One should drop cryptic hints that there are mysterious witnesses to the events and recently revealed evidence.

The narcissist has a very vivid imagination. Most of the drama takes place in the paranoid mind of the narcissist. His imagination runs amok. He finds himself snarled by horrifying scenarios, pursued by the vilest "certainties". The narcissist is his own worst persecutor and prosecutor. Let his imagination do the rest.

You don't have to do much except utter a vague reference, make an ominous allusion, delineate a possible turn of events. The narcissist will do the rest for you. He is like a small child in the dark, generating the very monsters that paralyze him with fear.

The narcissist may have been involved in tax evasion, in malpractice, in child abuse, in infidelity - there are so many possibilities, which offer a rich vein of attack. If done cleverly, noncommittally, gradually, and increasingly, the narcissist crumbles, disengages and disappears. He lowers his profile thoroughly in the hope of avoiding hurt and pain.

Many narcissists have been known to disown and abandon their whole life in response to a well-focused (and impeccably legal) campaign by their victims. They relocate, establish a new family, find another job, abandon a field of professional interest, avoid friends and acquaintances, even change their names.

*I want to emphasize that all these activities have to be pursued legally, preferably through the good services of law offices and in broad daylight. If done the wrong way, they might constitute extortion or blackmail, harassment and a host of other criminal offences.*

### II. Lure Him

Another way to neutralize the narcissist is to offer him continued Narcissistic Supply until the war is over and won by you. Dazzled by the drug of Narcissistic Supply, the narcissist immediately becomes docile and tamed, forgets his vindictiveness and triumphantly re-possesses his "property" and "territory".

Under the influence of Narcissistic Supply, the narcissist is unable to tell when he is being manipulated. He is blind, dumb and deaf. You can make a narcissist do anything by offering, withholding, or threatening to withhold Narcissistic Supply (adulation, admiration, attention, sex, awe, subservience, etc.).

### III. Threaten Him with Abandonment

The threat to abandon need not be explicit or conditional ("If you don't do something or if you do it – I will ditch you"). It is sufficient to confront the narcissist, to completely ignore him, to insist on respect for one's boundaries and wishes, or to shout back at him. The narcissist takes these signs of personal autonomy to be harbinger of impending separation and reacts with anxiety.

The narcissist is a living emotional pendulum. If he gets too close to someone emotionally, if he becomes intimate with someone, he fears ultimate and inevitable abandonment. He, thus, immediately distances himself, acts cruelly and brings about the very abandonment that he feared in the first place. This is called the Approach-Avoidance Repetition Complex.

In this paradox lies the key to coping with the narcissist. If, for instance, he is having a rage attack – rage back. This will provoke in him fears of being abandoned and calm him down instantaneously (and eerily).

Mirror the narcissist's actions and repeat his words. If he threatens – threaten back and credibly try to use the same language and content. If he leaves the house – do the same, disappear on him. If he is suspicious – act suspicious. Be critical, denigrating, humiliating, go down to his level – because that's the only way to penetrate his thick defences. Faced with his mirror image – the narcissist always recoils.

You will find that if you mirror him consistently and constantly, the narcissist becomes obsequious and tries to make amends, moving from one (cold and bitter, cynical and misanthropic, cruel and sadistic) pole to another (warm, even loving, fuzzy, engulfing, emotional, maudlin, and saccharine).

### IV. Manipulate Him

By playing on the narcissist's grandiosity and paranoia, it is possible to deceive and manipulate him effortlessly. Just offer him Narcissistic Supply – admiration, affirmation, adulation – and he is yours. Harp on his insecurities and his persecutory delusions – and he is likely to trust only you and cling to you for dear life.

But be careful not to overdo it! When asked how is the narcissist likely to react to continued mistreatment, I wrote this in one of my Pathological Narcissism FAQs:

*"The initial reaction of the narcissist to a perceived humiliation is a conscious rejection of the humiliating input. The narcissist tries to ignore it, talk it out of existence, or belittle its importance. If this crude mechanism of cognitive dissonance fails, the narcissist resorts to denial and repression of the humiliating material. He 'forgets' all about it, gets it out of his mind and, when reminded of it, denies it.*

*But these are usually merely stopgap measures. The disturbing data is bound to impinge on the narcissist's tormented consciousness. Once aware of its re-emergence, the narcissist uses fantasy to counteract and counterbalance it. He imagines all the horrible things that he would have done (or will do) to the sources of his frustration.*

*It is through fantasy that the narcissist seeks to redeem his pride and dignity and to re-establish his damaged sense of uniqueness and grandiosity. Paradoxically, the narcissist does not mind being humiliated if this were to make him more unique or to draw more attention to his person.*

*For instance: if the injustice involved in the process of humiliation is unprecedented, or if the humiliating acts or words place the narcissist in a unique position, or if they transform him into a public figure – the narcissist tries to encourage such behaviours and to elicit them from others.*

*In this case, he fantasizes how he defiantly demeans and debases his opponents by forcing them to behave even more barbarously than before, so that their unjust conduct is universally recognized as such and condemned and the narcissist is publicly vindicated and his self-respect restored. In short: martyrdom is as good a method of obtaining Narcissist Supply as any.*

*Fantasy, though, has its limits and once reached, the narcissist is likely to experience waves of self-hatred and self-loathing, the outcomes of helplessness and of realizing the depths of his dependence on Narcissistic Supply. These feelings culminate in severe self-directed aggression: depression, destructive, self-defeating behaviours or suicidal ideation.*

*These self-negating reactions, inevitably and naturally, terrify the narcissist. He tries to project them on to his environment. He may decompensate by developing obsessive-compulsive traits or by going through a psychotic microepisode.*

*At this stage, the narcissist is suddenly besieged by disturbing, uncontrollable violent thoughts. He develops ritualistic reactions to them: a sequence of motions, an act, or obsessive counter-thoughts. Or he might visualize his aggression, or experience auditory hallucinations. Humiliation affects the narcissist this deeply.*

*Luckily, the process is entirely reversible once Narcissistic Supply is resumed. Almost immediately, the narcissist swings from one pole to another, from being humiliated to being elated, from being put down to being reinstated, from being at the bottom of his own, imagined, pit to occupying the top of his own, imagined, hill."*

## What if I Want to Continue the Relationship?

### FIVE DON'T DO'S – How to Avoid the Wrath of the Narcissist

- Never disagree with the narcissist or contradict him;
- Never offer him any intimacy;
- Look awed by whatever attribute matters to him (for instance: by his professional achievements or by his good looks, or by his success with women and so on);
- Never remind him of life out there and if you do, connect it somehow to his sense of grandiosity;
- Do not make any comment, which might directly or indirectly impinge on his self-image, omnipotence, judgement, omniscience, skills, capabilities, professional record, or even omnipresence. Bad sentences start with: "I think you overlooked ... made a mistake here ... you don't know ... do you know ... you were not here yesterday so ... you cannot ... you should ... (perceived as rude imposition, narcissists react very badly to restrictions placed on their freedom) ... I (never mention the fact that you are a separate, independent entity, narcissists regard others as extensions of their selves, their internalization processes were screwed up and they did not differentiate properly)..." You get the gist of it.

### The TEN DO'S – How to Make Your Narcissist Dependent on You if you INSIST on Staying with Him

- Listen attentively to everything the narcissist says and agree with it all. Don't believe a word of it but let it slide as if everything is just fine, business as usual;
- Personally offer something absolutely unique to the narcissist which he cannot obtain anywhere else. Also be prepared to line up future Sources of Primary Narcissistic Supply for your

narcissist because you will not be IT for very long, if at all. If you take over the procuring function for the narcissist, he becomes that much more dependent on you which makes it a bit tougher for him to pull his haughty stuff – an inevitability, in any case;

- Be endlessly patient and go way out of your way to be accommodating, thus keeping the Narcissistic Supply flowing liberally, and keeping the peace (relatively speaking);
- Be endlessly giving. This one may not be attractive to you, but it is a take it or leave it proposition;
- Be absolutely emotionally and financially independent of the narcissist. Take what you need: the excitement and engulfment and refuse to get upset or hurt when the narcissist does or says something dumb, rude, or insensitive. Yelling back works really well but should be reserved for special occasions when you fear your narcissist may be on the verge of leaving you; the silent treatment is better as an ordinary response, but it must be carried out without any emotional content, more with the air of boredom and "I'll talk to you later, when I am good and ready, and when you are behaving in a more reasonable fashion";
- If your narcissist is cerebral and NOT interested in having much sex – then give yourself ample permission to have "hidden" sex with other people. Your cerebral narcissist will not be indifferent to infidelity so discretion and secrecy is of paramount importance;
- If your narcissist is somatic and you don't mind, join in on endlessly interesting group sex encounters but make sure that you choose properly for your narcissist. Narcissists are heedless and very undiscriminating in respect of sexual partners and that can get very problematic (STDs and blackmail come to mind);
- If you are a "fixer", then focus on fixing situations, preferably before they become "situations". Don't for one moment delude yourself that you can FIX the narcissist – it simply will not happen. Not because he is being stubborn – he just simply can't be fixed;
- If there is any fixing that can be done, it is to help your narcissist become aware of their condition, and this is VERY IMPORTANT, with no negative implications or accusations in the process at all. It is like living with a physically handicapped person and being able to discuss, calmly, unemotionally, what the limitations and benefits of the

handicap are and how the two of you can work with these factors, rather than trying to change them;

- FINALLY, and most important of all: KNOW YOURSELF. What are you getting from the relationship? Are you actually a masochist? A co-dependent perhaps? Why is this relationship attractive and interesting?

  Define for yourself what good and beneficial things you believe you are receiving in this relationship.

  Define the things that you find harmful TO YOU. Develop strategies to minimize the harm to yourself. Don't expect that you will cognitively be able to reason with the narcissist to change who they are. You may have some limited success in getting your narcissist to tone down on the really harmful behaviours THAT AFFECT YOU which emanate from the unchangeable WHAT the narcissist is. This can only be accomplished in a very trusting, frank and open relationship.

## The Paranoid

By far the most dangerous the lot. Lives in an inaccessible world of his own making. Cannot be reasoned with or cajoled. Thrives on threats, anxiety, and fear. Distorts every communication to feed his persecutory delusions.

[See the article "Avoiding Your Paranoid Ex" for coping strategies.]

## The Psychopath (Antisocial)

Stalking is a crime and stalkers are criminals. This simple truth is often ignored by mental health practitioners, by law enforcement agencies, and by the media. The horrid consequences of stalking are often underestimated and stalkers are mocked as eccentric and lonely weirdoes. Yet, stalking affects one fifth of all women and an unknown number of men – and often ends in violence and bloodshed.

A 1997 Review Paper titled "Stalking (Part I) An Overview of the Problem", Karen M. Abrams, MD, FRCPC1, Gail Erlick Robinson, MD, DPsych, FRCPC2, define stalking thus:

*"Stalking, or criminal harassment, is defined as the 'wilful, malicious, and repeated following or harassing of another person', usually requiring a 'credible threat of violence' against the victim or the victim's family (1). 'Harass' refers to wilful conduct directed at a person that seriously alarms, annoys, or distresses the person and which serves no legitimate purpose (2). Typically, the behaviour involves such things as loitering near the victim,*

approaching, making multiple phone calls, constantly surveilling, harassing the victim's employer or children, harming a pet, interfering with personal property, sabotaging dates, and sending threatening or sexually suggestive 'gifts' or letters. The harassment usually escalates, often beginning with phone calls that gradually become more threatening and aggressive in nature, and frequently ends in violent acts (3). In essence, the offender's behaviour is terrorizing, intimidating, and threatening, and restricts the freedom of and controls the victim.

In the US, there are individual state laws but no unified federal antistalking laws. Under the Criminal Code of Canada, it is a crime to knowingly or recklessly harass another person in any of the following ways: (1) by repeatedly following or communicating either directly or indirectly with that person or anyone known to them; (2) by watching where that person or anyone known to them resides, works, or happens to be; or (3) by engaging in any threatening conduct directed at that person or his or her family, if any of these cause the person to reasonably fear for his or her safety. In both the US and Canada, antistalking laws are in a state of flux."

Many criminals suffer from personality disorders – most prevalently, the Antisocial Personality Disorder, formerly known as "psychopathy". Co-morbidity – a "cocktail" of mental health disorders – is frequent. Most stalkers abuse substances (alcohol, drugs) and are prone to violence or other forms of aggression.

APD or AsPD was formerly called "psychopathy" or, more colloquially, "sociopathy". Some scholars, such as Robert Hare, still distinguish psychopathy from mere antisocial behaviour. The disorder appears in early adolescence but criminal behaviour and substance abuse often abate with age, usually by the fourth or fifth decade of life. It may have a genetic or hereditary determinant and afflicts mainly men. The diagnosis is controversial and regarded by some scholar as scientifically unfounded.

Psychopaths regard other people as objects to be manipulated and instruments of gratification and utility. They have no discernible conscience, are devoid of empathy and find it difficult to perceive other people's nonverbal cues, needs, emotions, and preferences. Consequently, the psychopath rejects other people's rights and his commensurate obligations. He is impulsive, reckless, irresponsible and unable to postpone gratification. He often rationalizes his behaviour showing an utter absence of remorse for hurting or defrauding others.

Their (primitive) defence mechanisms include splitting (they view the world – and people in it – as "all good" or "all evil"), projection (attribute their own shortcomings unto others) and Projective Identification (force others to behave the way they expect them to).

The psychopath fails to comply with social norms. Hence the criminal acts, the deceitfulness and identity theft, the use of aliases, the constant lying, and the conning of even his nearest and dearest for gain or pleasure. Psychopaths are unreliable and do not honour their undertakings, obligations, contracts, and responsibilities. They rarely hold a job for long or repay their debts. They are vindictive, remorseless, ruthless, driven, dangerous, aggressive, violent, irritable, and, sometimes, prone to magical thinking. They seldom plan for the long and medium terms, believing themselves to be immune to the consequences of their own actions.

Many psychopaths are outright bullies. Michigan psychologist Donald B. Saunders distinguishes between three types of aggressors: "family-only", "generally violent" (most likely to suffer from APD), and the "emotionally volatile". In an interview to Psychology Today, he described the "generally Violent" thus:

*"Type 2 men – the generally violent – use violence outside the home as well as in it. Their violence is severe and tied to alcohol; they have high rates of arrest for drunk driving and violence. Most have been abused as children and have rigid attitudes about sex roles. These men, Saunders explains, are calculating; they have a history with the criminal justice system and know what they can get away with."*

Bullies feel inadequate and compensates for it by being violent – verbally, psychologically, or physically. Some bullies suffer from personality and other mental health disorders. They feel entitled to special treatment, seek attention, lack empathy, are rageful and envious, and exploit and then discard their co-workers.

Bullies are insincere, haughty, unreliable, and lack empathy and sensitivity to the emotions, needs, and preferences of others whom they regard and treat as objects or instruments of gratification.

Bullies are ruthless, cold, and have alloplastic defences (and outside locus of control) – they blame others for their failures, defeats, or misfortunes. Bullies have low frustration and tolerance thresholds, get bored and anxious easily, are violently impatient, emotionally labile, unstable, erratic, and untrustworthy. They lack self-discipline, are egotistic, exploitative, rapacious, opportunistic, driven, reckless, and callous.

Bullies are emotionally immature and control freaks. They are consummate liars and deceivingly charming. Bullies dress, talk, and behave normally. Many of them are persuasive, manipulative, or even charismatic. They are socially adept, liked, and often fun to be around and the centre of attention. Only a prolonged and intensive interaction with them – sometimes as a victim – exposes their dysfunctions.

Though ruthless and, typically, violent, the psychopath is a calculating machine, out to maximize his gratification and personal profit. Psychopaths lack empathy and may even be sadistic – but understand well and instantly the language of carrots and sticks.

### Best Coping Strategy

- Convince your psychopath that messing with your life or with your nearest is going to cost him dearly;
- Do not threaten him. Simply, be unequivocal and firm about your desire to be left in peace and your intentions to involve the Law should he stalk, harass, or threaten you;
- Give him a choice between being left alone and becoming the target of multiple arrests, restraining orders, and worse;
- Take extreme precautions at all times and meet him accompanied by someone and in public places – and only if you have no other choice;
- Minimize contact and interact with him through professionals (lawyers, accountants, therapists, police officers, judges);
- Document every contact, every conversation, try to commit everything to writing. You may need it as evidence;
- Educate your children to be on their guard and to exercise caution and good judgement;
- Keep fully posted and updated your local law enforcement agencies, your friends, the media, and anyone else who would listen;
- Be careful with your personal information. Provide only the bare and necessary minimum. Remember: he has ways of finding out;
- Under no circumstances succumb to his romantic advances, accept his gifts, respond to personal communications, show interest in his affairs, help him out, or send him messages directly or through third parties. Maintain the No Contact rule;

- Equally, do not seek revenge. Do not provoke him, "punish him", taunt him, disparage him, bad-mouth or gossip about him or your relationship.

Return

# Coping with Stalking and Stalkers

## Getting Help

This article is meant to be a general guide to seeking and finding help. It does not contain addresses, contacts, and phone numbers. It is not specific to one state or country. Rather, it describes options and institutions which are common the world over. You should be the one to "fill in the blanks" and locate the relevant groups and agencies in your domicile.

Your first "fallback" option is YOUR FAMILY. They are, in many cases (though by no means always) your natural allies. They can provide you with shelter, money, emotional support, and advice. Don't hesitate to call on them in times of need.

YOUR FRIENDS and, to a lesser extent, YOUR COLLEAGUES AND NEIGHBOURS will usually lend you a sympathetic ear and will provide you with useful tips. Merely talking to them can not only ease the burden – but protect you from future abuse. Stalkers and paranoids thrive on secrecy and abhor public exposure.

Regrettably, resorting to the LEGAL SYSTEM – your next logical step – is bound to be a disappointing, disempowering, and invalidating experience. I wrote about it extensively in the essay "Pathologizing the Victim".

A 1997 Review Paper titled "Stalking (Part II) Victims' Problems With the Legal System and Therapeutic Considerations", Karen M. Abrams, MD, FRCPC1, Gail Erlick Robinson, MD, DPsych, FRCPC2 note:

*"Law-enforcement insensitivity toward domestic violence has already been well documented. Police often feel that, as opposed to serious crimes such as murder, domestic issues are not an appropriate police responsibility; 'private' misconduct should not be subject to public intervention, and, because few cases result in successful prosecution, pursuing domestic violence complaints is ultimately futile... This sense of futility, reinforced by the media and the courts, may be transmitted to the victim.*

*In cases involving ex-lovers, the police may have equal difficulty in being sympathetic to the issues involved. As in the case of Ms A, society often views stalking as a normal infatuation that will eventually resolve itself or as the actions of a rejected lover or lovesick individual, more to be empathized with than censured (2). Victims often report feeling that the police and society blame them for provoking harassment or making poor choices in relationships. Authorities may have particular difficulty understanding the woman who continues to have ambivalent feelings toward the offender...*

*In terms of the laws themselves, there is a history of ineffectiveness in dealing with crimes of stalking (1,5). The nature of the offences themselves makes investigations and prosecution difficult, because surveillance and phone calls often have no witnesses. Barriers to victims using civil actions against stalkers include dangerous time delays and financial requirements. Temporary restraining orders or peace bonds have been used most commonly and are generally ineffective, partly because law-enforcement agencies have limited resources to enforce such measures. Even if caught, violators receive, at most, minimal jail time or minor monetary penalties. Sometimes the offender just waits out the short duration of the order. Persistent, obsessed stalkers are usually not deterred."*

Still, it is crucial that you document the abuse and stalking and duly report them to the POLICE and to your BUILDING SECURITY. If your stalker is in jail, you should report him to the WARDENS and to his PAROLE OFFICER. It is important to resort to the COURTS in order to obtain restraining or cease and desist orders. Keep law enforcement officers and agencies fully posted. Don't hesitate to call upon them as often as you need to. It is their job. Hire a SECURITY EXPERT if the threat is credible or imminent.

You are well advised to rely on PROFESSIONAL ADVICE throughout your prolonged and arduous disentanglement from your paranoid and stalking ex. Use attorneys, accountants, private detectives, and therapists to communicate with him. Consult your LAWYER (or, if you can't afford one, apply for a pro bono lawyer provided by a civic association, or your state's legal aid). Ask him or her what are your rights, what kinds of legal redress you have, what safety precautions you should adopt – and what are the do's and don't do's of your situation.

Especially important is to choose the right THERAPIST for you and for your children. Check whether he or she has any experience with victims of stalking and with the emotional effects of constant threat and surveillance (fear, humiliation, ambivalence, helplessness, paranoid ideation). Stalking is a traumatic process and you may need intervention to ameliorate the post-traumatic stress effects it wreaks.

Join online and offline GROUPS AND ORGANIZATIONS FOR VICTIMS OF ABUSE AND STALKING. Peer support is critical. Helping others and sharing experiences and fears with other victims is a validating and empowering as well as a useful experience. Realizing that you are not alone, that you are not crazy, and that the whole situation is not your fault helps to restore your shattered self-esteem and puts things in perspective.

The SOCIAL SERVICES in your area are geared to deal with battering and stalking. They likely run shelters for victims of domestic violence and abuse, for instance.

Return

# Coping with Stalking and Stalkers

## Domestic Violence Shelters

Shelters are run, funded, and managed either by governments or by volunteer non-government organizations. According to a 1999 report published by the National Coalition Against Domestic Violence, there are well over 2000 groups involved in sheltering abused women and their off-spring.

Before you opt for moving with your children into a sheltered home or apartment, go through this check list.

1. It is important to make sure that the philosophy of the organizers of the shelters accords with your own. Some shelters, for instance, are run by feminist movements and strongly emphasize self-organization, co-operation, and empowerment through decision-making. Other shelters are supervised by the Church or other religious organizations and demand adherence to a religious agenda. Yet others cater to the needs of specific ethnic minorities or neighbourhoods.

2. Can you abide by the house rules? Are you a smoker? Some shelters are for non-smokers. What about boyfriends? Most shelters won't allow men on the premises. Do you require a special diet due to medical reasons? Is the shelter's kitchen equipped to deal with your needs?

3. Gather intelligence and be informed before you make your move. Talk to battered women who spent time in the shelter, to your social worker, to the organizers of the shelter. Check the local newspaper archive and visit the shelter at least twice: in daytime and at night.

4. How secure is the shelter? Does it allow visitation or any contact with your abusive spouse? Does the shelter have its own security personnel? How well is the shelter acquainted with domestic violence laws and how closely is it collaborating with courts, evaluators, and law enforcement agencies? Is recidivism among abusers tracked and

discouraged? Does the shelter have a good reputation among them? You wouldn't want to live in a shelter that is shunned by the police and the judicial system.

5. How does the shelter tackle the needs of infants, young children, and adolescents? What are the services and amenities it provides? What things should you bring with you when you make your exit – and what can you count on the shelter to make available? What should you pay for and what is free of charge? How well-staffed is the shelter? Is the shelter well-organized? Are the intake forms anonymous?

6. How accessible is the shelter to public transport, schooling, and to other community services?

7. Does the shelter have a batterer intervention program or workshop and a women's support group? In other words, does it provide counselling for abusers as well as ongoing succour for their victims? Are the programs run only by volunteers (laymen peers)? Are professionals involved in any of the activities and, if so, in what capacity (consultative, supervisory)? Additionally, does the shelter provide counselling for children, group and individual treatment modalities, education and play-therapy services, along with case management services? Is the shelter associated with outpatient services such vocational counselling and job training, outreach to high schools and the community, court advocacy, and mental health services or referrals?

8. Most important: don't forget that shelters are a temporary solution. These are transit areas and you are fully expected to move on. Not everyone is accepted. You are likely to be interviewed at length and screened for both your personal needs and compatibility with the shelter's guidelines. Is it really a crisis situation, are your life or health at risk – or are you merely looking to "get away from it all"? Even then, expect to be placed on a waiting list. Shelters are not vacation spots. They are in the serious business of defending the vulnerable.

When you move into a shelter, you must know in advance what your final destination is. Imagine and plan your life after the shelter. Do you intend to relocate? If so, would you need financial assistance? What about the children's education and friends? Can you find a job? Have everything sorted out. Only then, pack your things and leave your abuser.

Return

# Coping with Stalking and Stalkers

## Planning and Executing Your Getaway

Do not leave unprepared. Study and execute every detail of your getaway. This is especially important if your partner is violent. Be sure to make a Safety Plan – how to get out of the house unnoticed and the indispensable minimum items that you should carry with you, even on a short notice.

Here are the recommendations of the Province of Alberta in Canada:

Long before you actually leave, copy all important documents and store them in a safe place. These include: identity cards, health care and social insurance or security Cards, driver's license/registration, credit cards and bank cards, other personal identification (including picture ID), birth certificate, immunization card for the children, custody order, personal chequebook, last banking statement, and mortgage papers. Make a list of all computer passwords and access codes (for instance: ATM PINs).

When you leave the house, take with you these copied documents as well as the following personal items: prescribed medication, personal hygiene products, glasses/contact lenses, money (borrow from family members, a neighbour, colleague, or friends, if you have to), several changes of clothing (don't forget night wear and underwear), heirlooms, jewellery, photo albums (pictures that you want to keep), craft, needle work, hobby work.

The situation is inevitably more complicated if you are fleeing with your children. In this case, be sure to bring with you their various medications, soother, bottles, favourite toy or blanket, and clothing (again: night wear, underwear). Older kids may carry their own clothes and school books.

Make a list of the following and have it on you at all times: addresses and phone numbers of domestic violence shelters, police stations, night courts, community social services, schools in the vicinity, major media, and address and phone and fax numbers of your lawyer and his attorneys. Secure a detailed public transportation map.

Your best bet is to apply to a shelter for a safe place to stay the first few days and nights. [Read more about shelters here – Domestic Violence Shelters]

If you can afford to, your next step should be to hire a divorce attorney and file for interim custody. Your divorce papers can be served much later. Your first concern is to keep the children with you safely and legally. Your husband is likely to claim that you have kidnapped them.

But your escape should be only the tip of a long period of meticulous preparations.

We already mentioned that you should make copies of all important documents [see above]. Don't escape from your predicament penniless! Secretly put aside cash for an Escape Fund. Your husband is likely to block your checking account and credit cards. Ask around where you can stay the first week. Will your family or friends accept you? Apply to a domestic violence shelter and wait to be accepted. Be sure to know where you are going!

Make extra sets of keys and documents. Bundle these up with some clothes and keep these "reserve troves" with friends and family. Put one such "trove" in a safety deposit box and give the key to someone you trust. Secure transportation for the day or night of escape. Agree on codes and signals with friends and family ("If I don't call you by 10 PM, something has gone wrong", "If I call you and say that Ron is home, call the police").

You should wait until he is gone and only then leave home. Avoid confrontation over your departure. It can end badly. Do not inform him of your plans. Make excuses to slip away in the days and months before you actually leave. Get him used to your absence.

Should you get the police involved?

Return

# Coping with Stalking and Stalkers

## Getting Law Enforcement Authorities
## And the Police Involved

If you want the nightmare to end, there is a rule of thumb which requires courage and determination to implement:

Involve the police whenever possible.

Report his crimes as soon as you can and make sure you retain a copy of your complaint. Your abuser counts on your fear of him and on your natural propensity to keep domestic problems a secret. Expose him to scrutiny and penalties. This will make him re-consider his actions next time around.

Physical assault is a criminal offence as are rape and, in some countries, stalking and marital rape. If you have been physically or sexually assaulted, go to the nearest hospital and document your injuries. Be sure to obtain copies of the admission form, the medical evaluation report, and of any photographs and exam results (X-rays, computerized tomography-CT, biopsies, and so on).

If your abusive intimate partner verbally threatens you, your nearest and dearest, or your property or pets – this is also criminal conduct. To the best of your ability, get him on tape or make him repeat his threats in the presence of witnesses. Then promptly file a complaint with the police.

If your abuser forces you to remain indoors, in isolation, he is committing an offence. Forced confinement or imprisonment is illegal. While so incarcerated, failing to provide you with vital necessities – such as air, water, medical aid, and food – is yet another criminal act.

Damage to property rendering it inoperative or useless – is mischief. It is punishable by law. Same goes for cruelty to animals (let alone children).

If your partner swindled you out of funds or committed fraud, theft, or perjury (by falsifying your signature on a checking or credit card account, for instance) – report him to the police. Financial abuse is as pernicious as the physical variety.

In most countries, the police must respond to your complaint. They cannot just file it away or suppress it. They must talk to you and to your partner separately and obtain written and signed statements from both parties. The police officer on the scene must inform you of your legal options. The officer in charge must also furnish you with a list of domestic violence shelters and other forms of help available in your community.

If you suspect that a member of your family is being abused, the police, in most countries, can obtain a warrant permitting entry into the premises to inspect the situation. They are also authorized to help the victim relocate (leave) and to assist her in any way, including by applying on her behalf and with her consent to the courts to obtain restraining and emergency protection orders. A breach of either of these orders may be an indictable criminal offence as well as a civil offence.

If you decide to pursue the matter and if there are reasonable grounds to do so, the police will likely lay charges against the offender and accuse your partner of assault. Actually, your consent is only a matter of formality and is not strictly required. The police can charge an offender on the basis of evidence only.

If the team on the scene refuses to lay charges, you have the right to talk to a senior police officer. If you cannot sway them to act, you can lay charges yourself by going to the court house and filing with a Justice of the Peace (JP). The JP must let you lay charges. It is your inalienable right.

You cannot withdraw charges laid by the police and you most probably will be subpoenaed to testify against the abuser.

Should you get the courts involved?

Return

# Coping with Stalking and Stalkers

## Getting the Courts Involved
## Restraining Orders and Peace Bonds

Involve the courts whenever possible.

In many countries, the first step is to obtain a restraining order from a civil court as part of your divorce or custody proceedings or as a stand-alone measure.

In some countries, the police applies to the court for an emergency protection order on your behalf. The difference between a protection order and a restraining order is that the former is obtained following an incident of domestic violence involving injury or damage to property, it is available immediately, granted at the police's request, and issued even outside court hours.

Many restraining orders are granted ex parte, without the knowledge or presence of your abusive partner, based solely on a signed and sworn affidavit submitted by you. A typical emergency restraining order forbids the offender from visiting certain locations such as the children's schools, your workplace, or your home. It is later reviewed. At the review you should produce evidence of the abuse and witnesses. If the emergency or temporary order upheld it is fixed for a period of time at the judge's discretion.

Always carry the restraining order with you and leave copies at your place of employment and at your children's day-care and schools. You will have to show it to the police if you want to get your abuser arrested when he violates its terms. Breach of the restraining order is a criminal offence.

The wording of the order is not uniform – and it is crucial. "The police shall arrest" is not the same as "The police may arrest" the offender if he ignores the conditions set forth in the order. Don't forget to ask the court to forbid him to contact you by phone and other electronic means. Seek a new restraining order if you had moved and your place of residence or your workplace or the children's day-care or school changed.

If the abuser has visitation rights with the children, these should be specified in the order. Include a provision allowing you to deny the visit if he is intoxicated. The order can be issued against your abuser's family and friends as well if they harass and stalk you.

A restraining order is no substitute for taking precautionary measures to safeguard yourself and your children. Abusers often ignore the court's strictures and taunt you all the same. The situation can easily escalate and get out of hand. Be prepared for such unpleasant and dangerous eventualities.

Avoid empty and unlit areas, carry relevant emergency numbers with you at all times, install a personalized alarm system, wear comfortable shoes and clothes to allow you to run if attacked. Trust your senses – if you feel that you are being followed, go to a public place (restaurant, department store, cinema). Learn by rote the transit routes of all public transport around your home and workplace and make special arrangement with the cab operator nearest to you. You may also wish to consider buying a weapon or, at least, a spray can.

If you were physically or sexually assaulted or if you are being stalked or harassed, keep records of the incidents and a list of witnesses. Never hesitate to lay charges against your abuser, his family and friends. See your charges through by testifying against the offenders. Try not to withdraw the charges even if you worked out your problems. Abusers learn the hard way and a spell in jail (or even a fine) is likely to guarantee your future safety.

Based on a criminal police file, the criminal court can also force your abuser (and his family and friends if they have been harassing you) to sign a peace bond in the presence of a judge. It is a pledge of good behaviour, often requiring your abuser to stay away from your home and place of work for a period of 3-12 months. Some peace bonds forbid the abuser from carrying weapons.

Have the peace bond with you at all times and leave copies at your children's day-care and schools and at your place of employment. You will have to show it to the police if you want to get your abuser arrested when he violates its terms. Breach of the peace bond is a criminal offence.

Do not meet your abuser or speak to him while the restraining order or peace bond are in effect. The courts are likely to take a very dim view of the fact that you yourself violated the terms of these instruments of law issued for your protection and at your request.

There are many additional remedies the courts can apply. They can force your abusive partner to surrender to you households items and clothing, to grant you access to bank accounts and credit cards, to defray some costs, to pay alimony and child support, to submit to psychological counselling and evaluation, and to grant the police access to his home and workplace. Consult your family or divorce attorney as to what else can be done.

In theory, the courts are the victims' friends. The truth, however, is a lot more nuanced. If you are not represented, your chances to get protection and prevail (to have your day in court) are slim. The courts also show some institutional bias in favour of the abuser. Yet, despite these hurdles there is no substitute to getting the legal system to weigh in and restrain your abuser. Use it wisely and you will not regret it.

Return

# *Toxic Relationships*

## Abuse and Its Aftermath

**Relationships with Abusive Narcissists**

# Narcissists, Narcissistic Supply
## And Sources of Supply

*Question:* What is Narcissistic Supply?

*Answer:* We all search for positive cues from people around us. These cues reinforce in us certain behaviour patterns. There is nothing special in the fact that the narcissist does the same. However there are two major differences between the narcissistic and the normal personality.

The first is quantitative. The normal person is likely to welcome a moderate amount of attention – verbal and non-verbal – in the form of affirmation, approval, or admiration. Too much attention, though, is perceived as onerous. Though constructive criticism is accepted, destructive and negative criticism is avoided altogether.

The narcissist, in contrast, is the mental equivalent of an alcoholic. He is insatiable. He directs his whole behaviour, in fact his life, to obtaining pleasurable titbits of attention. He embeds them in a coherent, completely biased, picture of himself. He uses them to regulate his labile sense of self-worth and self-esteem.

To elicit constant interest, he projects to others a confabulated, fictitious version of himself, known as the False Self. The False Self is everything the narcissist is not: omniscient, omnipotent, charming, intelligent, rich, or well-connected.

The narcissist then proceeds to harvest reactions to this projected image from family members, friends, co-workers, neighbours, business partners and from colleagues. If these – the adulation, admiration, attention, fear, respect, applause, affirmation – are not forthcoming, the narcissist demands them, or extorts them. Money, compliments, a favourable critique, an appearance in the media, a sexual conquest are all converted into the same currency in the narcissist's mind. This currency is what I call Narcissistic Supply. The narcissist uses these inputs to regulate his fluctuating sense of self-worth.

The narcissist cathexes (emotionally invests) with grandiosity everything he owns or does: his nearest and dearest, his work, his environment. But, as time passes, this pathologically intense aura fades. The narcissist finds fault with things and people he had first thought impeccable. He energetically berates and denigrates that which he equally zealously exulted and praised only a short while before.

This inexorable and (to the outside world) disconcerting roller-coaster is known as the "Idealization-Devaluation Cycle". It involves serious cognitive and emotional deficits and a formidable series of triggered defence mechanisms.

It is important to distinguish between the various components of the process of Narcissistic Supply:

1. The *Trigger of Supply* is the person or object that provokes the source into yielding Narcissistic Supply by confronting the source with information about the narcissist's False Self.
2. The *Source of Narcissistic Supply* is the person that provides the Narcissistic Supply.
3. *Narcissistic Supply* is the reaction of the source to the trigger.

Publicity (celebrity or notoriety, being famous or being infamous) is a Trigger of Narcissistic Supply because it provokes people to pay attention to the narcissist (in other words, it moves sources to provide the narcissist with Narcissistic Supply). Publicity can be obtained by exposing oneself, by creating something, or by eliciting attention. The narcissist resorts to all three repeatedly (as drug addicts do to secure their daily dose). A mate or a companion is one such Source of Narcissistic Supply.

The narcissist homes in on Triggers and Sources of Narcissistic Supply – people, possessions, creative works, money – and imbues these sources and triggers with imputed uniqueness, perfection, brilliance, and grandiose qualities (omnipotence, omnipresence, omniscience). He filters out any data that contradict these fantastic misperceptions. He rationalizes, intellectualizes, denies, represses, projects and, in general, defends against contrarian information.

But the picture is more complicated. There are two categories of Narcissistic Supply and their Sources (NSSs):

The *Primary Narcissistic Supply* is attention, in both its public forms (fame, notoriety, infamy, celebrity) and its private, interpersonal, forms (adoration, adulation, applause, fear, repulsion). It is important to understand that attention of any kind – positive or negative – constitutes Primary Narcissistic Supply. Infamy is as sought after as fame, being notorious is as good as being renowned.

To the narcissist his "achievements" can be imaginary, fictitious, or only apparent, as long as others believe in them. Appearances count more than substance, what matters is not the truth but its perception.

*Triggers of Primary Narcissistic Supply* include, apart from being famous (celebrity, notoriety, fame, infamy), having an air of mystique (when the narcissist is considered to be mysterious), having sex and deriving from it a sense of masculinity/virility/femininity, and being close or connected to political, financial, military, or spiritual power or authority or actually yielding them.

*Sources of Primary Narcissistic Supply* are all those who provide the narcissist with Narcissistic Supply on a casual, random basis.

*Secondary Narcissistic Supply* includes: leading a normal life (a source of great pride for the narcissist), having a secure existence (economic security, social acceptability, upward mobility), and obtaining companionship.

Thus, having a mate, possessing conspicuous wealth, being creative, running a business (transformed into a Pathological Narcissistic Space), possessing a sense of anarchic freedom, being a member of a group or collective, having a professional or other reputation, being successful, owning property and flaunting one's status symbols all constitute Secondary Narcissistic Supply.

*Sources of Secondary Narcissistic Supply* are all those who provide the narcissist with Narcissistic Supply on a regular basis: spouse, friends, colleague, business partners, teachers, neighbours, and so on.

Both these Primary and Secondary Narcissistic Supply and their triggers and sources are incorporated in a *Narcissistic Pathological Space*.

**Question:** What are the functions of Narcissistic Supply in the narcissistic pathology?

**Answer:** The narcissist internalizes a "bad" object (typically, his mother) in his childhood. He harbours socially forbidden emotions towards this object: hatred, envy, and other forms of aggression. These feelings reinforce the narcissist's self-image as bad and corrupt. Gradually he develops a dysfunctional sense of self-worth. His self-confidence and self-image become unrealistically low and distorted.

In an effort to repress these "bad" feelings, the narcissist also suppresses all emotions. His aggression is channelled to fantasies or to socially legitimate outlets (dangerous sports, gambling, reckless driving, compulsive shopping). The narcissist views the world as a hostile, unstable, unrewarding, unjust, and unpredictable place.

He defends himself by loving a completely controllable object (himself), by projecting to the world an omnipotent and omniscient False Self, and by turning others to functions or to objects so that they pose no emotional risk. This reactive pattern is what we call pathological narcissism.

To exorcize his demons, the narcissist needs the world: its admiration, its adulation, its attention, its applause, even its penalties. The lack of a functioning personality on the inside is balanced by importing ego functions and boundaries from the outside.

The Primary Narcissistic Supply reaffirms the narcissist's grandiose fantasies, buttresses his False Self and, thus allows him to regulate his fluctuating sense of self-worth. The Narcissistic Supply contains information which pertains to the way the False Self is perceived by others and allows the narcissist to "calibrate" and "fine tune" it. The Narcissistic Supply also serves to define the boundaries of the False Self, to regulate its contents and to substitute for some of the functions normally reserved for a True, functioning, Self.

While it is easy to understand the function of the Primary Supply, Secondary Supply is a more complicated affair.

Interacting with the opposite sex and "doing business" are the two main Triggers of Secondary Narcissistic Supply (SNS). The narcissist mistakenly interprets his narcissistic needs as emotions. To him, pursuing a woman (a Source of Secondary Narcissistic Supply – SSNS), for instance, is what others call "love" or "passion".

Narcissistic Supply, both Primary and Secondary, is perishable goods. The narcissist consumes it and has to replenish it. As is the case with other drug addictions, to produce the same effect, he is forced to increase the dosage as he goes.

While the narcissist uses up his supply, his partner serves as a silent (and admiring) witness to the narcissist's "great moments" and "achievements". Thus, the narcissist's female friend "accumulates" the narcissist's "grand" and "illustrious past". When Primary Narcissistic Supply is low, she "releases" the supply she had accumulated. This she does by reminding the narcissist of those moments of glory that she had witnessed. She helps the narcissist to regulate his sense of self-worth.

This function – of Narcissistic Supply accumulation and release – is performed by all SSNSs, male or female, inanimate or institutional. The narcissist's co-workers, bosses, colleagues, neighbours, partners, and friends are all potential SSNSs. They all witness the narcissist's past accomplishments and can remind him of them when new supply runs dry.

**Question:** Why does the narcissist devalue his Source of Secondary Narcissistic Supply (SSNS)?

**Answer:** The narcissist realizes and resents his dependence on Narcissistic Supply. Moreover, deep inside, he is aware of the fact that his False Self is an untenable sham. Still, omnipotent as he holds himself to be, the narcissist believes in his ability to make it all come true, to asymptotically approximate his grandiose fantasies. He is firmly convinced that, given enough time and practice, he can and will become his lofty and ideal False Self.

Hence the narcissist's idea of progress: the frustrating and masochistic pursuit of an ever-receding mirage of perfection, brilliance, omniscience, omnipresence, and omnipotence. The narcissist dumps old Sources and Triggers of Supply because he is convinced that he is perpetually improving and that he deserves better and that "better" is just around the corner. He is driven by his own impossible Ego Ideal.

Narcissists are forever in pursuit of Narcissistic Supply. They are oblivious to the passage of time and are not constrained by any behavioural consistency, "rules" of conduct, or moral considerations. Signal to the narcissist that you are a willing source, and he is bound to try to extract Narcissistic Supply from you by any and all means.

This is a reflex. The narcissist would have reacted absolutely the same way to any other source because, to him, all sources are interchangeable.

Some Sources of Supply are ideal (from the narcissist's point of view): sufficiently intelligent, sufficiently gullible, submissive, reasonably (but not overly) inferior to the narcissist, in possession of a good memory (with which to regulate the flow of Narcissistic Supply), available but not imposing, not explicitly or overtly manipulative, undemanding, attractive (if the narcissist is somatic). In short: a Galathea-Pygmallion type.

But then, often abruptly and inexplicably, it is all over. The narcissist is cold, uninterested and remote.

One of the reasons is, as Groucho Marx put it, that the narcissist doesn't like to belong to those clubs which would accept him as a member. The narcissist devalues his Sources of Supply for the very qualities that made them such sources in the first place: their gullibility, their submissiveness, their (intellectual or physical) inferiority.

But there are many other reasons. For instance, the narcissist resents his dependency. He realizes that he is hopelessly and helplessly addicted to Narcissistic Supply and is in hock to its sources. By devaluing the sources of said supply (his spouse, his employer, his colleague, his friends) he ameliorates the dissonance.

Moreover, the narcissist perceives intimacy and sex as a threat to his uniqueness. Everyone needs sex and intimacy: it is the great equalizer. The narcissist resents this commonness. He rebels by striking out at the perceived founts of his frustration and "enslavement": his Sources of Narcissistic Supply.

Sex and intimacy are usually also connected to unresolved past conflicts with important Primary Objects (parents or caregivers). By constantly invoking these conflicts, the narcissist encourages transference and provokes the onset of approach-avoidance cycles. He blows hot and cold on his relationships.

Additionally, narcissists simply get tired of their sources. They get bored. There is no mathematical formula which governs this. It depends on numerous variables. Usually, the relationship lasts until the narcissist "gets used" to the source and its stimulating effects wear off or until a better Source of Supply presents itself.

*Question:* Could negative input serve as Narcissistic Supply (NS)?

*Answer:* Yes, it can. NS includes all forms of attention, both positive and negative: fame, notoriety, adulation, fear, applause, approval. Whenever the narcissist gets attention, positive or negative, whenever he is in the "limelight", it constitutes NS. If he can manipulate people or influence them – positively or negatively – it qualifies as NS.

Even quarrelling with people and confronting them constitute NS. Perhaps not the conflict itself, but the narcissist's ability to influence other people, to make them feel the way he wants, to manipulate them, to make them do something or refrain from doing it all count as forms of Narcissistic Supply. Hence the phenomenon of "serial litigators".

*Question:* Does the narcissist want to be liked?

*Answer:* Would you wish to be liked by your television set? To the narcissist, people are mere tools, Sources of Supply. If, in order to secure this supply, he must be liked by them, he acts likable, helpful, collegial, and friendly. If the only way is to be feared, he makes sure they fear him. He does not really care either way as long as he is being attended to. Attention – whether in the form of fame or infamy – is what it's all about. His world revolves around this constant mirroring. I am seen therefore I exist is his motto.

But the classic narcissist also craves punishment. His actions are aimed to elicit social opprobrium and sanctions. His life is a Kafkaesque, ongoing trial and the never-ending proceedings are in themselves the punishment. Being penalized (reprimanded, incarcerated, abandoned) serves to vindicate and validate the internal damning voices of the narcissist's sadistic, ideal and immature Superego (really, the erstwhile voices of his parents or other caregivers). It confirms his worthlessness. It relieves him from the inner conflict he endures when he is successful: the conflict between the gnawing feelings of guilt, anxiety, and shame and the need to relentlessly secure Narcissistic Supply.

*Question:* How does the narcissist treat his past Sources of Narcissistic Supply? Does he regard them as enemies?

*Answer:* One should be careful not to romanticize the narcissist. His remorse and good behaviour are always linked to fears of losing his sources.

Narcissists have no enemies. They have only Sources of Narcissistic Supply. An enemy means attention means supply. One holds sway over one's enemy. If the narcissist has the power to provoke emotions in you, then you are still a Source of Supply to him, regardless of which emotions are provoked.

The narcissist seeks out his old Sources of Narcissistic Supply when he has absolutely no other NS Sources at his disposal. Narcissists frantically try to recycle their old and wasted sources in such a situation. But the narcissist would not do even that had he not felt that he could still successfully extract a modicum of NS from the old source (even to attack the narcissist is to recognize his existence and to attend to him!!!).

If you are an old Source of Narcissistic Supply, first, get over the excitement of seeing the narcissist again. It may be flattering, perhaps sexually arousing. Try to overcome these feelings.

Then, simply ignore him. Don't bother to respond in any way to his offer to get together. If he talks to you – keep quiet, don't answer. If he calls you – listen politely and then say goodbye and hang up. Return his gifts unopened. Indifference is what the narcissist cannot stand. It indicates a lack of attention and interest that constitutes the kernel of negative NS to be avoided.

[Much more in "The Narcissist's Mother" and "The Development of the Narcissist"]

Return

# Narcissists, Disagreements and Criticism

*Question:* How do narcissists react to criticism?

*Answer:* Narcissistic injury is any threat (real or imagined) to the narcissist's grandiose and fantastic self-perception (False Self) as brilliant, perfect, omnipotent, omniscient, and entitled to special treatment and recognition, regardless of his actual accomplishments (or lack thereof).

The narcissist is forever trapped in the unresolved conflicts of his childhood (including the famous Oedipus Complex). This compels him to seek resolution by re-enacting these conflicts with significant others. But he is likely to return to the Primary Objects in his life (parents, authority figures, role models, or caregivers) to do either of two:

1. To "re-charge" the conflict "battery", or
2. When he fails to re-enact the conflict with another person.

The narcissist relates to his human environment through his unresolved conflicts. The energy of the tension thus created sustains him.

The narcissist is a person driven by parlously imminent eruptions, by the unsettling prospect of losing his precarious balance. Being a narcissist is a tightrope act. The narcissist must remain alert and on-edge. Only in a constant state of active conflict does he attain the requisite levels of mental arousal.

This periodical interaction with the objects of his conflicts sustains his inner turmoil, keeps the narcissist on his toes, infuses him with the intoxicating feeling that he is alive.

The narcissist perceives every disagreement, let alone criticism, as nothing short of a threat. Most narcissists react defensively to criticism and disagreement. They become conspicuously indignant, aggressive, and cold. They detach emotionally for fear of yet another (narcissistic) injury. They devalue the person who made the disparaging remark, the critical comment, the unflattering observation, the innocuous joke at the narcissist's expense.

By holding the critic in contempt, by diminishing the stature of the discordant conversant, the narcissist minimizes the impact of the disagreement or criticism on himself. This is known as cognitive dissonance.

The narcissist actively solicits Narcissistic Supply – adulation, compliments, admiration, subservience, attention, being feared – from others in order to sustain his fragile and dysfunctional Ego. Thus, he constantly courts possible rejection, criticism, disagreement, and even mockery.

The narcissist is, therefore, dependent on other people. He is aware of the risks associated with such all-pervasive and essential dependence. He resents his weakness and dreads possible disruptions in the flow of his drug: Narcissistic Supply. He is caught between the rock of his habit and the hard place of his frustration. No wonder he is prone to raging, lashing and acting out, and to pathological, all-consuming envy (all of these being expressions of pent-up aggression).

Like a trapped animal, the narcissist is constantly on the lookout for slights. He is hypervigilant: was this comment meant to demean him? Was this utterance a deliberate attack? He perceives every disagreement as criticism and every critical remark as complete and humiliating rejection – nothing short of a threat or a challenge. Gradually, his mind turns into a chaotic battlefield of paranoia and ideas of reference until he loses touch with reality and retreats to his own world of fantasized and unchallenged grandiosity.

When the disagreement or criticism or disapproval or approbation are public, though, the narcissist tends to regard them as Narcissistic Supply! Only when they are expressed in private does the narcissist rage against them.

The cerebral narcissist is as competitive and intolerant of criticism or disagreement as his somatic counterpart. The subjugation and subordination of others demand the establishment of his undisputed intellectual superiority or professional authority.

Alexander Lowen wrote an excellent exposition of this "hidden or tacit competition". The cerebral narcissist aspires to perfection. Thus, even the slightest and most inconsequential challenge to his authority is inflated by him. Hence, the disproportionateness of his reactions.

When confronting adversity fails, some narcissists resort to denial, which they apply to their "extensions" (family, business, workplace, friends) as well.

Take, for example, the narcissist's family. Narcissists often instruct, order, or threaten their children into hiding the truth of abuse, malfunction, maladaptation, fear, pervasive sadness, violence, mutual hatred and mutual repulsion which are the hallmarks of the narcissistic family.

"Not to wash the family's dirty linen in public" is a common exhortation. The whole family conforms to the fantastic, grandiose, perfect and superior narrative invented by the narcissist. The family becomes an extension of the False Self. This is an important function of these Sources of Secondary Narcissistic Supply.

Criticizing, disagreeing, or exposing these fictions and lies, penetrating the family's facade, are considered to be mortal sins. The sinner is immediately subjected to severe and constant emotional harassment, guilt trips and blame games, and to abuse, including physical abuse. This state of things is especially typical of families with sexual abuse.

Behaviour modification techniques are liberally used by the narcissist to ensure that the skeletons do stay in the family closets. An unexpected by-product of this atmosphere of concealment and falsity is mutiny. The narcissist's spouse or his adolescent children are likely to exploit the narcissist's vulnerabilities – his proneness to secrecy, self-delusion, and aversion to the truth – to rebel against him. The first thing to crumble in the narcissist's family is this shared psychosis: the mass denial and the secretiveness so diligently cultivated by him.

[Learn more about Narcissistic Rage]

Return

# The Unstable Narcissist

*Question:* Is the narcissist characterized by simultaneous instabilities in all the important aspects of his life?

*Answer:* The narcissist is a person who derives his Ego (and ego functions) from other people's reactions to an image he invents and projects, called the False Self (Narcissistic Supply). Since no absolute control over the quantity and quality of Narcissistic Supply is possible – it is bound to fluctuate – the narcissist's view of himself and of his world is correspondingly and equally volatile. As "public opinion" ebbs and flows, so do the narcissist's self-confidence, self-esteem, sense of self-worth, or, in other words, so does his Self. Even the narcissist's convictions are subject to a never-ending process of vetting by others.

The narcissistic personality is unstable in each and every one of its dimensions. It is the ultimate hybrid: rigidly amorphous, devoutly flexible, reliant for its sustenance on the opinion of people, whom the narcissist undervalues. A large part of this instability is subsumed under the Emotional Involvement Prevention Measures (EIPM), described in the Essay. The narcissist's lability is so ubiquitous and so dominant, that it might well be described as the ONLY stable feature of his personality.

The narcissist does everything with one goal in mind: to attract Narcissistic Supply (attention).

An example of this kind of behaviour:

The narcissist may study a given subject diligently and in great depth in order to impress people later with this newly acquired erudition. But, having served its purpose, the narcissist lets the knowledge thus acquired evaporate. The narcissist maintains a sort of a "short-term" cell or warehouse where he stores whatever may come handy in the pursuit of Narcissistic Supply. But he is almost never really interested in what he does, or studies, or experiences.

From the outside, this might be perceived as instability. But think about it this way: the narcissist is constantly preparing for life's "exams" and feels that he is on a permanent trial. It is common to forget material studied only in preparation for an exam or for a court appearance.

Short-term memory is perfectly normal. What sets the narcissist apart is the fact that, with him, this short-termism is a CONSTANT state of affairs and affects ALL his functions, not only those directly related to learning, or to emotions, or to experience, or to any single dimension of his life.

Thus, the narcissist learns, remembers and forgets not in line with his real interests or hobbies; he loves and hates not the real subjects of his emotions but one dimensional, utilitarian, cartoons constructed by him. He judges, praises and condemns – all from the narrowest possible point of view: the potential to extract Narcissistic Supply.

He asks not what he can do with the world and in it – but what can the world do for him as far as Narcissistic Supply is concerned. He falls in and out of love with people, workplaces, residences, vocations, hobbies, and interests because they seem to be able to provide more or less Narcissistic Supply and for no other reason.

Still, narcissists belong to two broad categories: the "compensatory stability" and the "enhancing instability" types.

### Compensatory Stability ("Classic") Narcissists

These narcissists isolate one or more (but never most) aspects of their lives and "make these aspect/s stable". They do not really emotionally invest themselves in maintaining these areas of their lives stable. Rather, this stability is safeguarded by artificial means: money, celebrity, power, fear. A typical example is a narcissist who changes numerous workplaces, a few careers, myriad hobbies, value systems or faiths. At the same time, he maintains (preserves) a relationship with a single woman (and even remains faithful to her). She is his "island of stability". To fulfil this role, she just needs to be physically present around him.

The narcissist is dependent upon "his" woman to maintain the stability lacking in all other areas of his life (to compensate for his instability). Yet, emotional closeness and intimacy are bound to threaten the narcissist. Thus, he is likely to distance himself from her and to remain detached and indifferent to most of her needs.

Despite this cruel emotional treatment, the narcissist considers her to be a source of sustenance and a fountain of empowerment. This mismatch between what he wishes to receive and what he is able to give, the narcissist prefers to deny, repress and bury deep in his unconscious.

This is why he is always shocked and devastated to learn of his wife's estrangement, infidelity, or intentions to divorce him. Possessed of no emotional depth, being completely clueless and one track minded, he cannot fathom the needs of others. In other words, he cannot empathize.

Another, even more common case is the "career narcissist". This narcissist marries, divorces and remarries with dizzying speed. Everything in his life is in constant flux: friends, emotions, judgements, values, beliefs, place of residence, affiliations, hobbies. Everything, that is, except his work.

His career is the island of compensating stability in his otherwise mercurial existence. This kind of narcissist is dogged by unmitigated ambition and devotion. He perseveres in one workplace or one job, patiently, persistently and blindly climbing up the corporate ladder and treading the career path. In his pursuit of job fulfilment and achievements, the workaholic narcissist is ruthless and unscrupulous, and, very often, successful.

### Enhancing Instability ("Borderline") Narcissist

The other kind of narcissist enhances instability in one aspect or dimension of his life by introducing instability in others. Thus, if such a narcissist resigns (or, more likely, is made redundant), he also relocates to another city or country. If he divorces, he is also likely to resign his job.

This added instability gives this type of narcissist the feeling that all the dimensions of his life are changing simultaneously, that he is being "unshackled", that a transformation is in progress. This, of course, is an illusion. Those who know the narcissist, no longer trust his frequent "conversions", "decisions", "crises", "transformations", "developments" and "periods". They see through his pretensions, protestations, and solemn declarations into the core of his instability. They know that he is not to be relied upon. They know that with narcissists, the temporary is the only permanence.

Narcissists hate routine. When a narcissist finds himself doing the same things over and over again, he gets depressed. He oversleeps, over-eats, over-drinks and, in general, engages in addictive, impulsive, reckless, and compulsive behaviours. This is his way of re-introducing risk and excitement into what he (emotionally) perceives to be a barren life.

The problem is that even the most exciting and varied existence becomes routine after a while. Living in the same country or apartment, meeting the same people, doing essentially the same things (even with changing content) all amount, in the eyes of the narcissist, to stultifying rote.

The narcissist feels entitled. He feels it is his right – due to his intellectual or physical superiority – to lead a thrilling, rewarding, kaleidoscopic life. He wants to force life itself, or at least people around him, to yield to his wishes and needs, supreme among them the need for stimulating variety.

This rejection of habit is part of a larger pattern of aggressive entitlement. The narcissist feels that the very existence of a sublime intellect (such as his) warrants concessions and allowances by others.

Thus, queuing in line is a waste of time better spent pursuing knowledge, inventing and creating. The narcissist feels that he deserves only the best medical treatment proffered by the most prominent medical authorities – lest the precious asset that he is should be lost to Mankind. The narcissist makes clear that he should not be bothered with trivial pursuits – these lowly functions are best assigned to the less gifted.

Entitlement is sometimes justified in a Picasso or an Einstein. But few narcissists are either. Their achievements are grotesquely incommensurate with their overwhelming sense of entitlement and with their grandiose self-image.

Of course, this overpowering sense of superiority often serves to mask and compensate for a cancerous complex of inferiority. Moreover, the narcissist infects others with his projected grandiosity and their feedback constitutes the edifice upon which he constructs his self-esteem. He regulates his sense of self-worth by rigidly insisting that he is above the madding crowd while deriving his Narcissistic Supply from the very people he holds in deep contempt.

But there is a second angle to this abhorrence of the predictable. Narcissists employ a host of Emotional Involvement Prevention Measures (EIPM's). Despising routine and avoiding it is one of these mechanisms. Their function is to prevent the narcissist from getting emotionally involved and, subsequently, hurt.

Their application results in an Approach-Avoidance Repetition Complex. The narcissist fears and loathes intimacy, stability and security and yet craves them. Consequently, he approaches and then avoids significant others or important tasks in a rapid succession of apparently inconsistent and disconnected cycles.

## The Two Loves of the Narcissist

Narcissists "love" their spouses or other significant others – as long as they continue to reliably provide them with Narcissistic Supply (in one word, with attention). Inevitably, they regard others as mere "sources", objects, or functions. Lacking empathy and emotional maturity, the narcissist's love is pathological. But the precise locus of the pathology depends on the narcissist's stability or instability in different parts of his life.

We are, therefore, faced with two pathological forms of narcissistic "love".

One type of narcissist "loves" others as one attaches to objects. He "loves" his spouse, for instance, simply because she exists and is available to provide him with Narcissistic Supply. He "loves" his children because they are part of his self-image as a successful husband and father. He "loves" his "friends" because – and only as long as – he can exploit them.

Such a narcissist reacts with alarm and rage to any sign of independence and autonomy in his "charges". He tries to "freeze" everyone around him in their "allocated" positions and "assigned roles". His world is rigid and immovable, predictable and static, fully under his control. He punishes for "transgressions" against this ordained order. He thus stifles life as a dynamic process of compromises and growth rendering it instead a mere theatre, a tableau vivant.

The other type of narcissist abhors monotony and constancy, equating them, in his mind, with death. He seeks upheaval, drama, and change, but only when they conform to his plans, designs, and views of the world and of himself. Thus, he does not encourage growth in his nearest and dearest. By monopolizing their lives, he, like the other kind of narcissist, also reduces them to mere objects, props in the exciting drama of his life.

This narcissist likewise rages at any sign of rebellion and disagreement. But, as opposed to the first sub-species, he seeks to animate others with his demented energy, grandiose plans, and megalomaniacal self-perception. An adrenaline junkie, his world is a whirlwind of comings and goings, reunions and separations, loves and hates, vocations adopted and discarded, schemes erected and dismantled, enemies turned friends and vice versa. His Universe is equally a theatre, but a more ferocious and chaotic one.

Where is love in all this? Where is the commitment to the loved one's welfare, the self-discipline, the extension of oneself to incorporate the beloved, the mutual growth?

These are nowhere to be seen. The narcissist's "love" is hate and fear disguised: fear of losing control and hatred of the very people his precariously balanced personality so depends on. The narcissist is egotistically committed only to his own well-being. To him, the objects of his "love" are interchangeable and inferior.

He idealizes his nearest and dearest not because he is smitten by emotion, but because he needs to captivate them and to convince himself that they are worthy Sources of Supply, despite their flaws and mediocrity. Once he deems them useless, he discards and devalues them cold-bloodedly. A predator, always on the lookout, he debases the coin of "love" as he corrupts everything else in himself and around him.

Return

# Inner Dialog, Cognitive Deficits
# And Introjects in Narcissism

*"Man can will nothing unless he has first understood that he must count no one but himself; that he is alone, abandoned on earth in the midst of his infinite responsibilities, without help, with no other aim than the one he sets himself, with no other destiny than the one he forges for himself on this earth."*
  [Jean Paul Sartre, Being and Nothingness, 1943]

The narcissist lacks empathy. He is, therefore, unable to meaningfully relate to other people and to truly appreciate what it is to be human. Instead, he withdraws inside, into a universe populated by avatars – simple or complex representations of parents, peers, role models, authority figures, and other members of his social milieu. There, in this twilight zone of simulacra, he develops "relationships" and maintains an on-going internal dialog with them.

All of us generate such representations of meaningful others and internalize these objects. In a process called introjection, we adopt, assimilate, and, later, manifest their traits and attitudes (the introjects).

But the narcissist is different. He is incapable of holding an external dialog. Even when he seems to be interacting with someone else – the narcissist is actually engaged in a self-referential discourse. To the narcissist, all other people are cardboard cut-outs, two dimensional animated cartoon characters, or symbols. They exist only in his mind. He is startled when they deviate from the script and prove to be complex and autonomous.

But this is not the narcissist's sole cognitive deficit.

The narcissist attributes his failures and mistakes to circumstances and external causes. This propensity to blame the world for one's mishaps and misfortunes is called "alloplastic defence". At the same time, the narcissist regards his successes and achievements (some of which are imaginary) as proofs of his omnipotence and omniscience. This is known in attribution theory as "defensive attribution".

Conversely, the narcissist traces other people's errors and defeats to their inherent inferiority, stupidity, and weakness. Their successes he dismisses as "being in the right place at the right time" – i.e., the outcome of luck and circumstance.

Thus, the narcissist falls prey to an exaggerated form of what is known in attribution theory as the "fundamental attribution error". Moreover, these fallacies and the narcissist's magical thinking are not dependent on objective data and tests of distinctiveness, consistency, and consensus.

The narcissist never questions his reflexive judgements and never stops to ask himself: are these events distinct or are they typical? Do they repeat themselves consistently or are they unprecedented? And what do others have to say about them?

The narcissist learns nothing because he regards himself as born perfect. Even when he fails a thousand times, the narcissist still feels the victim of happenstance. And someone else's repeated outstanding accomplishments are never proof of mettle or merit. People who disagree with the narcissist and try to teach him differently are, to his mind, biased or morons or both.

But the narcissist pays a dear price for these distortions of perception. Unable to gauge his environment with accuracy, he develops paranoid ideation and fails the reality test. Finally, he lifts the drawbridges and vanishes into a state of mind that can best be described as borderline psychosis.

*First published on the Suite 101 Narcissistic Personality Disorders Topic.*

Return

# The Narcissist as a Sadist

*Question:* What would cause a narcissist to victimize a significant other sadistically versus just discarding her when no longer useful?

*Answer:* The narcissist discards people when he becomes convinced that they can no longer provide him with Narcissistic Supply. This conviction, subjective and emotionally charged, does not have to be grounded in reality. Suddenly, because of boredom, disagreement, disillusion, a fight, an act, inaction, or a mood, the narcissist wildly swings from idealization to devaluation.

The narcissist then detaches immediately. He needs all the energy he can muster to obtain new Sources of Narcissistic Supply and would rather not spend these scarce resources over what he regards as human refuse, the pulp left after the extraction of Narcissistic Supply.

The narcissist would tend to display the sadistic aspect of his personality in one of two cases:

1. That the very acts of sadism generate Narcissistic Supply to be consumed by the narcissist ("I inflict pain, therefore I am superior"), or
2. That the victims of his sadism are still his only or major Sources of Narcissistic Supply but are perceived by him to be intentionally frustrating and withholding. Sadistic acts are his way of punishing them for not being docile, obedient, admiring and adoring as he expects them to be in view of his uniqueness, cosmic significance, and special entitlement.

The narcissist is not a full-fledged sadist, masochist, or paranoiac. He does not enjoy hurting his victims. He does not believe firmly that he is the focal point of persecution and the target of conspiracies.

But, he does enjoy punishing himself when it provides him with a sense of relief, exoneration and validation. This is his masochistic streak.

Because of his lack of empathy and his rigid personality, he often inflicts great (physical or mental) pain on meaningful others in his life and he enjoys their writhing and suffering. In this restricted sense he is a sadist.

To support his sense of uniqueness, greatness and (cosmic) significance, he is often hypervigilant. If he falls from grace, he attributes it to dark forces out to destroy him. If his sense of entitlement is not satisfied and he is ignored by others, he attributes it to the fear and feelings of inferiority that he provokes in them. So, to some extent, he is a paranoid.

The narcissist is as much an artist of pain as any sadist. The difference between them lies in their motivation. The narcissist tortures and abuses others as means to punish and to reassert superiority, omnipotence, and grandiosity. The sadist does it for pure (usually, sexually-tinged) pleasure. But both are adept at finding the chinks in people's armours. Both are ruthless and venomous in the pursuit of their prey. Both are unable to empathize with their victims, and are self-centred, and rigid.

The narcissist abuses his victim verbally, mentally, or physically (often, in all three ways). He infiltrates her defences, shatters her self-confidence, confuses and confounds her, demeans and debases her. He invades her territory, abuses her confidence, exhausts her resources, hurts her loved ones, threatens her stability and security, enmeshes her in his paranoid state of mind, frightens her out of her wits, withholds love and sex from her, prevents satisfaction and causes frustration, humiliates and insults her privately and in public, points out her shortcomings, criticizes her profusely and in a "scientific and objective" manner – and this is a partial list.

Very often, the narcissist's sadistic acts are disguised as an enlightened interest in the welfare of his victim. He plays the psychiatrist to her psychopathology (totally dreamt up by him). He acts the guru, the avuncular or father figure, the teacher, the only true friend, the old and the experienced – all these in order to weaken her defences and to lay siege to her disintegrating nerves. So subtle and poisonous is the narcissistic variant of sadism that it might well be regarded as the most dangerous of all.

Luckily, the narcissist's attention span is short and his resources and energy limited. In constant, effort-consuming and attention-diverting pursuit of Narcissistic Supply, the narcissist lets his victim go, usually before it had suffered irreversible damage. The victim is then free to rebuild her life from ruins. Not an easy undertaking this, but far better than the total obliteration which awaits the victims of the "true" sadist.

If one had to distil the quotidian existence of the narcissist in two pithy sentences, one would say:

The narcissist loves to be hated and hates to be loved.

Hate is the complement of fear and narcissists like being feared. It imbues them with an intoxicating sensation of omnipotence.

Many of them are veritably inebriated by the looks of horror or repulsion on people's faces: "They know that I am capable of anything."

The sadistic narcissist perceives himself as Godlike, ruthless and unscrupulous, capricious and unfathomable, devoid of emotions and asexual, omniscient, omnipotent and omnipresent, a plague, a devastation, an inescapable verdict.

He nurtures his ill-repute, stoking it and fanning the flames of gossip. It is an enduring asset. Hate and fear are sure-fire generators of attention. It is all about Narcissistic Supply, of course: the drug which narcissists consume and which, in turn, consumes them.

Deep inside, it is the horrid future and inescapable punishment that await the narcissist that are irresistibly appealing. Sadists are often also masochists. In sadistic narcissists, there is, actually, a burning desire – nay, need – to be punished. In the grotesque mind of the narcissist, his punishment is equally his vindication.

By being permanently on trial, the narcissist defiantly claims the high moral ground and the position of the martyr: misunderstood, discriminated against, unjustly roughed, outcast due to his very towering genius or other outstanding qualities.

To conform to the cultural stereotype of the "tormented artist", the narcissist provokes his own suffering. He is thus validated. His grandiose fantasies acquire a modicum of substance. "If I were not so special, they surely wouldn't have persecuted me so." The persecution of the narcissist proves to him his self-imputed uniqueness. To have "deserved" or to have provoked it, he must have been different and unique, for better or for worse.

The narcissist's aforementioned streak of paranoia makes his persecution inevitable. The narcissist is in constant conflict with "lesser beings": his spouse, his shrink, his boss, his colleagues, the police, the courts, his neighbours. Forced to stoop to their intellectual level, the narcissist feels like Gulliver: a giant shackled by Lilliputians. His life is a constant struggle against the self-contented mediocrity of his milieu. This is his fate which he accepts, though never stoically. It is his calling and the mission of his stormy life.

Deeper still, the narcissist has an image of himself as a worthless, bad and dysfunctional extension of others. In constant need of Narcissistic Supply, he feels humiliated by his dependency. The contrast between his grandiose fantasies and the reality of his habit, neediness and, often, failure (the Grandiosity Gap) is an emotionally corroding experience. It is a perpetual background noise of devilish, demeaning scorn. His inner voices "say" to him: "You are a fraud", "You are a nobody, a loser", "You deserve nothing", "If only they knew how worthless you are".

The narcissist attempts to silence these tormenting voices not by fighting them but by agreeing with them. Unconsciously – sometimes consciously – he "responds" to them: "I do agree with you. I am bad and worthless and deserving of the most severe punishment for my rotten character, disgraceful habits, my addiction and the constant sham that is my life. I will go and seek my doom. Now that I have complied, will you leave me alone? Will you let me be?"

Of course, they never do.

## Sadistic Personality Disorder

The Sadistic Personality Disorder made its last appearance in the DSM-III-TR and was removed from the DSM-IV and from its text revision, the DSM-IV-TR. Some scholars, notably Theodore Millon, regard its removal as a mistake and lobby for its reinstatement in future editions of the DSM.

The Sadistic Personality Disorder is characterized by a pattern of gratuitous cruelty, aggression, and demeaning behaviours which indicate the existence of deep-seated contempt for other people and an utter lack of empathy. Some sadists are "utilitarian": they leverage their explosive violence to establish a position of unchallenged dominance within a relationship. Unlike psychopaths, they rarely use physical force in the commission of crimes. Rather, their aggressiveness is embedded in an interpersonal context and is expressed in social settings, such as the family or the workplace.

This narcissistic need for an audience manifests itself in other circumstances. Sadists strive to humiliate people in front of witnesses. This makes them feel omnipotent. Power plays are important to them and they are likely to treat people under their control or entrusted to their care harshly: a subordinate, a child, a student, a prisoner, a patient, or a spouse are all liable to suffer the consequences of the sadist's "control freakery" and exacting "disciplinary" measures.

Sadists like to inflict pain because they find suffering, both corporeal and psychological, amusing. They torture animals and people because, to them, the sights and sounds of a creature writhing in agony are hilarious and pleasurable. Sadists go to great lengths to hurt others: they lie, deceive, commit crimes, and even make personal sacrifices merely so as to enjoy the cathartic moment of witnessing someone else's anguish.

Sadists are masters of abuse by proxy and ambient abuse. They terrorize and intimidate even their nearest and dearest into doing their bidding. They create an aura and atmosphere of unmitigated yet diffuse dread and consternation. This they achieve by promulgating complex "rules of the house" that restrict the autonomy of their dependants (spouses, children, employees, patients, clients, etc.). They have the final word and are the ultimate law. They must be obeyed, no matter how arbitrary and senseless are their rulings and decisions.

Most sadists are fascinated by gore and violence. They are vicarious serial killers: they channel their homicidal urges in socially acceptable ways by "studying" and admiring historical figures such as Hitler, for instance. They love guns and other weapons, are fascinated by death, torture, and martial arts in all their forms.

Return

# The Weapon of Language

*Question:* My wife was diagnosed as a narcissist. She twists everything and turns it against me. She distorts everything I ever said, ignores the context, and even invents her own endings. It is impossible to have a meaningful conversation with her because she won't commit to anything she says.

*Answer:* In the narcissist's surrealistic world, even language is pathologized. It mutates into a weapon of self-defence, a verbal fortification, a medium without a message, replacing words with duplicitous and ambiguous vocables.

Narcissists (and, often, by contagion, their unfortunate victims) don't talk, or communicate. They fend off. They hide and evade and avoid and disguise. In their planet of capricious and arbitrary unpredictability, of shifting semiotic and semantic dunes – they perfect the ability to say nothing in lengthy, Castro-like speeches.

The ensuing convoluted sentences are arabesques of meaninglessness, acrobatics of evasion, a lack of commitment elevated to an ideology. The narcissist prefers to wait and see what waiting brings. It is the postponement of the inevitable that leads to the inevitability of postponement as a strategy of survival.

It is often impossible to really understand a narcissist. The evasive syntax fast deteriorates into ever more labyrinthine structures. The grammar tortured to produce the verbal Doppler shifts essential to disguise the source of the information, its distance from reality, the speed of its degeneration into rigid "official" versions.

Buried under the lush flora and fauna of idioms without an end, the language erupts, like some exotic rash, an autoimmune reaction to its infection and contamination. Like vile weeds it spreads throughout, strangling with absent minded persistence the ability to understand, to feel, to agree, to disagree and to debate, to present arguments, to compare notes, to learn and to teach.

Narcissists, therefore, never talk to others – rather, they talk at others, or lecture them. They exchange subtexts, camouflage-wrapped by elaborate, florid, texts. They read between the lines, spawning a multitude of private languages, prejudices, superstitions, conspiracy theories, rumours, phobias and hysterias. Theirs is a solipsistic world: where communication is permitted only with oneself and the aim of language is to throw others off the scent or to obtain Narcissistic Supply.

This has profound implications. Communication through unequivocal, unambiguous, information-rich symbol systems is such an integral and crucial part of our world that its absence is not postulated even in the remotest galaxies which grace the skies of science fiction. In this sense, narcissists are nothing short of aliens. It is not that they employ a different language, a code to be deciphered by a new Freud. Their linguistic deficiency is also not the outcome of upbringing or socio-cultural background.

It is the fact that language is put by narcissists to a different use – not to communicate but to obscure, not to share but to abstain, not to learn but to defend and resist, not to teach but to preserve ever less tenable monopolies, to disagree without incurring wrath, to criticize without commitment, to agree without appearing to do so. Thus, an "agreement" with a narcissist is a vague expression of intent at a given moment – rather than the clear listing of long-term, iron-cast and mutual commitments.

The rules that govern the narcissist's universe are loopholed incomprehensibles, open to an exegesis so wide and so self-contradictory that it renders them meaningless. The narcissist often hangs himself by his own verbose Gordic knots, having stumbled through a minefield of logical fallacies and endured self-inflicted inconsistencies. Unfinished sentences hover in the air, like vapour above a semantic swamp.

In the case of the inverted narcissist, who had been suppressed and abused by overbearing caregivers, there is the strong urge not to offend. Intimacy and co-dependence are companions. Parental or peer pressures are irresistible and result in conformity and self-deprecation. Aggressive tendencies, strongly repressed in the social pressure cooker, teem under the veneer of forced civility and violent politeness. Constructive ambiguity, a non-committal "everyone is good and right", an atavistic variant of moral relativism and tolerance bred of fear and of contempt – are all at the service of this eternal vigilance against aggressive drives, at the disposal of a never ending peacekeeping mission.

With the classic narcissist, language is used cruelly and ruthlessly to ensnare one's enemies, to saw confusion and panic, to move others to emulate the narcissist (Projective Identification), to leave the listeners in doubt, in hesitation, in paralysis, to gain control, or to punish. Language is enslaved and forced to lie. The language is appropriated and expropriated. It is considered to be a weapon, an asset, a piece of lethal property, a traitorous mistress to be gang raped into submission.

To cerebral narcissists, language is a lover. The infatuation with its very sound leads to a pyrotechnic type of speech which sacrifices its meaning to its music. Its speakers pay more attention to the composition than to the content. They are swept by it, intoxicated by its perfection, inebriated by the spiralling complexity of its forms. Here, language is an inflammatory process. It attacks the very tissues of the narcissist's relationships with artistic fierceness. It invades the healthy cells of reason and logic, of cool headed argumentation and level headed debate.

Language is a leading indicator of the psychological and institutional health of social units, such as the family, or the workplace. Social capital can often be measured in cognitive (hence, verbal-lingual) terms. To monitor the level of comprehensibility and lucidity of texts is to study the degree of sanity of family members, co-workers, friends, spouses, mates, and colleagues. There can be no hale society without unambiguous speech, without clear communications, without the traffic of idioms and content that is an inseparable part of every social contract. Our language determines how we perceive our world. It IS our mind and our consciousness. The narcissist, in this respect, is a great social menace.

*First published on the Suite 101 Narcissistic Personality Disorders Topic.*

Return

# Other People's Pain

*Question:* Do narcissists actually enjoy the taunting, the sadistic behaviour, and the punishment that always follows?

*Answer:* Most narcissists enjoy an irrational and brief burst of relief after having suffered emotionally ("narcissistic injury") or after having sustained a loss. It is a sense of freedom, which comes with being unshackled. Having lost everything, the narcissist often feels that he has found himself, that he has been re-born, that he has been charged with natal energy, able to take on new challenges and to explore new territories. This elation is so addictive, that the narcissist often seeks pain, humiliation, punishment, scorn, and contempt – as long as they are public and involve the attention of peers and superiors. Being penalized accords with the tormenting inner voices of the narcissist which keep telling him that he is bad, corrupt, and worthy of punishment.

This is the masochistic streak in the narcissist. But the narcissist is also a sadist, albeit an unusual one. The narcissist inflicts pain and abuse on others. He devalues Sources of Supply, callously and offhandedly abandons them, and discards people, places, partnerships, and friendships unhesitatingly. Some narcissists, though by no means the majority, actually ENJOY abusing, taunting, tormenting, and freakishly controlling others ("gaslighting"). But most of them do these things absentmindedly, automatically, and, often, even without good reason.

What is unusual about the narcissist's sadistic behaviours – premeditated acts of tormenting others while enjoying their anguished reactions – is that they are goal orientated. "Pure" sadists have no goal in mind except the pursuit of pleasure: pain as an art form (remember the Marquis de Sade?). Conversely, the narcissist haunts and hunts his victims for a reason: he wants them to reflect his inner state. It is all part of a psychological defence mechanism called Projective Identification.

When the narcissist is angry, unhappy, disappointed, injured, or hurt, he feels unable to express his emotions sincerely and openly since to do so would be to admit his frailty, his neediness, and his weaknesses. He deplores his own humanity: his emotions, his vulnerability, his susceptibility, his gullibility, his inadequacies, and his failures. So, he makes use of other people to express his pain and his frustration, his pent up anger and his aggression.

He achieves this by mentally torturing other people to the point of madness, by driving them to violence, by forcing them to search for an outlet, for closure, and, sometimes, revenge. He causes people to lose their own character traits and adopt his own instead.

In reaction to his constant and well-targeted abuse, they become abusive, vengeful, ruthless, lacking empathy, obsessed, and aggressive. They mirror him faithfully and thus relieve him of the need to express himself directly.

Having constructed this hall of writhing human mirrors, the narcissist withdraws. His goal achieved, he lets go. As opposed to the sadist, he is not in it, indefinitely, for the pleasure. He abuses and traumatizes, humiliates and abandons, discards and ignores, insults and provokes only for the purpose of purging his inner demons. By possessing others, he purifies himself, cathartically, and exorcizes his demented self.

This accomplished, he acts almost with remorse. An episode of extreme abuse is followed by an act of great care and by mellifluous apologies. The Narcissistic Pendulum swings between the extremes of torturing others and soothing the resulting pain.

This incongruous behaviour, these "sudden" shifts between sadism and compassion, abuse and "love", ignoring and caring, abandoning and clinging, viciousness and remorse, the harsh and the tender are, perhaps, the most difficult to comprehend and to accept.

These swings produce in people around the narcissist emotional insecurity, an eroded sense of self-worth, fear, stress, and anxiety (often described as "walking on eggshells"). Gradually, emotional paralysis sets in and they come to occupy the same emotional wasteland inhabited by the narcissist, in effect his prisoners and hostages in more ways than one and even when he is long out of their lives.

### The Narcissism of Differences Big and Small

Freud coined the phrase "narcissism of small differences" in a paper titled "The Taboo of Virginity" that he published in 1917.

Referring to earlier work by British anthropologist Ernest Crawley, he said that we reserve our most virulent emotions – aggression, hatred, envy – towards those who resemble us the most. We feel threatened not by the Other with whom we have little in common – but by the "nearly-we", who mirror and reflect us.

The "nearly-he" imperils the narcissist's selfhood and challenges his uniqueness, perfection, and superiority: the fundaments of the narcissist's sense of self-worth. It provokes in him primitive narcissistic defences and leads him to adopt desperate measures to protect, preserve, and restore his balance. I call it the Array of Gulliver Defence Mechanisms.

The very existence of the "nearly-he" constitutes a narcissistic injury. The narcissist feels humiliated, shamed, and embarrassed not to be unique after all and he reacts with envy and aggression towards this source of frustration.

In doing so, he resorts to splitting, projection, and Projective Identification. He attributes to other people personal traits that he dislikes in himself and he forces them to behave in conformity with his expectations. In other words, the narcissist sees in others those parts of himself that he cannot countenance. He forces people around him to become him and to reflect his shameful behaviours, hidden fears, and forbidden wishes.

But how does the narcissist avoid the realization that what he loudly decries and derides is actually part of him? By exaggerating, or even dreaming up and creatively inventing, differences between his qualities and conduct and other people's. The more hostile he becomes towards the "nearly-he", the easier it is to distinguish himself from "the Other".

To maintain this differentiating aggression, the narcissist stokes the fires of hostility by obsessively and vengefully nurturing grudges and hurts (some of them imagined). He dwells on injustice and pain inflicted on him by these stereotypically "bad or unworthy" people. He devalues and dehumanizes them and plots revenge to achieve closure. In the process, he indulges in grandiose fantasies, aimed to boost his feelings of omnipotence and magical immunity.

In the process of acquiring an adversary, the narcissist blocks out information that threatens to undermine his emerging self-perception as righteous and offended. He begins to base his whole identity on the brewing conflict which is by now a major preoccupation and a defining or even all-pervasive dimension of his existence.

Very much the same dynamic applies to coping with major differences between the narcissist and others. He emphasizes the large disparities while transforming even the most minor ones into decisive and unbridgeable.

Deep inside, the narcissist is continuously subject to a gnawing suspicion that his self-perception as omnipotent, omniscient, and irresistible is flawed, confabulated, and unrealistic. When criticized, the narcissist actually agrees with the critic. In other words, there are only minor differences of opinion between the narcissist and his detractors. But this threatens the narcissist's internal cohesion. Hence the wild rage at any hint of disagreement, resistance, or debate.

Similarly, intimacy brings people closer together: it makes them more similar. There are only minor differences between intimate partners. The narcissist perceives this as a threat to his sense of uniqueness. He reacts by devaluing the cause of his fears: the mate, spouse, lover, or partner. He re-establishes the boundaries and the distinctions that were removed by intimacy. Thus restored, he is emotionally ready to embark on another round of idealization (the Approach-Avoidance Repetition Complex).

*First published on the Suite 101 Narcissistic Personality Disorders Topic.*

Return

# The Psychology of Torture

There is one place in which one's privacy, intimacy, integrity and inviolability are guaranteed: one's body, a unique temple and a familiar territory of sensa and personal history. The torturer invades, defiles and desecrates this shrine. He does so publicly, deliberately, repeatedly and, often, sadistically and sexually, with undisguised pleasure. Hence the all-pervasive, long-lasting, and, frequently, irreversible effects and outcomes of torture.

In a way, the torture victim's own body is rendered his worse enemy. It is corporeal agony that compels the sufferer to mutate, his identity to fragment, his ideals and principles to crumble. The body becomes an accomplice of the tormentor, an uninterruptible channel of communication, a treasonous, poisoned territory.

It fosters a humiliating dependency of the abused on the perpetrator. Bodily needs denied – sleep, toilet, food, water – are wrongly perceived by the victim as the direct causes of his degradation and dehumanization. As he sees it, he is rendered bestial not by the sadistic bullies around him but by his own flesh.

The concept of "body" can easily be extended to "family", or "home". Torture is often applied to kin and kith, compatriots, or colleagues. This intends to disrupt the continuity of "surroundings, habits, appearance, relations with others", as the CIA put it in one of its manuals. A sense of cohesive self-identity depends crucially on the familiar and the continuous. By attacking both one's biological body and one's "social body", the victim's psyche is strained to the point of dissociation.

Beatrice Patsalides describes this transmogrification thus in "Ethics of the Unspeakable: Torture Survivors in Psychoanalytic Treatment":

*"As the gap between the 'I' and the 'me' deepens, dissociation and alienation increase... Thoughts and dreams attack the mind and invade the body."*

Torture robs the victim of the most basic modes of relating to reality and, thus, is the equivalent of cognitive death. Space and time are warped by sleep deprivation. The self ("I") is shattered. The tortured have nothing familiar to hold on to: family, home, personal belongings, loved ones, language, name. Gradually, they lose their mental resilience and sense of freedom. They feel alien: unable to communicate, relate, attach, or empathize with others.

Torture splinters early childhood grandiose narcissistic fantasies of uniqueness, omnipotence, invulnerability, and impenetrability. But it enhances the fantasy of merger with an idealized and omnipotent (though not benign) other – the inflicter of agony. The twin processes of individuation and separation are reversed.

Torture is the ultimate act of perverted intimacy. The torturer invades the victim's body, pervades his psyche, and possesses his mind. Deprived of contact with others and starved for human interactions, the prey bonds with the predator. "Traumatic bonding", akin to the Stockholm Syndrome, is about hope and the search for meaning in the brutal and indifferent and nightmarish universe of the torture cell.

The abuser becomes the black hole at the centre of the victim's surrealistic galaxy, sucking in the sufferer's universal need for solace. The victim tries to "control" his tormentor by becoming one with him (introjecting him) and by appealing to the monster's presumably dormant humanity and empathy.

This bonding is especially strong when the torturer and the tortured form a dyad and "collaborate" in the rituals and acts of torture (for instance, when the victim is coerced into selecting the torture implements and the types of torment to be inflicted, or to choose between two evils).

The psychologist Shirley Spitz offers this powerful overview of the contradictory nature of torture in a seminar titled "The Psychology of Torture" [1989]:

*"Torture is an obscenity in that it joins what is most private with what is most public... A further obscenity of torture is the inversion it makes of intimate human relationships."*

Obsessed by endless ruminations, demented by pain and a continuum of sleeplessness, the victim regresses, shedding all but the most primitive defence mechanisms: splitting, narcissism, dissociation, Projective Identification, introjection, and cognitive dissonance. The victim constructs an alternative world, often suffering from depersonalization and derealization, hallucinations, ideas of reference, delusions, and psychotic episodes.

Sometimes the victim comes to crave pain – very much as self-mutilators do – because it is a proof and a reminder of his individuated existence otherwise blurred by the incessant torture.

Pain shields the sufferer from disintegration and capitulation. It preserves the veracity of his unthinkable and unspeakable experiences.

This dual process of the victim's alienation and addiction to anguish complements the perpetrator's view of his quarry as "inhuman", or "subhuman". The torturer assumes the position of the sole authority, the exclusive fount of meaning and interpretation, the source of both evil and good.

Torture is about reprogramming the victim to succumb to an alternative exegesis of the world, proffered by the abuser. It is an act of deep, indelible, traumatic indoctrination. The abused also swallows whole and assimilates the torturer's negative view of him and often, as a result, is rendered suicidal, self-destructive, or self-defeating.

Thus, torture has no cut-off date. The sounds, the voices, the smells, the sensations reverberate long after the episode has ended, both in nightmares and in waking moments. The victim's ability to trust other people – i.e., to assume that their motives are at least rational, if not necessarily benign – has been irrevocably undermined. Social institutions are perceived as precariously poised on the verge of an ominous, Kafkaesque mutation. Nothing is either safe or credible anymore.

Victims typically react by undulating between emotional numbing and increased arousal: insomnia, irritability, restlessness, and attention deficits. Recollections of the traumatic events intrude in the form of dreams, night terrors, flashbacks, and distressing associations.

The tortured develop compulsive rituals to fend off obsessive thoughts. Other psychological sequelae reported include cognitive impairment, reduced capacity to learn, memory disorders, sexual dysfunction, social withdrawal, inability to maintain long-term relationships, or even mere intimacy, phobias, ideas of reference and superstitions, delusions, hallucinations, psychotic microepisodes, and emotional flatness.

Depression and anxiety are very common. These are forms and manifestations of self-directed aggression. The sufferer rages at his own victimhood and the resulting multiple dysfunctions. He feels shamed by his new disabilities and responsible, or even guilty, somehow, for his predicament and the dire consequences borne by his nearest and dearest. His sense of self-worth and self-esteem are crippled.

In a nutshell, torture victims suffer from a Post-Traumatic Stress Disorder (PTSD). Their strong feelings of anxiety, guilt, and shame are also typical of victims of childhood abuse, domestic violence, and rape. They feel anxious because the perpetrator's behaviour is seemingly arbitrary and unpredictable – or mechanically and inhumanly regular.

They feel guilty and disgraced because, to restore a semblance of order to their shattered world and a modicum of dominion over their chaotic life, they need to transform themselves into the cause of their own degradation and the accomplices of their tormentors.

The CIA, in its "Human Resource Exploitation Training Manual – 1983" [reprinted in the April 1997 issue of Harper's Magazine], summed up the theory of coercion thus:

*"The purpose of all coercive techniques is to induce psychological regression in the subject by bringing a superior outside force to bear on his will to resist. Regression is basically a loss of autonomy, a reversion to an earlier behavioural level. As the subject regresses, his learned personality traits fall away in reverse chronological order. He begins to lose the capacity to carry out the highest creative activities, to deal with complex situations, or to cope with stressful interpersonal relationships or repeated frustrations."*

Inevitably, in the aftermath of torture, its victims feel helpless and powerless. This loss of control over one's life and body is manifested physically in impotence, attention deficits, and insomnia. This is often exacerbated by the disbelief many torture victims encounter, especially if they are unable to produce scars, or other "objective" proof of their ordeal. Language cannot communicate such an intensely private experience as pain.

Spitz makes the following observation:

*"Pain is also unsharable in that it is resistant to language... (W)hen we explore the interior state of physical pain we find that there is no object 'out there' – no external, referential content. Pain is not of, or for, anything. Pain is."*

Bystanders resent the tortured because they make them feel guilty and ashamed for having done nothing to prevent the atrocity. The victims threaten their sense of security and their much-needed belief in predictability, justice, and rule of law. The victims, on their part, do not believe that it is possible to effectively communicate to "outsiders" what they have been through. The torture chambers are "another galaxy". This is how Auschwitz was described by the author K. Zetnik in his testimony in the Eichmann trial in Jerusalem in 1961.

Kenneth Pope in "Torture", a chapter he wrote for the "Encyclopaedia of Women and Gender: Sex Similarities and Differences and the Impact of Society on Gender", quotes Harvard psychiatrist Judith Herman:

*"It is very tempting to take the side of the perpetrator. All the perpetrator asks is that the bystander do nothing. He appeals to the universal desire to see, hear, and speak no evil. The victim, on the contrary, asks the bystander to share the burden of pain. The victim demands action, engagement, and remembering."*

But, more often, continued attempts to repress fearful memories result in psychosomatic illnesses (conversion). The victim wishes to forget the torture, to avoid re-experiencing the often life threatening abuse and to shield his human environment from the horrors. In conjunction with the victim's pervasive distrust, this is frequently interpreted as hypervigilance, or even paranoia. It seems that the victims can't win. Torture is forever.

## Why Do People Torture?

We should distinguish functional torture from the sadistic variety. The former is calculated to extract information from the tortured or to punish them. It is measured, impersonal, efficient, and disinterested.

The latter – the sadistic variety – fulfils the emotional needs of the perpetrator.

People who find themselves caught up in anomic states – for instance, soldiers in war or incarcerated inmates – tend to feel helpless and alienated. They experience a partial or total loss of control. They have been rendered vulnerable, powerless, and defenceless by events and circumstances beyond their influence.

Torture amounts to exerting an absolute and all-pervasive domination over the victim's existence. It is a coping strategy employed by torturers who wish to reassert control over their lives and, thus, to re-establish their mastery and superiority. By subjugating the tortured, they regain their self-confidence and regulate their sense of self-worth.

Other tormentors channel their negative emotions – pent up aggression, humiliation, rage, envy, diffuse hatred – and displace them. The victim becomes a symbol of everything that's wrong in the torturer's life and the situation he finds himself caught in. The act of torture amounts to misplaced and violent venting.

Many perpetrate heinous acts out of a wish to conform. Torturing others is their way of demonstrating obsequious obeisance to authority, group affiliation, colleagueship, and adherence to the same ethical code of conduct and common values. They bask in the praise that is heaped on them by their superiors, fellow workers, associates, team mates, or collaborators. Their need to belong is so strong that it overpowers ethical, moral, or legal considerations.

Many offenders derive pleasure and satisfaction from sadistic acts of humiliation. To these, inflicting pain is fun. They lack empathy and so their victim's agonized reactions are merely cause for much hilarity.

Moreover, sadism is rooted in deviant sexuality. The torture inflicted by sadists is bound to involve perverted sex (rape, homosexual rape, voyeurism, exhibitionism, paedophilia, fetishism, and other paraphilias). Aberrant sex, unlimited power, excruciating pain, these are the intoxicating ingredients of the sadistic variant of torture.

Still, torture rarely occurs where it does not have the sanction and blessing of the authorities, whether local or national. A permissive environment is sine qua non. The more abnormal the circumstances, the less normative the milieu, the further the scene of the crime is from public scrutiny – the more is egregious torture likely to occur. This is especially true in totalitarian societies where the use of physical force to discipline or eliminate dissent is an acceptable practice.

*First published on the* Suite 101 *Narcissistic Personality Disorders Topic.*

Return

# Traumas as Social Interactions

We react to serious mishaps, life altering setbacks, disasters, abuse, and death by going through the phases of grieving. Traumas are the complex outcomes of psychodynamic and biochemical processes. But the particulars of traumas depend heavily on the interaction between the victim and his social milieu.

It would seem that while the victim moves from denial to helplessness, rage, depression and thence to acceptance of the traumatizing events – society demonstrates a diametrically opposed progression. This incompatibility, this mismatch of psychological phases is what leads to the formation and crystallization of trauma.

## PHASE I

### Victim – DENIAL

The magnitude of unfortunate events is often so overwhelming, their nature so alien, and their message so menacing that denial sets in as a defence mechanism aimed at self-preservation. The victim denies that the event occurred, that he or she is being abused, that a loved one had passed away, and so on.

### Society – ACCEPTANCE, MOVING ON

The victim's nearest ("society") – his colleagues, his employees, his clients, even his spouse, children, and friends – rarely experience the traumatizing events with the same shattering intensity. They are likely to accept the bad news and move on. Even at their most considerate and empathic, they are likely to lose patience with the victim's state of mind. They tend to ignore the victim, or chastise him, to mock, or to deride his feelings or behaviour, to collude to repress the painful memories, or to trivialize them.

### Summary

The mismatch between the victim's reactive patterns and emotional needs and society's matter-of-fact attitude hinders growth and healing. The victim requires society's help in avoiding a head-on confrontation with a reality he cannot digest. Instead, society serves as a constant and mentally destabilizing reminder of the root of the victim's unbearable agony (the Job Syndrome).

## PHASE II

### Victim – HELPLESSNESS

Denial gradually gives way to a sense of all-pervasive and humiliating helplessness, often accompanied by debilitating fatigue and mental disintegration. These are among the classic symptoms of PTSD (Post-Traumatic Stress Disorder). These are the bitter results of the internalization and integration of the harsh realization that there is nothing one can do to alter the outcomes of a natural, or man-made, catastrophe. The horror in confronting one's finiteness, meaninglessness, negligibility, and powerlessness is overpowering.

### Society – DEPRESSION

The more the members of society come to grips with the magnitude of the loss, or evil, or threat represented by the grief inducing events, the sadder they become. Depression is often little more than suppressed or self-directed anger. The anger, in this case, is belatedly induced by an identified or diffuse source of threat, or of evil, or by a loss. It is a higher level variant of the "fight or flight" reaction, tampered by the rational understanding that the "source" of the trauma is often impossible to tackle directly and to contain.

### Summary

Thus, when the victim is most in need, terrified by his helplessness and adrift, society is immersed in depression and unable to provide a holding and supporting environment. Growth and healing is again retarded by social interaction. The victim's innate sense of annulment is enhanced by the self-addressed anger (depression) of those around him.

## PHASE III

Both the victim and society react with RAGE to their predicaments. In an effort to narcissistically reassert himself, the victim develops a grandiose sense of anger directed at paranoidally selected, unreal, diffuse, and abstract targets (frustration sources). By being aggressive, the victim re-acquires mastery of the world and of himself.

Members of society use rage to re-direct the root cause of their depression (which is, as we said, self-directed anger) and to channel it safely. To ensure that this expressed aggression alleviates their depression, real targets are selected and real punishments meted out. In this respect, "social rage" differs from the victim's. The former is intended to sublimate aggression and channel it in a socially acceptable manner – the latter to reassert narcissistic self-love as an antidote to an all-devouring sense of helplessness.

In other words, society, by itself being in a state of rage, positively reinforces the narcissistic rage reactions of the grieving victim. This, in the long run, is counter-productive, inhibits personal growth, and prevents healing. It also erodes the reality test of the victim and encourages self-delusions, paranoidal ideation, and ideas of reference.

## PHASE IV

### Victim - DEPRESSION

As the consequences of narcissistic rage – both social and personal – grow more unacceptable, depression sets in. The victim internalizes his aggressive impulses. Self directed rage is safer but is the cause of great sadness and even suicidal ideation. The victim's depression is his way of conforming to social norms. It is also instrumental in ridding the victim of the unhealthy residues of narcissistic regression. It is when the victim acknowledges the malignancy of his rage (and its anti-social nature) that he adopts a depressive stance.

### Society - HELPLESSNESS

People around the victim ("society") also emerge from their phase of rage transformed. As they realize the futility of their rage, they feel more and more helpless and devoid of options. They grasp their limitations and the irrelevance of their good intentions. They accept the inevitability of loss and evil and Kafkaesquely agree to live under an ominous cloud of arbitrary judgement, meted out by impersonal powers.

### Summary

Again, the members of society are unable to help the victim to emerge from a self-destructive phase. His depression is enhanced by their apparent helplessness. Their introversion and inefficacy induce in the victim a feeling of nightmarish isolation and alienation. Healing and growth are once again retarded or even inhibited.

## PHASE V

### Victim - ACCEPTANCE, MOVING ON

Depression – when pathologically protracted and in conjunction with other mental health problems – sometimes leads to suicide. But more often, it allows the victim to process mentally hurtful and potentially harmful material and paves the way to acceptance. Withdrawal from social pressures enables the direct transformation of anger into other emotions, some of them socially unacceptable. The honest encounter between the victim and his own (possible) death often becomes a cathartic and self-empowering inner dynamic. The victim emerges ready to move on.

### Society - DENIAL

Society, on the other hand, having exhausted its reactive arsenal, resorts to denial. As memories fade and as the victim recovers and abandons his obsessive-compulsive dwelling on his pain, society feels morally justified to forget and forgive. This mood of historical revisionism, of moral leniency, of effusive forgiveness, of re-interpretation, and of a refusal to remember in detail leads to a repression and denial of the painful events by society.

### Summary

This final mismatch between the victim's emotional needs and society's reactions is less damaging to the victim. He is now more resilient, more flexible, and more willing to forgive and forget. Society's denial is really a denial of the victim. But, having ridden himself of more primitive narcissistic defences, the victim can do without society's acceptance and approval. Having endured the purgatory of grieving, he has now re-acquired his self, independent of society's acknowledgement.

Return

# How to Cope with a Narcissist?

No one should feel responsible for the narcissist's predicament. As far as he is concerned, others hardly exist – so enmeshed he is in himself and in the resulting misery of this very self-preoccupation. Others are objects on which he projects his wrath, rage, suppressed and mutating aggression and, finally, ill disguised violence. How should his closest, nearest and dearest cope with his eccentric vagaries?

The short answer is by abandoning him or by threatening to abandon him.

The threat to abandon need not be explicit or conditional ("If you don't do something or if you do it, I will ditch you"). It is sufficient to confront the narcissist, to completely ignore him, to insist on respect for one's boundaries and wishes, or to shout back at him. The narcissist takes these signs of personal autonomy to be harbingers of impending separation and reacts with anxiety.

The narcissist is tamed by the very same weapons that he uses to subjugate others. The spectre of being abandoned looms large over everything else. In the narcissist's mind, every discordant note presages solitude and the resulting confrontation with his orphaned self.

The narcissist is a person who is irreparably traumatized by the behaviour of the most important people in his life: his parents, role models, or peers. By being capricious, arbitrary, and sadistically judgemental, they moulded him into an adult, who fervently and obsessively tries to recreate the trauma in order to, this time around, resolve it (Repetition Complex).

Thus, on the one hand, the narcissist feels that his freedom depends upon re-enacting these early unsavoury experiences. On the other hand, he is terrified by this prospect. Realizing that he is doomed to go through the same traumas over and over again, the narcissist distances himself by using his aggression to alienate others, to humiliate people, and in general, to be emotionally absent.

This behaviour brings about the very consequence that the narcissist so fears: abandonment. But, this way, at least, the narcissist is able to convince himself (and others) that HE was the one who fostered the separation, that it was fully his choice and that he was not surprised. The truth is that, governed by his internal demons, the narcissist has no real choice. The dismal future of his relationships is preordained.

The narcissist is a binary person: the carrot is the stick in his case. If he gets too close to someone emotionally, he fears ultimate and inevitable abandonment. He, thus, distances himself, acts cruelly and brings about the very abandonment that he feared in the first place.

In this paradox lies the key to coping with the narcissist. If, for instance, he is having a rage attack – rage back. This will provoke in him fears of being abandoned and the resulting calm will be so total that it might seem eerie. Narcissists are known for these sudden tectonic shifts in mood and in behaviour.

Mirror the narcissist's actions and repeat his words. If he threatens – threaten back and credibly try to use the same language and content. If he leaves the house – leave it as well, disappear on him. If he is suspicious – act suspicious. Be critical, denigrating, humiliating, go down to his level – because that's the only way to penetrate his thick defences. Faced with his mirror image, the narcissist always recoils.

We must not forget that the narcissist behaves the way he does in order to engender and encourage abandonment. When mirrored, the narcissist dreads imminent and impending desertion, which is the inevitable result of his actions and words. This prospect so terrifies him that it induces in him an incredible alteration of behaviour.

He instantly succumbs and obsequiously tries to make amends, moving from one (cold and bitter, cynical and misanthropic, cruel and sadistic) pole to another (warm, even loving, fuzzy, engulfing, emotional, maudlin, and saccharine).

The other coping strategy is to give up on him.

Dump him and go about reconstructing your own life. Very few people deserve the kind of investment that is an absolute prerequisite to living with a narcissist. To cope with a narcissist is a full time, energy and emotion-draining job, which reduces people around him to insecure nervous wrecks. Who deserves such a sacrifice?

No one, to my mind, not even the most brilliant, charming, breathtaking, suave narcissist. The glamour and trickery wear thin and underneath them a monster lurks which irreversibly and adversely influences the lives of those around it for the worse.

Narcissists are incorrigibly and notoriously difficult to change. Thus, trying to "modify" them is doomed to failure. You should either accept them as they are or avoid them altogether. If one accepts the narcissist as he is, one should cater to his needs. His needs are part of who he is. Would you have ignored a physical handicap in another intimate partner? Would you not have assisted a quadriplegic? The narcissist is an emotional cripple. He needs constant adulation. He cannot help it. So, if one chooses to accept him, it is a package deal, the incessant provision of Narcissistic Supply included.

Return

# Narcissists and Women

*Question:* Do narcissists hate women?

*Answer:* Primary Narcissistic Supply (PNS) is any kind of Narcissistic Supply (NS) provided by people who are not "meaningful" or "significant" others. Adulation, attention, affirmation, fame, notoriety, sexual conquests are all forms of PNS.

Secondary NS (SNS) emanates from people who are in repetitive or continuous touch with the narcissist. It includes the important roles of Narcissistic Accumulation and Narcissistic Regulation, among others.

Narcissists abhor and dread getting emotionally intimate. The cerebral ones regard sex as a maintenance chore, something they have to do in order to keep their Source of Secondary Supply. The somatic narcissist treats women as objects and sex as a means to obtaining Narcissistic Supply.

Moreover, many narcissists tend to frustrate women. They refrain from having sex with them, tease them and then leave them, resist flirtatious and seductive behaviours and so on. Often, they invoke the existence of a girlfriend/fiancée/spouse as the "reason" why they cannot have sex or develop a relationship. But this is not out of loyalty and fidelity in the empathic and loving sense. This is because they wish (and often succeed) to sadistically frustrate the interested party.

But, this latter behaviour pertains only to cerebral narcissists not to somatic narcissists and to histrionics (Histrionic Personality Disorder – HPD) who use their body, sexuality, and seduction/flirtation to extract Narcissistic Supply from others.

Narcissists are misogynists. They team up with women who serve as Sources of SNS (Secondary Narcissistic Supply). The woman's chores are to accumulate past Narcissistic Supply (by witnessing the narcissist's "moments of glory") and release it in an orderly manner in order to regulate the fluctuating flow of primary supply and compensate for times of deficient supply.

Otherwise, cerebral narcissists are not interested in women.

Most of them are asexual (desire sex very rarely, if at all). They hold women in contempt and abhor the thought of being really intimate with them. Usually, they choose for partners submissive women whom they disdain for being well below their intellectual level.

This leads to a vicious cycle of neediness and self-contempt ("How come I am dependent on this inferior woman"). Hence the abuse. When Primary NS is available, the woman is hardly tolerated, as one would reluctantly pay the premium of an insurance policy.

Narcissists of all stripes do regard the "subjugation" of an attractive woman to be a Source of Narcissistic Supply, though.

Such conquests are status symbols, proofs of virility, and they allow the narcissist to engage in "vicarious" narcissistic behaviours, to express his narcissism through the "conquered" women, transforming them into instruments at the service of his narcissism, into his extensions. This is done by employing defence mechanisms such as Projective Identification.

The narcissist believes that being in love is actually merely going through the motions. To him, emotions are mimicry and pretence.

He says: "I am a conscious misogynist. I fear and loathe women and tend to ignore them to the best of my ability. To me they are a mixture of hunter and parasite."

Most male narcissists are misogynists. After all, they are the warped creations of women. Women gave birth to them and moulded them into what they are: dysfunctional, maladaptive, and emotionally dead. They are angry at their mothers and, by extension, at all women.

The narcissist's attitude to women is, naturally, complex and multi-layered but it can be described using four axes:
1. The Holy Whore
2. The Hunter Parasite
3. The Frustrating Object of Desire
4. Uniqueness Roles

The narcissist divides all women to saints (Madonnas) and whores. He finds it difficult to have sex ("dirty", "forbidden", "punishable", "degrading") with feminine significant others (spouse, intimate girlfriend). To him, sex and intimacy are mutually exclusive rather than mutually expressive or mutually reinforcing propositions.

Sex is reserved to "whores" (all other women in the world). This division resolves the narcissist's constant cognitive dissonance ("I want her but...", "I don't need anyone but..."). It also legitimizes his sadistic urges (abstaining from sex is a major and recurrent narcissistic "penalty" inflicted on female "transgressors"). It tallies well with the frequent idealization-devaluation cycles the narcissist goes through. The idealized females are sexless, the devalued ones "deserving" of their degradation (sex) and the contempt that, inevitably, follows thereafter.

The narcissist believes firmly that women are out to "hunt" men by genetic predisposition. As a result, he feels threatened (as any prey would). This, of course, is an intellectualization of the real state of affairs: the narcissist feels threatened by women and tries to justify this irrational fear by imbuing them with "objective", menacing qualities. The narcissist frequently "pathologizes" others in order to control them.

The narcissist believes that, once their prey is secured, women assume the role of "body snatchers". They abscond with the male's sperm, generate an endless stream of demanding children, and financially bleed the men in their lives to cater to their needs and to the needs of their dependants.

Put differently, women are parasites, leeches, whose sole function is to suck dry every man they find and tarantula-like decapitate him once no longer useful. This, of course, is exactly what the narcissist does to people. Thus, his view of women is a projection.

Heterosexual narcissists desire women as any other red-blooded male does or even more so due to their special symbolic nature in the narcissist's universe. Humbling a woman in acts of faintly sado-masochistic sex is a way of getting back at mother. But the narcissist is frustrated by his inability to meaningfully interact with women, by their apparent emotional depth and powers of psychological penetration (real or attributed) and by their sexuality.

Women's incessant demands for intimacy are perceived by the narcissist as threats. He recoils instead of getting closer. The cerebral narcissist also despises and derides sex, as we said before. Thus, caught in a seemingly intractable Repetition Complex, in approach-avoidance cycles, the narcissist becomes furious at the source of his frustration. Some narcissists set out to do some frustrating of their own. They tease (passively or actively), or they pretend to be asexual and, in any case, they turn down, rather cruelly, any feminine attempt to court them and to get closer.

Sadistically, they tremendously enjoy their ability to frustrate the desires, passions and sexual wishes of women. It makes them feel omnipotent and self-righteous. Narcissists regularly frustrate all women sexually and significant women in their lives both sexually and emotionally.

Somatic narcissists simply use women as objects and then discard them. They masturbate, using women as "flesh and blood sex dolls". The emotional background is identical. While the cerebral narcissist punishes through abstention, the somatic narcissist penalizes through excess.

The narcissist's mother kept behaving as though the narcissist was and is not special (to her). The narcissist's whole life is a pathetic and pitiful effort to prove her wrong. The narcissist constantly seeks confirmation from others that he is special: in other words that he is, that he actually exists.

Women threaten this quest. Sex is "bestial" and "common". There is nothing "special or unique" about sex. Women's sexual needs threaten to reduce the narcissist to the lowest common denominator: intimacy, sex and human emotions. Everybody and anybody can feel, copulate and breed. There is nothing in these activities to set the narcissist apart and above others. And yet women seem to be interested only in these pursuits. Thus, the narcissist emotionally believes that women are the continuation of his mother by other means and in different guises.

The narcissist hates women virulently, passionately and uncompromisingly. His hate is primal, irrational, the progeny of mortal fear and sustained abuse. Granted, most narcissists learn how to disguise, even repress these untoward feelings. But their hatred does get out of control and erupt from time to time.

Living with a narcissist is an arduous and eroding task. Narcissists are infinitely pessimistic, bad-tempered, paranoid and sadistic in an absent-minded and indifferent manner. Their daily routine is a rigmarole of threats, complaints, hurts, eruptions, moodiness and rage.

The narcissist rails against slights true and imagined. He alienates people. He humiliates them because this is his only weapon against his own humiliation wrought by their indifference. Gradually, wherever he is, the narcissist's social circle dwindles and then vanishes. Every narcissist is also a schizoid, to some extent. A schizoid is not a misanthrope. The narcissist does not necessarily hate people - he simply does not need them. He regards social interactions as a nuisance to be minimized.

The narcissist is torn between his need to obtain Narcissistic Supply (from others) and his fervent wish to be left alone. This wish springs from contempt and overwhelming feelings of superiority.

In the narcissist's psyche, there are fundamental conflicts between dependence, counter-dependence and contempt, neediness and devaluation, seeking and avoiding, turning on the charm to attract adulation and reacting wrathfully to the minutest "provocations". These conflicts lead to rapid cycling between gregariousness and self-imposed ascetic seclusion.

Such an unpredictable but always bilious and festering ambience, typical of the narcissist's "romantic" liaisons is hardly conducive to love or sex. Gradually, both become extinct. Relationships are hollowed out. Imperceptibly, the narcissist switches to asexual co-habitation.

But the vitriolic environment that the narcissist creates is only one hand of the equation. The other hand involves the woman herself.

As we said, heterosexual narcissists are attracted to women, but simultaneously repelled, horrified, bewitched and provoked by them. They seek to frustrate and humiliate them. Psychodynamically, the narcissist probably visits upon them his mother's sins, but such simplistic explanation does this complex subject great injustice.

Most narcissists are misogynists. Their sexual and emotional lives are perturbed and chaotic. They are not able to love in any true sense of the word, nor are they capable of developing any measure of intimacy. Lacking empathy, they are unable to offer to their partners emotional sustenance.

Do narcissists miss loving, would they have liked to love and are they angry with their parents for crippling them in this respect?

To the narcissist, these questions are incomprehensible. There is no way they can answer them. Narcissists have never loved. They do not know what is it that they are supposedly missing. Observing it from the outside, love seems to them to be a risible pathology.

Narcissists equate love with weakness. They hate being weak and they hate and despise weak people (e.g., the sick, the old and the young). They do not tolerate what they consider to be stupidity, disease and dependence and love seems to consist of all three. These are not sour grapes. They really feel this way.

Narcissists are angry men – but not because they never experienced love and probably never will. They are angry because they are not as powerful, awe inspiring and successful as they wish they were and, to their mind, deserve to be. Because their daydreams refuse so stubbornly to come true. Because they are their worst enemy. And because, in their unmitigated paranoia, they see adversaries plotting everywhere and they feel discriminated against and contemptuously ignored.

Many of them (the borderline narcissists) cannot conceive of life in one place with one set of people, doing the same thing, in the same field with one goal within a decades-old game plan. To them, this is the equivalent of death. They are most terrified of boredom and whenever faced with its daunting prospect, they inject drama or even danger into their lives. This way they feel alive.

The narcissist is a lonely wolf. He is a shaky platform, indeed, on which to base a family, or plans for the future.

Return

# The Inverted Narcissist

*With contributions by the members of the Narcissism List*

## Terminology

### Co-Dependents

There is great confusion regarding the terms co-dependent, counter-dependent, and dependent.

Like dependents (people with the Dependent Personality Disorder), co-dependents depend on other people for their emotional gratification and the performance of both inconsequential and crucial daily and psychological functions.

Co-dependents are needy, demanding, and submissive. They suffer from abandonment anxiety and, to avoid being overwhelmed by it, they cling to others and act immaturely. These behaviours are intended to elicit protective responses and to safeguard the "relationship" with their companion or mate upon whom they depend. Co-dependents appear to be impervious to abuse. No matter how badly they are mistreated, they remain committed.

This is where the "co" in "co-dependence" comes into play. By accepting the role of victims, co-dependents seek to control their abusers and manipulate them. It is a danse macabre in which both members of the dyad collaborate.

The Dependent Personality Disorder is a much disputed mental health diagnosis.

We are all dependent to some degree. We all like to be taken care of. When is this need judged to be pathological, compulsive, pervasive, and excessive? Clinicians who contributed to the study of this disorder use words such as "craving", "clinging", "stifling" (both the dependent and her partner), and "humiliating", or "submissive". But these are all subjective terms, open to disagreement and differences of opinion.

Moreover, virtually all cultures encourage dependency to varying degrees. Even in developed countries, many women, the very old, the very young, the sick, the criminal, and the mentally-handicapped are denied personal autonomy and are legally and economically dependent on others (or on the authorities). Thus, the Dependent Personality Disorder is diagnosed only when such behaviour does not conform to social or cultural norms.

Co-dependents, as they are sometimes known, are possessed with fantastic worries and concerns and are paralyzed by their abandonment anxiety and fear of separation. This inner turmoil renders them indecisive. Even the simplest everyday decision becomes an excruciating ordeal. This is why co-dependents rarely initiate projects or do things on their own.

Dependents typically go around eliciting constant and repeated reassurances and advice from myriad sources. This recurrent solicitation of succour is proof that the co-dependent seeks to transfer responsibility for his or her life to others, whether they have agreed to assume it or not.

This recoil and studious avoidance of challenges may give the wrong impression that the dependent is indolent or insipid. Yet, most dependents are neither. They are often fired by repressed ambition, energy, and imagination. It is their lack self-confidence that holds them back. They don't trust their own abilities and judgement.

Absent an inner compass and a realistic assessment of their positive qualities on the one hand and limitations on the other hand, dependents are forced to rely on crucial input from the outside. Realizing this, their behaviour becomes self-negating: they never disagree with meaningful others or criticizes them. They are afraid to lose their support and emotional nurturance.

Consequently, as I have written in the Open Site Encyclopaedia entry on this disorder:

*"The co-dependent moulds himself/herself and bends over backward to cater to the needs of his nearest and dearest and satisfy their every whim, wish, expectation, and demand. Nothing is too unpleasant or unacceptable if it serves to secure the uninterrupted presence of the co-dependent's family and friends and the emotional sustenance s/he can extract (or extort) from them.*

*The co-dependent does not feel fully alive when alone. S/he feels helpless, threatened, ill-at-ease, and child-like. This acute discomfort drives the co-dependent to hop from one relationship to another. The sources of nurturance are interchangeable. To the co-dependent, being with someone, with anyone, no matter whom – is always preferable to solitude."*

### Inverted Narcissist

Also called "covert narcissist", this is a co-dependent who depends exclusively on narcissists (narcissist-co-dependent). If you are living with a narcissist, have a relationship with one, if you are married to one, if you are working with a narcissist, etc. – it does NOT mean that you are an inverted narcissist.

To "qualify" as an inverted narcissist, you must CRAVE to be in a relationship with a narcissist, regardless of any abuse inflicted on you by him/her. You must ACTIVELY seek relationships with narcissists and ONLY with narcissists, no matter what your (bitter and traumatic) past experience has been. You must feel EMPTY and UNHAPPY in relationships with ANY OTHER kind of person. Only then, and if you satisfy the other diagnostic criteria of a Dependent Personality Disorder, can you be safely labelled an "inverted narcissist".

### Counter-Dependents

Counter-dependents reject and despise authority (they are contumacious) and often clash with authority figures (parents, bosses, or the law). Their sense of self-worth and their very self-identity are premised on and derived from (in other words, are dependent on) these acts of bravura and defiance. Counter-dependents are fiercely independent, controlling, self-centred, and aggressive.

These behaviour patterns are often the result of a deep-seated fear of intimacy. In an intimate relationship, the counter-dependent feels enslaved, ensnared, and captive. Counter-dependents are locked into Approach-Avoidance Repetition Complex cycles. Hesitant approach is followed by avoidance of commitment. They are "lone wolves" and bad team players.

Most "classical" (overt) narcissists are counter-dependents. Their emotions and needs are buried under a "scar tissue" which had formed, coalesced, and hardened during years of one form of abuse or another. Grandiosity, a sense of entitlement, a lack of empathy, and overweening haughtiness usually hide gnawing insecurity and a fluctuating sense of self-worth.

Counter-dependence is a reaction formation. The counter-dependent dreads his own weaknesses. He seeks to overcome them by projecting an image of omnipotence, omniscience, success, self-sufficiency, and superiority.

## Introduction

Co-dependence is an important and integral part of narcissism. Narcissists are either counter-dependent or co-dependent (inverted).

The DSM-IV-TR uses 9 criteria to define the Narcissistic Personality Disorder (NPD). It is sufficient to show signs of 5 of them to be diagnosed as a narcissist. Thus, theoretically, it is possible to have NPD without being grandiose.

Many scholars (Alexander Lowen, Jeffrey Satinover, Theodore Millon and others) suggested a "taxonomy" of pathological narcissism. They divided narcissists to sub-groups (very much as I do with my somatic versus cerebral narcissist dichotomy).

Lowen, for instance, talks about the "phallic" narcissist versus others. Satinover and Millon make a very important distinction between narcissists who were raised by "classically" abusive parents and those who were raised by doting and smothering or domineering mothers.

Glenn O. Gabbard in "Psychodynamic Psychiatry in Clinical Practice" [The DSM-IV-TR Edition. Comments on Cluster B Personality Disorders – Narcissistic. American Psychiatric Press, Inc., 2000] we find this:

"...These criteria (the DSM-IV-TR's) identify a certain kind of narcissistic patient – specifically, the arrogant, boastful, 'noisy' individual who demands to be in the spotlight. However, they fail to characterize the shy, quietly grandiose, narcissistic individual whose extreme sensitivity to slights leads to an assiduous avoidance of the spotlight."

The DSM-III-R alluded to at least two types of narcissists, but the DSM-IV-TR committee chose to delete this portion of the text:

"...included criterion, 'reacts to criticism with feelings of rage, shame, or humiliation (even not if expressed)' due to lack of 'specificity'."

Other theoreticians, clinicians and researchers similarly suggested a division between "the oblivious narcissist" (a.k.a. overt) and "the hypervigilant narcissist" (a.k.a. covert).

## The Inverted Narcissist

It is clear that there is, indeed, a hitherto neglected type of narcissist. It is the "self-effacing" or "introverted" narcissist. I call it the "inverted narcissist" (hereinafter: IN). Others call it "narcissist-co-dependent", "co-narcissist", or "N-magnet" (which erroneously implies the inverted narcissist's passivity and victimhood).

The Inverted Narcissist is a narcissist who, in many respects, is the mirror image of the "classical" narcissist. The psychodynamics of the inverted narcissist are not clear, nor are its developmental roots. Perhaps it is the product of an overweening Primary Object (parent) or caregiver. Perhaps excessive abuse leads to the repression of even the narcissistic and other defence mechanisms. Perhaps the IN's parents suppress every manifestation of grandiosity and of narcissism (very common in early childhood and adolescence), so that the narcissistic defence mechanism is "inverted" and internalized in this unusual form.

These narcissists are self-effacing, sensitive, emotionally fragile, and sometimes socially phobic. They derive all their self-esteem and sense of self-worth from the outside (from others), are pathologically envious (a transformation of aggression), are likely to intermittently engage in aggressive/violent behaviours, and are more emotionally labile than the classic narcissist.

There are, therefore, three "basic" types of narcissists:

1. *The offspring of neglecting parents* who default to narcissism as the predominant form of object relations (with themselves as the exclusive love object);

2. *The offspring of doting or domineering parents (often narcissists themselves)* – These children internalize their parents' voices in the form of a sadistic, ideal, immature Superego and spend their lives trying to be perfect, omnipotent, omniscient and to be judged "a success" by these parent-images and their later representations and substitutes (authority figures);

3. *The offspring of abusive parents* internalize the abusing, demeaning and contemptuous voices and spend their lives in an effort to elicit "counter-voices" from other people and thus to regulate their labile self-esteem and sense of self-worth.

All three types experience recurrent and Sisyphean failures. Shielded by their defence mechanisms, they constantly gauge reality wrongly, their actions and reactions become more and more rigid and the damage inflicted by them on themselves and on others is ever greater.

The narcissistic parent seems to employ a myriad primitive defence in his or her dealings with his or her children:

1. *Splitting, idealization, and devaluation* – Idealizing the child and devaluing him in cycles, which reflect the internal dynamics of the parent rather than anything the child does.
2. *Projective Identification* – Forcing the child to behave in a way which vindicates the parent's fears regarding himself or herself, his or her self-image and his or her self-worth. This is a particularly powerful and pernicious mechanism. If the narcissist parent fears his or her own deficiencies ("defects"), vulnerability, perceived weaknesses, susceptibility, gullibility, or emotions, he or she is likely to force the child to "feel" these rejected and (to him or her) repulsive emotions, to behave in ways strongly abhorred by the parent, to exhibit character traits the parent strongly rejects in himself or herself.
3. *Projection* – The child, in a way, becomes the "trash bin", the reflecting mirror of the parents' inhibitions, fears, self-loathing, self-contempt, perceived lack of self-worth, sense of inadequacy, rejected traits, repressed emotions, failures and emotional reticence. They attribute all these unwanted traits and emotions to the child.

Coupled with the parent's treatment of the child as the parent's extension, these psychological defences totally inhibit the psychological growth and emotional maturation of the child. The child becomes a reflection of the parent, a conduit through which the parent experiences and realizes himself or herself for better (hopes, aspirations, ambition, life goals) and for worse (weaknesses, "undesirable" emotions, "negative" traits).

Relationships between such parents and their progeny easily deteriorate to sexual or other modes of abuse because there are no functioning boundaries between them.

It seems that the child's reaction to a narcissistic parent can be either accommodation and assimilation, or rejection.

### Accommodation and Assimilation

The child accommodates, idealizes and internalizes (introjects) the narcissistic and abusive Primary Object (parent) successfully. This means that the child's "internal voice" is also narcissistic and abusive. The child tries to comply with its directives and with its explicit and perceived wishes.

The child becomes a masterful provider of Narcissistic Supply, a perfect match to the parent's personality, an ideal source, an accommodating, understanding and caring caterer to all the needs, whims, mood swings and cycles of the narcissist parent.

The child learns to endure devaluation and idealization with equanimity and adapt to the narcissist's cultish world view. The child, in short, becomes the ultimate extension. This is what we call an inverted narcissist.

We must not neglect the abusive aspect of such a relationship. The narcissistic parent always alternates between idealization and devaluation of his or her offspring. The child is likely to internalize these devaluing, abusive, critical, demeaning, berating, diminishing, minimizing, upbraiding, chastising voices.

The abusive parent (or caregiver) goes on to survive inside the child-turned-adult (as part of a sadistic and ideal Superego and an fantastic Ego Ideal). These internalized voices are so powerful that they inhibit even the development of reactive narcissism, the child's typical defence mechanism.

The child-turned-adult keeps looking for narcissists in order to feel whole, alive and wanted. He craves to be treated by a narcissist narcissistically. What others call abuse is, to him or her, familiar territory and constitutes Narcissistic Supply. To the inverted narcissist, the classic narcissist is a Source of Supply (Primary or Secondary) and his narcissistic behaviours constitute Narcissistic Supply. The IN feels dissatisfied, empty and unwanted when not "loved" by a narcissist.

The roles of Primary Source of Narcissistic Supply (PSNS) and Secondary Source of Narcissistic Supply (SSNS) are reversed. To the inverted narcissist, her narcissistic spouse is a Source of PRIMARY Narcissistic Supply.

But the child can also reject the narcissistic parent rather than accommodate him or her.

## Rejection

The child may react to the narcissism of the Primary Object (parent) with a peculiar type of rejection. He develops his own narcissistic personality, replete with grandiosity and lack of empathy – but his personality is antithetical to that of the narcissistic parent.

If the parent were a somatic narcissist, the child is likely to grow up to be a cerebral one. If his father prided himself on being virtuous, the son turns out sinful. If his narcissistic mother bragged about her frugality, her daughter would tend towards profligacy.

## An Attempted DSM-Style List of Criteria

It is possible to compose a DSM-IV-TR-like set of criteria for the inverted narcissist, using the classic narcissist's as a template. The two are, in many ways, flip sides of the same coin, or "the mould and the moulded" – hence the neologisms "mirror narcissist" or "inverted narcissist".

The narcissist tries to merge with an idealized but badly internalized object. He does so by "digesting" the meaningful others in his life and transforming them into extensions of his self. He uses various techniques to achieve this.

The inverted narcissist (IN), on the other hand, does not attempt, except in fantasy or in dangerous, masochistic sexual practice, to merge with an idealized external object. This is because she so successfully internalized the narcissistic Primary Object to exclude everyone else. The IN feels ill at ease in her relationships with non-narcissists because these dalliances are unconsciously perceived by her to constitute "betrayal", "cheating", an abrogation of the exclusivity clause she has with the narcissistic Primary Object.

This is the big difference between classical narcissists and their inverted sisters.

Classic narcissists of all stripes reject the Primary Object in particular (and object relations in general) in favour of a handy substitute: themselves.

Inverted narcissists accept the (narcissist) Primary Object and internalize it to the exclusion of all others (unless they are perceived to be faithful renditions, replicas of the narcissistic Primary Object).

### Criterion ONE

*Possesses a rigid sense of lack of self-worth.*

The classic narcissist has a badly regulated sense of self-worth. However this is not conscious. He goes through cycles of self-devaluation (and experiences them as dysphorias).

The IN's sense of self-worth does not fluctuate. It is rather stable – but it is very low. Whereas the narcissist devalues others – the IN devalues herself as an offering, a sacrifice to the narcissist. The IN pre-empts the narcissist by devaluing herself, by actively berating her own achievements, or talents. The IN is exceedingly distressed when singled out because of actual accomplishments or a demonstration of superior skills.

The inverted narcissist is compelled to filter all of her narcissistic needs through the primary narcissist in her life. Independence or personal autonomy are not permitted. The IN feels amplified by the narcissist's running commentary (because nothing can be accomplished by the IN without the approval of a primary narcissist in her life).

### Criterion TWO

*Pre-occupied with fantasies of unlimited success, power, brilliance and beauty or of an ideal love.*

This is the same as the DSM-IV-TR criterion for Narcissistic Personality Disorder but, with the IN, it manifests absolutely differently, i.e. the cognitive dissonance is sharper here because the IN is so absolutely and completely convinced of her worthlessness that these fantasies of grandeur are extremely painful "dissonances".

With the classical narcissist, the dissonance exists on two levels:
1. Between the unconscious feeling of lack of stable self-worth and the grandiose fantasies;
2. AND between the grandiose fantasies and reality (the Grandiosity Gap).

In comparison, the inverted narcissist can only vacillate between a sense of lack of self-worth and reality. No grandiosity is permitted, except in dangerous, forbidden fantasy. This shows that the IN is psychologically incapable of fully realizing her inherent potentials without a primary narcissist to filter the praise, adulation or accomplishments through. She must have someone to whom praise can be redirected.

The dissonance between the IN's certainty of self-worthlessness and genuine praise that cannot be deflected is likely to emotionally derail the inverted narcissist every time.

### Criterion THREE

*Believes that she is absolutely un-unique and un-special (i.e., worthless and not worthy of merger with the fantasized ideal) and that no one at all could understand her because she is innately unworthy of being understood. The IN becomes very agitated the more one tries to understand her because that also offends against her righteous sense of being properly excluded from the human race.*

A sense of worthlessness is typical of many other personality disorders (as well as the feeling that no one could ever understand them). The narcissist himself endures prolonged periods of self-devaluation, self-deprecation and self-doubt. This is part of the Narcissistic Cycle.

In this sense, the inverted narcissist is a partial narcissist. She is permanently fixated in a part of the Narcissistic Cycle, never to experience its complementary half: the narcissistic grandiosity and sense of entitlement.

The "righteous sense of being properly excluded" comes from the sadistic Superego in concert with an "overbearing, externally reinforced, conscience".

### Criterion FOUR

*Demands anonymity (in the sense of seeking to remain excluded at all costs) and is intensely irritated and uncomfortable with any attention being paid to her – similar to the Avoidant or the Schizoid.*

### Criterion FIVE

*Feels that she is undeserving and not entitled.*

Feels that she is inferior to others, lacking, insubstantial, unworthy, unlikable, unappealing, unlovable, someone to scorn and dismiss, or to ignore.

### Criterion SIX

*Is extinguishingly selfless, sacrificial, even unctuous in her interpersonal relationships and avoids the assistance of others at all costs. Can only interact with others when she can be seen to be giving, supportive, and expending an unusual effort to assist.*

Some narcissists behave the same way but only as a means to obtain Narcissistic Supply (praise, adulation, affirmation, attention). This must not be confused with the behaviour of the IN.

### Criterion SEVEN

*Lacks empathy. Is intensely attuned to others' needs, but only in so far as it relates to her own need to perform the required self-sacrifice, which in turn is necessary in order for the IN to obtain her Narcissistic Supply from the primary narcissist.*

By contrast, narcissists are never empathic. They are intermittently attuned to others only in order to optimize the extraction of Narcissistic Supply from them.

### Criterion EIGHT

*Envies others. Cannot conceive of being envied and becomes extremely agitated and uncomfortable if even brought into a situation where comparison might occur. Loathes and avoids competition at all costs, if there is any chance of actually winning it, or being singled out.*

### Criterion NINE

*Displays extreme shyness, lack of any real relational connections, is publicly self-effacing in the extreme, is internally highly moralistic and critical of others; is a perfectionist and engages in lengthy ritualistic behaviours, which can never be perfectly performed (is obsessive-compulsive, though not necessarily to the full extent exhibited in Obsessive-Compulsive Personality Disorder). Notions of being individualistic are anathema.*

## The Reactive Patterns of the Inverted Narcissist

The inverted narcissist does not suffer from a "milder" form of narcissism. Like the "classic" narcissists, inverted narcissism has degrees and shades. But it is much rarer and the DSM-IV-TR classical variety is the more prevalent.

The inverted narcissist is liable to react with rage whenever threatened, or...

...When envious of other people's achievements, their ability to feel wholeness, happiness, to accept rewards and successes; when her sense of self-worthlessness is diminished by a behaviour, a comment, an event, when her lack of self-worth and voided self-esteem is threatened. Thus, this type of narcissist might surprisingly react violently or wrathfully to GOOD things: a kind remark, a mission accomplished, a reward, a compliment, a proposition, or a sexual advance.

...When thinking about the past, when emotions and memories are evoked (usually negative ones) by certain music, a given smell, or sight.

...When her pathological envy leads to an all-pervasive sense of injustice and being discriminated against or deprived by a spiteful world.

...When she believes that she failed (and she always entertains this belief), that she is imperfect and useless and worthless, a good for nothing half-baked creature.

...When she realizes to what extent her inner demons possess her, constrain her life, torment her, and deform her and the hopelessness of it all.

When the inverted narcissist rages, she becomes verbally and emotionally abusive. She uncannily spots and attacks the vulnerabilities of her target, and mercilessly drives home the poisoned dagger of despair and self-loathing until it infects her adversary.

The calm after such a storm is even eerier, a thundering silence. The inverted narcissist regrets her behaviour and admits her feelings while apologizing profusely.

The inverted narcissist nurtures her negative emotions as yet another weapon of self-destruction and self-defeat. It is from this repressed self-contempt and sadistic self-judgement that the narcissistic rage springs forth.

One important difference between inverted narcissists and non-narcissists is that the former are less likely to react with PTSD (Post-Traumatic Stress Disorder) following the break-up of their relationships with their narcissists. They seem to be "desensitized" to the narcissist's unpredictable ways by their early upbringing.

Whereas the reactions of normal people to narcissistic behaviour patterns (and especially to the splitting and Projective Identification defence mechanisms and to the idealization devaluation cycles) is shock, profound hurt and disorientation – inverted narcissists show none of the above.

## The Life of the Inverted Narcissist

The IN is, usually, exceedingly and painfully shy as a child. Despite this Social Phobia, her grandiosity (absorbed from the parent) might direct her to seek "limelight" professions and occupations, which involve exposure, competition, "stage fright" and social friction.

The setting can vary from the limited (family) to the expansive (national media) – but, whatever it is, the result is constant conflict and feelings of discomfort, even terror and extreme excitement and thrill ("adrenaline rush"). This is because the IN's grandiosity is "imported" and not fully integrated. It is, therefore, not supportive of her "grandiose" pursuits (as is the case with the classical narcissist). On the contrary, the IN feels awkward, pitted on the edge of a precipice, contrived, and deceitful.

The inverted narcissist grows up in a stifling environment, whether it is an orthodox, hyper-religious, collectivist, or traditionalist culture, a monovalent, "black and white", doctrinarian and indoctrinating society – or a family which manifests all the above in a microcosm.

The inverted narcissist is cast in a negative (emergent) role within her family. Her "negativity" is attributed to her gender, the order of her birth, religious, social, or cultural dictates and commandments, her "character flaws", her relation to a specific person or event, her acts or inaction and so on.

In the words of one such IN:

*"In the religious culture I grew up in, women are SO suppressed, their roles are so carefully restricted. They are the representation, in the flesh, of all that is sinful, degrading, of all that is wrong with the world.*

*These are the negative gender/cultural images that were force fed to us the negative 'otherness' of women, as defined by men, was fed to me. I was so shy, withdrawn, unable to really relate to people at all from as early as I can remember."*

The IN is subjected and exposed either to an overbearing, overvalued parent, or to an aloof, detached, emotionally unavailable one – or to both – at an early stage of her life:

*"I grew up in the shadow of my father who adored me, put me on a pedestal, told me I could do or be anything I wanted because I was incredibly bright, BUT, he ate me alive, I was his property and an extension of him.*

*I also grew up with the mounting hatred of my narcissist brother who got none of this attention from our father and got no attention from our mother either. My function was to make my father look wonderful in the eyes of all outsiders, the wonderful parent with a genius Wunderkind as his last child, and the only child of the six that he was physically present to raise from the get go.*

*The overvaluation combined with being abjectly ignored or raged at by him when I stepped out of line even the tiniest bit, was enough to warp my personality."*

The IN is prevented from developing full-blown secondary narcissism. The IN is so heavily preoccupied in her pre-school years with satisfying the narcissistic parent, that the traits of grandiosity and self-love, even the need for Narcissistic Supply, remain dormant or repressed.

The IN simply "knows" that only the narcissistic parent can provide the requisite amount of Narcissistic Supply. The narcissistic parent is so controlling that any attempt to garner praise or adulation from any other source (without the approval of the parent) is severely punished by swift devaluation and even the occasional spanking or abuse (physical, emotional, or sexual).

This is a vital part of the conditioning that gives rise to inverted narcissism. Where the classical narcissist exhibits grandiosity, the IN is intensely uncomfortable with personal praise, and always wishes to divert praise away from herself onto her narcissist. This is why the IN can only truly feel anything when she is in a relationship with another narcissist. The IN is conditioned and programmed from the very beginning to be the perfect companion to the narcissist: to feed his Ego, to be purely his extension, to seek only praise and adulation if it brings greater praise and adulation to her narcissist.

## The Inverted Narcissist's Survival Guide

- Listen attentively to everything the narcissist says and agree with it all. Don't believe a word of it but let it slide as if everything is just fine, business as usual.
- Offer something absolutely unique to the narcissist which they cannot obtain anywhere else. Also be prepared to line up future Sources of Primary NS for your narcissist because you will not be IT for very long, if at all. If you take over the procuring function for the narcissist, they become that much more dependent on you which makes it a bit tougher for them to pull their haughty stuff – an inevitability, in any case.
- Be endlessly patient and go way out of your way to be accommodating, thus keeping the Narcissistic Supply flowing liberally, and keeping the peace (relatively speaking).
- Get tremendous personal satisfaction out of endlessly giving. This one may not be attractive to you, but it is a take it or leave it proposition.
- Be absolutely emotionally and financially independent of the narcissist. Take what you need: the excitement and engulfment (i.e., NS) and refuse to get upset or hurt when the narcissist does or says something dumb. Yelling back works really well but should be reserved for special occasions when you fear your narcissist may be on the verge of leaving you; the silent treatment is better as an ordinary response, but it must be devoid of emotional content, more with the air of boredom and "I'll talk to you later, when I am good and ready, and when you are behaving in a more reasonable fashion."
- If your narcissist is cerebral and not interested in having much sex, give yourself ample permission to have sex with other people. Your cerebral narcissist is not indifferent to infidelity, so discretion and secrecy is of paramount importance.
- If your narcissist is somatic and you don't mind, join in on group sex encounters but make sure that you choose properly for your narcissist. They are heedless and very undiscriminating in respect of sexual partners and that can get very problematic.

- If you are a "fixer", which most inverted narcissists are, focus on fixing situations, preferably before they become "situations". Don't for one moment delude yourself that you can actually fix the narcissist – it simply will not happen. Not because they are being stubborn – they just simply can't be fixed.
- If there is any fixing that can be done, it is to help your narcissist become aware of their condition, and (this is very important) with no negative implications or accusations in the process at all. It is like living with a physically handicapped person and being able to discuss, calmly, unemotionally, what the limitations and benefits of the handicap are and how the two of you can work with these factors, rather than trying to change them.
- Finally, and most important of all for the inverted narcissist: get to know yourself. What are you getting from the relationship? Are you actually a masochist? Why is this relationship attractive and interesting?

  Define for yourself what good and beneficial things you believe you are receiving in this relationship. Define the things that you find harmful to you. Develop strategies to minimize the harm to yourself.

  Don't expect that you will cognitively be able to reason with the narcissist to change who he is. You may have some limited success in getting your narcissist to tone down on the really harmful behaviours that affect you, which emanate from the unchangeable essence of the narcissist. This can only be accomplished in a very trusting, frank and open relationship.

The inverted narcissist can have a reasonably good, long lasting relationship with the narcissist. You must be prepared to give your narcissist a lot of space and leeway.

You don't really exist for him as a fully realized person – no one does. They are not fully realized people so they cannot possibly have the skills, no matter how smart or sexy, to be a complete person in the sense that most adults are complete.

### Somatic versus Cerebral Inverted Narcissists

The inverted narcissist is really an erstwhile narcissist internalized by the IN. Inevitably, we are likely to find among the inverted the same propensities, predilections, preferences and inclinations that we do among proper narcissists.

The cerebral IN is an IN whose Source of vicarious Primary Narcissistic Supply lies – through the medium and mediation of a narcissist – in the exercise of his intellectual faculties. A somatic IN would tend to make use of her body, sex, shape or health in trying to secure NS for "her" narcissist.

The inverted narcissist feeds on the primary narcissist and this is her Narcissistic Supply. So these two typologies can essentially become a self-supporting, symbiotic system.

In reality though, both the narcissist and the inverted narcissist need to be quite well aware of the dynamics of this relationship in order to make it work as a successful long-term arrangement. It might well be that this symbiosis would only work between a cerebral narcissist and a cerebral invert. The somatic narcissist's incessant sexual dalliances would be far too threatening to the equanimity of the cerebral invert for there to be much chance of this succeeding, even for a short time.

It would seem that only opposing types of narcissist can get along when two classic narcissists are involved in a couple. It follows, syllogistically, that only identical types of narcissist and inverted narcissist can survive in a couple. In other words: the best, most enduring couples of narcissist and his inverted narcissist mate would involve a somatic narcissist and a somatic IN – or a cerebral narcissist and a cerebral IN.

### Coping with Narcissists and Non-Narcissists

The inverted narcissist is a person who grew up enthralled by the narcissistic parent. This parent engulfed and subsumed the child's being to such an extent that the child's personality was irrevocably shaped by this immersion, damaged beyond hope of repair. The child was not even able to develop defence mechanisms such as narcissism to cope with the abusive parent.

The end result is an inverted narcissistic personality. The traits of this personality are primarily evident in the context of romantic relationships. The child was conditioned by the narcissistic parent to only be entitled to feel whole, useful, happy, and productive when the child augmented or mirrored to the parent the parent's False Self. As a result the child is shaped by this engulfment and cannot feel complete in any significant adult relationship unless they are with narcissists.

### The Inverted Narcissist in
### Relationship with the Narcissist

The inverted narcissist is drawn to significant relationships with other narcissists in her adulthood. These relationships are usually spousal primary relationships but can also be friendships with narcissists outside of the primary love relationship.

In a primary relationship, the inverted narcissist attempts to re-create the parent-child relationship. The IN thrives on mirroring to the narcissist his grandiose fantasies and in so doing the IN obtains her own Narcissistic Supply (which is the dependence of the narcissist upon the IN for his Secondary Narcissistic Supply).

The IN must have this form of relationship with a narcissist in order to feel whole. The IN goes as far as needed to ensure that the narcissist is happy, cared for, properly adored, as she feels is the narcissist's right. The IN glorifies and lionizes her narcissist, places him on a pedestal, endures any and all narcissistic devaluation with calm equanimity, impervious to the overt slights of the narcissist.

Narcissistic rage is handled deftly by the inverted narcissist. The IN is exceedingly adept at managing every aspect of her life, tightly controlling all situations, so as to minimize the potential for the inevitable narcissistic rages of her narcissist.

The IN wishes to be subsumed by the narcissist. The IN only feels truly loved and alive in this kind of relationship. The IN is loath to abandon her relationships with narcissists. The relationship only ends when the narcissist withdraws completely from the symbiosis. Once the narcissist has determined that the IN is of no further use, and withholds all Narcissistic Supply from the IN, only then does the IN reluctantly move on to another relationship.

The IN is most likely to equate sexual intimacy with engulfment. This can be easily misread to mean that the IN is herself a somatic narcissist, but it would be incorrect. The IN can endure years of minimal sexual contact with her narcissist and still be able to maintain the self-delusion of intimacy and engulfment. The IN finds a myriad of other ways to "merge" with the narcissist, becoming intimately, though only in support roles, involved with the narcissist's business, career, or any other activity where the IN can feel that they are needed by the narcissist and are indispensable.

The IN is an expert at doling out Narcissistic Supply and even goes as far as procuring Primary Narcissistic Supply for their narcissist (even where this means finding another lover for the narcissist, or participating in group sex with the narcissist).

Usually though, the IN seems most attracted to the cerebral narcissist and finds him easier to manage than the somatic narcissist. The cerebral narcissist is uninterested in sex and this makes life considerably easier for the IN, i.e., the IN is less likely to "lose" her cerebral narcissist to another primary partner. A somatic narcissist may be prone to changing partners with greater frequency or wish to have no partner, preferring to have multiple, casual sexual relationships of no apparent depth which never last very long.

The IN regards relationships with narcissists as the only true and legitimate form of primary relationship. The IN is capable of having primary relationships with non-narcissists. But without the engulfment and the drama, the IN feels unneeded, unwanted and emotionally uninvolved.

### When Can a *Classic Narcissist* Become an Inverted Narcissist?

A classic narcissist can become an inverted narcissist in one (or more) of the following (typically cumulative) circumstances:

1. Immediately following a life crisis and a narcissistic injury (divorce, devastating financial loss, death of a parent, or a child, imprisonment, loss of social status and, in general, any other narcissistic injury); or
2. When the injured narcissist then meets another classic narcissist who restores a sense of meaning and superiority (uniqueness) to his life. The injured narcissist derives Narcissistic Supply vicariously, by proxy, through the "dominant" narcissist.
3. As part of an effort to secure a particularly desired Source of Narcissistic Supply. The conversion from classic to inverted narcissism serves to foster an attachment (bonding) between the narcissist and his source. When the narcissist judges that the source is his and can be taken for granted, he reverts to his former, classically narcissistic self.

Such a "conversion" is always temporary. It does not last and the narcissist reverts to his "default" or dominant state.

### When Can an Inverted Narcissist Become a *Classic Narcissist*?

The inverted narcissist can become a classic narcissist in one (or more) of the following (typically cumulative) circumstances:

1. Immediately following a life crisis that involves the incapacitation or dysfunction of the inverted narcissist's partner (sickness, accident, demotion, divorce, devastating financial loss, death of a parent, or a child, imprisonment, loss of social status and, in general, any other narcissistic injury); or

2. When the inverted narcissist, injured and disillusioned, then meets another inverted narcissist who restores a sense of meaning and superiority (uniqueness) to her life. The injured narcissist derives Narcissistic Supply from the inverted narcissist.
3. As part of an effort to secure a particularly desired Source of Narcissistic Supply. The conversion from inverted to classic narcissism serves to foster an attachment (bonding) between the narcissist and her source. When the narcissist judges that the source is hers and can be taken for granted, she reverts to her former, inverted narcissistic self.

Such a "conversion" is always temporary. It does not last and the narcissist reverts to her "default" or dominant state.

## Relationships between the
## Inverted Narcissist and Non-Narcissists

The inverted narcissist can maintain relationships outside of the symbiotic primary relationship with a narcissist. But the IN does not "feel" loved because she finds the non-narcissist not "engulfing" or not "exciting". Thus, the IN tends to devalue her non-narcissistic primary partner as less worthy of the IN's love and attention.

The IN may be able to sustain a relationship with a non-narcissist by finding other narcissistic symbiotic relationships outside of this primary relationship. The IN may, for instance, have a narcissistic friend or lover, to whom she pays extraordinary attention, ignoring the real needs of the non-narcissistic partner.

Consequently, the only semi-stable primary relationship between the IN and the non-narcissist occurs where the non-narcissist is very easy going, emotionally secure and not needing much from the IN at all by way of time, energy or commitment to activities requiring the involvement of both parties. In a relationship with this kind of non-narcissist, the IN may become a workaholic or very involved in outside activities that exclude the non-narcissist spouse.

It appears that the inverted narcissist in a relationship with a non-narcissist is behaviourally indistinguishable from a true narcissist. The only important exception is that the IN does not rage at his non-narcissist partner – she instead withdraws from the relationship even further. This passive-aggressive reaction has been noted, though, with narcissists as well.

## Inverted Narcissists Talk about Themselves

### Competition and (Pathological) Envy

*"I have a dynamic that comes up with every single person I get close to, where I feel extremely competitive toward and envious of the other person. But I don't ACT competitive, because at the very outset, I see myself as the loser in the competition. I would never dream of trying to beat the other person, because I know deep in my heart that they would win and I would be utterly humiliated. There are fewer things on earth that feel worse to me than losing a contest and having the other person gloat over me, especially if they know how much I cared about not losing. This is one thing that I actually feel violent about. I guess I tend to project the grandiosity part of the NPD package onto the other person rather than on a False Ego of my own. So most of the time I'm stuck in a state of deep resentment and envy toward her. To me, she's always far more intelligent, likable, popular, talented, self-confident, emotionally developed, morally good, and attractive than I am. And I really hate her for that, and feel humiliated by it. So it's incredibly hard for me to feel happy for this person when she has a success, because I'm overcome with humiliation about myself. This has ruined many a close relationship. I tend to get this way about one person at a time, usually the person who is playing the role of 'my better half', best friends or lovers/partners. So it's not like I'm unable to be happy for anyone, ever, or that I envy every person I meet. I don't get obsessed with how rich or beautiful movie stars are or anything like that. It only gets projected onto this partner-person, the person I'm depending on the most in terms of supplies (attention, reassurance, security, building up my self-esteem, etc.)...*

*...The really destructive thing that happens is, I see her grandiose traits as giving her the power to have anything and anyone she wants. So I feel a basic insecurity, because why should she stay with a loser like me, when she's obviously so out of my league? So really, what I'm envious of is the power that all that talent, social ability, beauty, etc., gives her to have CHOICES – the choice to stay or leave me. Whereas I am utterly dependent on her. It's this emotional inequality that I find so humiliating."*

*"I agree with the inverted narcissist designation – sometimes I've called myself a 'closet narcissist'. That is, I've internalized the value system of grandiosity, but have not applied the grandiose identity to myself.*

I believe I SHOULD BE those grandiose things, but at the same time, I know I'm not and I'm miserable about it. So people don't think of me as having an inflated Ego – and indeed I don't – but scratch the surface, and you'll find all these inflated expectations. I mean to say that perhaps the parents suppressed every manifestation of grandiosity (very common in early childhood) and of narcissism – so that the defence mechanism that narcissism is was 'inverted' and internalized in this unusual form."

"Maybe there aren't two discrete states (NPD vs. 'regular' low self-esteem) – maybe it's more of a continuum. And maybe it's just the degree and depth of the problem that distinguishes one from the other.

My therapist describes NPD as 'the inability to love oneself'. As she defines it, the 'narcissistic wound' is a deep wounding of the sense of self, the image of oneself. That doesn't mean that other disorders – or for that matter, other life stressors – can't also cause low self-esteem. But I think NPD IS low self-esteem...

That's what the disorder is really about – an image of yourself that is profoundly negative, and the inability to attain a normal and healthy self-image..."

"Yes, I'm a survivor of child abuse. But remember that not all abuse is alike. There are different kinds of abuse, and different effects. My XXX's style of abuse had to do with trying to annihilate me as a separate person. It also had to do with the need to put all his negative self-image onto me – to see in me what he hated in himself. So I got to play the role of the loser that he secretly feared he was. I was flipped back and forth in those roles – sometimes I'd be a Source of NS for him, and other times I was the receptacle of all his pain and rage. Sometimes my successes were used to reflect back on him, to show off to the rest of the family. Other times, my successes were threatening to my father, who suddenly feared that I was superior to him and had to be squelched.

I experience emotions that most people I know don't feel. Or maybe they do feel them, but to far less extreme intensity. For example, the envy and comparison/competition I feel toward others. I guess most of us have experienced rivalry, jealousy, being compared to others. Most of us have felt envy at another's success. Yet most people I know seem able to overcome those feelings to some extent, to be able to function normally. In a competition, for example, they may be driven to do their best so they can win. For me, the fear of losing and being humiliated is so intense that I avoid competition completely. I am terrified of showing people that I care about doing well, because it's so shaming for me if I lose. So I underachieve and pretend I don't care. Most people I know may envy another person's good luck or success, but it doesn't prevent them from also being happy for them and supporting them. But for me, when I'm in a competitive dynamic with someone, I can't hear about any of their successes, or compliments they've received, etc. I don't even like to see the person doing good things, like bringing Thanksgiving leftovers to the sick old guy next door, because those things make me feel inferior for not thinking of doing that myself (and not having anyone in my life that I'd do that for). It's just so incredibly painful for me to see evidence of the other person's good qualities, because it immediately brings up my feeling of inferiority. I can't even stand to date someone, who looks really good, because I'm jealous of their good looks! So this deep and obsessive envy has destroyed my joy in other people. All the things about other people that I love and take pleasure in is a double-edged sword because I also hate them for it, for having those good qualities (while, presumably, I don't).

I don't know – do you think this is garden-variety low self-esteem? I know plenty of people who suffer from lack of confidence, from timidity, social awkwardness, hatred of their body, feeling unlovable, etc. But they don't have this kind of hostile, corrosive resentment of another person for being all the wonderful things that they can't be, or aren't allowed to be, etc. And one thing I hate is when people are judgemental of me about how I feel, as though I can help it. It's like, 'You shouldn't be so selfish, you should feel happy for her that she's successful', etc. They don't understand that I would love to feel those things, but I can't. I can't stop the incredible pain that explodes in me when these feelings get triggered, and I often can't even HIDE the feelings. It's just so overwhelming. I feel so damaged sometimes. There's more, but that's the crux of it for me, anyway."

### Getting Compliments

"I love getting compliments and rewards, and do not react negatively to them. In some moods, when my self-hate has gotten triggered, I can sometimes get to places where I'm inconsolable, because I get stuck in bitterness and self-pity, and so I doubt the sincerity or the reliability of the good thing that someone is saying to me (to try to cheer me up or whatever). But, if I'm in a reasonable mood and someone offers me something good, I'm all too happy to accept it! I don't have a stake in staying miserable."

### The Partiality of the Condition

"I do agree that it's (atypical or inverted narcissism) not MILDER. But how I see it is that it's PARTIAL. The part that's there is just as destructive as it is in the typical narcissist. But there are parts missing from that total, full-blown disorder – and I see that as healthy, actually. I see it as parts of myself that WEREN'T infected by the pathology, that are still intact.

In my case, I did not develop the overweening Ego part of the disorder. So in a sense, what you have with me is the naked pathology, with no covering: no suaveness, no charm, no charisma, no confidence, no persuasiveness, but also no excuses, no lies, no justifications for my feelings. Just the ugly self-hate, for all to see. And the self-hate part is just as bad as it is with a full-blown narcissist, so again, it's not milder.

But because I don't have the denial part of the disorder, I have a lot more insight, a lot more motivation to do something about my problems (i.e., I 'self-refer' to therapy), and therefore, I think, a lot more hope of getting better than people whose defence involves totally denying they even have a problem."

"When my full-blown XXX's pathological envy would get triggered, he would respond by putting down the person he was envious of – or by putting down the accomplishment itself, or whatever good stuff the other person had. He'd trivialize it, or outright contradict it, or find some way to convince the other person (often me) that the thing they're feeling good about isn't real, or isn't worthwhile, or is somehow bad, etc. He could do this because the inflated ego defence was fully formed and operating with him.

When MY pathological envy gets triggered, I will be bluntly honest about it. I'll say something self-pitying, such as: 'You always get the good stuff, and I get nothing'; 'You're so much better than I'; 'People like you better – you have good social skills and I'm a jerk'; and so on. Or I might even get hostile and sarcastic: 'Well, it must be nice to have so many people worshipping you, isn't it?' I don't try to convince myself that the other person's success isn't real or worthwhile, etc. Instead, I'm totally flooded with the pain of feeling utterly inferior and worthless – and there's no way for me to convince myself or anyone else otherwise. I'm not saying that the things I say are pleasant to hear – and it is still manipulative of me to say them, because the other person's attention is drawn away from their joy and onto my pain and hostility. And instead of doubting their success's worth or reality, they feel guilty about it, or about talking about it, because it hurts me so much. So from the other person's point of view, maybe it's not any easier to live with a partial narcissist than with a full-blown, in that their joys and successes lead to pain in both cases. It's certainly not easier for me, being flooded with rage and pain instead of being able to hide behind a delusion of grandeur. But from my therapist's point of view, I'm much better off because I know I'm unhappy - it's in my face all the time. So I'm motivated to work on it and change it. And time has borne her words out.

Over the past several years that I've worked on this issue, I have changed a great deal in how I deal with it. Now when the envy gets triggered, I don't feel so entwined with the other person - I recognize that it's my OWN pain getting triggered, not something they are doing to me. And so I can acknowledge the pain in a more responsible way, taking ownership of it by saying, 'The jealousy feelings are getting triggered again, and I'm feeling worthless and inferior. Can you reassure me that I'm not?' That's a lot better than making some snide, hostile, or self-pitying comment that puts the other person on the defensive or makes them feel guilty... I do prefer the term 'partial' because that's what it feels like to me. It's like a building that's partially built - the house of narcissism. For me, the structure is there, but not the outside, so you can see inside the skeleton to all the junk that's inside. It's the same junk that's inside a full-blown narcissist, but their building is completed, so you can't see inside. Their building is a fortress, and it's almost impossible to bring it down. My defences aren't as strong ... which makes my life more difficult in some ways because I REALLY feel my pain. But it also means that the house can be brought down more easily, and the junk inside cleaned out..."

### Thinking about the Past and the World

"I don't usually get rageful about the past. I feel sort of emotionally cut-off from the past, actually. I remember events very clearly, but usually can't remember the feelings. When I do remember the feelings, my reaction is usually one of sadness, and sometimes of relief that I can get back in touch with my past. But not rage. All my rage seems to get displaced on the current people in my life."

"...When I see someone being really socially awkward and geeky, passive-aggressive, indirect and victim-like, it does trigger anger in me because I identify with that person and I don't want to. I try to put my negative feelings onto them, to see that person as the jerk, not me – that's what a narcissist does, after all. But for me it doesn't completely work because I know, consciously, what I'm trying to do. And ultimately, I'm not kidding anyone, least of all myself."

### Self-Pity and Depression

"More self-pity and depression here – not so much rage. One of the things that triggers my rage more than anything else is the inability to control another person, the inability to dominate them and force my reality on them. I feel impotent, humiliated, forced back on my empty self. Part of what I'm feeling here is envy: that person who can't be controlled clearly has a self and I don't, and I just hate them for it. But it's also a power struggle – I want to get Narcissistic Supply by being in control and on top and having the other person submissive and compliant..."

### Regretting, Admitting Mistakes

"I regret my behaviour horribly, and I DO admit my feelings. I am also able, in the aftermath, to have empathy for the feelings of the person I've hurt, and I'm horribly sad about it, and ashamed of myself. It's as though I'd been possessed by a demon, acted out all this abusive horrible stuff, and then, after the departure of the demon, I'm back in my right mind and it's like, 'What have I DONE???' I don't mean I'm not responsible for what I did (i.e., a demon made me do it). But when I'm triggered, I have no empathy – I can only see my projection onto that person, as a huge threat to me, someone who must be demolished. But when my head clears, I see that person's pain, hurt, fear – and I feel terrible. I want to make it up to them. And that feeling is totally sincere – it's not an act. I'm genuinely sorry for the pain I've caused the other person."

### Rage

"I wouldn't say that my rage comes from repressed self-contempt (mine is not repressed – I'm totally aware of it). And it's not missing atonement either, since I do atone. The rage comes from feeling humiliated, from feeling that the other person has somehow sadistically and gleefully made me feel inferior, that they're getting off on being superior, that they're mocking me and ridiculing me, that they have scorn and contempt for me and find it all very amusing. That – whether real or imagined (usually imagined) – is what causes my rage."

### Pursuing Relationships with Narcissists

"There are some very few of us who actually seek out relationships with narcissists. We do this with the full knowledge that we are not wanted, despised even. We persist and pursue no matter the consequences, no matter the cost.

I am an 'inverted narcissist'. It is because as a child I was 'imprinted/fixated' with a particular pattern involving relationships. I was engulfed so completely by my father's personality and repressed so severely by various other factors in my childhood that I simply didn't develop a recognisable personality. I existed purely as an extension of my father. I was his genius Wunderkind. He ignored my mother and poured all his energy and effort into me. I did not develop full-blown secondary narcissism... I developed into the perfect 'other half' of the narcissists moulding me. I became the perfect, eager co-dependent. And this is an imprint, a pattern in my psyche, a way of (not) relating to the world of relationships by only being able to truly relate to one person (my father) and then one kind of person – the narcissist.

He is my perfect lover, my perfect mate, a fit that is so slick and smooth, so comfortable and effortless, so filled with meaning and actual feelings – that's the other thing. I cannot feel on my own. I am incomplete. I can only feel when I am engulfed by another (first it was my father) and now – well now it has to be a narcissist. Not just any narcissist either. He must be exceedingly smart, good looking, have adequate reproductive equipment and some knowledge on how to use it and that's about it.

When I am engulfed by someone like this I feel completed, I can actually FEEL. I am whole again. I function as a sibyl, an oracle, an extension of the narcissist. His fiercest protector, his purveyor/procurer of NS, the secretary, organizer, manager, etc. I think you get the picture and this gives me INTENSE PLEASURE.

So the answer to your question: 'Why would anyone want to be with someone who doesn't want them back?' The short answer is, 'Because there is no one else remotely worth looking at.'"

### Making Amends

"I mostly apologize, and I give the person space to talk about what hurt them so that (1) they get to express their anger or hurt to me, and (2) I can understand better and know better how not to hurt them (if I can avoid it) the next time there's a conflict. Sometimes the hurt I cause is unintentional – maybe I've been insensitive or forgetful or something, in which case I feel more certain that I can avoid repeating the hurtful behaviour, since I didn't want to hurt them in the first place. If the hurt I caused has to do with my getting my trigger pulled and going into a rage, then that hurt was quite deliberate, although at the time I was unable to experience the other person as vulnerable or capable of being hurt by me. And I do realize that if that trigger is pulled again, it might happen again. But I also hope that there'll be a LITTLE TINY window where the memory of the conversation will come back to me while I'm in my rage, and I'll remember that the person really IS vulnerable. I hope that by hearing over and over that the person actually does feel hurt by what I say while in rages, that I might remember that when I am triggered and raging. So, mostly I apologize and try to communicate with the other person. I don't verbally self-flagellate, because that's manipulative. Not to say I never do that – in fact I've had a dynamic with people where I verbally put myself down and try to engage the other person into arguing me out of it.

But if I'm in the middle of apologizing to the other person for hurting them, then I feel like this is their moment, and I don't want to turn the focus toward getting them to try to make me feel better. I will talk about myself, but only in an attempt to communicate, so that we can understand each other better. I might say, 'I got triggered about such-and-such, and you seemed so invulnerable that it enraged me', etc. – and the other person might react with, 'But I was feeling vulnerable, I just couldn't show it', etc. – and we'll go back and forth like that. So it's not like I don't think my feelings count, and I do want the other person to UNDERSTAND my feelings, but I don't want to put the other person in the role of taking care of my feelings in that moment, because they have just been hurt by me and I'm trying to make it up to them, not squeeze more stuff OUT of them..."

"So when I've been a real jerk to someone, I want them to feel like it's OK to be pissed off at me, and I want them to know that I am interested in and focused on how they feel, not just on how I feel. As for gifts – I used to do that, but eventually I came to feel that that was manipulative, too, that it muddled things because then the other person would feel like they couldn't be angry anymore, since after all, I've just brought them this nice gift. I also feel that in general, gift-giving is a sweet and tender thing to do, and I don't want to sully that tenderness by associating it with the hurt that comes from abusive behaviour."

### Why Narcissists?

"I am BUILT this way. I may have overstated it by saying that I have 'no choice' because, in fact I do.

The choice is - live in an emotionally deadened monochrome world where I can reasonably interact with normal people OR I can choose to be with a narcissist in which case my world is Technicolor, emotionally satisfying, alive and wondrous (also can be turbulent and a real roller coaster ride for the unprepared, not to mention incredibly damaging for people who are not inverted narcissists and who fall into relationships with narcissists). As I have walked on both sides of the street, and because I have developed coping mechanisms that protect me really quite well, I can reasonably safely engage in a primary, intimate relationship with a narcissist without getting hurt by it.

The real WHY of it all is that I learned, as a young child, that being 'eaten alive' by a narcissist parent, to the point where your existence is but an extension of his own, was how all relationships ought to work. It is a psychological imprint - my 'love map', it is what feels right to me intrinsically. A pattern of living - I don't know how else to describe it so you and others will understand how very natural and normal this is for me. It is not the torturous existence that most of the survivors of narcissism are recounting on this list.

My experiences with narcissists, to me, ARE NORMAL for me. Comfortable like an old pair of slippers that fit perfectly. I don't expect many people to attempt to do this, to 'make themselves into' this kind of person. I don't think anyone could, if they tried.

It is my need to be engulfed and merged that drives me to these relationships and when I get those needs met I feel more normal, better about myself. I am the outer extension of the narcissist. In many ways I am a vanguard, a public two-way warning system, fiercely defending my narcissist from harm, and fiercely loyal to him, catering to his every need in order to protect his fragile existence. These are the dynamics of my particular version of engulfment. I don't need anyone to take care of me. I need only to be needed in this very particular way, by a narcissist who inevitably possesses the ability to engulf in a way that normal, fully realized adults cannot. It is somewhat paradoxical - I feel freer and more independent with a narcissist than without one. I achieve more in my life when I am in this form of relationship. I try harder, work harder, am more creative, think better of myself, excel in most every aspect of my life."

"...I go ahead and cater to him and pretend that his words don't hurt, and later, I engage in an internal fight with myself for being so damned submissive. It's a constant battle and I can't seem to decide which voice in my head I should listen to... I feel like a fool, yet, I would rather be a fool with him than a lonely, well-rounded woman without him. I've often said that the only way that we can stay together is because we feed off of each other. I give him everything he needs and he takes it. Seeing him happy and pleased is what gives me pleasure. I feel very successful then."

### Partial NPD

"I do think it's uncommon for girls to develop these patterns, as they are usually trained to be self-effacing. I certainly was! However, I have a lot of the very same underlying patterns that full-blown, obnoxiously egotistical NP's have, but I am not egotistical because I didn't develop the pattern of inflated Ego and grandiosity. All the rest of it is there, though: fragile Ego, lack of a centre or self, super-sensitive to criticism and rejections, pathological, obsessive envy, comparisons and competitive attitudes toward others, a belief that everyone in the world is either superior or inferior to me, and so on.

Sometimes I kind of wish I had developed the inflated Ego of a complete NP, because then I would at least be able to hide from all the pain I feel.

But at the same time, I'm glad I didn't, because those people have a much lower chance of recovery – how can they recover if they don't acknowledge anything is wrong? Whereas it's pretty clear to me I have problems, and I've spent my life working on them and trying to change myself and heal."

### Narcissist-Non Narcissist
### And Narcissist-Inverted Narcissist Couples

"Can a N and a non-N ever maintain a long lasting marriage? It would seem that a non-N would have too much self-esteem to lend himself to a lifetime of catering and pandering to an N's unending need for unearned adoration and glory. I, as a non-N... got tired of these people and their unremitting attempts to drain my psyche within a relatively short period of time and abandoned them as soon as I realized what I was dealing with to preserve my own sanity."

"It depends on the non-narcissist, really. Narcissism is a RIGID, systemic pattern of responses. It is so all-pervasive and all-encompassing that it is a PERSONALITY disorder. If the non-narcissist is co-dependent, for instance, then the narcissist is a perfect match for him and the union will last..."

"You have to pimp for the narcissist, intellectually, and sexually. If your narcissist is somatic, you are much better off lining up the sex partners than leaving it to him. Intellectual pimping is more varied. You can think of wonderful things and then subtly string out the idea, in the most delicate of packages and watch the narcissist cogitate their way to 'their' brilliant discovery whilst you bask in the glow of their perfection and success... The point of this entire exercise is to assure YOUR supply, which is the narcissist himself, not to punish yourself by giving away a great idea or abase yourself because, of course, YOU are not worthy of having such a great idea on your own – but who knows, it may seem that way to the inverted narcissist. It really depends on how self-aware the inverted is."

"The only rejection you need to fear is the possibility of losing the narcissist and if one is doing everything else right, this is very unlikely to happen! So by 'emotionally independent' I am talking about being self-assured, doing your own thing, having a life, feeling strong and good about yourself, getting emotional sustenance from other people. I mean, let's face it, a drug is a drug is a habit. Habits just are, and what they ARE NOT are the be all and end all of love, commitment and serene symmetrical, balanced emotional perfection that is the ideal of the romanticized 'love-for-a-lifetime' all-American relationship dream."

"(I am) terribly turned on by narcissists. The most exciting moments of my life in every venue have been with narcissists. It is as if living and loving with normal people is a grey thing by comparison, not fuelled by sufficient adrenaline. I feel like a junkie, now, that I no longer permit myself the giddy pleasure of the RUSH I used to know when I was deeply and hopelessly involved with an N. I am like a lotus-eater. And I always felt guilty about this and also sorry that I ever succumbed that first time to my first narcissist lover."

"I am exactly this way and I feel exactly as you do, that the world is a sepia motion picture but when I am intimately involved with a narcissist, it breaks out into three-dimensional Technicolor and I can see and feel in ways that are not available to me otherwise. In my case I developed this (inverted narcissism) as a result of being the favourite of my father who so completely absorbed me into his personality that I was not able to develop a sense of separation. So I am stuck in this personality matrix of needing to be engulfed, adored by and completely taken over by a narcissist in my life. In turn, I worship, defend, regulate and procure Narcissistic Supply for my narcissist. It is like the mould and the moulded."

"In my case, I realize that while I can't stop loving my current narcissist, it isn't necessary for me to avoid as long as I can understand. In my way of looking at it, he is deserving of love, and since I can give him love without it hurting me, then as long as he needs it, he shall have it."

"My personal theory is that dogmatic religious culture is a retarding influence on the growth and maturation of those heavily involved - more and more autonomy (and hence personal responsibility) seems to be blithely sacrificed to the group mind/spirit. It is as though the church members become one personality and that personality is narcissistic and the individual just folds under the weight of that kind of group pressure - particularly if you are a child."

"If I displayed behaviour that made my XXX look good to others, I was insipidly overvalued. When I dared be something other than who she wanted me to be, the sarcastic criticism and total devaluation was unbelievable. So, I learned to be all things to all people. I get a heavenly high from surrendering my power to a narcissist, to catering to them, in having them overvalue and need me, and it is the only time that I truly feel alive..."

"We have very little choice in all of this. We are as vacant and warped as the narcissist. XXX is wont to say, 'I don't HAVE a personality disorder, I AM a personality disorder.' It defines who we are and how we will respond. You will always and ONLY have real feelings when you are with a narcissist. It is your love map, it is the programming within your psyche. Does it need to control your behaviour? Not necessarily. Knowing what you are can at least give you the opportunity to forecast the effect of an action before you take it. So, loveless black and white may be the very healthiest thing for you for the foreseeable future. I tend to think of these episodes with narcissists as being cyclic. You will likely need to cut loose for a while when your child is older.

DO NOT feel ashamed please! Should a physically handicapped person feel ashamed of their handicap? No and neither should we. The trouble with us is that we are fooled into thinking that these relationships are 'guilty pleasures'. They feel so very good for a time but they are more akin to addiction satisfaction rather than being the 'right match' or an 'appropriate relationship'. I am still very conflicted myself about this. I wrote a few months ago that it was like having a caged very dangerous animal inside of me. When I get near narcissists, the animal smells its own kind and it wants out. I very carefully 'micro-manage' my life. This means that I daily do fairly regular reality checks and keep a very tight reign on my self and my behaviours. I am also obsessive-compulsive."

"I feel as though I'm constantly on an emotional roller coaster. I may wake up in a good mood, but if my N partner does or says something, which is hurtful to me, my mood changes immediately. I now feel sad, empty, afraid. All I want to do at this point is anything that will make him say something NICE to me.

Once he does, I'm back on top of the world. This pattern of mood changes, or whatever you may call them, can take place several times a day. Each and every day. I've gotten to the point where I'm not sure that I can trust myself to feel any one way, because I know that I have no control over myself. He has the control. It's scary, yet I've sort of come to depend on him determining how I am going to feel."

"When I was first involved with my cerebral narcissist I was like this but after awhile I just learned to become more emotionally distant (the ups and downs were just too much) and find emotional gratification with other people, mostly girl friends and one of two male friends. I make a point of saying ... that the invert must be or become emotionally and financially independent (if you don't do this he will eat you up and when he has finished with you and you are nothing but a husk, you will be expelled from his life in one big vomit). It is really important for you to start to take responsibility for your own emotional wellness without regard to how he treats you. Remember that the narcissist has the emotional maturity of a two-year old! Don't expect much in the way of emotional depth or support in your relationship – he simply is not capable of anything that sophisticated."

Return

# The Spouse/Mate/Partner of the Narcissist

*Question:* What kind of a spouse/mate/partner is likely to be attracted to a narcissist?

*Answer:*

**The Victims**

On the face of it, there is no partner or mate, who typically "binds" with a narcissist. They come in all shapes and sizes. The initial phases of attraction, infatuation and falling in love are pretty normal. The narcissist puts on his best face – the other party is blinded by budding love. A natural selection process occurs only much later, as the relationship develops and is put to the test.

Living with a narcissist can be exhilarating, is always onerous, often harrowing. Surviving a relationship with a narcissist indicates, therefore, the parameters of the personality of the survivor. She (or, more rarely, he) is moulded by the relationship into The Typical Narcissistic Mate/Partner/Spouse.

First and foremost, the narcissist's partner must have a deficient or a distorted grasp of her self and of reality. Otherwise, she (or he) is bound to abandon the narcissist's ship early on. The cognitive distortion is likely to consist of belittling and demeaning herself, while aggrandizing and adoring the narcissist.

The partner is, thus, placing herself in the position of the eternal victim: undeserving, punishable, a scapegoat. Sometimes, it is very important to the partner to appear moral, sacrificial and victimized. At other times, she is not even aware of this predicament. The narcissist is perceived by the partner to be a person in the position to demand these sacrifices from her because he is superior in many ways (intellectually, emotionally, morally, professionally, or financially).

The status of professional victim sits well with the partner's tendency to punish herself, namely: with her masochistic streak.

She feels that the tormented life with the narcissist is just what she deserves.

In this respect, the partner is the mirror image of the narcissist. By maintaining a symbiotic relationship with him, by being totally dependent upon her source of masochistic supply (which the narcissist most reliably constitutes and most amply provides), the partner enhances certain traits and encourages certain behaviours, which are at the very core of narcissism.

The narcissist is never whole without an adoring, submissive, available, self-denigrating partner. His very sense of superiority, indeed his False Self, depends on it. His sadistic Superego switches its attentions from the narcissist (in whom it often provokes suicidal ideation) to the partner, thus finally obtaining an alternative source of sadistic satisfaction.

It is through self-denial that the partner survives. She denies her wishes, hopes, dreams, aspirations, sexual, psychological and material needs, choices, preferences, values, and much else besides. She perceives her needs as threatening because they might engender the wrath of the narcissist's God-like supreme figure.

The narcissist is rendered in her eyes even more superior through and because of this self-denial. Self-denial undertaken to facilitate and ease the life of a "great man" is more palatable. The "greater" the man (the narcissist), the easier it is for the partner to ignore her own self, to dwindle, to degenerate, to turn into an appendix of the narcissist and, finally, to become nothing but an extension, to merge with the narcissist to the point of oblivion and of merely dim memories of herself.

The two collaborate in this macabre dance. The narcissist is formed by his partner inasmuch as he forms her. Submission breeds superiority and masochism breeds sadism. The relationship is characterized by emergentism: within the couple, roles are allocated almost from the start and any deviation meets with an aggressive, even violent reaction.

The predominant state of the partner's mind is utter confusion. Even the most basic relationships – with husband, children, or parents – remain bafflingly obscured by the giant shadow cast by the intensive interaction with the narcissist. A suspension of judgement is part and parcel of a suspension of individuality, which are both prerequisites to and the outcomes of living with a narcissist. The partner no longer knows what is true and right and what is wrong and forbidden.

The narcissist recreates for the partner the sort of emotional ambience that led to his own formation in the first place: capriciousness, fickleness, arbitrariness, emotional (and physical or sexual) abandonment. The world becomes hostile and ominous and the partner has only one thing left to cling to: the narcissist.

And cling she does. If there is anything which can safely be said about those who emotionally team up with narcissists, it is that they are overtly and overly dependent.

The partner doesn't know what to do – and this is only too natural in the mayhem that is the relationship with the narcissist. But the typical partner also does not know what she wants and, to a large extent, who she is and what she wishes to become.

These unanswered questions hamper the partner's ability to gauge reality. Her primordial sin is that she fell in love with an image, not with a real person. It is the voiding of the image that is mourned when the relationship ends.

The break-up of a relationship with a narcissist is, therefore, very emotionally charged. It is the culmination of a long chain of humiliations and of subjugation. It is the rebellion of the functioning and healthy parts of the partner's personality against the tyranny of the narcissist.

The partner is likely to have totally misread and misinterpreted the whole interaction (I hesitate to call it a relationship). This lack of proper interface with reality might be labelled "pathological".

Why is it that the partner seeks to prolong her pain? What is the source and purpose of this masochistic streak? Upon the break-up of the relationship, the partner (but not the narcissist, who usually refuses to provide closure) engage in a tortuous and drawn out post mortem.

But the question who did what to whom (and even why) is irrelevant. What is relevant is to stop mourning oneself, start smiling again and love in a less subservient, hopeless, and pain-inflicting manner.

## The Abuse

Abuse is an integral, inseparable part of the Narcissistic Personality Disorder.

The narcissist idealizes and then DEVALUES and discards the object of his initial idealization. This abrupt, heartless devaluation IS abuse. The narcissist exploits, lies, insults, demeans, ignores (the "silent treatment"), manipulates, and controls others.

There are many forms of abuse. To love too much is to abuse. It is tantamount to treating someone as one's extension, an object, or an instrument of gratification. To be over-protective, not to respect privacy, to be brutally honest, with a morbid sense of humour, or consistently tactless is to abuse. To expect too much, to denigrate, to ignore someone are all modes of abuse. There is physical abuse, verbal abuse, psychological abuse, sexual abuse. The list is long.

Narcissists are masters of abusing surreptitiously ("ambient abuse"). They are "stealth abusers". You have to actually live with one in order to witness the abuse.

There are two important categories of abuse:

1. *Overt Abuse* – The open and explicit abuse of another person. Threatening, coercing, battering, lying, berating, demeaning, chastising, insulting, humiliating, exploiting, ignoring ("silent treatment"), devaluing, unceremoniously discarding, verbal abuse, physical abuse and sexual abuse are all forms of overt abuse.

2. *Covert or Controlling Abuse* – Narcissism is almost entirely about control. It is a primitive and immature reaction to the circumstances of the narcissist's life (usually in his childhood) in which he was rendered helpless. It is about re-asserting one's identity, re-establishing predictability, mastering the environment, both human and physical.

   The bulk of narcissistic behaviours can be traced to this panicky reaction to the potential for loss of control. Narcissists are hypochondriacs (and difficult patients) because they are afraid to lose control over their body, their appearance, and their proper functioning. They are obsessive-compulsive in their efforts to subdue their physical habitat and render it foreseeable. They stalk people and harass them as a means of "being in touch": another form of narcissistic control.

But why the panic?

The narcissist is a solipsist. To him, nothing exists except himself. Meaningful others are his extensions, assimilated by him, they are internal objects - not external ones. Thus, losing control of a significant other is equivalent to losing the use of a limb, or of one's brain. It is terrifying.

Independent or disobedient people evoke in the narcissist the realization that something is wrong with his worldview, that he is not the centre of the world or its prime mover and that he cannot control what, to him, are internal representations.

To the narcissist, losing control means going insane. Because other people are mere elements in the narcissist's mind, being unable to manipulate them literally means losing it (his mind). Imagine, if you suddenly were to find out that you cannot manipulate your memories or control your thoughts... It would have felt nightmarish!

Moreover, it is often only through manipulation and extortion that the narcissist can secure his Narcissistic Supply (NS). Controlling his Sources of Narcissistic Supply is a (mental) life or death question for the narcissist. The narcissist is a drug addict (his drug being Narcissistic Supply) and he goes to great lengths to obtain the next dose.

In his frantic efforts to maintain control or re-assert it, the narcissist resorts to a myriad of fiendishly inventive stratagems and mechanisms. Here is a partial list:

### Unpredictability

The narcissist acts unpredictably, capriciously, inconsistently and irrationally. This serves to demolish in others their carefully crafted worldview. They become dependent upon the next twist and turn of the narcissist, his inexplicable whims, his outbursts, denial, or smiles.

In other words: the narcissist makes sure that HE is the only stable entity in the lives of others by shattering the rest of their world through his seemingly insane behaviour. He guarantees his presence in their lives by destabilizing them.

In the absence of a self, there are no likes or dislikes, preferences, predictable behaviour or characteristics. It is not possible to know the narcissist. There is no one there.

The narcissist was conditioned from an early age of abuse and trauma to expect the unexpected. His was a world in which (sometimes sadistic) capricious caretakers and peers often behaved arbitrarily. He was trained to deny his True Self and nurture a False one.

Having invented himself, the narcissist sees no problem in re-inventing that which he designed in the first place. The narcissist is his own repeated creator – hence his grandiosity.

Moreover, the narcissist is a man for all seasons, forever adaptable, constantly imitating and emulating role models, a human sponge, a perfect mirror, a chameleon, a non-entity that is, at the same time, all entities combined.

The narcissist is best described by Heidegger's phrase: "Being and Nothingness". Into this reflective vacuum, this sucking black hole, the narcissist attracts the Sources of his Narcissistic Supply.

To an observer, the narcissist appears to be fractured or discontinuous.

Pathological narcissism has been compared to the Dissociative Identity Disorder (formerly the Multiple Personality Disorder). By definition, the narcissist has at least two selves, the True and False ones. His personality is very primitive and disorganized. Living with a narcissist is a nauseating experience not only because of what he is, but because of what he is NOT. He is not a fully formed human, but a dizzyingly kaleidoscopic gallery of ephemeral images, which melt into each other seamlessly. It is incredibly disorienting.

It is also exceedingly problematic. Promises made by the narcissist are easily disowned by him. His plans are transient. His emotional ties a simulacrum. Most narcissists have one island of stability in their life (spouse, family, their career, a hobby, their religion, country, or idol) pounded by the turbulent currents of an otherwise stochastic existence.

The narcissist does not keep agreements, does not adhere to laws or social norms, and regards consistency and predictability as demeaning traits.

Thus, to invest in a narcissist is a purposeless, futile and meaningless activity. To the narcissist, every day is a new beginning, a hunt, a new cycle of idealization or devaluation, a newly invented self. There is no accumulation of credits or goodwill because the narcissist has no past and no future. He occupies an eternal and timeless present. He is a fossil caught in the frozen ashes of a volcanic childhood.

What to do?

Refuse to accept such behaviour. Demand reasonably predictable and rational actions and reactions. Insist on respect for your boundaries, predilections, preferences, and priorities.

## Disproportional Reactions

One of the favourite tools of manipulation in the narcissist's arsenal is the disproportionality of his reactions. He reacts with supreme rage to the slightest slight. He punishes severely for what he perceives to be an offence against him, no matter how minor. He throws a temper tantrum over any discord or disagreement, however gently and considerately expressed. Immediately thereafter, he may act attentive, charming and seductive (even over-sexed, if need be). This ever-shifting emotional landscape ("affective dunes") coupled with an inordinately harsh and arbitrarily applied "penal code" are both promulgated by the narcissist. Neediness and dependence on the source of all justice meted – the narcissist – are thus guaranteed.

What to do?

Demand a just and proportional treatment. Reject or ignore unjust and capricious behaviour.

If you are up to the inevitable confrontation, react in kind. Let him taste some of his own medicine.

### Dehumanization and Objectification

People have a need to believe in the empathic skills and basic good-heartedness of others. By dehumanizing and objectifying people the narcissist attacks the very foundations of the social treaty. This is the "alien" aspect of narcissists: they may be excellent imitations of fully formed adults but they are emotionally non-existent, or, at best, immature.

This is so horrid, so repulsive, so phantasmagoric that people recoil in terror. It is then, with their defences absolutely down, that they are the most susceptible and vulnerable to the narcissist's control. Physical, psychological, verbal and sexual abuse are all forms of dehumanization and objectification.

What to do?

Never show your abuser that you are afraid of him. Do not negotiate with bullies. They are insatiable. Do not succumb to blackmail.

If things get rough – disengage, involve law enforcement officers, friends and colleagues, or threaten him (legally).

Do not keep your abuse a secret. Secrecy is the abuser's weapon.

Never give him a second chance. React with your full arsenal to the first transgression.

### Abuse of Information

From the first moments of an encounter with another person, the narcissist is on the prowl. He collects information with the intention of abusing it later in order to extract Narcissistic Supply. The more he knows about his potential Source of Supply, the better able he is to coerce, manipulate, charm, extort or convert her "to the cause". The narcissist does not hesitate to misuse the information he gleaned, regardless of its intimate nature or the circumstances in which he obtained it. This is a powerful tool in his armoury.

What to do?

Be guarded. Don't be too forthcoming in a first or casual meeting. First, gather intelligence on your interlocutor.

Be yourself. Don't misrepresent your wishes, boundaries, preferences, priorities, and red lines.

Do not behave inconsistently. Do not go back on your word. Be firm and resolute.

### Impossible Situations

The narcissist engineers impossible, dangerous, unpredictable, unprecedented, or highly specific situations in which he is sorely and indispensably needed. The narcissist's knowledge, his skills or his traits become the only ones applicable, or the most useful to coping with these artificial predicaments. It is a form of control by proxy.

What to do?

Stay away from such quagmires. Scrutinize every offer and suggestion, no matter how innocuous.

Prepare back-up plans. Keep others informed of your whereabouts and appraised of your situation.

Be vigilant and doubting. Do not be gullible and suggestible. Better safe than sorry.

### Control by Proxy

If all else fails, the narcissist recruits friends, colleagues, mates, family members, the authorities, institutions, neighbours, or the media – in short, third parties – to do his bidding. He uses them to cajole, coerce, threaten, stalk, offer, retreat, tempt, convince, harass, communicate and otherwise manipulate his target. He controls these unaware instruments exactly as he plans to control his ultimate prey. He employs the same mechanisms and devices. And he dumps his props unceremoniously when the job is done.

Another form of control by proxy is to engineer situations in which abuse is inflicted upon another person. Such carefully crafted scenarios involve embarrassment and humiliation as well as social sanctions (condemnation, opprobrium, or even physical punishment). Society, or a social group become the instruments of the narcissist.

What to do?

Often the abuser's proxies are unaware of their role. Expose him. Inform them. Demonstrate to them how they are being abused, misused, and plain used by the abuser.

Trap your abuser. Treat him as he treats you. Involve others. Bring it into the open. Nothing like sunshine to disinfest abuse.

Gaslighting or stealth or ambient abuse is the fostering, propagation and enhancement of an atmosphere of fear, intimidation, instability, unpredictability and irritation. There are no acts of traceable or provable explicit abuse, nor any manipulative settings of control. Yet, the irksome feeling remains, a disagreeable foreboding, a premonition, a bad omen.

In the long-term, such an environment erodes one's sense of self-worth and self-esteem. Self-confidence is shaken badly. Often, the victims become paranoid or schizoid and thus are exposed even more to criticism and judgement. The roles are thus reversed: the victim is considered mentally disordered and the narcissist the suffering soul or the victim.

What to do?

Run! Get away! Ambient abuse often develops into overt and violent abuse.

You don't owe anyone an explanation but you owe yourself a life. Bail out of the relationship. Leave him now.

## Indifference and Decompensation in Pathological Narcissism

The narcissist lacks empathy. Consequently, he is not really interested in the lives, emotions, needs, preferences, and hopes of people around him. Even his nearest and dearest are, to him, mere instruments of gratification. They require his undivided attention only when they "malfunction" - when they become disobedient, independent, or critical. He loses all interest in them if they cannot be "fixed" (for instance, when they are terminally ill or develop a modicum of personal autonomy and independence).

Once he gives up on his erstwhile Sources of Supply, the narcissist proceeds to promptly and peremptorily devalue and discard them. This is often done by simply ignoring them - a facade of indifference that is known as the "silent treatment" and is, at heart, hostile and aggressive. Indifference is, therefore, a form of devaluation. People find the narcissist "cold", "inhuman", "heartless", "clueless", "robotic or machine-like".

Early on in life, the narcissist learns to disguise his socially-unacceptable indifference as benevolence, equanimity, cool-headedness, composure, or superiority. "It is not that I don't care about others" - he shrugs off his critics - "I am simply more level-headed, more resilient, more composed under pressure... They mistake my equanimity for apathy."

The narcissist tries to convince people that he is compassionate. His profound lack of interest in his spouse's life, vocation, interests, hobbies, and whereabouts he cloaks as benevolent altruism. "I give her all the freedom she can wish for!" – he protests – "I don't spy on her, follow her, or nag her with endless questions. I don't bother her. I let her lead her life the way she sees fit and don't interfere in her affairs!" He makes a virtue out of his emotional truancy.

All very commendable but when taken to extremes such benign neglect turns malignant and signifies the voidance of true love and attachment. The narcissist's emotional (and, often, physical) absence from all his relationships is a form of aggression and a defence against his own thoroughly repressed feelings.

In rare moments of self-awareness, the narcissist realizes that without his input – even in the form of feigned emotions – people will abandon him. He then swings from cruel aloofness to maudlin and grandiose gestures intended to demonstrate the "larger than life" nature of his sentiments. This bizarre pendulum only proves the narcissist's inadequacy at maintaining adult relationships. It convinces no one and repels many.

The narcissist's guarded detachment is a sad reaction to his unfortunate formative years. Pathological narcissism is thought to be the result of a prolonged period of severe abuse by primary caregivers, peers, or authority figures. In this sense, pathological narcissism is, therefore, a reaction to trauma. Narcissism IS a form of Post-Traumatic Stress Disorder that got ossified and fixated and mutated into a personality disorder.

All narcissists are traumatized and all of them suffer from a variety of post-traumatic symptoms: abandonment anxiety, reckless behaviours, anxiety and mood disorders, somatoform disorders, and so on. But the presenting signs of narcissism rarely indicate post-trauma. This is because pathological narcissism is an EFFICIENT coping (defence) mechanism. The narcissist presents to the world a facade of invincibility, equanimity, superiority, skilfulness, cool-headedness, invulnerability, and, in short: indifference.

This front is penetrated only in times of great crises that threaten the narcissist's ability to obtain Narcissistic Supply. The narcissist then "falls apart" in a process of disintegration known as decompensation. The dynamic forces which render him paralyzed and fake – his vulnerabilities, weaknesses, and fears – are starkly exposed as his defences crumble and become dysfunctional. The narcissist's extreme dependence on his social milieu for the regulation of his sense of self-worth is painfully and pitifully evident as he is reduced to begging and cajoling.

At such times, the narcissist acts out self-destructively and anti-socially. His mask of superior equanimity is pierced by displays of impotent rage, self-loathing, self-pity, and crass attempts at manipulation of his friends, family, and colleagues. His ostensible benevolence and caring evaporate. He feels caged and threatened and he reacts as any animal would do – by striking back at his perceived tormentors, at his hitherto "nearest" and "dearest".

## The Malignant Optimism of the Abused

I often come across sad examples of the powers of self-delusion that the narcissist provokes in his victims. It is what I call "malignant optimism". People refuse to believe that some questions are unsolvable, some diseases incurable, some disasters inevitable. They see a sign of hope in every fluctuation. They read meaning and patterns into every random occurrence, utterance, or slip of tongue. They are deceived by their own pressing need to believe in the ultimate victory of good over evil, health over sickness, order over disorder. Life appears otherwise so meaningless, so unjust and so arbitrary... So, they impose upon it a design, progress, aims, and paths. This is magical thinking.

"If only he tried hard enough", "If he only really wanted to heal", "If only we found the right therapy", "If only his defences were down", "There MUST be something good and worthy under his hideous facade", "NO ONE can be that evil and destructive", "He must have meant it differently", "God, or a higher being, or the spirit, or the soul is the solution and the answer to our prayers", "He is not responsible for what he is – his narcissism is the product of a difficult childhood, of abuse, and of his monstrous parents."

The Pollyanna defences of the abused are aimed against the emerging and horrible understanding that humans are mere specks of dust in a totally indifferent universe, the playthings of evil and sadistic forces, of which the narcissist is one and that finally the victims' pains means nothing to anyone but themselves.

The narcissist holds such malignant optimism in barely disguised contempt. To him, it is a sign of weakness. It gives off the scent of prey. It is a gaping vulnerability. He uses and abuses this human need for order, good, and meaning as he uses and abuses all other human needs. Gullibility, selective blindness, malignant optimism – these are the weapons of the beast. And the abused are hard at work to provide it with its arsenal.

Return

# Investing in a Narcissist

*Question:* In what type of narcissist is it worthwhile to invest emotionally?

*Answer:* This, obviously, is a matter of value judgement. Narcissism is a powerful force, akin to the psychological element in drug addiction. The narcissist is sustained by ever increasing amounts of Narcissistic Supply. Adoration, approval, attention and the maintenance of an audience are the nourishment without which the narcissist shrivels.

Depending on how talented the narcissist is, Narcissistic Supply could be the by-product of real achievements. The narcissist usually applies his skills and exploits his natural advantages where they provide him with the highest narcissistic rewards. For instance: he writes books to gain public acclaim not because he has something to say or because he cannot contain his emotions or his message – but in order to garner the attention of the public and the media. Still, narcissists are, mostly, gifted and, therefore, are able to contribute to society at large. They become artists, authors, political leaders, business leaders, or entertainers in order to bask in the limelight.

Some narcissists could be judged "worthy of sacrifice". They benefit their community "more" than they harm it. Those nearest and dearest pay a price – which is deemed more than amply compensated for by the contributions of the narcissist to the well-being of his community. But it is always a close call.

Return

# The Double Reflection

## Narcissistic Couples and Narcissistic Types

*Question:* Can two narcissists establish a long-term, stable relationship?

*Answer:* Two narcissists of the same type (somatic, cerebral, classic, compensatory, or inverted) cannot maintain a stable, long-term, full-fledged, and functional relationship.

Consider two types of narcissists: the somatic narcissist and the cerebral narcissist. The somatic type relies on his body and sexuality as Sources of Narcissistic Supply. The cerebral narcissist uses his intellect, his intelligence and his professional achievements to obtain the same.

Narcissists are either predominantly cerebral or overwhelmingly somatic. In other words, they either generate their Narcissistic Supply by using their bodies or by flaunting their minds.

The somatic narcissist flashes his sexual conquests, parades his possessions, puts his muscles on ostentatious display, brags about his physical aesthetics or sexual prowess or exploits, is often a health freak and a hypochondriac. The cerebral narcissist is a know-it-all, haughty and intelligent "computer". He uses his awesome intellect, or knowledge (real or pretended) to secure adoration, adulation and admiration. To him, his body and its maintenance are a burden and a distraction.

Both types are autoerotic (psychosexually in love with themselves, with their bodies or with their brains). Both types prefer masturbation to adult, mature, interactive, multi-dimensional and emotion-laden sex.

The cerebral narcissist is often celibate (even when he has a girlfriend or a spouse). He prefers pornography and sexual auto-stimulation to the real thing. The cerebral narcissist is sometimes a latent (hidden, not yet outed) homosexual.

The somatic narcissist uses other people's bodies to masturbate. Sex with him – pyrotechnics and acrobatics aside - is likely to be an impersonal and emotionally alienating and draining experience. The partner is often treated as an object, an extension of the somatic narcissist, a sex toy or a sex slave.

It is a mistake to assume type-constancy. In other words, all narcissists are both cerebral and somatic. In each narcissist, one of the types is dominant. So, the narcissist is either largely cerebral – or dominantly somatic. But the other, recessive (manifested less frequently) type, is there. It is lurking, waiting to erupt.

The narcissist swings between his dominant type and his recessive type which manifests mainly after a major narcissistic injury or life crisis.

The cerebral narcissist brandishes his brainpower, exhibits his intellectual achievements, basks in the attention given to his mind and to its products. He hates his body and neglects it. It is a nuisance, a burden, a derided appendix, an inconvenience, a punishment. The cerebral narcissist is asexual (rarely has sex, often years apart). He masturbates regularly and very mechanically. His fantasies are homosexual or paedophiliac or tend to objectify his partner (rape, group sex). He stays away from women because he perceives them to be ruthless predators who are out to consume him.

The cerebral narcissist typically goes through a few major life crises. He gets divorced, goes bankrupt, does time in prison, is threatened, harassed and stalked, is often devalued, betrayed, denigrated and insulted. He is prone to all manner of chronic illnesses.

Invariably, following every life crisis, the somatic narcissist in him takes over. The cerebral narcissist suddenly becomes a lascivious lecher. When this happens, he maintains a few relationships – replete with abundant and addictive sex – going simultaneously. He sometimes participates in and initiates group sex and mass orgies. He exercises, loses weight and hones his body into an irresistible proposition.

This outburst of unrestrained, primordial lust wanes in a few months and he settles back into his cerebral ways. No sex, no women, no body.

These total reversals of character stun his mates. His girlfriend or spouse finds it impossible to digest this eerie transformation from the gregarious, darkly handsome, well-built and sexually insatiable person that swept her off her feet – to the bodiless, bookwormish hermit with not an inkling of interest in either sex or other carnal pleasures.

The cerebral narcissist misses his somatic half, but finding a balance is a doomed quest. The satyr that is the somatic narcissist is forever trapped in the intellectual cage of the cerebral one, the Brain.

Thus, if both members of the couple are cerebral narcissists, for instance if both of them are scholars, the resulting competition prevents them from serving as ample Sources of Narcissistic Supply to each other. Finally the mutual admiration society crumbles.

Consumed by the pursuit of their narcissistic gratification, they have no time or energy or will left to cater to the narcissistic needs of their partner. Moreover, the partner is perceived as a dangerous and vicious contender for a scarce resource: extant Sources of Narcissistic Supply. This may be less true if the two narcissists work in totally unrelated academic or intellectual fields.

But if the narcissists involved are of different types, if one of them is cerebral and the other one somatic, a long-term partnership based on the mutual provision of Narcissistic Supply can definitely survive.

Example: if one of the narcissists is somatic (uses his/her body as a source of narcissistic gratification) and the other one cerebral (uses his intellect or his professional achievements as such a source), there is nothing to destabilize such collaboration. It is even potentially emotionally rewarding.

The relationship between these two narcissists resembles the one that exists between an artist and his art or a collector and his collection. This can and does change, of course, as the narcissists involved grow older, flabbier and less agile intellectually. The somatic narcissist is also prone to multiple sexual relationships and encounters intended to support his somatic and sexual self-image. These may subject the relationship to fracturing strains. But, all in all, a stable and enduring relationship can – and often does – develop between dissimilar narcissists.

Return

# Narcissistic Parents

*Question:* What are the effects that narcissistic parents have on their offspring?

*Answer:* At the risk of over-simplification: narcissism tends to breed narcissism – but only a minority of the children of narcissistic parents become narcissists. This may be due to a genetic predisposition or to different life circumstances (like being the firstborn). Still, MOST narcissists have one or more narcissistic parents or caregivers.

The narcissistic parent regards his or her child as a multi-faceted Source of Narcissistic Supply. The child is considered to be and treated as an extension of the narcissist parent. It is through the child that the narcissist seeks to settle "open scores" with the world. The child is supposed to realize the unfulfilled dreams, wishes, and fantasies of the narcissistic parent.

This "life by proxy" can develop in two ways: the narcissist can either merge with his child or be ambivalent about him. The ambivalence is the result of a conflict between the narcissist's wish to attain his narcissistic goals through the child and his pathological (destructive) envy of the child and his accomplishments.

To ameliorate the unease bred by this emotional ambivalence, the narcissistic parent resorts to a myriad control mechanisms. These can be grouped into: *guilt-driven* ("I sacrificed my life for you..."), *co-dependent* ("I need you, I cannot cope without you..."), *goal-driven* ("We have a common goal which we can and must achieve") and *explicit* ("If you do not adhere to my principles, beliefs, ideology, religion, values, if you do not obey my instructions – I will punish you").

This exercise of control helps to sustain the illusion that the child is a part of the narcissist. But maintaining the illusion calls for extraordinary levels of control (on the part of the parent) and obedience (on the part of the child). The relationship is typically symbiotic and emotionally turbulent.

The child fulfils another important narcissistic function: the provision of Narcissistic Supply. There is no denying the implied (though imaginary) immortality in having a child. The early (natural) dependence of the child on his caregivers serves to assuage their abandonment anxiety.

The narcissist tries to perpetuate this dependence, using the aforementioned control mechanisms. The child is the ultimate Secondary Narcissistic Source of Supply. He is always present, he admires the narcissist, he witnesses the narcissist's moments of triumph and grandeur.

Owing to his wish to be loved, the child can be extorted into constant giving. To the narcissist, a child is a dream come true, but only in the most egotistical sense. When the child is perceived as "reneging" on his main obligation (to provide his narcissistic parent with a constant supply of attention), the parent's emotional reaction is harsh and revealing.

It is when the narcissistic parent is disenchanted with his child that we see the true nature of this pathological relationship. The child is totally objectified. The narcissist reacts to a breach in the unwritten contract between them with wells of aggression and aggressive transformations: contempt, rage, emotional and psychological abuse, and even physical violence. He tries to annihilate the real "disobedient" child and substitute it with the subservient, edifying, former version.

Return

# Narcissists and Children

*Question:* My husband positively detests children. When a child enters the room, I can see him arching like a cat, ready to do battle. Needless to say we are childless.

*Answer:* The narcissist sees in children feigned innocence, relentless and ruthless manipulation, the cunning of the weak. They are ageless. Their narcissism is disarming in its directness, in its cruel and absolute lack of empathy. They demand with insistence, punish absent-mindedly, idealize and devalue capriciously. They have no loyalty. They do not love, they cling. Their dependence is a mighty weapon and their neediness – a drug. They have no time, neither before, nor after. To them, existence is a play, they are the actors, and we all are but the props. They raise and drop the curtain of their mock emotions at will. The bells of their laughter often tintinnabulate. They are the fresh abode of good and evil, and pure they are.

Children, to the narcissist, are both mirrors and competitors. They reflect authentically the narcissist's constant need for adulation and attention. Their grandiose fantasies of omnipotence and omniscience are crass caricatures of his internal world. The way they abuse others and mistreat them hits close to home. Their innocuous charm, their endless curiosity, their fount of energy, their sulking, nagging, boasting, bragging, lying, and manipulating are mutations of the narcissist's own behaviour. He recognizes his thwarted self in them. When they make their entrance, all attention is diverted. Their fantasies endear them to their listeners. Their vainglorious swagger often causes smiles. Their trite stupidities are invariably treated as pearls of wisdom. Their nagging is yielded to, their threats provoke to action, their needs accommodated urgently. The narcissist stands aside, an abandoned centre of attention, the dormant eye of an intellectual storm, all but ignored and neglected. He watches the child with envy, with rage, with wrath. He hates the child's effortless ability to defeat him.

Children are loved by their mothers, as the narcissist was not. They are bundled emotions, and happiness and hope. The narcissist is jealous of them, infuriated by his deprivation, fearful of the sadness and hopelessness that they provoke in him. Like music, they reify a threat to the precariously balanced emotional black hole that is the narcissist. They are his past, his dilapidated and petrified True Self, his wasted potentials, his self-loathing and his defences. They are his pathology projected.

The narcissist revels in his Orwellian narcissistic newspeak. Love is weakness, happiness is a psychosis, hope is malignant optimism. Children defy all this. They are proof positive of how different it could all have been.

But what the narcissist consciously experiences is disbelief. He cannot understand how anyone can love these thuggish brats, their dripping noses, gelatinous fat bodies, whitish sweat, and bad breath. How can anyone stand their cruelty and vanity, their sadistic insistence and blackmail, their prevarication and deceit? In truth, no one except their parents can.

As far as the narcissist knows, children are always derided by everyone except their parents. To him, there is something sick and sickening in a mother's affections. There is a maddening blindness involved, an addiction, a psychotic episode, it's sick, this bond, it's nauseous. The narcissist hates children. He hates them for being him.

Return

# The Narcissist and His Family

*Question:* Is there a typical relationship between the narcissist and his family?

*Answer:* We are all members of a few families in our lifetime: the one that we are born to and the one(s) that we create. We all transfer hurts, attitudes, fears, hopes and desires – a whole emotional baggage – from the former to the latter. The narcissist is no exception.

The narcissist has a dichotomous view of humanity: people are either Sources of Narcissistic Supply (and, then, idealized and over-valued) or do not fulfil this function (and, therefore, are valueless, devalued). The narcissist gets all the love that he needs from himself. From the outside he requires approval, affirmation, admiration, adoration, attention – in other words, externalized ego boundary functions.

He does not require – nor does he seek – his parents' or his siblings' love, or to be loved by his children. He casts them as the audience in the theatre of his inflated grandiosity. He wishes to impress them, shock them, threaten them, infuse them with awe, inspire them, attract their attention, subjugate them, or manipulate them.

He emulates and simulates an entire range of emotions and employs every means to achieve these effects. He lies (narcissists are pathological liars: their very Self is a False one). He acts the pitiful, or, its opposite, the resilient and reliable. He stuns and shines with outstanding intellectual brilliance or physical capacities and achievements, or he adopts behaviour patterns appreciated by other members of the family. When confronted with (younger) siblings or with his own children, the narcissist is likely to go through three phases:

At first, he perceives his offspring or siblings as a threat to his Narcissistic Supply, competitors for the attention of his spouse, or mother, as the case may be. They intrude on his turf and invade the Pathological Narcissistic Space. The narcissist does his best to belittle them, hurt (even physically) and humiliate them and then, when these reactions prove ineffective or counterproductive, he retreats into an imaginary world of omnipotence. A period of emotional absence and detachment ensues.

His aggression having failed to elicit Narcissistic Supply, the narcissist proceeds to indulge himself in daydreaming, delusions of grandeur, planning of future coups, nostalgia and hurt (the Lost Paradise Syndrome). The narcissist reacts this way to the birth of his children or to the introduction of new foci of attention to the family cell (even to a new pet!).

Whoever the narcissist perceives to be in competition with for scarce Narcissistic Supply is relegated to the role of the enemy. Where the uninhibited expression of the aggression and hostility aroused by this predicament is illegitimate or impossible, the narcissist prefers to stay away. Rather than attack his offspring or siblings, he sometimes immediately disconnects, detaches himself emotionally, becomes cold and uninterested, or directs transformed anger at his mate or at his parents (the more "legitimate" targets).

Other narcissists see the opportunity in the "mishap". They seek to manipulate their parents (or their mate) by "taking over" the newcomer. Such narcissists monopolize their siblings or their newborn children. This way, indirectly, they benefit from the attention directed at the infants. The sibling or offspring become vicarious Sources of Narcissistic Supply and proxies for the narcissist.

An example: by being a good father to his offspring or a good brother to his siblings, the narcissist secures the grateful admiration of the mother ("What an outstanding father/brother he is"). He also assumes part of or all the credit for baby's/sibling's achievements. This is a process of annexation and assimilation of the other, a strategy that the narcissist makes use of in most of his relationships.

As siblings or progeny grow older, the narcissist begins to see their potential for becoming edifying, reliable and satisfactory Sources of Narcissistic Supply. His attitude, then, is completely transformed. The former threats have now become promising potentials. He cultivates those whom he trusts to be the most rewarding. He encourages them to idolize him, to adore him, to be awed by him, to admire his deeds and capabilities, to learn to blindly trust and obey him, in short to surrender to his charisma and to become submerged in his folie-de-grandeur.

It is at this stage that the risk of child abuse – up to and including outright incest – is heightened. The narcissist is auto-erotic. He is the preferred object of his own sexual attraction. His siblings and his children share his genetic material. Molesting or having intercourse with them is as close as the narcissist gets to having sex with himself.

Moreover, the narcissist perceives sex in terms of annexation. The sexual partner is "assimilated" and becomes an extension of the narcissist, a fully controlled and manipulated object. Sex, to the narcissist, is the ultimate act of depersonalization and objectification of the other. He actually masturbates with other people's bodies.

Minors pose little danger of criticizing the narcissist or confronting him. They are perfect, malleable and abundant Sources of Narcissistic Supply. The narcissist derives gratification from having coital relations with adulating, physically and mentally inferior, inexperienced and dependent "bodies".

These roles – allocated to them explicitly and demandingly or implicitly and perniciously by the narcissist – are best fulfilled by ones whose mind is not yet fully formed and independent. The older the siblings or offspring, the more they become critical, even judgemental, of the narcissist. They are better able to put into context and perspective his actions, to question his motives, to anticipate his moves.

As they mature, they often refuse to continue to play the mindless pawns in his chess game. They hold grudges against him for what he has done to them in the past, when they were less capable of resistance. They can gauge his true stature, talents and achievements – which, usually, lag far behind the claims that he makes.

This brings the narcissist a full cycle back to the first phase. Again, he perceives his siblings or sons/daughters as threats. He quickly becomes disillusioned and devaluing. He loses all interest, becomes emotionally remote, absent and cold, rejects any effort to communicate with him, citing life's pressures and the preciousness and scarceness of his time.

He feels burdened, cornered, besieged, suffocated, and claustrophobic. He wants to get away, to abandon his commitments to people who have become totally useless (or even damaging) to him. He does not understand why he has to support them, or to suffer their company and he believes himself to have been deliberately and ruthlessly trapped.

He rebels either passively-aggressively (by refusing to act or by intentionally sabotaging the relationships) or actively (by being overly critical, aggressive, unpleasant, verbally and psychologically abusive and so on). Slowly – to justify his acts to himself – he gets immersed in conspiracy theories with clear paranoid hues.

To his mind, the members of the family conspire against him, seek to belittle or humiliate or subordinate him, do not understand him, or stymie his growth. The narcissist usually finally gets what he wants and the family that he has created disintegrates to his great sorrow (due to the loss of the Narcissistic Space) – but also to his great relief and surprise (how could they have let go someone as unique as he?).

This is the cycle: the narcissist feels threatened by arrival of new family members – he tries to assimilate or annex his siblings or offspring – he obtains Narcissistic Supply from them – he overvalues and idealizes these newfound sources – as sources grow older and independent, they adopt anti narcissistic behaviours – the narcissist devalues them – the narcissist feels stifled and trapped – the narcissist becomes paranoid – the narcissist rebels and the family disintegrates.

This cycle characterizes not only the family life of the narcissist. It is to be found in other realms of his life (his career, for instance). At work, the narcissist, initially, feels threatened (no one knows him, he is a nobody). Then, he develops a circle of admirers, cronies and friends which he "nurtures and cultivates" in order to obtain Narcissistic Supply from them. He overvalues them (he regards them as the brightest, the most loyal, with the biggest chances to climb the corporate ladder and other superlatives).

But following some anti-narcissistic behaviours on their part (a critical remark, a disagreement, a refusal, however polite, to do the narcissist's bidding), the narcissist devalues all these previously idealized individuals. Now that they have dared oppose him, they are judged by him to be stupid, cowardly, lacking in ambition, skills and talents, common (the worst expletive in the narcissist's vocabulary), with an unspectacular career ahead of them.

The narcissist feels that he is misallocating his scarce and invaluable resources (for instance, his time). He feels besieged and suffocated. He rebels and erupts in a serious of self-defeating and self-destructive behaviours, which lead to the disintegration of his life.

Doomed to build and to ruin, attach and detach, appreciate and depreciate, the narcissist is predictable in his "death wish". What sets him apart from other suicidal types is that his wish is granted to him in small, tormenting doses throughout his anguished life.

## Custody and Visitation

A parent diagnosed with full-fledged Narcissistic Personality Disorder (NPD) should be denied custody and should be granted only restricted rights of visitation under supervision.

Narcissists accord the same treatment to children and adults. They regard both as Sources of Narcissistic Supply, mere instruments of gratification: they idealize them at first and then devalue them in favour of alternative, safer and more subservient, sources. Such treatment is traumatic and can have long-lasting emotional effects.

The narcissist's inability to acknowledge and abide by the personal boundaries set by others puts the child at heightened risk of abuse - verbal, emotional, physical, and, often, sexual. His possessiveness and panoply of indiscriminate negative emotions - transformations of aggression, such as rage and envy - hinder the narcissist's ability to act as a "good enough" parent. His propensities for reckless behaviours, substance abuse, and sexual deviance endanger the child's welfare, or even his or her life.

## The Roots of Paedophilia

Paedophiles are attracted to prepubescent children and act on their sexual fantasies. It is a startling fact that the aetiology of this paraphilia is unknown. Paedophiles come from all walks of life and have no common socio-economic background. Contrary to media-propagated myths, most of them had not been sexually abused in childhood and the vast majority of paedophiles are also drawn to adults of the opposite sex (are heterosexuals).

Only a few belong to the Exclusive Type: the ones who are tempted solely by kids. Nine tenths of all paedophiles are male. They are fascinated by preteen females, teenage males, or (more rarely) both.

Moreover, at least one fifth (and probably more) of the population have paedophiliac fantasies. The prevalence of child pornography and child prostitution prove it. Paedophiles start out as "normal" people and are profoundly shocked and distressed to discover their illicit sexual preference for the pre-pubertal. The process and mechanisms of transition from socially acceptable sexuality to much-condemned (and criminal) paedophilia are still largely mysterious.

Paedophiles seem to have narcissistic and antisocial (psychopathic) traits. They lack empathy for their victims and express no remorse for their actions. They are in denial and, being pathological confabulators, they rationalize their transgressions, claiming that the children were merely being educated for their own good and, anyhow, derived great pleasure from it.

The paedophile's ego-syntony rests on his alloplastic defences. He generally tends to blame others (or the world or the "system") for his misfortunes, failures, and deficiencies. Paedophiles frequently accuse their victims of acting promiscuously, of "coming on to them", of actively tempting, provoking, and luring (or even trapping) them.

The paedophile - similar to the autistic patient - misinterprets the child's body language and inter-personal cues. His social communication skills are impaired and he fails to adjust information gained to the surrounding circumstances (for instance, to the kid's age and maturity).

Coupled with his lack of empathy, this recurrent inability to truly comprehend others causes the paedophile to objectify the targets of his lasciviousness. Paedophilia is, in essence, auto-erotic. The paedophile uses children's bodies to masturbate with. Hence the success of the Internet among paedophiles: it offers disembodied, anonymous, masturbatory sex. Children in cyberspace are mere representations - often nothing more than erotic photos and screen names.

It is crucial to realize that paedophiles are not enticed by the children themselves, by their bodies, or by their budding and nubile sexuality (remember Nabokov's Lolita?). Rather, paedophiles are drawn to what children symbolize, to what preadolescents stand for and represent.

To the paedophile...

### Sex with Children is "Free" and "Daring"

Sex with sub-teens implies freedom of action with impunity. It enhances the paedophile's magical sense of omnipotence and immunity. By defying the authority of the state and the edicts of his culture and society, the paedophile experiences an adrenaline rush to which he gradually becomes addicted. Illicit sex becomes the outlet for his urgent need to live dangerously and recklessly.

The paedophile is on a quest to reassert control over his life. Studies have consistently shown that paedophilia is associated with anomic states (war, famine, epidemics) and with major life crises (failure, relocation, infidelity of spouse, separation, divorce, unemployment, bankruptcy, illness, death of the offender's nearest and dearest). It is likely – though hitherto unsubstantiated by research – that the typical paedophile is depressive and with a borderline personality (low organization and fuzzy personal boundaries). Paedophiles are reckless and emotionally labile. The paedophile's sense of self-worth is volatile and dysregulated. He is likely to suffer from abandonment anxiety and be a co-dependent or counter-dependent.

Paradoxically, it is by seemingly losing control in one aspect of his life (sex) that the paedophile re-acquires a sense of mastery. The same mechanism is at work in the development of eating disorders. An inhibitory deficit is somehow magically perceived as omnipotence.

### Sex with Children is Corrupt and Decadent

The paedophile makes frequent (though unconscious) use of projection and Projective Identification in his relationships with children. He makes his victims treat him the way he views himself – or attributes to them traits and behaviours that are truly his.

The paedophile is aware of society's view of his actions as vile, corrupt, forbidden, evil, and decadent (especially if the paedophiliac act involves incest). He derives pleasure from the sleazy nature of his pursuits because it tends to sustain his view of himself as "bad", "a failure", "deserving of punishment", and "guilty".

In extreme (mercifully uncommon) cases, the paedophile projects these torturous feelings and self-perceptions onto his victims. The children defiled and abused by his sexual attentions thus become "rotten", "bad objects", guilty and punishable. This leads to sexual sadism, lust rape, and snuff murders.

### Sex with Children is a Re-Enactment of a Painful Past

Many paedophile truly bond with their prey. To them, children are the reification of innocence, genuineness, trust, and faithfulness – qualities that the paedophile wishes to nostalgically recapture.

The relationship with the child provides the paedophile with a "safe passage" to his own, repressed and fearful, inner child. Through his victim, the paedophile gains access to his suppressed and thwarted emotions. It is a fantasy-like second chance to re-enact his childhood, this time benignly. The paedophile's dream to make peace with his past comes true transforming the interaction with the child to an exercise in wish fulfilment.

### Sex with Children is a Shared Psychosis

The paedophile treats "his" chosen child as an object, an extension of himself, devoid of a separate existence and denuded of distinct needs. He finds the child's submissiveness and gullibility gratifying. He frowns on any sign of personal autonomy and regards it as a threat. By intimidating, cajoling, charming, and making false promises, the abuser isolates his prey from his family, school, peers, and from the rest of society and, thus, makes the child's dependence on him total.

To the paedophile, the child is a "transitional object" – a training ground on which to exercise his adult relationship skills. The paedophile erroneously feels that the child will never betray and abandon him, therefore guaranteeing "object constancy".

The paedophile – stealthily but unfailingly – exploits the vulnerabilities in the psychological makeup of his victim. The child may have low self-esteem, a fluctuating sense of self-worth, primitive defence mechanisms, phobias, mental health problems, a disability, a history of failure, bad relations with parents, siblings, teachers, or peers, or a tendency to blame herself, or to feel inadequate (autoplastic neurosis). The kid may come from an abusive family or environment – which conditioned her or him to expect abuse as inevitable and "normal". In extreme and rare cases the victim is a masochist, possessed of an urge to seek ill-treatment and pain.

The paedophile is the guru at the centre of a cult. Like other gurus, he demands complete obedience from his "partner". He feels entitled to adulation and special treatment by his child-mate. He punishes the wayward and the straying lambs. He enforces discipline.

The child finds himself in a twilight zone. The paedophile imposes on him a shared psychosis, replete with persecutory delusions, "enemies", mythical narratives, and apocalyptic scenarios if he is flouted. The child is rendered the joint guardian of a horrible secret.

The paedophile's control is based on ambiguity, unpredictability, fuzziness, and ambient abuse. His ever-shifting whims exclusively define right versus wrong, desirable and unwanted, what is to be pursued and what to be avoided. He alone determines rights and obligations and alters them at will.

The typical paedophile is a micro-manager. He exerts control over the minutest details and behaviours. He punishes severely and abuses withholders of information and those who fail to conform to his wishes and goals.

The paedophile does not respect the boundaries and privacy of the (often reluctant and terrified) child. He ignores his or her wishes and treats children as objects or instruments of gratification. He seeks to control both situations and people compulsively.

The paedophile acts in a patronizing and condescending manner and criticises often. He alternates between emphasizing the minutest faults (devaluation) and exaggerating the looks, talents, traits, and skills (idealization) of the child. He is wildly unrealistic in his expectations – which legitimizes his subsequent abusive conduct when he is inevitably disappointed or frustrated.

Narcissistic paedophiles claim to be infallible, superior, talented, skilful, omnipotent, and omniscient. They often lie and confabulate to support these unfounded claims and to justify their actions. Most paedophiles suffer from cognitive deficits and reinterpret reality to fit their fantasies.

In extreme cases, the paedophile feels above the law – any kind of law. This grandiose and haughty conviction leads to criminal acts, incestuous or polygamous relationships, and recurrent friction with the authorities.

### The Paedophile Regards Sex with Children as an Ego-Booster

Sub-teen children are, by definition, "inferior". They are physically weaker, dependent on others for the fulfilment of many of their needs, cognitively and emotionally immature, and easily manipulated. Their fund of knowledge is limited and their skills restricted. His relationships with children buttress the paedophile's twin grandiose delusions of omnipotence and omniscience. Compared to his victims, the paedophiles is always the stronger, the wiser, the most skilful and well-informed.

### Sex with Children Guarantees Companionship

Inevitably, the paedophile considers his child-victims to be his best friends and companions. Paedophiles are lonely, erotomanic, people.

The paedophile believes that he is in love with (or simply loves) the child. Sex is merely one way to communicate his affection and caring. But there are other venues.

To show his keen interest, the common paedophile keeps calling the child, dropping by, writing e-mails, giving gifts, providing services, doing unsolicited errands "on the kid's behalf", getting into relationships with the preteen's parents, friends, teachers, and peers, and, in general, making himself available (stalking) at all times. The paedophile feels free to make legal, financial, and emotional decisions for the child.

The paedophile intrudes on the victim's privacy, disrespects the child's express wishes and personal boundaries and ignores his or her emotions, needs, and preferences. To the paedophile, "love" means enmeshment and clinging coupled with an overpowering separation anxiety (fear of being abandoned).

Moreover, no amount of denials, chastising, threats, and even outright hostile actions convince the erotomaniac that the child is not in love with him. He knows better and will make the world see the light as well. The child and his guardians are simply unaware of what is good for the kid. The paedophile determinedly sees it as his task to bring life and happiness into the child's dreary and unhappy existence.

Thus, regardless of overwhelming evidence to the contrary, the paedophile is convinced that his feelings are reciprocated – in other words, that the child is equally infatuated with him or her. He interprets everything the child does (or refrains from doing) as coded messages confessing to and conveying the child's interest in and eternal devotion to the paedophile and to the "relationship".

Some (by no means all) paedophiles are socially-inapt, awkward, schizoid, and suffer from a host of mood and anxiety disorders. They may also be legitimately involved with the child (e.g., stepfather, former spouse, teacher, gym instructor, sibling) – or with his parents (for instance, a former boyfriend, a one night stand, colleagues or co-workers). They are driven by their all-consuming loneliness and all-pervasive fantasies.

Consequently, paedophiles react badly to any perceived rejection by their victims. They turn on a dime and become dangerously vindictive, out to destroy the source of their mounting frustration. When the "relationship" looks hopeless, some paedophiles violently embark on a spree of self-destruction or criminal acts, such as kidnapping and worse.

Paedophilia is to some extent a culture-bound syndrome, defined as it is by the chronological age of the child involved. Ephebophilia, for instance – the exclusive sexual infatuation with teenagers – is not considered to be a form of paedophilia (or even paraphilia).

In some cultures, societies and countries (Afghanistan, for instance) the age of consent is as low as 12. The marriageable age in Britain until the end of the nineteenth century was 10. Paedophilia is a common and socially-condoned practice in certain tribal societies and isolated communities (the Island of Pitcairn).

It would, therefore, be wise to redefine paedophilia as an attraction to or sexual acts with prepubescent children or with people of the equivalent mental age (e.g., retarded) in contravention of socially, legally, and culturally accepted practices.

Return

# Narcissists, Sex and Fidelity

## The Somatic and the Cerebral Narcissist

*Question:* Are narcissists mostly hyperactive or hypoactive sexually and to what extent are they likely to be unfaithful in marriage?

*Answer:* Broadly speaking, there are two types of narcissists, loosely corresponding to the two categories mentioned in the question.

Sex, to the narcissist, is an instrument designed to increase the number of Sources of Narcissistic Supply. If it happens to be the most efficient weapon in the narcissist's arsenal, he makes profligate use of it. In other words: if the narcissist cannot obtain adoration, admiration, approval, applause, or any other kind of attention by other means (e.g., intellectually), he resorts to sex.

He then becomes a satyr (or a nymphomaniac) and indiscriminately engages in sex with multiple partners. His sex partners are considered by him to be objects – Sources of Narcissistic Supply. It is through the processes of successful seduction and sexual conquest that the narcissist derives his badly needed narcissistic "fix".

The narcissist is likely to perfect his techniques of courting and regard his sexual exploits as a form of art. He usually discloses this side of him – in great detail – to others, to an audience, expecting to win their approval and admiration. Because the Narcissistic Supply in his case is in the very act of conquest and (what he perceives to be) subordination, the narcissist is forced to hop from one partner to another.

Some narcissists prefer "complicated" situations. If men – they prefer virgins, married women, frigid or lesbian women, etc. The more "difficult" the target, the more rewarding the narcissistic outcome. Such a narcissist may be married, but he does not regard his extra-marital affairs as either immoral or a breach of any explicit or implicit contract between him and his spouse.

He keeps explaining to anyone who cares to listen that his other sexual partners are nothing to him, meaningless, that he is merely taking advantage of them and that they do not constitute a threat to his great marriage and should not be taken seriously by his spouse. In his mind a clear separation exists between the honest "woman of his life" (really, a Madonna-saint) and the "whores" that he is having sex with.

With the exception of the meaningful women in his life, he tends to view all females in a bad light. His behaviour, thus, achieves a dual purpose: securing Narcissistic Supply, on the one hand and re-enacting old, unresolved conflicts and traumas (abandonment by Primary Objects and the Oedipal Conflict, for instance).

When inevitably abandoned by his spouse, the narcissist is veritably shocked and hurt. This is the sort of crisis, which might drive him to psychotherapy. Still, deep inside, he feels compelled to continue to pursue precisely the same path. His abandonment is cathartic, purifying. Following a period of deep depression and suicidal ideation, the narcissist is likely to feel cleansed, invigorated, unshackled, ready for the next round of hunting.

But there is another type of narcissist. The cerebral narcissist also has bouts of sexual hyperactivity in which he trades sexual partners and tends to regard them as objects. However, with him, this is a secondary behaviour. It appears mainly after major narcissistic traumas and crises.

A painful divorce, a devastating and disgraceful personal or financial upheaval – and this type of narcissist adopts the view that the "old" (intellectual) solutions do not work anymore. He frantically gropes and searches for new ways to attract attention, to restore his False Self (his grandiosity) and to secure a subsistence level of Narcissistic Supply.

Sex is handy and is a great source of the right kind of supply: it is immediate, sexual partners are interchangeable, the solution is comprehensive (it encompasses all the aspects of the narcissist's being), natural, highly charged, adventurous, and pleasurable. Thus, following a life crisis, the cerebral narcissist is likely to be deeply immersed in sexual activities, very frequently and almost to the exclusion of all other matters.

However, as the memories of the crisis fade, as the narcissistic wounds heal, as the Narcissistic Cycle re-commences and the balance is restored, this second type of narcissist reveals his true colours. He abruptly loses interest in sex and in all his sexual partners. The frequency of his sexual activities deteriorates from a few times a day to a few times a year. He reverts to intellectual pursuits, sports, politics, voluntary activities – anything but sex.

This kind of narcissist is afraid of encounters with the opposite sex and is even more afraid of emotional involvement or commitment that he fancies himself prone to develop following a sexual encounter. In general, such a narcissist withdraws not only sexually, but also emotionally. If married – he loses all overt interest in his spouse, sexual or otherwise. He confines himself to his world and makes sure that he is sufficiently busy to preclude any interaction with his nearest (and supposedly dearest).

He becomes completely entangled in "big projects", lifelong plans, a vision, or a cause – all very rewarding narcissistically and all very demanding and time consuming. In such circumstances, sex inevitably becomes an obligation, a necessity, or a maintenance chore reluctantly undertaken to preserve his Sources of Supply (e.g., his marriage).

The cerebral narcissist does not enjoy sex and by far prefers masturbation or "objective", emotionless sex, like going to prostitutes. Actually, he uses his mate or spouse as an "alibi", a shield against the attentions of other women, an insurance policy which preserves his virile image while making it socially and morally commendable for him to avoid any intimate or sexual contact with others.

Ostentatiously ignoring women other than his wife (a form of aggression) he feels righteous in saying: "I am a faithful husband". At the same time, he feels hostility towards his spouse for ostensibly preventing him from freely expressing his sexuality, for depriving him of carnal pleasures he could have had with others.

The narcissist's inner dialog goes something like this: "I am married/attached to this woman. Therefore, I am not allowed to be in any form of contact with other women which might be interpreted as more than casual or businesslike. This is why I refrain from having anything to do with women – because I am being faithful, as opposed to immoral men. However, I do not like this situation. I envy my free peers. They can have as much sex and romance as they want to, while I am confined to this marriage, chained by my wife, my freedom curbed. I am angry at her and I will punish her by abstaining from having sex with her."

Thus frustrated, the narcissist minimizes all manner of intercourse with his close circle (spouse, children, parents, siblings, very intimate friends): sexual, verbal, or emotional. He limits himself to the rawest exchanges of information and isolates himself socially.

His reclusion insures against a future hurt and skirts the intimacy that he so dreads. But, again, this way he also secures abandonment and the replay of old, unresolved, conflicts. Finally, he really is left alone by everyone, with no Secondary Sources of Supply.

In his quest to find new sources, he again embarks on ego-mending bouts of sex, followed by the selection of a spouse or a mate (a Secondary Narcissistic Supply Source). Then the cycle re-commence: a sharp drop in sexual activity, emotional absence and cruel detachment leading to abandonment.

Most cerebral narcissists, though, are sexually faithful to their spouses. The typical cerebral narcissist alternates between what appears to be hyper-sexuality and asexuality (really, forcefully repressed sexuality). In the second phase, he feels no sexual urges, bar the most basic. He is, therefore, not compelled to "cheat" upon his mate, betray her, or violate the marital vows. He is much more interested in preventing a worrisome dwindling of the kind of Narcissistic Supply that really matters. Sex, he says to himself, contentedly, is for those who can do no better.

Somatic narcissists lean towards verbal exhibitionism. They tend to brag in graphic details about their conquests and exploits. In extreme cases, they might introduce "live witnesses" and revert to total, classical exhibitionism. This sits well with their tendency to "objectify" their sexual partners, to engage in emotionally-neutral sex (group sex, for instance) and to indulge in autoerotic sex.

The exhibitionist sees himself reflected in the eyes of his beholders. This constitutes the main sexual stimulus, this is what turns him on. This outside "look" is also what defines the narcissist. There is bound to be a connection. One (the exhibitionist) may be the culmination, the "pure case" of the other (the narcissist).

Return

# The Extra-Marital Narcissist

*Question:* My husband has a liaison with another woman. He has been diagnosed with Narcissistic Personality Disorder. What should I do?

*Answer:* Narcissists are people who fail to maintain a stable sense of self-worth. Very often somatic narcissists (narcissistic who use their bodies and their sexuality to secure Narcissistic Supply) tend to get involved in extra-marital affairs. The new "conquests" sustain their grandiose fantasies and their distorted and unrealistic self-image.

It is, therefore, nigh impossible to alter this particular behaviour of a somatic narcissist. Sexual interactions serve as a constant, reliable, easy to obtain Source of Narcissistic Supply. It is the only Source of such Supply if the narcissist is not cerebral (does not rely on his intellect, intelligence, or professional achievements for Narcissistic Supply).

You should set up rigid, strict and VERY WELL DEFINED rules of engagement. Ideally, all contacts between your spouse and his lover should be immediately and irrevocably severed. But this is usually too much to ask for. So, you should make crystal clear when is she allowed to call, whether she is allowed to write to him at all and in which circumstances, what are the subjects she is allowed to broach in her correspondence and phone calls, when is he allowed to see her and what other modes of interaction are permissible.

CLEAR AND PAINFUL SANCTIONS in case the above rules are violated must be promulgated. Both rules and sanctions MUST BE APPLIED RIGOROUSLY AND MERCILESSLY and MUST BE SET IN WRITING IN UNEQUIVOCAL TERMS.

The problem is that the narcissist never really separates from his Sources of Narcissistic Supply until and unless they cease to be ones. Narcissists never really say good-bye. His lover is likely to still have an emotional hold on him.

Help him by telling him what will be the price that he stands to pay if he does not obey the rules and sanctions you have agreed on. Tell him that you cannot live like this any longer, that if he does not get rid of this presence – of the echoes of his past, really – he will be squandering his present, he will be forfeiting you. Don't be afraid to lose him. If he prefers this woman to you, it is important for you to know it. If he prefers you to her, your nightmare is over (at least until the next round).

If you insist on staying with him, you must also be prepared to serve as a Source of Narcissistic Supply, an alternative to the supply provided by his former lover. You must brace yourself: serving as a Narcissistic Supply Source is an onerous task, a full time job and a very ungrateful one at that. The narcissist's thirst for adulation, admiration, worship, approval, and attention is unquenchable. It is a Sisyphean, mind-numbing effort, which heralds only additional demands and disgruntled, critical, humiliating tirades by the narcissist.

That you are afraid to confront reality is normal. You are afraid to set clear alternatives and boundaries. You are afraid that he will leave you. You are afraid that he will prefer her to you. AND YOU MAY WELL BE RIGHT. But if this is the case and you go on living with him and tormenting yourself, it is unhealthy.

If you find it difficult to confront the fact that it is all over between you, that your relationship is an empty shell, that your husband is with another woman, do not hesitate to seek help from professionals and non-professionals alike. But do not let this situation fester into psychological gangrene. Amputate now while you can.

Return

# Mourning the Narcissist

*Question:* If the narcissist is as abusive as you say, why do we react so badly when he leaves?

*Answer:* At the commencement of the relationship, the narcissist is a dream-come-true. He is often intelligent, witty, charming, good looking, an achiever, empathetic, in need of love, loving, caring, attentive and much more besides. He is the perfect bundled answer to the nagging questions of life: finding meaning, companionship, compatibility, and happiness. He is, in other words, ideal.

It is difficult to let go of this idealized figure. Relationships with narcissists inevitably and invariably end with the dawn of a double realization. The first is that one has been (ab)used by the narcissist and the second is that one was regarded by the narcissist as a disposable, dispensable and interchangeable instrument (object).

The assimilation of this new gained knowledge is an excruciating process, often unsuccessfully completed. People get fixated at different stages. They fail to come to terms with their rejection as human beings – the most total form of rejection there is.

We all react to loss. Loss makes us feel helpless and objectified. When our loved ones die, we feel that Nature or God or Life treated us as playthings. When we divorce (especially if we did not initiate the break-up), we often feel that we have been exploited and abused in the relationship, that we are being "dumped", that our needs and emotions are ignored. In short, we again feel objectified.

Losing the narcissist is no different to any other major loss in life. It provokes a cycle of bereavement and grief (as well as some kind of mild Post-Traumatic Stress Syndrome in cases of severe abuse). This cycle has four phases: denial, rage, sadness and acceptance.

Denial can assume many forms. Some go on pretending that the narcissist is still a part of their life, even going to the extreme of "interacting" with the narcissist by pretending to "communicate" with him or to "meet" him (through others, for instance). Extreme cases of such denial are known as erotomania.

Others develop persecutory delusions, thus incorporating the narcissist into their life and psyche as an ominous and dark presence, as a "bad object". This ensures "his" continued "interest" in them – however malevolent and threatening that "interest" is perceived to be. These are radical denial mechanisms, which border on the psychotic and often resolve into brief psychotic micro-episodes.

More benign and transient forms of denial include the development of ideas of reference. The narcissist's every move or utterance is interpreted as directed at the suffering person, his ex, and to carry a hidden message which can be "decoded" only by the recipient.

Others deny the very narcissistic nature of the narcissist. They attribute his abusive conduct to ignorance, mischief, lack of self-control (due to childhood abuse or trauma), or benign intentions. This denial mechanism leads them to believe that the narcissist is really not a narcissist at all but someone who is merely not aware of his "true" essence, or someone who innocently enjoys mind games and toying with people's lives, or an unwitting part of a dark conspiracy to defraud and abuse gullible victims.

Often the narcissist is depicted as obsessed or possessed – imprisoned by his "invented" condition and, really, deep inside, a nice and gentle and lovable person.

At the healthier end of the spectrum of denial reactions we find the classical denial of loss: the disbelief, the hope that the narcissist may return, the suspension and repression of all information to the contrary.

Denial in mentally healthy people quickly evolves into rage. There are a few types of rage. Rage can be focussed and directed at the narcissist, at other facilitators of the loss, such as the narcissist's lover, or at specific circumstances. It can be directed at oneself – which often leads to depression, suicidal ideation, self-mutilation and, in some cases, suicide. Or, it can be diffuse, all-pervasive, all-encompassing and engulfing. Such loss-related rage can be intense and in bursts or osmotic and permeate the whole emotional landscape.

Rage gives place to sadness. It is the sadness of the trapped animal, an existential angst mixed with acute depression. It involves dysphoria (inability to rejoice, to be optimistic, or expectant) and anhedonia (inability to experience pleasure or to find meaning in life). It is a paralyzing sensation, which slows one down and enshrouds everything in the grey veil of randomness. Everything suddenly looks meaningless and empty.

This, in turn, gives place to gradual acceptance, renewed energy, and bouts of activity. The narcissist is gone both physically and mentally. The void left in his wake still hurts and pangs of regret and hope still exist. But, on the whole, the narcissist is transformed into a narrative, a symbol, another life experience, or a (tedious) cliché. He is no longer omnipresent and his former victim entertains no delusions as to the one-sided and abusive nature of the relationship or as to the possibility and desirability of its renewal.

Return

# Back to La-la Land

Relationships with narcissists peter out slowly and tortuously. Narcissists do not provide closure. They stalk. They cajole, beg, promise, persuade, and, ultimately, succeed in doing the impossible yet again: sweep you off your feet, though you know better than to succumb to their spurious and superficial charms.

So, you go back to your "relationship" and hope for a better ending. You walk on eggshells. You become the epitome of submissiveness, a perfect Source of Narcissistic Supply, the ideal mate or spouse or partner or colleague. You keep your fingers crossed.

But how does the narcissist react to the resurrection of the bond?

It depends on whether you have re-entered the liaison from a position or strength, or of vulnerability and weakness.

The narcissist casts all interactions with other people in terms of conflicts or competitions to be won. He does not regard you as a partner – but as an adversary to be subjugated and defeated. Thus, as far as he is concerned, your return to the fold is a triumph, proof of his superiority and irresistibility.

If he perceives you as autonomous, dangerously independent, and capable of bailing out and abandoning him – the narcissist acts the part of the sensitive, loving, compassionate, and empathic counterpart. Narcissists respect strength, they are awed by it. As long as you maintain a "no nonsense" attitude, placing the narcissist on probation, he is likely to behave himself.

If, on the other hand, you have resumed contact because you have capitulated to his threats or because you are manifestly dependent on him financially or emotionally – the narcissist will pounce on your frailty and exploit your fragility to the maximum. Following a perfunctory honeymoon, he will immediately seek to control and abuse you.

In both cases, the narcissist's thespian reserves are ultimately exhausted and his true nature and feelings emerge. The facade crumbles and beneath it lurks the same old heartless falsity that is the narcissist. His gleeful smugness at having bent you to his wishes and rules, his all-consuming sense of entitlement, his sexual depravity, his aggression, pathological envy, and rage – all erupt uncontrollably.

The prognosis for the renewed affair is far worse if it follows a lengthy separation in which you have made a life for yourself with your own interests, pursuits, set of friends, needs, wishes, plans, and obligations, independent of your narcissistic ex.

The narcissist cannot countenance your separateness. To him, you are a mere instrument of gratification or an extension of his bloated False Self. He resents your pecuniary wherewithal, is insanely jealous of your friends, refuses to accept your preferences or compromise his own, in envious and dismissive of your accomplishments.

Ultimately, the very fact that you have survived without his constant presence seems to deny him his much-needed Narcissistic Supply. He rides the inevitable cycle of idealization and devaluation. He berates you, humiliates you publicly, threatens you, destabilizes you by behaving unpredictably, fosters ambient abuse, and uses others to intimidate and humble you ("abuse by proxy").

You are then faced with a tough choice:

To leave again and give up all the emotional and financial investments that went into your attempt to resurrect the relationship – or to go on trying, subject to daily abuse and worse?

It is a well-known landscape. You have been here before. But this familiarity doesn't make it less nightmarish.

Return

# Surviving the Narcissist

*Question:* Is there a point in waiting for the narcissist to heal? Can he ever get better?

*Answer:* The victims of the narcissist's abusive conduct resort to fantasies and self-delusions to salve their pain.

### Rescue Fantasies

"It is true that he is a chauvinistic narcissist and that his behaviour is unacceptable and repulsive. But all he needs is a little love and he will be straightened out. I will rescue him from his misery and misfortune. I will give him the love that he lacked as a child. Then his narcissism will vanish and we will live happily ever after."

### Loving a Narcissist

I believe in the possibility of loving the narcissist if one accepts him unconditionally, in a disillusioned and expectation-free manner.

Narcissists are narcissists. Take them or leave them. Some of them are lovable. Most of them are highly charming and intelligent. The source of the misery of the victims of the narcissist is their disappointment, their disillusionment, their abrupt and tearing and tearful realization that they fell in love with an ideal of their own making, a phantasm, an illusion, a fata morgana. This "waking up" is traumatic. The narcissist always remains the same. It is the victim who changes.

It is true that narcissists present a luring facade in order to captivate Sources of Narcissistic Supply. But this facade is easy to penetrate because it is inconsistent and too perfect. The cracks are evident from day one but often ignored. Then there are those who KNOWINGLY and WILLINGLY commit their emotional wings to the burning narcissistic candle.

This is the catch-22. To try to communicate emotions to a narcissist is like discussing atheism with a religious fundamentalist.

Narcissists have emotions, very strong ones, so terrifyingly overpowering and negative that they hide them, repress, block and transmute them. They employ myriad defence mechanisms to cope with their repressed emotions: Projective Identification, splitting, projection, intellectualization, rationalization.

Any effort to relate to the narcissist emotionally is doomed to failure, alienation and rage. Any attempt to "understand" (in retrospect or prospectively) narcissistic behaviour patterns, reactions, or the narcissist's inner world in emotional terms is equally hopeless. Narcissists should be regarded as a force of nature or an accident waiting to happen.

The Universe has no master-plot or mega-plan to deprive anyone of happiness. Being born to narcissistic parents, for instance, is not the result of a conspiracy. It is a tragic event, for sure. But it cannot be dealt with emotionally, without professional help, or haphazardly. Stay away from narcissists, or face them aided by your own self-discovery through therapy. It can be done.

Narcissists have no interest in emotional or even intellectual stimulation by significant others. Such feedback is perceived as a threat. Significant others in the narcissist's life have very clear roles: the accumulation and dispensation of past Primary Narcissistic Supply in order to regulate current Narcissistic Supply. Nothing less but definitely nothing more. Proximity and intimacy breed contempt. A process of devaluation is in full operation throughout the life of the relationship.

A passive witness to the narcissist's past accomplishments, a dispenser of accumulated Narcissistic Supply, a punching bag for his rages, a co-dependent, a possession (though not prized but taken for granted) and nothing much more. This is the ungrateful, FULL TIME, draining job of being the narcissist's significant other.

But people are not instruments. To regard them as such is to devalue them, to reduce them, to restrict them, to prevent them from realizing their potential. Inevitably, narcissists lose interest in their instruments, these truncated versions of full-fledged humans, once they cease to serve them in their pursuit of glory and fame.

Consider "friendship" with a narcissist as an example of such thwarted relationships. One cannot really get to know a narcissist "friend". One cannot be friends with a narcissist and one cannot love a narcissist. Narcissists are addicts. They are no different to drug addicts. They are in pursuit of gratification through the drug known as Narcissistic Supply. Everything and EVERYONE around them is an object, a potential source (to be idealized) or not (and, then to be cruelly discarded).

Narcissists home in on potential suppliers like cruise missiles. They are excellent at imitating emotions, at exhibiting the right behaviours on cue, and at manipulating.

All generalizations are false, of course, and there are bound to be some happy relationships with narcissists [I discuss the narcissistic couple in The Double Reflection]. One example of a happy marriage is when a somatic narcissist teams up with a cerebral one or vice versa.

Narcissists can be happily married to submissive, subservient, self-deprecating, echoing, mirroring and indiscriminately supportive spouses. They also do well with masochists. But it is difficult to imagine that a healthy, normal person would be happy in such a folie-a-deux ("madness in twosome" or shared psychosis).

It is also difficult to imagine a benign and sustained influence on the narcissist of a stable, healthy mate/spouse/partner. [I dedicated to this issue The Narcissist's Spouse/Mate/Partner]

BUT many a spouse/friend/mate/partner like to BELIEVE that, given sufficient time and patience, they will be the ones to rid the narcissist of his inner demons. They think that they can "rescue" the narcissist, shield him from his (distorted) self, as it were.

The narcissist makes use of this naiveté and exploits it to his benefit. The natural protective mechanisms, which are provoked in normal people by love are cold bloodedly used by the narcissist to extract yet more Narcissistic Supply from his writhing victim.

The narcissist affects his victims by infiltrating their psyches, by penetrating their defences. Like a virus, it establishes a new genetic strain within his/her victims. It echoes through them, it talks through them, it walks through them. It is like the invasion of the body snatchers.

You should be careful to separate your self from the narcissist's seed inside you, this alien growth, this spiritual cancer that is the result of living with a narcissist. You should be able to tell apart the real you and the parts assigned to you by the narcissist. To cope with him/her, the narcissist forces you to "walk on eggshells" and develop a False Self of your own. It is nothing as elaborate as his False Self, but it is there, in you, as a result of the trauma and abuse inflicted upon you by the narcissist.

Thus, perhaps we should talk about VoNPD, another mental health diagnostic category: Victims of NPD.

They experience shame and anger at their past helplessness and submissiveness. They are hurt and sensitized by the harrowing experience of sharing a simulated existence with a simulated person, the narcissist. They are scarred and often suffer from Post-Traumatic Stress Disorder (PTSD). Some of them lash out at others, offsetting their frustration with bitter aggression.

Like his disorder, the narcissist is all-pervasive. Being the victim of a narcissist is a condition no less pernicious than being a narcissist. Great mental efforts are required to abandon a narcissist and physical separation is only the first (and least important) step.

One can abandon a narcissist – but the narcissist is slow to abandon his victims. He is there, lurking, rendering existence unreal, twisting and distorting with no respite, an inner, remorseless voice, lacking in compassion and empathy for its victim.

The narcissist is there in spirit long after he had vanished in the flesh. This is the real danger that the victims of the narcissist face: that they become like him, bitter, self-centred, lacking in empathy. This is the last bow of the narcissist, his curtain call, by proxy as it were.

## Narcissistic Tactics

The narcissist tends to surround himself with his inferiors (in some respect: intellectually, financially, physically). He limits his interactions with them to the plane of his superiority. This is the safest and fastest way to sustain his grandiose fantasies of omnipotence and omniscience, brilliance, ideal traits, perfection and so on.

People are interchangeable and the narcissist does not distinguish one individual from another. To him they are all inanimate elements of "his audience" whose job is to reflect his False Self. This generates a perpetual and permanent cognitive dissonance:

The narcissist despises the very people who sustain his ego boundaries and functions. He cannot respect people so expressly and clearly inferior to him – yet he can never associate with people evidently on his level or superior to him, the risk of narcissistic injury in such associations being too great. Equipped with a fragile Ego, precariously teetering on the brink of narcissistic injury, the narcissist prefers the safe route. But he feels contempt for himself and for others for having preferred it.

Some narcissists are also psychopaths (suffer from the Antisocial Personality Disorder) and/or sadists. Antisocials don't really enjoy hurting others – they simply don't care one way or the other. But sadists do enjoy it.

Classical narcissists do not enjoy wounding others – but they do enjoy the sensation of unlimited power and the validation of their grandiose fantasies when they do harm others or are in the position to do so. It is more the POTENTIAL to hurt others than the actual act that turns them on.

### The Never-Ending Story

Even the official termination of a relationship with a narcissist is not the end of the affair. The ex "belongs" to the narcissist. She is an inseparable part of his Pathological Narcissistic Space. This possessive streak survives the physical separation.

Thus, the narcissist is likely to respond with rage, seething envy, a sense of humiliation and invasion and violent-aggressive urges to an ex's new boyfriend, or new job (to her new life without him). Especially since it implies a "failure" on his part and, thus negates his grandiosity.

But there is a second scenario:

If the narcissist firmly believes (which is very rare) that the ex does not and will never represent any amount, however marginal and residual, of any kind (Primary or Secondary) of Narcissistic Supply, he remains utterly unmoved by anything she does and anyone she may choose to be with.

Narcissists do feel bad about hurting others and about the unsavoury course their lives tend to assume. Their underlying (and subconscious) ego-dystony (feeling bad about themselves) was only recently discovered and described. But the narcissist feels bad only when his Supply Sources are threatened because of his behaviour or following a narcissistic injury in the course of a major life crisis.

The narcissist equates emotions with weakness. He regards the sentimental and the emotional with contempt. He looks down on the sensitive and the vulnerable. He derides and despises the dependent and the loving. He mocks expressions of compassion and passion. He is devoid of empathy. He is so afraid of his True Self that he would rather disparage it than admit to his own faults and "soft spots".

He likes to talk about himself in mechanical terms ("machine", "efficient", "punctual", "output", "computer"). He suppresses his human side diligently and with dedication. To him being human and survival are mutually exclusive propositions. He must choose and his choice is clear. The narcissist never looks back, unless and until forced to by life's circumstances.

All narcissists fear intimacy. But the cerebral narcissist deploys strong defences against it: "scientific detachment" (the narcissist as the eternal observer), intellectualizing and rationalizing his emotions away, intellectual cruelty [see FAQ regarding inappropriate affect], intellectual "annexation" (he regards others as his extension, property, or turf), objectifying the other, and so on. Even emotions that he does express (pathological envy, rage) have the not wholly unintended effect of alienating rather than creating intimacy.

## Abandoning the Narcissist

The narcissist initiates his own abandonment because of his fear of it. He is so terrified of losing his Sources of Narcissistic Supply (and of being emotionally hurt) that he would rather "control", "master", or "direct" the potentially destabilizing situation. Remember: the personality of the narcissist has a low level of organization. It is precariously balanced.

Being abandoned could cause a narcissistic injury so grave that the whole edifice can come crumbling down. Narcissists usually entertain suicidal ideation in such cases. But, if the narcissist had initiated and directed his own abandonment, if it is perceived as a goal he had set to himself – he can and does avoid all these untoward consequences.

[See the section about Emotional Involvement Prevention Mechanisms in the Essay]

## The Dynamics of the Relationship

The narcissist lives in a fantasized world of ideal beauty, incomparable (imaginary) achievements, wealth, brilliance and unmitigated success. The narcissist denies his reality constantly. This is what I call the Grandiosity Gap: the abyss between his sense of entitlement grounded in his inflated grandiose fantasies – and his incommensurate reality and meagre accomplishments.

The narcissist's partner is perceived by him to be merely a Source of Narcissistic Supply, an instrument, an extension of himself. It is inconceivable that – blessed by the constant presence of the narcissist – such a tool would malfunction. The needs and grievances of the partner are perceived by the narcissist as threats and slights.

The narcissist considers his very presence in the relationship as nourishing and sustaining. He feels entitled to the best others can offer without investing in maintaining his relationships or in catering to the well-being of his "suppliers".

To rid himself of deep-set feelings of (rather justified) guilt and shame, he pathologizes the partner. He projects his own mental illness unto her. Through the intricate mechanism of Projective Identification he forces her to play an emergent role of "the sick" or "the weak" or "the naive" or "the dumb" or "the no good". What he denies in himself, what he is loath to face in his own personality, he attributes to others and moulds them to conform to his prejudices against himself.

The narcissist must have the best, the most glamorous, stunning, talented, head turning, mind-boggling spouse in the entire world. Nothing short of this fantasy will do. To compensate for the shortcomings of his real life spouse, he invents an idealized figure and relates to it instead.

Then, when reality conflicts too often and too evidently with this figment, he reverts to devaluation. His behaviour turns on a dime and becomes threatening, demeaning, contemptuous, berating, reprimanding, destructively critical and sadistic – or cold, unloving, detached, and "clinical". He punishes his real life spouse for not living up to his fantasy, for "refusing" to be his Galathea, his Pygmalion, his ideal creation. The narcissist then plays a wrathful and demanding God.

## Moving On

To preserve one's mental health – one must abandon the narcissist. One must move on.

Moving on is a process, not a decision or an event. First, one has to acknowledge and accept painful reality. Such acceptance is a volcanic, shattering, agonizing series of nibbling thoughts and strong resistances. Once the battle is won, and harsh and agonizing realities are assimilated, one can move on to the learning phase.

## Learning

We label. We educate ourselves. We compare experiences. We digest. We have insights.

Then we decide and we act. This is "to move on". Having gathered sufficient emotional sustenance, knowledge, support and confidence, we face the battlefields of our relationships, fortified and nurtured. This stage characterizes those who do not mourn – but fight; do not grieve – but replenish their self-esteem; do not hide – but seek; do not freeze – but move on.

## Grieving

Having been betrayed and abused, we grieve. We grieve for the image we had of the traitor and abuser – the image that was so fleeting and so wrong, yet so dear to us. We mourn the damage. We experience the fear of never being able to love or to trust again – and we grieve this loss, too. At one stroke, we lost someone we trusted and even loved, we lost our trusting and loving selves and we lost the trust and love that we felt. Can anything be worse?

The emotional process of grieving has many phases.

At first, we are dumbfounded, shocked, inert, immobile. We play dead to avoid our inner monsters. We are ossified in our pain, cast in the mould of our reticence and fears. Then we feel enraged, indignant, rebellious and hateful. Then we accept. Then we cry. And then – some of us – learn to forgive and to pity. And this is called healing.

All stages are absolutely necessary and good for you. It is bad not to rage back, not to shame those who shamed us, to deny, to pretend, to evade. But it is equally bad to get fixated on our rage. Permanent grieving is the perpetuation of our abuse by other means.

By endlessly recreating our harrowing experiences, we unwillingly collaborate with our abuser to perpetuate his or her evil deeds. It is by moving on that we defeat our abuser, minimizing him and his importance in our lives. It is by loving and by trusting anew that we annul that which was done to us. To forgive is never to forget. But to remember is not necessarily to re-experience.

## Forgiving and Forgetting

Forgiving is an important capability. It does more for the forgiver than for the forgiven. But it should not be a universal, indiscriminate behaviour. It is legitimate not to forgive sometimes. It depends, of course, on the severity or duration of what was done to you.

In general, it is unwise and counterproductive to apply to life "universal" and "immutable" principles. Life is too chaotic to succumb to rigid edicts. Sentences which start with "never" or "always" are not very credible and often lead to self-defeating, self-restricting and self-destructive behaviours.

Conflicts are an important and integral part of life. One should never seek them out, but when confronted with a conflict, one should not avoid it. It is through conflicts and adversity as much as through care and love that we grow.

Human relationships are dynamic. We must assess our friendships, partnerships, even our marriages periodically. In and by itself, a common past is insufficient to sustain a healthy, nourishing, supportive, caring and compassionate relationship. Common memories are a necessary but not a sufficient condition. We must gain and regain our friendships on a daily basis. Human relationships are a constant test of allegiance and empathy.

## Remaining Friends with the Narcissist

Can't we act civilized and remain on friendly terms with our narcissist ex?

Never forget that narcissists (full fledged ones) are nice and friendly only when:

a. They want something from you – Narcissistic Supply, help, support, votes, money... They prepare the ground, manipulate you and then come out with the "small favour" they need or ask you blatantly or surreptitiously for Narcissistic Supply ("What did you think about my performance...", "Do you think that I really deserve the Nobel Prize?");

b. They feel threatened and they want to neuter the threat by smothering it with oozing pleasantries;

c. They have just been infused with an overdose of Narcissistic Supply and they feel magnanimous and magnificent and ideal and perfect. To show magnanimity is a way of flaunting one's impeccable divine credentials. It is an act of grandiosity. You are an irrelevant prop in this spectacle, a mere receptacle of the narcissist's overflowing, self-contented infatuation with his False Self.

This beneficence is transient. Perpetual victims often tend to thank the narcissist for "little graces". This is the Stockholm Syndrome: hostages tend to emotionally identify with their captors rather than with the police. We are grateful to our abusers and tormentors for ceasing their hideous activities and allowing us to catch our breath.

Some people say that they prefer to live with narcissists, to cater to their needs and to succumb to their whims because this is the way they have been conditioned in early childhood. It is only with narcissists that they feel alive, stimulated and excited. The world glows in Technicolor in the presence of a narcissist and decays to sepia colours in his absence.

I see nothing inherently "wrong" with that. The test is this: if someone were to constantly humiliate and abuse you verbally using Archaic Chinese, would you have felt humiliated and abused? Probably not. Some people have been conditioned by the narcissistic Primary Objects in their lives (parents or caregivers) to treat narcissistic abuse as Archaic Chinese, to turn a deaf ear.

This technique is effective in that it allows the inverted narcissist (the narcissist's willing mate) to experience only the good aspects of living with a narcissist: his sparkling intelligence, the constant drama and excitement, the lack of intimacy and emotional attachment (some people prefer this). Every now and then the narcissist breaks into abuse in Archaic Chinese. So what, who understands Archaic Chinese anyway, says the inverted narcissist to herself.

I have only one nagging doubt, though:

If the relationship with a narcissist is so rewarding, why are inverted narcissists so unhappy, so ego-dystonic, so in need of help (professional or otherwise)? Aren't they victims who are simply experiencing the Stockholm Syndrome (Trauma Bonding, identifying with the kidnapper rather than with the Police) and who are then in denial of their own torment?

## Narcissists and Abandonment

Narcissists are terrified of being abandoned exactly as are co-dependents and borderlines.

But their solution is different.

Co-dependents cling. Borderlines are emotionally labile and react disastrously to the faintest hint of being abandoned.

Narcissists facilitate their own abandonment. They make sure that they are abandoned.

This way they achieve two goals:

1. Getting it over with – The narcissist has a very low threshold of tolerance to uncertainty and inconvenience, emotional or material. Narcissists are very impatient and "spoiled". They cannot delay gratification or impending doom. They must have it all now, good or bad.

2. By bringing the feared abandonment about, the narcissist can lie to himself persuasively. "She didn't abandon me, it is I who abandoned her. I controlled the situation. It was all my doing, so I was really not abandoned, was I now?" In time, the narcissist adopts this "official version" as the truth. He might say: "I abandoned her emotionally and sexually long before she left."

[This is one of the important <u>Emotional Involvement Prevention Mechanisms (EIPM)</u> that I write about in the Essay]

**Why the Failing Relationships?**

Narcissists hate happiness and joy and ebullience and vivaciousness – in short, they hate life itself.

The roots of this bizarre propensity can be traced to a few psychological dynamics, which operate concurrently (it is very confusing to be a narcissist).

First, there is pathological envy.

The narcissist is constantly envious of other people: their successes, their property, their character, their education, their children, their ideas, the fact that they are capable of feeling, their good moods, their past, their future, their present, their spouses, their mistresses or lovers, their location...

Almost anything can be the trigger of a bout of biting, acidulous envy. But there is nothing, which reminds the narcissist more of the totality of his envious experiences than happiness. Narcissists lash out at happy people out of their own nagging sense of deprivation.

Then there is narcissistic hurt.

The narcissist regards himself as the centre of the world and the epicentre of the lives of his closest, nearest and dearest. He is the source of all emotions, responsible for all developments, positive and negative alike, the axis, the prime cause, the only cause, the mover, the shaker, the broker, the pillar, forever indispensable.

It is therefore a bitter and sharp rebuke to this grandiose fantasy to see someone else happy for reasons that have nothing to do with the narcissist. It painfully serves to illustrate to him that he is but one of many causes, phenomena, triggers and catalysts in other people's lives; that there are things happening outside the orbit of his control or initiative; that he is not privileged or unique.

The narcissist uses Projective Identification. He channels his negative emotions through other people, his proxies. He induces unhappiness and gloom in others to enable him to experience his own misery. Inevitably, he attributes the source of such sadness either to himself, as its cause – or to the "pathology" of the sad person.

"You are constantly depressed, you should really see a therapist", is a common advice he doles out.

The narcissist – in an effort to maintain the depressive state until it serves some cathartic purpose – strives to perpetuate it by constantly reminding the depressed person of its existence. "You look sad/bad/pale today. Is anything wrong? Can I help you? Things haven't been going so well lately?"

Last but not least is the exaggerated fear of losing control.

The narcissist feels that he controls his human environment mostly by manipulation and mainly by emotional extortion and distortion. This is not far from reality. The narcissist suppresses any sign of emotional autonomy. He feels threatened and belittled by an emotion not directly or indirectly fostered by him or by his actions. Counteracting someone else's happiness is the narcissist's way of reminding everyone: "I am here, I am omnipotent, you are at my mercy and you will feel happy only when I tell you to."

### Living with a Narcissist

You cannot change people, at least not in the real, profound, deep sense. You can only adapt to them and adapt them to you. If you do find your narcissist rewarding at times – you should consider doing these:

1. Determine your limits and boundaries. How much and in which ways can you adapt to him (i.e., accept him AS HE IS) and to which extent and in which ways would you like him to adapt to you (i.e., accept you as you are). Act accordingly. Accept what you have decided to accept and reject the rest. Change in you what you are willing and able to change – and ignore the rest. Conclude an unwritten contract of co-existence (could be written if you are more formally inclined).

2. Try to maximize the number of times that "...his walls are down", that you "...find him totally fascinating and everything I desire". What makes him be and behave this way? Is it something that you say or do? Is it preceded by events of a specific nature? Is there anything you can do to make him behave this way more often?

Remember, though:

Sometimes we mistake guilt and self-assumed blame for love.

Committing suicide for someone else's sake is not love.

Sacrificing yourself for someone else is not love.

It is domination through co-dependence.

You control your narcissist by giving, as much as he controls you through his pathology.

Your unconditional generosity sometimes prevents him from facing his True Self and thus healing.

It is impossible to have a relationship with a narcissist that is meaningful to the narcissist.

It is, of course, possible to have a relationship with a narcissist that is meaningful to you [see The Inverted Narcissist].

You modify your behaviour in order to secure the narcissist's continuing love, not in order to be abandoned.

This is the root of the perniciousness of this phenomenon:

The narcissist is a meaningful, crucially significant figure ("object") in the inverted narcissist's life.

This is the narcissist's leverage over the inverted narcissist. And since the inverted narcissist is usually very young when making the adaptation to the narcissist – it all boils down to fear of abandonment and death in the absence of care and sustenance.

The inverted narcissist's accommodation of the narcissist is as much a wish to gratify one's narcissist (parent) as the sheer terror of forever withholding gratification from one's self.

## The Need to be Hopeful

I understand the need to be hopeful.

There are gradations of narcissism. This book deals with the extreme and ultimate form of narcissism, the Narcissistic Personality Disorder (NPD). The prognosis for those merely with narcissistic traits or a narcissistic style is far better than the healing prospects of a full-fledged narcissist.

We often confuse shame with guilt.

Narcissists feel shameful when confronted with a failure. They feel (narcissistically) injured. Their omnipotence is threatened, their sense of perfection and uniqueness is questioned. They are enraged, engulfed by self-reprimand, self-loathing and internalized violent urges.

The narcissist punishes himself for failing to be God – not for mistreating others.

The narcissist makes an effort to communicate his pain and shame in order to elicit the Narcissistic Supply he needs to restore and regulate his failing sense of self-worth. In doing so, the narcissist resorts to the human vocabulary of empathy. The narcissist will say anything to obtain Narcissistic Supply. It is a manipulative ploy – not a confession of real emotions or an authentic description of internal dynamics.

Yes, the narcissist is a child – but a very young one.

Yes, he can tell right from wrong – but is indifferent to both.

Yes, a process of "re-parenting" (what Kohut called a "self-object") is required to foster growth and maturation. In the best of cases, it takes years and the prognosis is dismal.

Yes, some narcissists make it. And their mates or spouses or children or colleagues or lovers rejoice.

But is the fact that people survive tornadoes a reason to go out and seek one?

The narcissist is very much attracted to vulnerability, to unstable or disordered personalities or to his inferiors. Such people constitute secure Sources of Narcissistic Supply. The inferior offer adulation. The mentally disturbed, the traumatized, the abused become dependent and addicted to him. The vulnerable can be easily and economically manipulated without fear of repercussions.

"A healed narcissist" is a contradiction in terms, an oxymoron (though there may be exceptions, of course).

Still, healing (not only of narcissists) is dependent upon and derived from a sense of security in a relationship.

The narcissist is not particularly interested in healing. He tries to optimize his returns, taking into consideration the scarcity and finiteness of his resources. Healing, to him, is simply a bad business proposition.

In the narcissist's world being accepted or cared for (not to mention loved) is a foreign language. It is meaningless.

One might recite the most delicate haiku in Japanese and it would still remain meaningless to a non-Japanese.

That non-Japanese are not adept at Japanese does not diminish the value of the haiku or of the Japanese language, needless to say.

Narcissists damage and hurt but they do so offhandedly and naturally, as an after-thought and reflexively.

They are aware of what they are doing to others – but they do not care.

Narcissists feel that they are entitled to their pleasure and gratification (Narcissistic Supply is often obtained by subjugating and subsuming others).

They feel that others are less than human, mere extensions of the narcissist, or instruments to fulfil the narcissist's wishes and obey his often capricious commands.

The narcissist feels that no evil can be inflicted on machines, instruments, or extensions. He feels that his needs justify his actions.

Return

# The Cyber Narcissist

To the narcissist, the Internet is an alluring and irresistible combination of playground and hunting grounds, the gathering place of numerous potential Sources of Narcissistic Supply, a world where false identities are the norm and mind games the bon ton. And it is beyond the reach of the law, the pale of social norms, or the strictures of civilized conduct.

The somatic finds cyber-sex and cyber-relationships aplenty. The cerebral claims false accomplishments, sham skills, erudition and talents. Both, if minimally communicative, end up at the instantly gratifying epicentre of a cult of fans, followers, stalkers, erotomaniacs, denigrators, and plain nuts. The constant attention and attendant quasi-celebrity feed and sustain their grandiose fantasies and inflated self-image.

The Internet is an extension of the real-life Narcissistic Pathological Space but without its risks, injuries, and disappointments. In the virtual universe of the Web, the narcissist vanishes and reappears with ease, often adopting a myriad aliases and nicknames. He can thus fend off criticism, abuse, disagreement, and disapproval effectively and in real time while simultaneously preserving the precarious balance of his infantile personality. Narcissists are, therefore, prone to Internet addiction.

The positive characteristics of the Net are largely lost on the narcissist. He is not keen on expanding his horizons, fostering true relationships, or getting in real contact with other people. The narcissist is forever the provincial because he filters everything through the narrow lens of his addiction. He measures others – and idealizes or devalues them – according to one criterion only: how useful they might be as Sources of Narcissistic Supply.

The Internet is an egalitarian medium where people are judged by the consistency and quality of their contributions rather than by the content or bombast of their claims. But the narcissist is driven to distracting discomfiture by a lack of clear and commonly accepted hierarchy (with himself at the pinnacle). He fervently and aggressively tries to impose the "natural order" – either by monopolizing the interaction or, if that fails, by becoming a major disruptive influence.

But the Internet may also be the closest many narcissists get to psychodynamic therapy. Because it is still largely text-based, the Web is populated by disembodied entities. By interacting with these intermittent, unpredictable, ultimately unknowable, ephemeral, and ethereal voices the narcissist is compelled to project unto them his own experiences, fears, hopes, and prejudices.

Transference (and counter-transference) are quite common on the Net and the narcissist's defence mechanisms, notably projection and Projective Identification, are frequently aroused. The therapeutic process is set in motion by the unbridled, uncensored, and brutally honest reactions to the narcissist's repertory of antics, pretensions, delusions, and fantasies.

The narcissist – ever the intimidating bully – is not accustomed to such resistance. Initially, it may heighten and sharpen his paranoia and lead him to compensate by extending and deepening his grandiosity. Some narcissists withdraw altogether, reverting to the schizoid posture. Others become openly antisocial and seek to subvert, sabotage, and destroy the online sources of their frustration. A few retreat and confine themselves to the company of adoring sycophants and unquestioning groupies.

But a long exposure to the culture of the Net – irreverent, sceptical, and populist – usually exerts a beneficial effect even on the staunchest and most rigid narcissist. Far less convinced of his own superiority and infallibility, the online narcissist mellows and begins, albeit hesitantly, to listen to others and to collaborate with them.

Return

# Narcissism, Other Mental Health Disorders, Substance Abuse, and Reckless Behaviours

## Co-Morbidity and Dual Diagnosis

*Question:* The symptoms that you describe are common to so many people that I know... Does this mean that they are all narcissists?

*Answer:* The classification of Axis II personality disorders – deeply ingrained, maladaptive, lifelong behaviour patterns – in the Diagnostic and Statistical Manual, fourth edition, text revision [American Psychiatric Association. DSM-IV-TR, Washington, 2000] – or the DSM-IV-TR for short – has come under sustained and serious criticism from its inception in 1952.

The DSM-IV-TR adopts a categorical approach, postulating that personality disorders are *"qualitatively distinct clinical syndromes"* [p. 689]. This is widely doubted. Even the distinction made between "normal" and "disordered" personalities is increasingly being rejected. The "diagnostic thresholds" between normal and abnormal are either absent or weakly supported.

The polythetic form of the DSM's Diagnostic Criteria – only a subset of the criteria is adequate grounds for a diagnosis – generates unacceptable diagnostic heterogeneity. In other words, people diagnosed with the same personality disorder may have only one diagnostic criterion in common.

The DSM fails to clarify the exact relationship between Axis II and Axis I disorders and the way chronic childhood and developmental problems interact with personality disorders.

The differential diagnoses are vague and the personality disorders are insufficiently demarcated. The result is excessive co-morbidity (multiple Axis II diagnoses in the same patient).

The DSM contains little discussion of what distinguishes normal character (personality), personality traits, or personality style (Millon) from personality disorders. The DSM does not incorporate personality disorders induced by circumstances (reactive personality disorders, such as Milman's proposed "Acquired Situational Narcissism"). Nor does it efficaciously cope with personality disorders that are the result of medical conditions (such as brain injuries, metabolic conditions, or protracted poisoning).

The DSM suffers from a dearth of documented clinical experience regarding both the disorders themselves and the utility of various treatment modalities.

A few personality disorders are "not otherwise specified": a catchall, basket "category".

Cultural bias is evident in certain personality disorders (such as the Antisocial and the Schizotypal).

The emergence of dimensional alternatives to the categorical approach is acknowledged in the DSM-IV-TR itself:

*"An alternative to the categorical approach is the dimensional perspective that personality disorders represent maladaptive variants of personality traits that merge imperceptibly into normality and into one another."* [p. 689]

The following issues – long neglected in the DSM – are likely to be tackled in future editions as well as in current research:

- The longitudinal course of the disorder(s) and their temporal stability from early childhood onwards;
- The genetic and biological underpinnings of personality disorder(s);
- The development of personality psychopathology during childhood and its emergence in adolescence;
- The interactions between physical health and disease and personality disorders;
- The effectiveness of various treatments: talk therapies as well as psychopharmacology.

The Diagnostic and Statistical Manual [American Psychiatric Association. DSM-IV-TR, Washington, 2000] defines "personality" as:

*"...enduring patterns of perceiving, relating to, and thinking about the environment and oneself ... exhibited in a wide range of important social and personal contexts."*

Patients suffering from personality disorders have these things in common:

They are persistent, relentless, stubborn, and insistent (except those suffering from the Schizoid or the Avoidant personality disorders).

They feel entitled to – and vociferously demand – preferential treatment and privileged access to resources and personnel. They often complain about multiple symptoms. They get involved in "power plays" with authority figures (such as physicians, therapists, nurses, social workers, bosses, and bureaucrats) and rarely obey instructions or observe rules of conduct and procedure.

They hold themselves to be superior to others or, at the very least, unique. Many personality disorders involve an inflated self-perception and grandiosity. Such subjects are incapable of empathy (the ability to appreciate and respect the needs and wishes of other people). In therapy or medical treatment, they alienate the physician or therapist by treating her as inferior to them.

Patients with personality disorders are self-centred, self-preoccupied, repetitive, and, thus, boring.

Subjects with personality disorders seek to manipulate and exploit others. They trust no one and have a diminished capacity to love or intimately share because they do not trust or love themselves. They are socially maladaptive and emotionally unstable.

No one knows whether personality disorders are the tragic outcomes of nature or the sad follow-up to a lack of nurture by the patient's environment.

Generally speaking, though, most personality disorders start out in childhood and early adolescence as mere problems in personal development. Exacerbated by repeated abuse and rejection, they then become full-fledged dysfunctions. Personality disorders are rigid and enduring patterns of traits, emotions, and cognitions. In other words, they rarely "evolve" and are stable and all-pervasive, not episodic. By "all-pervasive", I mean to say that they affect every area in the patient's life: his career, his interpersonal relationships, his social functioning.

Personality disorders cause unhappiness and are usually co-morbid with mood and anxiety disorders. Most patients are ego-dystonic (except narcissists and psychopaths). They dislike and resent who they are, how they behave, and the pernicious and destructive effects they have on their nearest and dearest. Still, personality disorders are defence mechanisms writ large. Thus, few patients with personality disorders are truly self-aware or capable of life transforming introspective insights.

Patients with personality disorder typically suffer from a host of other psychiatric problems (example: depressive illnesses, or obsessions-compulsions). They are worn-out by the need to reign in their self-destructive and self-defeating impulses.

Patients with personality disorders have alloplastic defences and an external locus of control. In other words: rather than accept responsibility for the consequences of their actions, they tend to blame other people or the outside world for their misfortune, failures, and circumstances. Consequently, they fall prey to paranoid persecutory delusions and anxieties. When stressed, they try to pre-empt (real or imaginary) threats by changing the rules of the game, introducing new variables, or by trying to manipulate their environment to conform to their needs. They regard everyone and everything as mere instruments of gratification.

Patients with Cluster B personality disorders (Narcissistic, Antisocial, Borderline, and Histrionic) are mostly ego-syntonic, even though they are faced with formidable character and behavioural deficits, emotional deficiencies and lability, and overwhelmingly wasted lives and squandered potentials. Such patients do not, on the whole, find their personality traits or behaviour objectionable, unacceptable, disagreeable, or alien to their selves.

There is a clear distinction between patients with personality-disorders and patients with psychoses (schizophrenia-paranoia and the like). As opposed to the latter, the former have no hallucinations, delusions or thought disorders. At the extreme, subjects who suffer from the Borderline Personality Disorder experience brief psychotic "microepisodes", mostly during treatment. Patients with personality disorders are also fully oriented, with clear senses (sensorium), good memory and a satisfactory general fund of knowledge.

*Question:* Does narcissism often occur with other mental health disorders (co-morbidity) or with substance abuse (dual diagnosis)?

*Answer:* NPD (Narcissistic Personality Disorder) is often diagnosed with other mental health disorders (such as the Borderline, Histrionic, or Antisocial Personality Disorders). This is called "co-morbidity". NPD is also often accompanied by substance abuse and other reckless and impulsive behaviours and this co-occurrence is called "dual diagnosis".

**The Schizoid and Paranoid Personality Disorders**

The basic dynamic of this particular brand of co-morbidity goes like this:

1. The narcissist feels superior, unique, entitled and better than his fellow men. He thus tends to despise them, to hold them in contempt and to regard them as lowly and subservient beings.
2. The narcissist feels that his time is invaluable, his mission of cosmic importance, his contributions to humanity priceless. He, therefore, demands total obedience and catering to his ever-changing needs. Any demands on his time and resources are deemed to be both humiliating and wasteful.
3. But the narcissist is DEPENDENT on input from other people for the performance of certain ego functions (such as the regulation of his sense of self-worth). Without Narcissistic Supply (adulation, adoration, attention), the narcissist shrivels and withers and is dysphoric (depressed).
4. The narcissist resents this dependence. He is furious at himself for his neediness and – in a typical narcissistic manoeuvre (called "alloplastic defence") – he blames OTHERS for his anger. He displaces his rage and its roots.
5. Many narcissists are also paranoid. This means that they are afraid of people and of what people might do to them. Wouldn't you be scared and paranoid if your very life depended continually on the goodwill of others? The narcissist's very life depends on others providing him with Narcissistic Supply. He becomes suicidal if they stop doing so.
6. To counter this overwhelming feeling of helplessness (dependence on Narcissistic Supply), the narcissist becomes a control freak. He sadistically manipulates others to satisfy his needs. He derives pleasure from the utter subjugation of his human environment.
7. Finally, the narcissist is a latent masochist. He seeks punishment, castigation and ex-communication. This self-destruction is the only way to validate powerful voices he had internalized as a child ("You are a bad, rotten, hopeless child").

The narcissistic landscape is fraught with contradictions. The narcissist depends on people – but hates and despises them. He wants to control them unconditionally – but is also looking to punish himself savagely. He is terrified of persecution ("persecutory delusions") – but seeks the company of his own "persecutors" compulsively.

The narcissist is the victim of incompatible inner dynamics, ruled by numerous vicious circles, pushed and pulled simultaneously by irresistible forces. A minority of narcissists choose the Schizoid Solution. They choose, in effect, to disengage, both emotionally and socially.

[Read more about the narcissist's reactions to deficient Narcissistic Supply: The Delusional Way Out]

[Read more about Schizoid Narcissists in FAQ 51]

## HPD (Histrionic Personality Disorder) and Somatic NPD

Somatic narcissists acquire their Narcissistic Supply by making use of their bodies, of sex, of physical of physiological achievements, traits, health, exercise, or relationships. They possess many Histrionic features.

[Read the DSM-IV-TR (2000) definition of the Histrionic Personality Disorder]

## Narcissists and Depression

[Read Frequently Asked Question 9 to learn more about depression and the narcissist]

## Dissociative Identity Disorder and NPD

Is the True Self of the narcissist the equivalent of the host personality in the DID (Dissociative Identity Disorder) – and the False Self one of the fragmented personalities, also known as "alters"?

The False Self is a mere construct rather than a full-fledged self. It is the locus of the narcissist's fantasies of grandiosity, his feelings of entitlement, omnipotence, magical thinking, omniscience and magical immunity. But it lacks many other functional and structural elements.

Moreover, it has no "cut-off" date. DID alters have a date of inception, usually as a reaction to trauma or abuse (they have an "age"). The False Self is a process, not an entity, it is a reactive pattern and a reactive formation. The False Self is not a self, nor is it false. It is very real, more real to the narcissist than his True Self.

As Kernberg observed, the narcissist actually vanishes and is replaced by a False Self. There is NO True Self inside the narcissist. The narcissist is a hall of mirrors – but the hall itself is an optical illusion created by the mirrors. Narcissism is reminiscent of a painting by Escher.

In DID, the patient's emotions are segregated into personality-like internal constructs ("entities"). The notion of "unique separate multiple whole personalities" is untrue. DID is a continuum. The subject's inner language breaks down into polyglottal chaos. In

DID, emotions cannot communicate with each other for fear of provoking overwhelming pain (and its fatal consequences). So, they are being kept apart by various mechanisms (a host or birth personality, a facilitator, a moderator and so on).

All personality disorders involve a modicum of dissociation. But the narcissistic solution is to emotionally disappear altogether. Hence, the tremendous, insatiable need of the narcissist for external approval. The narcissist exists ONLY as a reflection. Since he is forbidden to love his True Self, he chooses to have no self at all. It is not dissociation – it is a vanishing act.

NPD is a total, "pure" solution: self-extinguishing, self-abolishing, and entirely fake.

### NPD and Attention Deficit Hyperactivity Disorder

NPD has been associated with Attention Deficit / Hyperactivity Disorder (ADHD, or ADD) and with RAD (Reactive Attachment Disorder). The rationale is that children suffering from ADHD are unlikely to develop the attachment necessary to prevent a narcissistic regression (Freud) or adaptation (Jung).

Bonding and object relations ought to be affected by ADHD. Research to supports this intuitive linkage has yet to come to light, though. Still, many psychotherapists and psychiatrists use it as a working hypothesis. Another proposed dynamic is between autistic disorders (such as Asperger's Syndrome) and narcissism.

### Narcissism and Bipolar Disorder

The manic phase of Bipolar I Disorder is often misdiagnosed as Narcissistic Personality Disorder (NPD).

Bipolar patients in the manic phase exhibit many of the signs and symptoms of pathological narcissism: hyperactivity, self-centredness, lack of empathy, and control freakery. During this recurring chapter of the disease, the patient is euphoric, has grandiose fantasies, spins unrealistic schemes, and has frequent rage attacks (is irritable) if her or his wishes and plans are (inevitably) frustrated.

The manic phases of the bipolar disorder, however, are limited in time while NPD is not. Furthermore, the mania is followed by – usually protracted – depressive episodes. The narcissist is also frequently dysphoric. But whereas the bipolar sinks into deep self-deprecation, self-devaluation, unbounded pessimism, all-pervasive guilt and anhedonia, the narcissist, even when depressed, never forgoes his narcissism: his grandiosity, sense of entitlement, haughtiness, and lack of empathy.

Narcissistic dysphorias are much shorter and reactive: they constitute a response to the Grandiosity Gap. In plain words, the narcissist is dejected when confronted with the abyss between his inflated self-image and grandiose fantasies and the drab reality of his life: his failures, lack of accomplishments, disintegrating interpersonal relationships, and low status. Yet, one dose of Narcissistic Supply is enough to elevate the narcissists from the depth of misery to the heights of manic euphoria.

Not so with the bipolar. The source of her or his mood swings is assumed to be brain biochemistry – not the availability of Narcissistic Supply. Whereas the narcissist is in full control of his faculties, even when maximally agitated, the bipolar often feels that s/he has lost control of his/her brain ("flight of ideas"), his/her speech, his/her attention span (distractibility), and his/her motor functions.

The bipolar is prone to reckless behaviours and substance abuse only during the manic phase. The narcissist does drugs, drinks, gambles, shops on credit, indulges in unsafe sex or in other compulsive behaviours both when elated and when deflated.

As a rule, the bipolar's manic phase interferes with his/her social and occupational functioning. Many narcissists, in contrast, reach the highest rungs of their community, church, firm, or voluntary organization. Most of the time, they function flawlessly – though the inevitable blowups and the grating extortion of Narcissistic Supply usually put an end to the narcissist's career and social liaisons.

The manic phase of bipolar sometimes requires hospitalization and, more frequently than admitted, involves psychotic features. Narcissists are never hospitalized as the risk for self-harm is minute. Moreover, psychotic microepisodes in narcissism are decompensatory in nature and appear only under unendurable stress (e.g., in intensive therapy).

The bipolar's mania provokes discomfort in both strangers and in the patient's nearest and dearest. His/her constant cheer and compulsive insistence on interpersonal, sexual, and occupational, or professional interactions engenders unease and repulsion. Her/his lability of mood – rapid shifts between uncontrollable rage and unnatural good spirits – is downright intimidating. The narcissist's gregariousness, by comparison, is calculated, "cold", controlled, and goal-orientated (the extraction of Narcissistic Supply). His cycles of mood and affect are far less pronounced and less rapid.

The bipolar's swollen self-esteem, overstated self-confidence, obvious grandiosity, and delusional fantasies are akin to the narcissist's and are the source of the diagnostic confusion. Both types of patients purport to give advice, carry out an assignment, accomplish a mission, or embark on an enterprise for which they are uniquely unqualified and lack the talents, skills, knowledge, or experience required.

But the bipolar's bombast is far more delusional than the narcissist's. Ideas of reference and magical thinking are common and, in this sense, the bipolar is closer to the schizotypal than to the narcissistic.

There are other differentiating symptoms:

Sleep disorders – notably acute insomnia – are common in the manic phase of bipolar and uncommon in narcissism. So is "manic speech": pressured, uninterruptible, loud, rapid, dramatic (includes singing and humorous asides), sometimes incomprehensible, incoherent, chaotic, and lasts for hours. It reflects the bipolar's inner turmoil and his/her inability to control his/her racing and kaleidoscopic thoughts.

As opposed to narcissists, bipolar in the manic phase are often distracted by the slightest stimuli, are unable to focus on relevant data, or to maintain the thread of conversation. They are "all over the place" – simultaneously initiating numerous business ventures, joining a myriad organization, writing umpteen letters, contacting hundreds of friends and perfect strangers, acting in a domineering, demanding, and intrusive manner, totally disregarding the needs and emotions of the unfortunate recipients of their unwanted attentions. They rarely follow up on their projects.

The transformation is so marked that the bipolar is often described by his/her closest as "not himself/herself". Indeed, some bipolars relocate, change name and appearance, and lose contact with their "former life". Antisocial or even criminal behaviour is not uncommon and aggression is marked, directed at both others (assault) and oneself (suicide). Some biploars describe an acuteness of the senses, akin to experiences recounted by drug users: smells, sounds, and sights are accentuated and attain an unearthly quality.

As opposed to narcissists, bipolars regret their misdeeds following the manic phase and try to atone for their actions. They realize and accept that "something is wrong with them" and seek help. During the depressive phase they are ego-dystonic and their defences are autoplastic (they blame themselves for their defeats, failures, and mishaps).

Finally, pathological narcissism is already discernible in early adolescence. The full-fledged bipolar disorder – including a manic phase – rarely occurs before the age of 20. The narcissist is consistent in his pathology – not so the bipolar. The onset of the manic episode is fast and furious and results in a conspicuous metamorphosis of the patient.

[More about this topic here:

Stormberg, D., Roningstam, E., Gunderson, J., & Tohen, M. (1998) Pathological Narcissism in Bipolar Disorder Patients. Journal of Personality Disorders, 12, 179-185;

Roningstam, E. (1996), Pathological Narcissism and Narcissistic Personality Disorder in Axis I Disorders. Harvard Review of Psychiatry, 3, 326-340]

### Narcissism and Asperger's Disorder

Asperger's Disorder is often misdiagnosed as Narcissistic Personality Disorder (NPD), though evident as early as age 3 (while pathological narcissism cannot be safely diagnosed prior to early adolescence).

In both cases, the patient is self-centred and engrossed in a narrow range of interests and activities. Social and occupational interactions are severely hampered and conversational skills (the give and take of verbal intercourse) are primitive. The Asperger's patient's body language – eye to eye gaze, body posture, facial expressions – is constricted and artificial, akin to the narcissist's. Nonverbal cues are virtually absent and their interpretation in others lacking.

Yet, the gulf between Asperger's and pathological narcissism is vast.

The narcissist switches between social agility and social impairment voluntarily. His social dysfunctioning is the outcome of conscious haughtiness and the reluctance to invest scarce mental energy in cultivating relationships with inferior and unworthy others. When confronted with potential Sources of Narcissistic Supply, however, the narcissist easily regains his social skills, his charm, and his gregariousness.

Many narcissists reach the highest rungs of their community, church, firm, or voluntary organization. Most of the time, they function flawlessly – though the inevitable blowups and the grating extortion of Narcissistic Supply usually put an end to the narcissist's career and social liaisons.

The Asperger's patient often wants to be accepted socially, to have friends, to marry, to be sexually active, and to sire offspring. He just doesn't have a clue as to how to go about it. His affect is limited. His initiative – for instance, to share his experiences with nearest and dearest or to engage in foreplay – is thwarted. His ability to divulge his emotions stilted. He is incapable or reciprocating and is largely unaware of the wishes, needs, and feelings of his interlocutors or counterparties.

Inevitably, Asperger's patients are perceived by others to be cold, eccentric, insensitive, indifferent, repulsive, exploitative or emotionally-absent. To avoid the pain of rejection, they confine themselves to solitary activities – but, unlike the schizoid, not by choice. They limit their world to a single topic, hobby, or person and dive in with the greatest, all-consuming intensity, excluding all other matters and everyone else. It is a form of hurt-control and pain regulation.

Thus, while the narcissist avoids pain by excluding, devaluing, and discarding others, the Asperger's patient achieves the same result by withdrawing and by passionately incorporating in his universe only one or two people and one or two subjects of interest. Both narcissists and Asperger's patients are prone to react with depression to perceived slights and injuries, but Asperger's patients are far more at risk of self-harm and suicide.

The use of language is another differentiating factor.

The narcissist is a skilled communicator. He uses language as an instrument to obtain Narcissistic Supply or as a weapon to obliterate his "enemies" and discarded sources with. Cerebral narcissists derive Narcissistic Supply from the consummate use they make of their innate verbosity.

Not so the Asperger's patient. He is equally verbose at times (and taciturn on other occasions) but his topics are few and, thus, tediously repetitive. He is unlikely to obey conversational rules and etiquette (for instance, to let others speak in turn). Nor is the Asperger's patient able to decipher nonverbal cues and gestures or to monitor his own misbehaviour on such occasions. Narcissists are similarly inconsiderate – but only towards those who cannot possibly serve as Sources of Narcissistic Supply.

[More about Autism Spectrum Disorders here:

McDowell, Maxson J. (2002) The Image of the Mother's Eye: Autism and Early Narcissistic Injury, Behavioural and Brain Sciences (Submitted);

Benis, Anthony – "Toward Self & Sanity: On the Genetic Origins of the Human Character" – Narcissistic-Perfectionist Personality Type (NP) with special reference to infantile autism;
Stringer, Kathi (2003) An Object Relations Approach to Understanding Unusual Behaviours and Disturbances;
James Robert Brasic, MD, MPH (2003) Pervasive Developmental Disorder: Asperger Syndrome]

## Narcissism and Generalized Anxiety Disorder (GAD)

Anxiety disorders – and especially Generalized Anxiety Disorder (GAD) – are often misdiagnosed as Narcissistic Personality Disorder (NPD).

Anxiety is uncontrollable and excessive apprehension. Anxiety disorders usually come replete with obsessive thoughts, compulsive and ritualistic acts, restlessness, fatigue, irritability, difficulty concentrating, and somatic manifestations (such as an increased heart rate, sweating, or, in Panic Attacks, chest pains).

By definition, narcissists are anxious for social approval or attention (Narcissistic Supply). The narcissist cannot control this need and the attendant anxiety because he requires external feedback to regulate his labile sense of self-worth. This dependence makes most narcissists irritable. They fly into rages and have a very low threshold of frustration.

Like patients who suffer from panic attacks and Social Phobia (another Anxiety Disorder), narcissists are terrified of being embarrassed or criticized in public. Consequently, most narcissists fail to function well in various settings (social, occupational, romantic, etc.).

Many narcissists develop obsessions and compulsions. Like sufferers of GAD, narcissists are perfectionists and preoccupied with the quality of their performance and the level of their competence. As the Diagnostic and Statistical Manual [DSM-IV-TR, pp. 473] puts it, GAD patients (especially children):

"... (A)re typically overzealous in seeking approval and require excessive reassurance about their performance and their other worries."

This applies equally well to narcissists. Both classes of patients are paralyzed by the fear of being judged as imperfect or lacking. Narcissists as well as patients with anxiety disorders constantly fail to measure up to an inner, harsh, and sadistic critic and a grandiose, inflated self-image.

The narcissistic solution is to avoid comparison and competition altogether and to demand special treatment. The narcissist's sense of entitlement is incommensurate with the narcissist's true accomplishments. He withdraws from the rat race because he does not deem his opponents, colleagues, or peers worthy of his efforts. As opposed to narcissists, patients with anxiety disorders are invested in their work and their profession. To be exact, they are over-invested. Their preoccupation with perfection is counter-productive and, ironically, renders them underachievers.

It is easy to mistake the presenting symptoms of certain anxiety disorders as pathological narcissism. Both types of patients are worried about social approbation and seek it actively. Both present a haughty or impervious facade to the world. Both are dysfunctional and weighed down by a history of personal failure on the job and in the family. But the narcissist is ego-dystonic: he is proud and happy of who he is. The anxious patient is distressed and is looking for help and a way out of his or her predicament. Hence the differential diagnosis.

[Bibliography:

Goldman, Howard G. - Review of General Psychiatry, 4th ed. - London, Prentice-Hall International, 1995 - p. 279-282;

Gelder, Michael et al., eds. - Oxford Textbook of Psychiatry, 3rd ed. - London, Oxford University Press, 2000 - p. 160-169;

Klein, Melanie - The Writings of Melanie Klein - Ed. Roger Money-Kyrle, 4 vols. - New York, Free Press, 1964-75;

Kernberg O. - Borderline Conditions and Pathological Narcissism - New York, Jason Aronson, 1975;

Millon, Theodore (and Roger D. Davis, contributor) - Disorders of Personality: DSM IV and Beyond, 2nd ed. - New York, John Wiley and Sons, 1995;

Millon, Theodore - Personality Disorders in Modern Life - New York, John Wiley and Sons, 2000;

Schwartz, Lester - Narcissistic Personality Disorders - A Clinical Discussion - Journal of American Psychoanalytic Association, 22 (1974) - p. 292-305;

Vaknin, Sam - Malignant Self Love - Narcissism Revisited, 8th revised impression - Skopje and Prague, Narcissus Publications, 2007]

## BPD, NPD and Other Cluster B Personal Disorders

In the DSM, there are 10 distinct personality disorders (Paranoid, Schizoid, Schizotypal, Antisocial, Borderline, Histrionic, Narcissistic, Avoidant, Dependent, Obsessive-Compulsive) and one catchall category, Personality Disorders NOS (Not Otherwise Specified).

Personality disorders with marked similarities are grouped into clusters.

Cluster A (the Odd or Eccentric Cluster) includes the Paranoid, Schizoid, and Schizotypal personality disorders.

Cluster B (the Dramatic, Emotional, or Erratic Cluster) is comprised of the Antisocial, Borderline, Histrionic, and Narcissistic personality disorders.

Cluster C (the Anxious or Fearful Cluster) encompasses the Avoidant, Dependent, and Obsessive-Compulsive personality disorders.

The Clusters are not valid theoretical constructs and have never been verified or rigorously tested. They constitute merely convenient shorthand and so provide little additional insight into their component personality disorders.

The personality disorders in Cluster B are ubiquitous. You are far more likely to have come across a Borderline or a Narcissist or a Psychopath than across a Schizotypal, for instance.

First, an overview of Cluster B:

Borderline Personality Disorder is marked by instability. The patient is a roller-coaster of emotions (this is called emotional lability). She (most Borderlines are women) fails to maintain stable relationships and dramatically attaches to, clings, and violently detaches from a seemingly inexhaustible stream of lovers, spouses, intimate partners, and friends. Self-image is volatile, one's sense of self-worth is fluctuating and precarious, affect is unpredictable and inappropriate, and impulse control is impaired (the patient's threshold of frustration is low).

The Antisocial Personality Disorder involves contemptuous disregard for others. The psychopath ignores or actively violates other people's rights, choices, wishes, preferences, and emotions.

The Narcissistic Personality Disorder is founded on a sense of fantastic grandiosity, brilliance, perfection, and power (omnipotence). The narcissist lacks empathy, is exploitative, and compulsively seeks Narcissistic Supply (attention, admiration, adulation, being feared, etc.) to buttress his False Self – a confabulated "person" aimed at inspiring awe and extracting compliance and subservience from others.

Finally, the Histrionic Personality Disorder also revolves around attention-seeking but is usually confined to sexual conquests and displays of the histrionic's capacity to irresistibly seduce others.

Each personality disorder (PD) has its own form of Narcissistic Supply:

- *HPD (Histrionic PD)* – Derive their supply from their heightened sexuality, seductiveness, flirtatiousness, from serial romantic and sexual encounters, from physical exercises, and from the shape and state of their body;
- *NPD (Narcissistic PD)* – Derive their supply from garnering attention, both positive (adulation, admiration) and negative (being feared, notoriety);
- *BPD (Borderline PD)* – Derive their supply from the presence of others (they suffer from separation anxiety and are terrified of being abandoned);
- *AsPD (Antisocial PD)* – Derive their supply from accumulating money, power, control, and having (sometimes sadistic) "fun".

Seductive behaviour alone is NOT necessarily indicative of Histrionic PD. Somatic narcissists behave this way as well.

The differential diagnoses between the various personality disorders are blurred. It is true that some traits are much more pronounced (or even qualitatively different) in specific disorders. For example: delusional, expansive, and all-pervasive grandiose fantasies are typical of the narcissist. But, in a milder form, they also appear in many other personality disorders, such as the Paranoid, the Schizotypal, and the Borderline. A sense of entitlement is common to ALL Cluster B disorders.

It would seem that personality disorders occupy a continuum.

### Abandonment, NPDs and Other Personality Disorders

Both narcissists and borderlines are afraid of abandonment. Only their coping strategies differ. Narcissists do everything they can to bring about their own rejection (and thus "control" it and "get it over with"). Borderlines do everything they can either to avoid relationships in the first place, or to prevent abandonment once in a relationship by clinging to the partner or by emotionally extorting his continued presence and commitment.

### NPD and BPD – Suicide

Narcissists almost never act on their suicidal ideation, while borderlines do so incessantly (by cutting, self injury, or mutilation). But both tend to become suicidal under severe and prolonged stress.

NPDs can suffer from brief reactive psychoses in the same way that borderlines suffer from psychotic microepisodes.

There are some differences between NPD and BPD, though:

a. The narcissist is way less impulsive;

b. The narcissist is less self-destructive, rarely self-mutilates, and practically never attempts suicide;

c. The narcissist is more stable (displays reduced emotional lability, maintains stability in interpersonal relationships and so on).

## Narcissist vs. Psychopath

We all heard the terms "psychopath" or "sociopath". These are the old names for a patient with the Antisocial Personality Disorder (AsPD). It is hard to distinguish narcissists from psychopaths. The latter may simply be a less inhibited and less grandiose form of the former. Indeed, the DSM-V Committee is considering to abolish this differential diagnosis altogether.

Still, there are some important nuances setting the two disorders apart:

As opposed to most narcissists, psychopaths are either unable or unwilling to control their impulses or to delay gratification. They use their rage to control people and manipulate them into submission.

Psychopaths, like narcissists, lack empathy but many of them are also sadistic: they take pleasure in inflicting pain on their victims or in deceiving them. They even find it funny!

Psychopaths are far less able to form interpersonal relationships, even the twisted and tragic relationships that are the staple of the narcissist.

Both the psychopath and the narcissist disregard society, its conventions, social cues and social treaties. But the psychopath carries this disdain to the extreme and is likely to be a scheming, calculated, ruthless, and callous career criminal. Psychopaths are deliberately and gleefully evil while narcissists are absent-mindedly and incidentally evil.

Psychopaths really do not need other people while narcissists are addicted to Narcissistic Supply (the admiration, attention, and envy of others).

Millon and Davis (supra) add [p. 299-300]:

*"When the egocentricity, lack of empathy, and sense of superiority of the narcissist cross-fertilize with the impulsivity, deceitfulness, and criminal tendencies of the antisocial, the result is a psychopath, an individual who seeks the gratification of selfish impulses through any means without empathy or remorse."*

As opposed to what Scott Peck says, narcissists are not evil - they lack the intention to cause harm (mens rea). As Millon notes, certain narcissists *"incorporate moral values into their exaggerated sense of superiority. Here, moral laxity is seen (by the narcissist) as evidence of inferiority, and it is those who are unable to remain morally pure who are looked upon with contempt."*

[Millon, Th., Davis, R. – Personality Disorders in Modern Life, John Wiley and Sons, 2000]

Narcissists are simply indifferent, callous and careless in their conduct and in their treatment of others. Their abusive conduct is off-handed and absent-minded, not calculated and premeditated like the psychopath's.

## NPD and Neuroses

The personality disordered patient maintains ALLOPLASTIC defences (reacts to stress by attempting to change the external environment or by shifting blame to it). Neurotics have AUTOPLASTIC defences (react to stress by attempting to change their internal processes, or by assuming blame). Many personality disorders also TEND to be ego-syntonic (i.e., to be perceived by the patient as acceptable, unobjectionable and part of the self) while neurotics tend to be ego-dystonic (the opposite).

## The Hated-Hating Personality Disordered

One needs only to read scholarly texts to learn how despised, derided, hated and avoided patients with personality disorders are even by mental health practitioners. Many people don't even realize that they have a personality disorder. Their social ostracism makes them feel victimized, wronged, discriminated against and hopeless. They don't understand why they are so detested, shunned and abandoned.

They cast themselves in the role of victims and attribute mental disorders to others ("pathologizing"). They employ the primitive defence mechanisms of splitting and projection augmented by the more sophisticated mechanism of Projective Identification.

In other words:

They "split off" from their personality the bad feelings of hating and being hated because they cannot cope with negative emotions. They project these undesirable emotions unto others ("He hates me, I don't hate anyone", "I am a good soul, but he is a psychopath", "He is stalking me, I just want to stay away from him", "He is a con-artist, I am the innocent victim").

Then they FORCE others to behave in a way that JUSTIFIES their expectations and their view of the world (Projective Identification followed by counter Projective Identification).

Some narcissists, for instance, firmly "believe" that women are evil predators, out to suck their lifeblood and then abandon them. So, they try and make their partners fulfil this prophecy. They try and make sure that the women in their lives behave exactly in this manner, that they do not abnegate and ruin the narcissist's craftily, elaborately, and studiously designed Weltanschauung (worldview).

Such narcissists tease women and betray them and bad mouth them and taunt them and torment them and stalk them and haunt them and pursue them and subjugate them and frustrate them until these women do, indeed, abandon them. The narcissist then feels vindicated and validated – totally ignoring HIS contribution to this recurrent pattern.

The personality disordered patient is full of negative emotions, with aggression and its transmutations, hatred and pathological envy. He is constantly seething with rage, jealousy, and other corroding sentiments. Unable to release these emotions (personality disorders are defence mechanisms against "forbidden" feelings), such patients split them, project them and force others to behave in a way which LEGITIMIZES and RATIONALIZES this overwhelming negativity. "No wonder I hate everyone – look how people repeatedly mistreat me." The personality disordered are doomed to incur self-inflicted injuries. They generate the very hate that legitimizes their hatred, which fosters their social ex-communication.

### The Negativistic (Passive-Aggressive) Personality Disorder

The Negativistic (Passive-Aggressive) Personality Disorder is not yet recognized by the DSM Committee. It makes its appearances in Appendix B of the Diagnostic and Statistical Manual, titled "Criteria Sets and Axes Provided for Further Study".

Some people are perennial pessimists and have "negative energy" and negativistic attitudes ("good things don't last", "it doesn't pay to be good", "the future is behind me"). Not only do they disparage the efforts of others, but they make it a point to resist demands to perform in workplace and social settings and to frustrate people's expectations and requests, however reasonable and minimal they may be. Such persons regard every requirement and assigned task as impositions, reject authority, resent authority figures (boss, teacher, parent-like spouse), feel shackled and enslaved by commitment, and oppose relationships that bind them in any manner.

Passive-aggressiveness wears a multitude of guises: procrastination, malingering, perfectionism, forgetfulness, neglect, truancy, intentional inefficiency, stubbornness, and outright sabotage. This repeated and advertent misconduct has far reaching effects. Consider the Negativist in the workplace: he or she invests time and efforts in obstructing their own chores and in undermining relationships. But, these self-destructive and self-defeating behaviours wreak havoc throughout the workshop or the office.

People diagnosed with the Negativistic (Passive-Aggressive) Personality Disorder resemble narcissists in some important respects. Despite the obstructive role they play, passive-aggressives feel unappreciated, underpaid, cheated, and misunderstood. They chronically complain, whine, carp, and criticize. They blame their failures and defeats on others, posing as martyrs and victims of a corrupt, inefficient, and heartless system (in other words, they have alloplastic defences and an external locus of control).

Passive-aggressives sulk and give the "silent treatment" in reaction to real or imagined slights. They suffer from ideas of reference (believe that they are the butt of derision, contempt, and condemnation) and are mildly paranoid (the world is out to get them, which explains their personal misfortune). In the words of the DSM: *"They may be sullen, irritable, impatient, argumentative, cynical, sceptical and contrary."* They are also hostile, explosive, lack impulse control, and, sometimes, reckless.

Inevitably, passive-aggressives are envious of the fortunate, the successful, the famous, their superiors, those in favour, and the happy. They vent this venomous jealousy openly and defiantly whenever given the opportunity. But, deep at heart, passive-aggressives are craven. When reprimanded, they immediately revert to begging forgiveness, kowtowing, or maudlin protestations, turning on their charm, and promising to behave and perform better in the future.

### The Borderline Narcissist - A Psychotic?

Kernberg suggested a "borderline" diagnosis. It is somewhere between psychotic and neurotic (actually between the psychotic and the personality disordered):

- The neurotic has autoplastic defences ("Something's wrong with me");
- The personality disordered has alloplastic defences ("Something's wrong with the world");

• Psychotics believe that "something's wrong with those who say that something's wrong with me".

Some personality disorders have a psychotic streak. Borderlines have psychotic episodes. Narcissists react with psychosis to life crises and in treatment ("psychotic microepisodes" which can last for days).

### Pathological Narcissism, Psychosis and Delusions

One of the most important symptoms of pathological narcissism (the Narcissistic Personality Disorder) is grandiosity. Grandiose fantasies (megalomaniac delusions of grandeur) permeate every aspect of the narcissist's personality. They are the reason that the narcissist feels entitled to special treatment which is typically incommensurate with his real accomplishments. The Grandiosity Gap is the abyss between the narcissist's self-image (as reified by his False Self) and reality.

When Narcissistic Supply is deficient, the narcissist decompensates and acts out in a variety of ways. Narcissists often experience psychotic micro-episodes during therapy and when they suffer narcissistic injuries in a life crisis. But can the narcissist "go over the edge"? Do narcissists ever become psychotic?

Some terminology first:

The narrowest definition of PSYCHOSIS, according to the DSM-IV-TR, is *"restricted to delusions or prominent hallucinations, with the hallucinations occurring in the absence of insight into their pathological nature"*.

And what are delusions and hallucinations?

A DELUSION is *"a false belief based on incorrect inference about external reality that is firmly sustained despite what almost everyone else believes and despite what constitutes incontrovertible and obvious proof or evidence to the contrary"*.

A HALLUCINATION is a *"sensory perception that has the compelling sense of reality of a true perception but that occurs without external stimulation of the relevant sensory organ"*.

Granted, the narcissist's hold on reality is tenuous (narcissists sometimes fail the reality test). Admittedly, narcissists often seem to believe in their own confabulations. They are unaware of the pathological nature and origin of their self-delusions and are, thus, technically delusional (though they rarely suffer from hallucinations, disorganized speech, or disorganized or catatonic behaviour). In the strictest sense of the word, narcissists appear to be psychotic.

But, actually, they are not. There is a qualitative difference between benign (though well-entrenched) self-deception or even malignant con-artistry – and "losing it".

Pathological narcissism should not be construed as a form of psychosis because:

1. The narcissists is usually fully aware of the difference between true and false, real and make-belief, the invented and the extant, right and wrong. The narcissist consciously chooses to adopt one version of the events, an aggrandizing narrative, a fairy-tale existence, a "what-if" counterfactual life. He is emotionally invested in his personal myth. The narcissist feels better as fiction than as fact – but he never loses sight of the fact that it is all just fiction.

2. Throughout, the narcissist is in full control of his faculties, cognisant of his choices, and goal-orientated. His behaviour is intentional and directional. He is a manipulator and his delusions are in the service of his stratagems. Hence his chameleon-like ability to turn his guises, his conduct, and his convictions on a dime.

3. Narcissistic delusions rarely persist in the face of blanket opposition and reams of evidence to the contrary. The narcissist usually tries to convert his social milieu to his point of view. He attempts to condition his nearest and dearest to positively reinforce his delusional False Self. But, if he fails, he modifies his profile on the fly. He "plays it by ear". His False Self is extemporaneous: a perpetual work of art, permanently reconstructed in a reiterative process designed around intricate and complex Feedback Loops.

Though the narcissistic personality is rigid, its content is always in flux. Narcissists forever re-invent themselves, adapt their consumption of Narcissistic Supply to the "marketplace", attuned to the needs of their "suppliers". Like the performers that they are, they resonate with their "audience", giving it what it expects and wants. They are efficient instruments for the extraction and consumption of human reactions.

As a result of this interminable process of fine tuning, narcissists have no loyalties, no values, no doctrines, no beliefs, no affiliations, and no convictions. Their only constraint is their addiction to human attention, positive or negative.

Psychotics, by comparison, are fixated on a certain view of the world and of their place in it. They ignore any and all information that might challenge their delusions. Gradually, they retreat into the inner recesses of their tormented mind and become dysfunctional.

Narcissists can't afford to shut out the world because they so heavily depend on it for the regulation of their labile sense of self-worth. Owing to this dependence, they are hypersensitive and hypervigilant, alert to every bit of new data. They are continuously busy rearranging their self-delusions to incorporate new information in an ego-syntonic manner.

This is why the Narcissistic Personality Disorder is insufficient grounds for claiming a "diminished capacity" (insanity) defence. Narcissists are never divorced from reality – they crave it, and need it, and consume it in order to maintain the precarious balance of their disorganized, borderline-psychotic personality. All narcissists, even the freakiest ones, can tell right from wrong, act with intent, and are in full control of their faculties and actions.

**Masochism and Narcissism**

Isn't seeking punishment a form of assertiveness and self-affirmation?

Author Cheryl Glickauf-Hughes, in the American Journal of Psychoanalysis [June 97, 57:2, p. 141-148] wrote:

*"Masochists tend to defiantly assert themselves to the narcissistic parent in the face of criticism and even abuse. For example, one masochistic patient's narcissistic father told him as a child that if he said 'one more word' that he would hit him with a belt and the patient defiantly responded to his father by saying 'One more word!'. Thus, what may appear, at times, to be masochistic or self-defeating behaviour may also be viewed as self-affirming behaviour on the part of the child toward the narcissistic parent."*

*Masochistic Personality Disorder*

The Masochistic Personality Disorder made its last appearance in the DSM-III-TR and was removed from the DSM-IV and from its text revision, the DSM-IV-TR. Some scholars, notably Theodore Millon, regard its removal as a mistake and lobby for its reinstatement in future editions of the DSM.

The masochist has been taught from an early age to hate himself and consider himself unworthy of love and worthless as a person. Consequently, he or she is prone to self-destructive, punishing, and self-defeating behaviours. Though capable of pleasure and possessed of social skills, the masochist avoids or undermines pleasurable experiences. He does not admit to enjoying himself, seeks suffering, pain, and hurt in relationships and situations, rejects help and resents those who offer it. He actively renders futile attempts to assist or ameliorate or mitigate or solve his problems and predicaments.

These self-penalizing behaviours are self-purging: they intend to relieve the masochist of overwhelming, pent-up anxiety. The masochist's conduct is equally aimed at avoiding intimacy and its benefits: companionship and support.

Masochists tend to choose people and circumstances that inevitably and predictably lead to failure, disillusionment, disappointment, and mistreatment. Conversely, they tend to avoid relationships, interactions, and circumstances that are likely to result in success or gratification. They reject, disdain, or even suspect people who consistently treat them well. Masochists find caring, loving persons sexually unattractive.

The masochist typically adopts unrealistic goals and thus guarantees underachievement. Masochists routinely fail at mundane tasks, even when these are crucial to their own advancement and personal objectives and even when they adequately carry out similar assignments on behalf of others. The DSM gives this example: *"Helps fellow students write papers, but is unable to write his or her own."*

When the masochist fails at these attempts at self-sabotage, he reacts with rage, depression, and guilt. He is likely to "compensate" for his undesired accomplishments and happiness by having an accident or by engaging in behaviours that produce abandonment, frustration, hurt, illness, or physical pain. Some masochists make harmful self-sacrifices, uncalled for by the situation and unwanted by the intended beneficiaries or recipients.

The Projective Identification defence mechanism is frequently at play. The masochist deliberately provokes, solicits, and incites angry, disparaging, and rejecting responses from others in order to feel on "familiar territory": humiliated, defeated, devastated, and hurt.

### The Inverted Narcissist – A Masochist?

The inverted narcissist (IN) is more of a co-dependent than a masochist. Strictly speaking masochism is sexual (as in sado-masochism). But the colloquial term means "seeking gratification through self-inflicted pain or punishment". This is not the case with co-dependents or IN's.

The inverted narcissist is a specific variant of co-dependent that derives gratification from her relationship with a narcissistic or a psychopathic (antisocial personality disordered) partner. But her gratification has nothing to do with the (very real) emotional (and, at times, physical) pain inflicted upon her by her mate.

Rather the IN is gratified by the re-enactment of past abusive relationships. In the narcissist, the IN feels that she has found a lost parent. The IN seeks to re-create old unresolved conflicts through the agency of the narcissist. There is a latent hope that this time the IN will get it "right", that THIS emotional liaison or interaction will not end in bitter disappointment and lasting agony. Yet, by choosing a narcissist for her partner, the IN ensures an identical outcome time and again. Why should one choose to repeatedly FAIL in her relationships is an intriguing question. Partly, it has to do with the comfort of familiarity. The IN is used since childhood to failing relationships. It seems that the IN prefers predictability to emotional gratification and to personal development. There are also strong elements of self-punishment and self-destruction added to the combustible mix that is the dyad narcissist-inverted narcissist.

## Narcissists and Sexual Perversions

Narcissism has long been thought to be a form of paraphilia (sexual deviation or perversion). It has been closely associated with incest and paedophilia.

Incest is an AUTOEROTIC act and, therefore, narcissistic. When a father makes love to his daughter – he is making love to himself because she IS 50% himself. It is a form of masturbation and reassertion of control over oneself.

[I analyzed the relationship between narcissism and homosexuality in FAQ: Homosexual and Transsexual Narcissists]

## Narcissism, Substance Abuse, and Reckless Behaviours

Pathological narcissism is an addiction to Narcissistic Supply, the narcissist's drug of choice. It is, therefore, not surprising that other addictive and reckless behaviours: workaholism, alcoholism, drug abuse, pathological gambling, compulsory shopping, or reckless driving – piggyback on this primary dependence.

The narcissist – like other types of addicts – derives pleasure from these exploits. But they also sustain and enhance his grandiose fantasies as "unique", "superior", "entitled", and "chosen". They place him above the laws and pressures of the mundane and away from the humiliating and sobering demands of reality. They render him the centre of attention - but also place him in "splendid isolation" from the madding and inferior crowd.

Such compulsory and wild pursuits provide a psychological exoskeleton. They are a substitute to quotidian existence. They afford the narcissist with an agenda, with timetables, goals, and faux achievements. The narcissist - the adrenaline junkie - feels that he is in control, alert, excited, and vital. He does not regard his condition as dependence. The narcissist firmly believes that he is in charge of his addiction, that he can quit at will and on short notice.

The narcissist denies his cravings for fear of "losing face" and subverting the flawless, perfect, immaculate, and omnipotent image he projects. When caught red handed, the narcissist underestimates, rationalizes, or intellectualizes his addictive and reckless behaviours - converting them into an integral part of his grandiose and fantastic False Self.

Thus, a drug abusing narcissist may claim to be conducting first hand research for the benefit of humanity - or that his substance abuse results in enhanced creativity and productivity. The dependence of some narcissists becomes a way of life: busy corporate executives, race car drivers, athletes, or professional gamblers come to mind.

The narcissist's addictive behaviours take his mind off his inherent limitations, inevitable failures, painful and much-feared rejections, and the Grandiosity Gap: the abyss between the image he projects (the False Self) and injurious reality. They relieve his anxiety and resolve the tension between his unrealistic expectations and inflated self-image and his incommensurate achievements, position, status, recognition, intelligence, wealth, and physique.

Thus, there is no point in treating the dependence and recklessness of the narcissist without first treating the underlying personality disorder. The narcissist's addictions serve deeply ingrained emotional needs. They intermesh seamlessly with the pathological structure of his disorganized personality, with his character faults, and primitive defence mechanisms.

Techniques such as "12 steps" may prove efficacious in treating the narcissist's grandiosity, rigidity, sense of entitlement, exploitativeness, and lack of empathy. This is because - as opposed to traditional treatment modalities - the emphasis is on tackling the narcissist's psychological makeup, rather than on mere behaviour modification.

The narcissist's overwhelming need to feel omnipotent and superior can be co-opted in the therapeutic process. Overcoming an addictive behaviour can be – truthfully – presented by the therapist as a rare and impressive feat, worthy of the narcissist's unique mettle.

Narcissists fall for these transparent pitches surprisingly often. But this approach can backfire. Should the narcissist relapse – an almost certain occurrence – he will feel ashamed to admit his fallibility, need for emotional sustenance, and impotence. He is likely to avoid treatment altogether and convince himself that now, having succeeded once to get rid of his addiction, he is self-sufficient and omniscient.

Return

# Narcissism and Evil

In his bestselling "People of the Lie", Scott Peck claims that narcissists are evil. Are they?

The concept of "evil" in this age of moral relativism is slippery and ambiguous. The "Oxford Companion to Philosophy" [Oxford University Press, 1995] defines it thus:

*"The suffering which results from morally wrong human choices."*

To qualify as evil a person (Moral Agent) must meet these requirements:

a. That he can and does consciously choose between the (morally) right and wrong and constantly and consistently prefers the latter;

b. That he acts on his choice irrespective of the consequences to himself and to others.

Clearly, evil must be premeditated. Francis Hutcheson and Joseph Butler argued that evil is a by-product of the pursuit of one's interest or cause at the expense of other people's interests or causes. But this ignores the critical element of conscious choice among equally efficacious alternatives. Moreover, people often pursue evil even when it jeopardizes their well-being and obstructs their interests. Sadomasochists even relish this orgy of mutual assured destruction.

Narcissists satisfy both conditions only partly. Their evil is utilitarian. They are evil only when being malevolent secures a certain outcome. Sometimes, they consciously choose the morally wrong - but not invariably so. They act on their choice even if it inflicts misery and pain on others. But they never opt for evil if they are to bear the consequences. They act maliciously because it is expedient to do so, not because it is "in their nature".

The narcissist is able to tell right from wrong and to distinguish between good and evil. In the pursuit of his interests and causes, he sometimes chooses to act wickedly. Lacking empathy, the narcissist is rarely remorseful. Because he feels entitled, exploiting others is second nature. The narcissist abuses others absent-mindedly, offhandedly, as a matter of fact.

The narcissist objectifies people and treats them as expendable commodities to be discarded after use. Admittedly, that, in itself, is evil. Yet, it is the mechanical, thoughtless, heartless face of narcissistic abuse – devoid of human passions and of familiar emotions – that renders it so alien, so frightful and so repellent.

We are often shocked less by the actions of narcissist than by the way he acts. In the absence of a vocabulary rich enough to capture the subtle hues and gradations of the spectrum of narcissistic depravity, we default to habitual adjectives such as "good" and "evil". Such intellectual laziness does this pernicious phenomenon and its victims little justice.

### Why are We Fascinated by Evil and Evildoers?

The common explanation is that one is fascinated with evil and evildoers because, through them, one vicariously expresses the repressed, dark, and evil parts of one's own personality. Evildoers, according to this theory, represent the "shadow" nether lands of our selves and, thus, they constitute our antisocial alter egos. Being drawn to wickedness is an act of rebellion against social strictures and the crippling bondage that is modern life. It is a mock synthesis of our Dr. Jekyll with our Mr. Hyde. It is a cathartic exorcism of our inner demons.

Yet, even a cursory examination of this account reveals its flaws.

Far from being taken as a familiar, though suppressed, element of our psyche, evil is mysterious. Though preponderant, villains are often labelled "monsters" – abnormal, even supernatural aberrations. It took Hanna Arendt two thickset tomes to remind us that evil is banal and bureaucratic, not fiendish and omnipotent.

In our minds, evil and magic are intertwined. Sinners seem to be in contact with some alternative reality where the laws of Man are suspended. Sadism, however deplorable, is also admirable because it is the reserve of Nietzsche's Supermen, an indicator of personal strength and resilience. A heart of stone lasts longer than its carnal counterpart.

Throughout human history, ferocity, mercilessness, and lack of empathy were extolled as virtues and enshrined in social institutions such as the army and the courts. The doctrine of Social Darwinism and the advent of moral relativism and deconstruction did away with ethical absolutism. The thick line between right and wrong thinned and blurred and, sometimes, vanished.

Evil nowadays is merely another form of entertainment, a species of pornography, a sanguineous art. Evildoers enliven our gossip, colour our drab routines and extract us from dreary existence and its depressive correlates. It is a little like collective self-injury. Self-mutilators report that parting their flesh with razor blades makes them feel alive and reawakened. In this synthetic universe of ours, evil and gore permit us to get in touch with real, raw, painful life.

The higher our desensitized threshold of arousal, the more profound the evil that fascinates us. Like the stimuli-addicts that we are, we increase the dosage and consume added tales of malevolence and sinfulness and immorality. Thus, in the role of spectators, we safely maintain our sense of moral supremacy and self-righteousness even as we wallow in the minutest details of the vilest crimes.

Return

# The Psychology of Mass and Serial Killers

Countess Erszebet Bathory was a breathtakingly beautiful, unusually well-educated woman, married to a descendant of Vlad Dracula of Bram Stoker fame. In 1611, she was tried – though, being a noblewoman, not convicted – in Hungary for slaughtering 612 young girls. The true figure may have been 40-100, though the Countess recorded in her diary more than 610 girls and 50 bodies were found in her estate when it was raided.

The girls were not killed outright. They were kept in a dungeon and repeatedly pierced, prodded, pricked, and cut. The Countess may have bitten chunks of flesh off their bodies while they were alive. She is said to have bathed and showered in their blood in the mistaken belief that she could thus slow down the aging process.

The Countess was notorious as an inhuman sadist long before her hygienic fixation. She once ordered the mouth of a talkative servant sewn. It is rumoured that in her childhood she witnessed a gypsy being sewn into a horse's stomach and left to die.

Her servants were executed, their bodies burnt and their ashes scattered. Being royalty, she was merely confined to her bedroom until she died in 1614. For a hundred years after her death, by royal decree, mentioning her name in Hungary was a crime.

Cases like Barothy's give the lie to the assumption that serial killers are a modern – or even post-modern – phenomenon, a cultural-societal construct, a by-product of urban alienation, Althusserian interpellation, and media glamorization. Serial killers are, indeed, largely made, not born. But they are spawned by every culture and society, moulded by the idiosyncrasies of every period as well as by their personal circumstances and genetic makeup.

Still, every crop of serial killers mirrors and reifies the pathologies of the milieu, the depravity of the Zeitgeist, and the malignancies of the Leitkultur. The choice of weapons, the identity and range of the victims, the methodology of murder, the disposal of the bodies, the geography, the sexual perversions and paraphilias – are all informed and inspired by the slayer's environment, upbringing, community, socialization, education, peer group, sexual orientation, religious convictions, and personal narrative. Movies like "Born Killers", "Man Bites Dog", "Copycat", and the Hannibal Lecter series capture this truth.

Serial killers are the quiddity and quintessence of malignant narcissism.

Yet, to some degree, we all are narcissists. Primary narcissism is a universal and inescapable developmental phase. Narcissistic traits are common and often culturally condoned. To this extent, serial killers are merely our reflection through a glass darkly.

In their book "Personality Disorders in Modern Life", Theodore Millon and Roger Davis attribute pathological narcissism to *"a society that stresses individualism and self-gratification at the expense of community... In an individualistic culture, the narcissist is 'God's gift to the world'. In a collectivist society, the narcissist is 'God's gift to the collective'."*

Lasch described the narcissistic landscape thus [in "The Culture of Narcissism: American Life in an age of Diminishing Expectations", 1979]:

*"The new narcissist is haunted not by guilt but by anxiety. He seeks not to inflict his own certainties on others but to find a meaning in life."*

The narcissist's pronounced lack of empathy, off-handed exploitativeness, grandiose fantasies and uncompromising sense of entitlement make him treat all people as though they were objects (he "objectifies" people). The narcissist regards others either as useful conduits for and Sources of Narcissistic Supply (attention, adulation, etc.) – or as extensions of himself.

Similarly, serial killers often mutilate their victims and abscond with trophies – usually, body parts. Some of them have been known to eat the organs they have ripped – an act of merging with the dead and assimilating them through digestion. They treat their victims as some children do their rag dolls.

Killing the victim – often capturing him or her on film before the murder – is a form of exerting unmitigated, absolute, and irreversible control over it. The serial killer aspires to "freeze time" in the still perfection that he has choreographed. The victim is motionless and defenceless. The killer attains long sought "object permanence". The victim is unlikely to run on the serial assassin, or vanish as earlier objects in the killer's life (e.g., his parents) have done.

In malignant narcissism, the True Self of the narcissist is replaced by a false construct, imbued with omnipotence, omniscience, and omnipresence. The narcissist's thinking is magical and infantile. He feels immune to the consequences of his own actions. Yet, this very source of apparently superhuman fortitude is also the narcissist's Achilles heel.

The narcissist's personality is chaotic. His defence mechanisms are primitive. The whole edifice is precariously balanced on pillars of denial, splitting, projection, rationalization, and Projective Identification. Narcissistic injuries – life crises, such as abandonment, divorce, financial difficulties, incarceration, public opprobrium – can bring the whole thing tumbling down. The narcissist cannot afford to be rejected, spurned, insulted, hurt, resisted, criticized, or disagreed with.

Likewise, the serial killer is trying desperately to avoid a painful relationship with his object of desire. He is terrified of being abandoned or humiliated, exposed for what he is and then discarded. Many killers often have sex – the ultimate form of intimacy – with the corpses of their victims. Objectification and mutilation allow for unchallenged possession.

Devoid of the ability to empathize, permeated by haughty feelings of superiority and uniqueness, the narcissist cannot put himself in someone else's shoes, or even imagine what it means. The very experience of being human is alien to the narcissist whose invented False Self is always to the fore, cutting him off from the rich panoply of human emotions.

Thus, the narcissist believes that all people are narcissists. Many serial killers believe that killing is the way of the world. Everyone would kill if they could or were given the chance to do so. Such killers are convinced that they are more honest and open about their desires and, thus, morally superior. They hold others in contempt for being conforming hypocrites, cowed into submission by an overweening establishment or society.

The narcissist seeks to adapt society in general – and meaningful others in particular – to his needs. He regards himself as the epitome of perfection, a yardstick against which he measures everyone, a benchmark of excellence to be emulated. He acts the guru, the sage, the "psychotherapist", the "expert", the objective observer of human affairs. He diagnoses the "faults" and "pathologies" of people around him and "helps" them "improve", "change", "evolve", and "succeed" – i.e., conform to the narcissist's vision and wishes.

Serial killers also "improve" their victims – slain, intimate objects – by "purifying" them, removing "imperfections", depersonalizing and dehumanizing them. This type of killer saves its victims from degeneration and degradation, from evil and from sin, in short: from a fate worse than death.

The killer's megalomania manifests at this stage. He claims to possess, or have access to, higher knowledge and morality. The killer is a special being and the victim is "chosen" and should be grateful for it. The killer often finds the victim's ingratitude irritating, though sadly predictable.

In his seminal work, "Aberrations of Sexual Life" (originally: "Psychopathia Sexualis"), quoted in the book "Jack the Ripper" by Donald Rumbelow, Kraft-Ebbing offers this observation:

*"The perverse urge in murders for pleasure does not solely aim at causing the victim pain and – most acute injury of all – death, but that the real meaning of the action consists in, to a certain extent, imitating, though perverted into a monstrous and ghastly form, the act of defloration. It is for this reason that an essential component ... is the employment of a sharp cutting weapon; the victim has to be pierced, slit, even chopped up... The chief wounds are inflicted in the stomach region and, in many cases, the fatal cuts run from the vagina into the abdomen. In boys an artificial vagina is even made... One can connect a fetishistic element too with this process of hacking ... inasmuch as parts of the body are removed and ... made into a collection."*

Yet, the sexuality of the serial, psychopathic, killer is self-directed. His victims are props, extensions, aides, objects, and symbols. He interacts with them ritually and, either before or after the act, transforms his diseased inner dialog into a self-consistent extraneous catechism. The narcissist is equally auto-erotic. In the sexual act, he merely masturbates with other – living – people's bodies.

The narcissist's life is a giant Repetition Complex. In a doomed attempt to resolve early conflicts with significant others, the narcissist resorts to a restricted repertoire of coping strategies, defence mechanisms, and behaviours. He seeks to recreate his past in each and every new relationship and interaction. Inevitably, the narcissist is invariably confronted with the same outcomes. This recurrence only reinforces the narcissist's rigid reactive patterns and deep-set beliefs. It is a vicious, intractable, cycle.

Correspondingly, in some cases of serial killers, the murder ritual seemed to have recreated earlier conflicts with meaningful objects, such as parents, authority figures, or peers. The outcome of the replay is different to the original, though. This time, the killer dominates the situation.

The killings allow him to inflict abuse and trauma on others rather than be abused and traumatized. He outwits and taunts figures of authority – the police, for instance. As far as the killer is concerned, he is merely "getting back" at society for what it did to him. It is a form of poetic justice, a balancing of the books, and, therefore, a "good" thing. The murder is cathartic and allows the killer to release hitherto repressed and pathologically transformed aggression – in the form of hate, rage, and envy.

But repeated acts of escalating gore fail to alleviate the killer's overwhelming anxiety and depression. He seeks to vindicate his negative introjects and sadistic Superego by being caught and punished. The serial killer tightens the proverbial noose around his neck by interacting with law enforcement agencies and the media and thus providing them with clues as to his identity and whereabouts. When apprehended, most serial assassins experience a great sense of relief.

Serial killers are not the only objectifiers – people who treat others as objects. To some extent, leaders of all sorts – political, military, or corporate – do the same. In a range of demanding professions – surgeons, medical doctors, judges, law enforcement agents – objectification efficiently fends off attendant horror and anxiety.

Yet, serial killers are different. They represent a dual failure – of their own development as full-fledged, productive individuals – and of the culture and society they grow in. In a pathologically narcissistic civilization - social anomies proliferate. Such societies breed malignant objectifiers - people devoid of empathy – also known as "narcissists".

*First published on the* <u>*Suite 101*</u> *Narcissistic Personality Disorders Topic.*

Return

# Transformations of Aggression

*Question:* Why is he so aggressive? Is it pent-up sadism? Is he born this way? It's like he hates everyone, all the time. How can I avoid this aspect of his personality?

*Answer:* Prone to magical thinking, the narcissist is deeply convinced of the transcendental meaning of his life. He fervently believes in his own uniqueness and "mission". He constantly searches for clues regarding the hidden, though inevitable, meaning of his personal life. The narcissist is forever a "public persona", even when alone, in the confines of his bedroom. His every move, his every act, his every decision and every scribbling is of momentous consequence. The narcissist often documents his life with vigil, for the benefit of future biographers. His every utterance and shred of correspondence are carefully orchestrated as befitting a historical figure of import.

This grandiose background leads to an exaggerated sense of entitlement. The narcissist feels that he is worthy of special and immediate treatment by the most qualified persons. His time is too precious to be wasted on bureaucratic trifles, misunderstandings, underlings, and social conventions. His mission is urgent. Other people are expected both to share the narcissist's self-assessment and to behave accordingly: to accommodate his needs, instantly comply with his wishes, and succumb to his whims.

But the world does not always accommodate, comply, and succumb. It often resists the wishes of the narcissist, mocks his comportment, or, worst of all, ignores him. The narcissist reacts to this with a cycle of frustration and aggression.

Still, it is not always possible to express naked aggression. It may be dangerous, or counterproductive, or plain silly. Even the narcissist cannot attack his boss, or a policeman, or the neighbourhood bully with impunity. So, the narcissist's aggression wears many forms. The narcissist suddenly becomes brutally "honest", or bitingly "humorous", or smotheringly "helpful", or sexually "experimental", or socially "reclusive", or behaviourally "different", or finds yet another way to express his scathing and repressed hostility.

The narcissist's favourite sadistic cocktail is brutal honesty coupled with "helpful advice" and "concern" for the welfare of the person thus attacked. The narcissist blurts out, often unprovoked, hurtful observations. These statements are invariably couched in a socially impeccable context.

For instance, "Do you know you have bad breath? You will be much more popular had you treated it", "You are really too fat, you should take care of yourself, you are not young, you know, who knows what this is doing to your heart", "These clothes do not complement you. Let me give you the name of my tailor...", "You are behaving very strangely lately, I think that talk therapy combined with medication may do wonders", and so on.

The misanthropic and schizoid narcissist at once becomes sociable and friendly when he spots an opportunity to hurt someone or to avenge himself. He then resorts to humour: black, thwarted, poignant, biting, sharpened and agonizing. Thinly disguises barbs follow thinly disguised threats cloaked in "jokes" or "humorous anecdotes".

Another favourite trick is to harp on the insecurities, fears, weaknesses, and deficiencies of the target of aggression. If married to a jealous spouse, the narcissist emphasizes his newfound promiscuity and need to experiment sexually. If his business partner has been traumatized by a previous insolvency, the narcissist berates him for being too cautious or insufficiently entrepreneurial while forcing the partnership to assume outlandish and speculative business risks. If co-habiting with a gregarious mate, the narcissist acts the recluse, the hermit, the social misfit, or the misunderstood visionary, thus forcing the partner to give up her social life.

The narcissist is seething with enmity and venom. He is a receptacle of unbridled hatred, animosity, and hostility. When he can, the narcissist often turns to physical violence. But the non-physical manifestations of his pent-up bile are even more terrifying, more all-pervasive, and more lasting. Beware of narcissists bearing gifts. They are bound to explode in your face, or poison you. The narcissist hates you wholeheartedly and thoroughly simply because you are. Remembering this has a survival value.

## The Adrenaline Junkie

Narcissistic Supply is exciting. When it is available, the narcissist feels elated, omnipotent, omniscient, handsome, sexy, adventurous, invincible, and irresistible. When it is missing, the narcissist first enters a manic phase of trying to replenish his supply and, if he fails, the narcissist shrivels, withdraws and is reduced to a zombie-like state of numbness.

Some people – and all narcissists – are addicted to excitement, to the adrenaline rush, to the danger inevitably and invariably involved. They are the adrenaline junkies. All narcissists are adrenaline junkies, but not all adrenaline junkies are narcissists.

Narcissistic Supply is the narcissist's particular sort of thrill. Deficient Narcissistic Supply is tantamount to the absence of excitement and thrills in non-narcissistic adrenaline junkies.

Originally, in early childhood, Narcissistic Supply is meant to help the narcissist regulate his volatile sense of self-worth and self-esteem. But Narcissistic Supply, regardless of its psychodynamic functions, also simply feels good. The narcissist grows addicted to the gratifying effects of Narcissistic Supply. He reacts with anxiety when constant, reliable provision is absent or threatened.

Thus, Narcissistic Supply always comes with excitement, on the one hand and with anxiety on the other hand.

When unable to secure "normal" Narcissistic Supply – adulation, recognition, fame, celebrity, notoriety, infamy, affirmation, or mere attention – the narcissist resorts to "abnormal" Narcissistic Supply. He tries to obtain his drug – the thrills, the good feeling that comes with Narcissistic Supply – by behaving recklessly, by succumbing to substance abuse, or by living dangerously.

Narcissists faced with a chronic state of deficient Narcissistic Supply become criminals, or race car drivers, or gamblers, or soldiers, or investigative journalists. They defy authority. They avoid safety, routine and boredom: no safe sex, no financial prudence, no stable marriage or career. They become peripatetic and itinerant. They change jobs, or lovers, or vocations, or avocations, or residences, or friendships often.

But sometimes even these extreme and demonstrative steps are not enough. When confronted with a boring, routine existence, with a chronic and permanent inability to secure Narcissistic Supply and excitement, these people compensate by inventing thrills where there are none.

They become paranoid, full of delusional persecutory notions and ideas of reference. Or they develop phobias: fear of flying, of heights, of enclosed or open spaces, of cats or spiders. Fear is a good substitute to the excitement they so crave and that eludes them.

Anxiety leads to the frenetic search for Narcissistic Supply. Obtaining the supply causes a general, albeit transient, sense of wellbeing, relief and release as the anxiety is alleviated. This cycle is addictive.

But what generates the anxiety in the first place? Are people born adrenaline junkies or do they become ones?

No one knows for sure. It may be genetically determined. We may discover one day that adrenaline junkies, conditioned by defective genes, develop special neural and biochemical paths, an unusual sensitivity to adrenaline. Or, it may indeed be the sad outcome of abuse and trauma during the formative years. The brain is plastic and easily influenced by recurrent bouts of capricious and malicious treatment.

*First published on the Suite 101 Narcissistic Personality Disorders Topic.*

Return

# The Narcissist's Victims

*Question:* You describe the narcissist as a cunning, immoral extortionist. How does the narcissist affect people around him?

*Answer:* Sooner, or later, everyone around the narcissist is bound to become his victim. People are sucked – voluntarily or involuntarily – into the turbulence that constitutes his life, into the black hole that is his personality, into the whirlwind, which makes-up his interpersonal relationships.

Different people are adversely affected by different aspects of the narcissist's life and psychological makeup. Some trust him and rely on him, only to be bitterly disappointed. Others love him and discover that he cannot reciprocate. Yet others are forced to live vicariously, through him.

There are three categories of victims:

*Victims of the narcissist's instability* – The narcissist leads an unpredictable, vicissitudinal, precarious, often dangerous life. His ground is ever shifting: geographically as well as mentally. He changes addresses, workplaces, vocations, avocations, interests, friends and enemies with a bewildering speed. He baits authority and challenges it.

He is, therefore, prone to conflict: likely to be a criminal, a rebel, a dissident, or a critic. He gets bored easily, trapped in cycles of idealization and devaluation of people, places, hobbies, jobs, values. He is mercurial, unstable, and unreliable. His family suffers: his spouse and children have to wander with him in his private desert, endure the Via Dolorosa that he incessantly walks.

They live in constant fear and trepidation: what next? where next? who is next? To a lesser extent, this is the case with the narcissist's friends, bosses, colleagues, or with his country. These biographical vacillations and mental oscillations deny the people around him autonomy, unperturbed development and self-fulfilment, their path to self-recognition and contentment.

To the narcissist, other humans are mere instruments, Sources of Narcissistic Supply. He sees no reason to consider their needs, wishes, wants, desires and fears. He derails their life with ease and ignorance. Deep inside he knows that he is wrong to do so because they might retaliate – hence, his persecutory delusions.

*Victims of the narcissist's misleading signals* – These are the victims of the narcissist's deceiving emotional messages. The narcissist mimics real emotions artfully. He exudes the air of someone really capable of loving or of being hurt, of one passionate and soft, empathic and caring. Most people are misled into believing that he is even more humane than average.

They fall in love with the mirage, the fleeting image, with the fata morgana of a lush emotional oasis in the midst of their emotional desert. They succumb to the luring proposition that he is. They give in, give up, and give everything only to be discarded ruthlessly when deemed by the narcissist to be no longer useful.

Riding high on the crest of the narcissist's over-valuation only to crash into the abysmal depths of his devaluation, these victims lose control over their emotional life. The narcissist drains them, exhausts their resources, sucks the blood-life of Narcissistic Supply out of their dwindling, depleted selves.

This emotional roller coaster is so harrowing that the experience borders on the truly traumatic. To remove doubt: this behaviour pattern is not confined to matters of the heart. The narcissist's employer, for instance, is misled by his apparent seriousness, industriousness, ambition, willing to sacrifice, honesty, thoroughness and a host of other utterly fake qualities.

These apparent traits are false because they are directed at securing Narcissistic Supply rather than at doing a good job. The narcissist's clients and suppliers may suffer from the same illusion.

The narcissist's fraudulent emanations are not restricted to messages with emotional content. They may contain wrong or false or partial information. The narcissist does not hesitate to lie, deceive, or "reveal" (misleading) half-truths. He appears to be intelligent, charming and, therefore, reliable. He is a convincing conjurer of words, signs, behaviours, and body language.

The above two classes of victims are casually exploited and then discarded by the narcissist. As far as the narcissist is concerned, no more malice is involved in this behaviour pattern than in any other interaction with an instrument. No more premeditation and contemplation than in breathing. These are victims of narcissistic reflexes. Perhaps this is what makes it all so repulsively horrific: the offhanded nature of the damage inflicted.

Not so the third category of victims.

These are the *victims upon whom the narcissist designs*, maliciously and intentionally, to inflict his wrath and bad intentions. The narcissist is both sadistic and masochistic. In hurting others he always seeks to hurt himself. In punishing them he wishes to be penalized. Their pains are his.

Thus, he attacks figures of authority and social institutions with vicious, uncontrolled, almost insane rage – only to accept his due punishment (their reaction to his venomous diatribes or antisocial actions) with incredible complacency, or even relief. He engages in vitriolic humiliation of his kin and folk, of regime and government, of his firm or of the law – only to suffer pleasurably in the role of the outcast, the ex-communicated, the exiled, and the imprisoned martyr or dissident.

The punishment of the narcissist does little to compensate his randomly (rather incomprehensibly) selected victims. The narcissist forces individuals and groups of people around him to pay a heavy toll, materially, in reputation, and emotionally. He is ruinous, and disruptive.

In behaving so, the narcissist seeks not only to be punished, but also to maintain emotional detachment (Emotional Involvement Preventive Measures, EIPMs). Threatened by intimacy and by the predatory cosiness of routine and mediocrity, the narcissist lashes back at what he perceives to be the sources of this dual threat. He attacks those whom he thinks take him for granted, those who fail to recognize his superiority, those who consider him "average" and "normal".

And they, alas, include just about everyone he knows.

Return

# Narcissism by Proxy

*Question:* Is narcissism "contagious"? Can one "catch" narcissism by living with a narcissist?

*Answer:* Clinicians use the word "epidemiology" to describe the prevalence of psychopathologies. There is some merit in examining the incidence of personality disorders in the general population. Mental health is the visible outcome of an intricate interplay between nature and nurture, genetics and culture, the brain and one's upbringing and socialization.

Yet are personality disorders communicable diseases?

The answer is more complex than a simple "yes" or "no". Personality disorders are not contagious in the strict, rigorous, medical sense. They are not communicated by pathogens from one individual to another. They lack many of the basic features of biological epidemics. Still, they are communicated.

First, there is the direct, interpersonal, influence.

A casual encounter with a narcissist is likely to leave a bad aftertaste, bewilderment, hurt, or anger. But these transient reactions have no lasting effect and they fade with time. Not so with a more protracted exposure: marriage, partnership, cohabitation, working or studying together and the like.

Narcissism brushes off. Our reactions to the narcissist, the initial ridicule, the occasional rage, or the frustration tend to accumulate and form the sediment of deformity. Gradually, the narcissist distorts the personalities of those he is in constant touch with, casts them in his defective mould, limits them, redirects them, and inhibits them. When sufficiently cloned, the narcissist uses the people he affected as narcissistic proxies, narcissistic vehicles of vicarious narcissism.

The narcissist provokes in us emotions, which are predominantly negative and unpleasant. The initial reaction, as we said, is likely to be ridicule. The narcissist is pompous, incredibly self-centred, falsely grandiose, spoiled and odd (even his manner of speech is likely to be constrained and archaic). Thus, he often elicits smirks in lieu of admiration.

But the entertainment value is fast over. The narcissist's behaviour becomes tiresome, irksome and cumbersome. Ridicule is supplanted by ire and, then, by overt anger. The narcissist's inadequacies are so glaring and his denial and other defence mechanisms so primitive that we constantly feel like screaming at him, reproaching him, or even striking at him literally as well as figuratively.

Ashamed of these reactions, we begin to feel guilty. We find ourselves attached to a mental pendulum, swinging between repulsion and guilt, rage and pity, lack of empathy and remorse. Slowly we acquire the very characteristics of the narcissist that we so deplore. We become as tactless as he is, as devoid of empathy and of consideration, as ignorant of the emotional makeup of other people, and as one track minded. Exposed to the sick halo of the narcissist, we are "infected".

The narcissist invades our personality. He makes us react the way he would have liked to have reacted, had he dared, or had he known how (a mechanism known as Projective Identification). We are exhausted by his eccentricity, by his extravagance, by his grandiosity, by his constant entitlement.

The narcissist incessantly, adamantly, even aggressively makes demands upon his human environment. He is addicted to his Narcissistic Supply: admiration, adoration, approval, attention. He forces others to lie to him and over-rate his achievements, his talents, and his merits. Living in a narcissistic cult or fantasyland, he compels his closest, nearest and dearest to join him there.

The resulting depletion, exhaustion, desperation and weakening of the will are fully taken advantage of by the narcissist. He penetrates these reduced defences and, like a Trojan horse, spews forth his lethal charge. Gradually, those in proximity to him, find themselves imitating and emulating his personality traits. The narcissist also does not refrain from intimidating them into compliance with his commands.

The narcissist coerces people around him by making subtle uses of processes such as reinforcement and conditioning. As they seek to avoid the unpleasant consequences of not succumbing to his wishes, people put up with his demands and are subjected to his whims. Not to endure his terrifying rages, they "cut corners", pretend, participate in his charade, lie, and become subsumed in his grandiose fantasies.

Rather than be aggressively nagged, they reduce themselves and minimize their profiles, rendering themselves invisible. By doing all this they delude themselves into believing that they have escaped the worst consequences.

But the worst is yet to come. The narcissist is confined, constrained, restrained and inhibited by the unique structures of his personality and of his disorder. There are many behaviours which he cannot engage in, many reactions and actions "prohibited", many desires stifled, many fears insurmountable.

The narcissist uses others as an outlet for all these repressed emotions and behaviour patterns. Having invaded their personalities, having altered them by methods of attrition and erosion, having made them compatible with his own disorder, having secured the submission and compliance of his victims, he moves on to occupy their shells. Then he makes them do what he has always dreamt of doing, what he has often desired, what he has constantly feared to do.

Using the same compelling procedures, he drives his mates, spouse, partners, colleagues, children, or co-workers into collaborating in the expression of the repressed side of his personality. At the same time, he negates their vague suspicion that their personality has been replaced by his when committing these acts.

The narcissist can, thus, derive, vicariously, through the lives of others, the Narcissistic Supply that he so craves. He induces in his army of zombies criminal, romantic, or heroic, impulses. He makes his bots travel far and fast, breach all norms, gamble against all odds, fear none and nothing – in short: he transforms them into that which he could never be.

The narcissist thrives on the attention, admiration, fascination, or horrified reactions lavished upon his proxies. He consumes the Narcissistic Supply flowing through these human conduits of his own making. Such a narcissist is likely to use sentences like "I made him", "He was nothing before he met me", "He is my creation", "She learned everything she knows from me and at my expense", and so on.

Sufficiently detached – both emotionally and legally – the narcissist flees the scene when the going gets tough. Often, these behaviours, acts and emotions induced by the proximity to the narcissist result in harsh consequences. An emotional or legal crisis, a physical or material catastrophe are common outcomes of doing the narcissist's bidding.

The narcissist's prey is not equipped to deal with the crises that are the narcissist's daily bread and which, now, he or she are forced to confront as the narcissist's proxy. The behaviour and emotions induced by the narcissist are alien and the victim experiences a cognitive dissonance. This only aggravates the situation. But the narcissist is rarely there to watch his clones writhe and suffer.

At the first sign of trouble, he goes missing. This vanishing act is not necessarily physical or geographical. The narcissist is actually better at disappearing emotionally and at evading his moral and legal obligations (despite his constant self-righteous moralizing).

It is then and there that his family and coterie discover his true colours: he uses and discards people offhandedly. To him, people are either "functional" and "useful" in his pursuit of Narcissistic Supply – or they are not. But, in both cases, he regards them not as human but as objects, or mere abstractions. Of all the hurts that the narcissist inflicts on his nearest and ostensibly dearest, this abrupt and contemptuous disregard is, probably, the strongest and most enduring one.

## When Victims Become Narcissists

Some people adopt the role of a professional victim. In doing so, they become self-centred, devoid of empathy, abusive, and exploitative. In other words, they become narcissists. The role of "professional victims" – people whose existence and very identity rest solely and entirely on their victimhood – is well researched in victimology. It doesn't make for nice reading.

These victim "pros" are often more cruel, vengeful, vitriolic, lacking in compassion and violent than their abusers. They make a career of it. They identify with this role to the exclusion of all else. This is precisely what I call "Narcissistic Contagion" or "Narcissism by Proxy".

Those affected entertain the (false) notion that they can compartmentalize their narcissistic behaviour and direct it only at the narcissist. In other words, they trust in their ability to segregate their conduct and to be verbally abusive towards the narcissist while civil and compassionate with others, to act with malice where the narcissist is concerned and with Christian charity towards all others.

They cling to the "faucet theory". They believe that they can turn on and off their negative feelings, their abusive outbursts, their vindictiveness and vengefulness, their blind rage, their non-discriminating judgement. This, of course, is untrue. These behaviours spill over into daily transactions with innocent neighbours, colleagues, family members, co-workers, or customers.

One cannot be partly or temporarily vindictive and judgemental any more than one can be partly or temporarily pregnant. To their horror, these victims discover that they have been transmuted and transformed into their worst nightmare: into narcissists.

Return

# Facilitating Narcissism

*"The new narcissist is haunted not by guilt but by anxiety. He seeks not to inflict his own certainties on others but to find a meaning in life."*
[Christopher Lasch - The Culture of Narcissism: American Life in an Age of Diminishing Expectations, 1979]

*"A characteristic of our times is the predominance, even in groups traditionally selective, of the mass and the vulgar. Thus, in intellectual life, which of its essence requires and presupposes qualification, one can note the progressive triumph of the pseudo-intellectual, unqualified, unqualifiable..."*
[Jose Ortega y Gasset - The Revolt of the Masses, 1932]

We are surrounded by malignant narcissists. How come this disorder has hitherto been largely ignored? How come there is such a dearth of research and literature regarding this crucial family of pathologies? Even mental health practitioners are woefully unaware of it and unprepared to assist its victims.

The sad answer is that narcissism meshes well with our culture. [See: Lasch - The Cultural Narcissist]

It is a kind of a "background narcissistic radiation", permeating every social and cultural interaction. It is hard to distinguish pathological narcissists from ambitious, self-assertive, self-confident, self-promoting, eccentric, or highly individualistic persons. Hard sell, greed, envy, self-centredness, exploitativeness, diminished empathy are all socially condoned features of Western civilization.

Our society is atomized, the outcome of individualism gone awry. It encourages narcissistic leadership and role models.

Its sub-structures - institutionalized religion, political parties, civic organizations, the media, corporations - are all suffused with narcissism and pervaded by its pernicious outcomes. [See: Collective Narcissism]

The very ethos of materialism and capitalism upholds certain narcissistic traits, such as reduced empathy, exploitation, a sense of entitlement, or grandiose fantasies ("vision"). [More about this in It is My World]

Narcissists are aided, abetted and facilitated by four types of people and institutions: the adulators, the blissfully ignorant, the self-deceiving and those deceived by the narcissist.

The adulators are fully aware of the nefarious and damaging aspects of the narcissist's behaviour but believe that they are more than offset by his positive traits and by the benefits – to themselves, to their collective, or to society at large. They engage in an explicit trade-off between some of their principles and values and their personal profit, or the greater good. In a curious inversion of judgement, they cast the perpetrator as the victim of a smear campaign orchestrated by the abused or attribute the offender's predicament to bigotry.

They seek to help the narcissist, promote his agenda, shield him from harm, connect him with like-minded people, do his chores for him and, in general, create the conditions and the environment for his success. This kind of alliance is especially prevalent in political parties, the government, multinationals, religious organizations and other hierarchical collectives.

The blissfully ignorant are simply unaware of the "bad sides" of the narcissist – and make sure they remain oblivious to them. They look the other way, or pretend that the narcissist's behaviour is normative, or turn a blind eye to his egregious misbehaviour. They are classic deniers of reality. Some of them maintain a generally rosy outlook premised on the inbred benevolence of Mankind. Others simply cannot tolerate dissonance and discord. They prefer to live in a fantastic world where everything is harmonious and smooth and evil is banished. They react with rage to any information to the contrary and block it out instantly. Once they form an opinion that the accusations against the narcissist are overblown, malicious, and false – it becomes immutable. "I have made up my mind, – they seem to be broadcasting – now don't confuse me with the facts." This type of denial is well evidenced in dysfunctional families.

The self-deceivers are fully aware of the narcissist's transgressions and malice, his indifference, exploitativeness, lack of empathy, and rampant grandiosity – but they prefer to displace the causes, or the effects of such misconduct. They attribute it to externalities ("a rough patch"), or judge it to be temporary. They even go as far as accusing the victim for the narcissist's lapses, or for defending herself ("she provoked him").

In a feat of cognitive dissonance, they deny any connection between the acts of the narcissist and their consequences ("His wife abandoned him because she was promiscuous, not because of anything he did to her"). They are swayed by the narcissist's undeniable charm, intelligence, or attractiveness. But the narcissist needs not invest resources in converting them to his cause: he does not deceive them. They are self-propelled into the abyss that is narcissism. The inverted narcissist, for instance, is a self-deceiver.

The deceived are people – or institutions, or collectives – deliberately taken for a premeditated ride by the narcissist. He feeds them false information, manipulates their judgement, proffers plausible scenarios to account for his indiscretions, soils the opposition, charms them, appeals to their reason, or to their emotions, and promises the Moon.

Again, the narcissist's incontrovertible powers of persuasion and his impressive personality play a part in this predatory ritual. The deceived are especially hard to deprogram. They are often themselves encumbered with narcissistic traits and find it impossible to admit a mistake, or to atone.

They are likely to stay on with the narcissist to his – and their – bitter end.

Regrettably, the narcissist rarely pays the price for his offences. His victims pick up the tab. But even here the malignant optimism of the abused never ceases to amaze.

*First published on the Suite 101 Narcissistic Personality Disorders Topic.*

Return

# Narcissists in Positions of Authority

*"He knows not how to rule a kingdom, that cannot manage a province; nor can he wield a province, that cannot order a city; nor he order a city, that knows not how to regulate a village; nor he a village, that cannot guide a family; nor can that man govern well a family that knows not how to govern himself; neither can any govern himself unless his reason be lord, will and appetite her vassals; nor can reason rule unless herself be ruled by God, and be obedient to Him."*
   [Hugo Grotius, Jurist]

*Question:* Are narcissists in position of authority likely to take advantage of their patients/students/subordinates?

*Answer:* Being in a position of authority secures the uninterrupted flow of Narcissistic Supply. Fed by the awe, fear, subordination, admiration, adoration and obedience of his underlings, parish, students, or patients, the narcissist thrives in such circumstances. The narcissist aspires to acquire authority by any means available to him. He may achieve it by making use of some outstanding traits or skills such as his intelligence, or through an asymmetry built into a relationship. The narcissistic medical doctor or mental health professional and his patients, the narcissistic guide, teacher, or mentor and his students, the narcissistic leader, guru, pundit, or psychic and his followers or admirers, or the narcissistic business tycoon, boss, or employer and his subordinates – all are instances of such asymmetry. The rich, powerful, more knowledgeable narcissists occupy a Pathological Narcissistic Space.

   These types of relationships – based on the unidirectional and unilateral flow of Narcissistic Supply – border on abuse. The narcissist, in pursuit of an ever-increasing supply, of an ever-larger dose of adoration, and an ever-bigger fix of attention, gradually loses his moral constraints. With time, it gets harder to obtain Narcissistic Supply. The sources of such supply are human and they become weary, rebellious, tired, bored, disgusted, repelled, or plainly amused by the narcissist's incessant dependence, his childish craving for attention, his exaggerated or even paranoid fears which lead to obsessive-compulsive behaviours. To secure their continued collaboration in the procurement of his much-needed supply the narcissist might resort to emotional extortion, straight blackmail, abuse, or misuse of his authority.

The temptation to do so, though, is universal. No doctor is immune to the charms of certain female patients, nor are university professors asexual. What prevent them from immorally, cynically, callously and consistently abusing their positions are ethical imperatives embedded in them through socialization and empathy. They have learned the difference between right and wrong and, having internalized it, they choose right when they face a moral dilemma. They empathize with other human beings, "putting themselves in their shoes", and refrain from doing unto others what they do not wish to be done to them.

In these two crucial points narcissists differ from other humans.

Their socialization process – usually the product of problematic early relationships with Primary Objects (parents, or caregivers) – is often perturbed and results in social dysfunctioning. And they are incapable of empathizing: as far as they are concerned, people exist only to supply them with Narcissistic Supply. Those unfortunate few who do not comply with this overriding dictum must be made to alter their ways and if even this fails, the narcissist loses interest in them and classifies them as "sub-human, animals, service-providers, functions, symbols" and worse. Hence the abrupt shifts from over-valuation to devaluation of others. While bearing the gift of Narcissistic Supply the "other" is idealized by the narcissist. The narcissist shifts to the opposite pole (devaluation) when Narcissistic Supply dries up or when he estimates that it is about to.

As far as the narcissist is concerned, there is no moral dimension to abusing others – only a pragmatic one: will he be punished for doing so? The narcissist is atavistically responsive to fear and lacks any in-depth understanding of what it is to be a human being. Trapped in his pathology, the narcissist resembles an alien on drugs, a junkie of Narcissistic Supply devoid of the kind of language, which renders human emotions intelligible and communicable.

### Narcissistic Leaders

*"It was precisely that evening in Lodi that I came to believe in myself as an unusual person and became consumed with the*

*ambition to do the great things that until then had been but a fantasy."*
[Napoleon Bonaparte, "Thoughts"]

*"They may all e called Heroes, in as much as they have derived their purposes and their vocation not from the calm regular course of things, sanctioned by the existing order, but from a concealed fount, from that inner Spirit, still hidden beneath the surface, which impinges on the outer world as a shell and bursts it into pieces – such were Alexander, Caesar, Napoleon... World-historical men – the Heroes of an epoch – must therefore be recognized as its clear-sighted ones: their deeds, their words are the best of their time... Moral claims which are irrelevant must not be brought into collision with World-historical deeds... So mighty a form must trample down many an innocent flower – crush to pieces many an object in its path."*
[G.W.F. Hegel, "Lectures on the Philosophy of History"]

*"Such beings are incalculable, they come like fate without cause or reason, inconsiderately and without pretext. Suddenly they are here like lightning too terrible, too sudden, too compelling and too 'different' even to be hated... What moves them is the terrible egotism of the artist of the brazen glance, who knows himself to be justified for all eternity in his 'work' as the mother is justified in her child...*

*In all great deceivers a remarkable process is at work to which they owe their power. In the very act of deception with all its preparations, the dreadful voice, expression, and gestures, they are overcome by their belief in themselves; it is this belief which then speaks, so persuasively, so miracle-like, to the audience."*
[Friedrich Nietzsche, "The Genealogy of Morals"]

The narcissistic leader is the culmination and reification of his period, culture, and civilization. He is likely to rise to prominence in narcissistic societies.

The malignant narcissist invents and then projects a False, fictitious, Self for the world to fear, or to admire. He maintains a tenuous grasp on reality to start with and this is further exacerbated by the trappings of power. The narcissist's grandiose self-delusions and fantasies of omnipotence and omniscience are supported by real life authority and the narcissist's predilection to surround himself with obsequious sycophants.

The narcissist's personality is so precariously balanced that he cannot tolerate even a hint of criticism and disagreement. Most narcissists are paranoid and suffer from ideas of reference (the delusion that they are being mocked or discussed when they are not). Thus, narcissists often regard themselves counterfactually as "victims of persecution".

The narcissistic leader fosters and encourages a personality cult with all the hallmarks of an institutional religion: priesthood, rites, rituals, temples, worship, catechism, mythology. The leader is this religion's ascetic saint. He monastically denies himself earthly pleasures (or so he claims) in order to be able to dedicate himself fully to his calling.

The narcissistic leader is a monstrously inverted Jesus, sacrificing his life and denying himself so that his people – or humanity at large – should benefit. By surpassing and suppressing his humanity, the narcissistic leader becomes a distorted version of Nietzsche's "Superman".

But being a-human or super-human also means being a-sexual and a-moral.

In this restricted sense, narcissistic leaders are post-modernist and moral relativists. They project to the masses an androgynous figure and enhance it by engendering the adoration of nudity and all things "natural" – or by strongly repressing these feelings. But what they refer to as "nature" is not natural at all.

The narcissistic leader invariably proffers an aesthetic of decadence and evil carefully orchestrated and artificial – though it is not perceived this way by him or by his followers. Narcissistic leadership is about reproduced copies, not about originals. It is about the manipulation of symbols – not about veritable atavism or true conservatism.

In short: narcissistic leadership is about theatre, not about life. To enjoy the spectacle (and be subsumed by it), the leader demands the suspension of judgement, depersonalization, and de-realization. Catharsis is tantamount, in this narcissistic dramaturgy, to self-annulment.

Narcissism is nihilistic not only operationally, or ideologically. Its very language and narratives are nihilistic. Narcissism is conspicuous nihilism – and the cult's leader serves as a role model, annihilating the Man, only to re-appear as a pre-ordained and irresistible Force of Nature.

Narcissistic leadership often poses as a rebellion against the "old ways": against the hegemonic culture, the upper classes, the established religions, the superpowers, the corrupt order. Narcissistic movements are puerile, a reaction to narcissistic injuries inflicted upon a narcissistic (and rather psychopathic) toddler nation-state, or group, or upon the leader.

Minorities or "others" – often arbitrarily selected – constitute a perfect, easily identifiable, embodiment of all that is "wrong". They are accused of being antiquated, of being eerily disembodied, cosmopolitan, part of the establishment, or "decadent". They are hated on religious and socio-economic grounds, or because of their race, sexual orientation, origin... They are castigated as different, as narcissistic (feel and act as morally superior), they are everywhere, they are defenceless, they are credulous, they are adaptable (and thus can be co-opted to collaborate in their own destruction). They are the perfect hate figures. Narcissists thrive on hatred and pathological envy.

This is precisely the source of the fascination with Hitler, diagnosed by Erich Fromm – together with Stalin – as a malignant narcissist. He was an inverted human. His unconscious was his conscious. He acted out our most repressed drives, fantasies, and wishes. He provides us with a glimpse of the horrors that lie beneath our social veneer, the barbarians at our personal gates, and what it was like before we invented civilization. Hitler forced us all through a time warp and many did not emerge. He was not the devil. He was one of us. He epitomized what Arendt aptly called the banality of evil: just an ordinary, mentally disturbed failure, a member of a mentally disturbed and failing nation, who lived through disturbed and failing times. He was the perfect mirror, a channel, a voice, and the very depth of our souls.

The narcissistic leader prefers the sparkle and glamour of well-orchestrated illusions to the tedium and method of real accomplishments. His reign is all smoke and mirrors, devoid of substances, consisting of mere appearances and mass delusions. In the aftermath of his regime – the narcissistic leader having died, been deposed, or voted out of office – it all unravels. The tireless and constant prestidigitation ceases and the entire edifice crumbles. What looked like an economic miracle turns out to have been a fraud-laced bubble. Loosely-held empires disintegrate. Laboriously assembled business conglomerates go to pieces. "Earth shattering" and "revolutionary" scientific discoveries and theories are discredited. Social experiments end in mayhem.

It is important to understand that the use of violence must be ego-syntonic. It must accord with the self-image of the narcissist. It must abet and sustain his grandiose fantasies and feed his sense of entitlement. It must conform to the narcissistic narrative.

Thus, a narcissist who regards himself as the benefactor of the poor, a member of the common folk, the representative of the disenfranchised, the champion of the dispossessed against the corrupt elite – is more unlikely to resort to violence against the poor, the disenfranchised, and the dispossessed.

The pacific mask crumbles when the narcissist becomes convinced that the very people he purported to speak for, his constituency, his grassroots fans, the Prime Sources of his Narcissistic Supply have turned against him. At first, in a desperate effort to maintain the fiction underlying his chaotic personality, the narcissist strives to explain away the sudden reversal of sentiment. "The people are being duped by (the media, big industry, foreign powers, the military, the elite, etc.)", "They don't really know what they are doing", "They will have a rude awakening and revert to form", etc. When these flimsy attempts to patch a tattered personal mythology fail, the narcissist is injured. Narcissistic injury inevitably leads to narcissistic rage and to a terrifying display of unbridled aggression. The pent-up frustration and hurt translate into devaluation. That which was previously idealized is now discarded with contempt and hatred.

This primitive defence mechanism is called "splitting". To the narcissist, things and people are either entirely bad (evil) or entirely good. "You are either with me or against me" is a common refrain. The narcissist projects onto others his own shortcomings and negative emotions, thus transforming himself, in his mind, into a totally good object. A narcissistic leader is likely to justify the butchering of his own people by claiming that they intended to kill him, undo the revolution, devastate the economy, or the country, etc.

The "small people", the "rank and file", the "loyal soldiers" of the narcissist – his flock, his nation, his employees – they pay the price. The disillusionment and disenchantment are agonizing. The process of reconstruction, of rising from the ashes, of overcoming the trauma of having been deceived, exploited and manipulated – is drawn-out. It is difficult to trust again, to have faith, to love, to be led, to collaborate. Feelings of shame and guilt engulf the erstwhile followers of the narcissist. This is his sole legacy: a massive Post-Traumatic Stress Disorder.

### The Cult of the Narcissist

The narcissist is the guru at the centre of a cult. Like other gurus, he demands complete obedience from his flock: his spouse, his offspring, other family members, friends, and colleagues. He feels entitled to adulation and special treatment by his followers. He punishes the wayward and the straying lambs. He enforces discipline, adherence to his teachings, and common goals. The less accomplished he is in reality – the more stringent his mastery and the more pervasive the brainwashing.

The – often involuntary – members of the narcissist's mini-cult inhabit a twilight zone of his own construction. He imposes on them a shared psychosis, replete with persecutory delusions, "enemies", mythical narratives, and apocalyptic scenarios if he is flouted.

The narcissist's control is based on ambiguity, unpredictability, fuzziness, and ambient abuse. His ever-shifting whims exclusively define right versus wrong, desirable and unwanted, what is to be pursued and what to be avoided. He alone determines the rights and obligations of his disciples and alters them at will.

The narcissist is a micro-manager. He exerts control over the minutest details and behaviours. He punishes severely and abuses withholders of information and those who fail to conform to his wishes and goals.

The narcissist does not respect the boundaries and privacy of his reluctant adherents. He ignores their wishes and treats them as objects or instruments of gratification. He seeks to control both situations and people compulsively.

He strongly disapproves of others' personal autonomy and independence. Even innocuous activities, such as meeting a friend or visiting one's family require his permission. Gradually, he isolates his nearest and dearest until they are fully dependent on him emotionally, sexually, financially, and socially.

He acts in a patronizing and condescending manner and criticizes often. He alternates between emphasizing the minutest faults (devaluation) and exaggerating the talents, traits, and skills (idealization) of the members of his cult. He is wildly unrealistic in his expectations – which, when he is inevitably let down, legitimizes his subsequent abusive conduct.

The narcissist claims to be infallible, superior, talented, skilful, omnipotent, and omniscient. He often lies and confabulates to support these unfounded claims. Within his cult, he expects awe, admiration, adulation, and constant attention commensurate with his outlandish stories and assertions. He reinterprets reality to fit his fantasies.

His thinking is dogmatic, rigid, and doctrinaire. He does not countenance free thought, pluralism, or free speech and doesn't brook criticism and disagreement. He demands – and often gets –

complete trust and the relegation to his capable hands of all decision-making.

He forces the participants in his cult to be hostile to critics, the authorities, institutions, his personal enemies, or the media – if they try to uncover his actions and reveal the truth. He closely monitors and censors information from the outside, exposing his captive audience only to selective data and analyzes.

The narcissist's cult is "missionary" and "imperialistic". He is always on the lookout for new recruits – his spouse's friends, his daughter's girlfriends, his neighbours, new colleagues at work. He immediately attempts to "convert" them to his "creed" – to convince them how wonderful and admirable he is. In other words, he tries to render them Sources of Narcissistic Supply.

Often, his behaviour on these "recruiting missions" is different to his conduct within the "cult". In the first phases of wooing new admirers and proselytizing to potential "conscripts" – the narcissist is attentive, compassionate, empathic, flexible, self-effacing, and helpful. At home, among the "veterans" he is tyrannical, demanding, wilful, opinionated, aggressive, and exploitative.

As the leader of his congregation, the narcissist feels entitled to special amenities and benefits not accorded the "rank and file". He expects to be waited on hand and foot, to make free use of everyone's money and dispose of their assets liberally, and to be cynically exempt from the rules that he himself established (if such violation is pleasurable or gainful).

In extreme cases, the narcissist feels above the law – any kind of law. This grandiose and haughty conviction leads to criminal acts, incestuous or polygamous relationships, and recurrent friction with the authorities.

Hence the narcissist's panicky and sometimes violent reactions to "dropouts" from his cult. There's a lot going on that the narcissist wants kept under wraps. Moreover, the narcissist stabilizes his fluctuating sense of self-worth by deriving Narcissistic Supply from his victims. Abandonment threatens the narcissist's precariously balanced personality.

Add to that the narcissist's paranoid and schizoid tendencies, his lack of introspective self-awareness, and his stunted sense of humour (lack of self-deprecation) and the risks to the grudging members of his cult are clear.

The narcissist sees enemies and conspiracies everywhere. He often casts himself as the heroic victim (martyr) of dark and stupendous forces. In every deviation from his tenets he espies malevolent and ominous subversion. He, therefore, is bent on disempowering his devotees. By any and all means.

## The Professions of the Narcissist

The narcissist naturally gravitates towards those professions which guarantee the abundant and uninterrupted provision of Narcissistic Supply. He seeks to interact with people from a position of authority, advantage, or superiority. He thus elicits their automatic admiration, adulation, and affirmation – or, failing that, their fear and obedience.

Several vocations meet these requirements: teaching, the priesthood, show business, corporate management, the medical professions, politics, and sports. It is safe to predict that narcissists would be over-represented in these occupations.

The cerebral narcissist is likely to emphasize his intellectual prowess and accomplishments (real and imaginary) in an attempt to solicit supply from awe-struck students, devoted parishioners, admiring voters, obsequious subordinates, or dependent patients. His somatic counterpart derives his sense of self-worth from body building, athletic achievements, tests of resilience or endurance, and sexual conquests.

The narcissistic medical doctor or mental health professional and his patients, the narcissistic guide, teacher, or mentor and his students, the narcissistic leader, guru, pundit, or psychic and his followers or admirers, and the narcissistic business tycoon, boss, or employer and his underlings are all instances of Pathological Narcissistic Spaces.

This is a worrisome state of affairs. Narcissists are liars. They misrepresent their credentials, knowledge, talents, skills, and achievements. A narcissist medical doctor would rather let patients die than expose his ignorance. A narcissistic therapist often traumatizes his clients with his acting out, rage, exploitativeness, and lack of empathy. Narcissistic businessmen bring ruin on their firms and employees.

Nor is the narcissist deterred by possible punishment or regards himself subject to Man-made laws. His sense of entitlement coupled with the conviction of his own superiority lead him to believe in his invincibility, invulnerability, immunity, and divinity. The narcissist holds human edicts, rules, and regulations in disdain and human penalties in contempt. He regards human needs and emotions as weaknesses to be predatorily exploited.

Return

# The Narcissist in the Workplace

*Question:* The narcissist turns the workplace into a duplicitous hell. What to do?

*Answer:* To a narcissistic employer, the members of his "staff" are Secondary Sources of Narcissistic Supply. Their role is to accumulate Narcissistic Supply (i.e., to remember events that support the grandiose self-image of the narcissist) and to regulate the Narcissistic Supply of the narcissist during dry spells: to adulate, adore, admire, agree, provide attention and approval, and, generally, serve as an audience to him.

The staff (or should we say "stuff"?) is supposed to remain passive. The narcissist is not interested in anything but the simplest function of mirroring. When the mirror acquires a personality and a life of its own, the narcissist is incensed. When independent-minded, an employee might be in danger of being sacked by his narcissistic employer (an act which demonstrates the employer's omnipotence).

The employee's presumption to be the employer's equal by trying to befriend him (friendship is possible only among equals) injures the employer narcissistically. He is willing to accept his employees only as underlings, whose very position serves to support his grandiose fantasies.

But his grandiosity is so tenuous and rests on such fragile foundations, that any hint of equality, disagreement or need (any intimation that the narcissist "needs" friends, for instance) threatens the narcissist profoundly. The narcissist is exceedingly insecure. It is easy to destabilize his impromptu "personality". His harsh reactions are merely in self-defence.

Classic narcissistic behaviour is when idealization is followed by devaluation. The devaluing attitude develops as a result of disagreements or simply because time has eroded the employee's capacity to serve as a FRESH Source of Supply.

The veteran employee, now taken for granted by his narcissistic employer, becomes uninspiring as a source of adulation, admiration and attention. The narcissist always seeks new thrills and stimuli.

The narcissist is notorious for his low threshold of resistance to boredom. His behaviour is impulsive and his biography tumultuous precisely because of his need to introduce uncertainty and risk to what he regards as "stagnation" or "slow death" (i.e., routine). Most interactions in the workplace are part of the rut – and thus constitute a reminder of this routine – deflating the narcissist's grandiose fantasies.

Narcissists do many unnecessary, wrong and even dangerous things in pursuit of the stabilization of their inflated self-image.

Narcissists feel suffocated by intimacy, or by the constant reminders of the REAL, nitty-gritty world out there. It reduces them, makes them realize the Grandiosity Gap between their fantasies and reality. It is a threat to the precarious balance of their personality structures ("false" and invented) and treated by them as a menace or a nuisance.

Narcissists forever shift the blame, pass the buck, and engage in cognitive dissonance. They "pathologize" the other, foster feelings of guilt and shame in her, demean, debase and humiliate in order to preserve their sense of superiority.

Narcissists are pathological liars. They think nothing of it because their very Self is False and their own confabulation.

Here are a few useful guidelines:

• Never disagree with the narcissist or contradict him;
• Never offer him any intimacy;
• Look awed by whatever attribute matters to him (for instance: by his professional achievements or by his good looks, or by his success with women and so on);
• Never remind him of life out there and if you do, connect it somehow to his sense of grandiosity. You can aggrandize even your office supplies, the most mundane thing conceivable by saying: "These are the BEST art materials ANY workplace is going to have", "We get them EXCLUSIVELY", etc.;
• Do not make any comment, which might directly or indirectly impinge on the narcissist's self-image, omnipotence, superior judgement, omniscience, skills, capabilities, professional record, or even omnipresence. Bad sentences start with: "I think you overlooked ... made a mistake here ... you don't know ... do you know ... you were not here yesterday so ... you cannot ... you should ... (interpreted as rude imposition, narcissists react very badly to perceived restrictions placed on their freedom) ... I (never mention the fact that you are a separate,

independent entity, narcissists regard others as extensions of their selves)..."

Manage your narcissistic boss. Notice patterns in his bullying. Is he more aggressive on Monday mornings and more open to suggestions on Friday afternoon? Is he amenable to flattery? Can you modify his conduct by appealing to his morality, superior knowledge, good manners, cosmopolitanism, or upbringing? Manipulating the narcissist is the only way to survive in such a tainted workplace.

Can the narcissist be harnessed? Can his energies be channelled productively?

This would be a deeply flawed – and even dangerous – strategy. Various management gurus purport to teach us how to harness this force of nature known as malignant or pathological narcissism. Narcissists are driven, visionary, ambitious, exciting and productive, says Michael Maccoby, for instance. To ignore such a resource is a criminal waste. All we need to do is learn how to "handle" them.

Yet, this prescription is either naive or disingenuous. Narcissists cannot be "handled", or "managed", or "contained", or "channelled". They are, by definition, incapable of team work. They lack empathy, are exploitative, envious, haughty and feel entitled, even if such a feeling is commensurate only with their grandiose fantasies and when their accomplishments are meagre.

Narcissists dissemble, conspire, destroy and self-destruct. Their drive is compulsive, their vision rarely grounded in reality, their human relations a calamity. In the long run, there is no enduring benefit to dancing with narcissists – only ephemeral and, often, fallacious, "achievements".

Return

# Dr. Watson and Mr. Hastings

## The Narcissist and His Friends

*Question:* Do narcissists have friends?

*Answer:* "Who's the fairest of them all?" – asks the Bad Queen in the fairy tale. Having provided the wrong answer, the mirror is smashed to smithereens. Not a bad allegory for how the narcissist treats his "friends".

Literature helps us grasp the intricate interactions between the narcissist and members of his social circle.

Both Sherlock Holmes and Hercules Poirot, the world's most renowned fiction detectives, are quintessential narcissists. Both are also schizoids: they have few friends and are largely confined to their homes, engaged in solitary activities. Both have fatuous, sluggish, and anodyne sidekicks who slavishly cater to their whims and needs and provide them with an adulating gallery – Holmes' Dr. Watson and Poirot's poor Hastings.

Both Holmes and Poirot assiduously avoid the "competition" – equally sharp minds who seek their company for a fertilizing intellectual exchange among equals. They feel threatened by the potential need to admit to ignorance and confess to error. Both gumshoes are self-sufficient and consider themselves peerless.

The Watsons and Hastings of this world provide the narcissist with an obsequious, unthreatening, audience and with the kind of unconditional and unthinking obedience that confirms to him his omnipotence. They are sufficiently vacuous to make the narcissist look sharp and omniscient – but not so asinine as to be instantly discernible as such. They are the perfect backdrop, never likely to attain centre stage and overshadow their master.

Moreover, both Holmes and Poirot sadistically – and often publicly – taunt and humiliate their Sancho Panzas, explicitly chastising them for being dim-witted. Narcissism and sadism are psychodynamic cousins and both Watson and Hastings are perfect victims of abuse: docile, understanding, malignantly optimistic, self-deluding, and idolizing.

Narcissists can't empathize or love and, therefore, have no friends. The narcissist is one track minded. He is interested in securing Narcissistic Supply from Narcissistic Supply Sources. He is not interested in people as such. He is a solipsist, and recognizes only himself as human. To the narcissist, all others are three dimensional cartoons, tools and instruments in the tedious and Sisyphean task of generating Narcissistic Supply and consuming it.

The narcissist over-values people (when they are judged to be potential sources of such supply), uses them, devalues them (when no longer able to supply him) and discards them nonchalantly. This behaviour pattern tends to alienate and to distance people from him.

Gradually, the social circle of the narcissist dwindles (and ultimately vanishes). People around him who are not turned off by the ugly succession of his acts and attitudes are rendered desperate and fatigued by the turbulent nature of the narcissist's life.

Those few still loyal to him, gradually abandon him because they can no longer withstand and tolerate the ups and downs of his career, his moods, his confrontations and conflicts with authority, his chaotic financial state and the dissolution of his emotional affairs. The narcissist is a human roller coaster – fun for a limited time, nauseating in the long run.

This is one aspect of the process of narcissistic confinement.

Ever sensitive to outside opinion, the narcissist's behaviour, choices, acts, attitudes, beliefs, interests, in short: his very life is curtailed by it. The narcissist derives his ego functions from observing his reflection in other people's eyes. Gradually, he homes in on the right mixture of texts and actions, which elicit Narcissistic Supply from his environment.

Anything which might – however remotely – endanger the availability or the quantity of the narcissist's Narcissistic Supply is excised. The narcissist avoids certain situations (for instance: where he is likely to encounter opposition, or criticism, or competition). He refrains from certain activities and actions (which are incompatible with his projected False Self). And he steers clear of people he deems insufficiently amenable to his charms.

To avoid narcissistic injury, the narcissist employs a host of Emotional Involvement Prevention Measures (EIPMs). He becomes rigid, repetitive, predictable, boring, limits himself to "safe subjects" (such as, endlessly, himself) and to "safe conduct", and often rages hysterically when confronted with unexpected situations or with the slightest resistance to his preconceived course of action.

The narcissist's rage is not so much a reaction to offended grandiosity as it is the outcome of panic. The narcissist maintains a precarious balance, a mental house of cards, poised on a precipice. His equilibrium is so delicate that anything and anyone can upset it: a casual remark, a disagreement, a slight criticism, a hint, or a fear.

The narcissist magnifies it all into monstrous, ominous, proportions. To avoid these (not so imagined) threats, the narcissist prefers to "stay at home". He limits his social intercourse. He abstains from daring, trying, or venturing out. He is crippled. This, indeed, is the very essence of the malignancy that is at the heart of narcissism: the fear of flying.

Return

# For the Love of God

*"1 But know this, that in the last days perilous times will come: 2 For men will be lovers of themselves, lovers of money, boasters, proud, blasphemers, disobedient to parents, unthankful, unholy, 3 unloving, unforgiving, slanderers, without self-control, brutal, despisers of good, 4 traitors, headstrong, haughty, lovers of pleasure rather than lovers of God, 5 having a form of godliness but denying its power. And from such people turn away! 6 For of this sort are those who creep into households and make captives of gullible women loaded down with sins, led away by various lusts, 7 always learning and never able to come to the knowledge of the truth. 8 Now as Jan'nes and Jam'bres resisted Moses, so do these also resist the truth: men of corrupt minds, disapproved concerning the faith; 9 but they will progress no further, for their folly will be manifest to all, as theirs also was."*
[The Second Epistle of Paul the Apostle to Timothy 3:1-9]

*Question:* I think that my priest is a narcissist. Can men of God be narcissists?

*Answer:* God is everything the narcissist ever wants to be: omnipotent, omniscient, omnipresent, admired, much discussed, and awe inspiring. God is the narcissist's wet dream, his ultimate grandiose fantasy. But God comes handy in other ways as well.

The narcissist alternately idealizes and devalues figures of authority.

In the idealization phase, he strives to emulate them, he admires them, imitates them (often ludicrously), and defends them. They cannot go wrong, or be wrong. The narcissist regards them as bigger than life, infallible, perfect, whole, and brilliant. But as the narcissist's unrealistic and inflated expectations are inevitably frustrated, he begins to devalue his former idols.

Now they are "human" (to the narcissist, a derogatory term). They are small, fragile, error-prone, pusillanimous, mean, dumb, and mediocre. The narcissist goes through the same cycle in his relationship with God, the quintessential authority figure.

But often, even when disillusionment and iconoclastic despair set in, the narcissist continues to pretend to love God and follow Him. The narcissist maintains this deception because his continued proximity to God confers on him authority. Priests, leaders of the congregation, preachers, evangelists, cultists, politicians, intellectuals – all derive authority from their allegedly privileged relationship with God.

Religious authority allows the narcissist to indulge his sadistic urges and to exercise his misogynism freely and openly. Such a narcissist is likely to taunt and torment his followers, hector and chastise them, humiliate and berate them, abuse them spiritually, or even sexually. The narcissist whose source of authority is religion is looking for obedient and unquestioning slaves upon whom to exercise his capricious and wicked mastery. The narcissist transforms even the most innocuous and pure religious sentiments into a cultish ritual and a virulent hierarchy. He preys on the gullible. His flock become his hostages.

Religious authority also secures the narcissist's Narcissistic Supply. His coreligionists, members of his congregation, his parish, his constituency, his audience are transformed into loyal and stable Sources of Narcissistic Supply. They obey his commands, heed his admonitions, follow his creed, admire his personality, applaud his personal traits, satisfy his needs (sometimes even his carnal desires), revere and idolize him.

Moreover, being a part of an immanent "bigger thing" is very gratifying narcissistically. Being a particle of God, being immersed in His grandeur, experiencing His power and blessings first hand, communing with him are all Sources of unending Narcissistic Supply. The narcissist becomes God by observing His commandments, following His instructions, loving Him, obeying Him, succumbing to Him, merging with Him, communicating and communing with Him, or even by defying Him (the greater the narcissist's adversary – the more grandiosely important the narcissist feels).

Like everything else in the narcissist's life, he mutates God into a kind of inverted narcissist. God becomes his dominant Source of Supply. He forms a personal relationship with this overwhelming and overpowering entity in order to overwhelm and overpower others. He becomes God vicariously, by the proxy of his relationship with Him. He idealizes God, then devalues Him, then abuses Him. This is the classic narcissistic pattern and even God himself cannot escape it.

*First published on the* <u>Suite 101</u> *Narcissistic Personality Disorders Topic.*

Return

# *Toxic Relationships*

## Abuse and Its Aftermath

**Case Studies**

# Adolescent Narcissist

Donovan, 16 years old, is incapable of loving and, therefore, has never loved you, his stepmother (or, for that matter, anyone else, himself included) in his entire life. His natural capacity to love and to return love was all but eliminated by his horrid childhood. We practice loving first and foremost through our parents. If they fail us, if they turn out to be unpredictable, capricious, violent, or unjust - this capacity is stunted forever. This is what happened to Donovan: the ideal figures of his childhood proved to be much less than ideal. Abuse is a very poor breeding ground for healthy emotions.

Granted, Donovan - being the brilliant and manipulative person that he is - knows how to perfectly simulate and emulate LOVE. He acts lovingly - but this is a mere act and it should not be confused with the real thing. Donovan shows love in order to achieve goals: money, a warm house, food on the table, adoration (Narcissistic Supply). Once these are available from other sources, the first ones are discarded callously, cold-heartedly, cruelly and abruptly.

You have been a temporary stopover for Donovan, the equivalent of a full board hotel (no chores, no requirements on his time). Not only was he able to secure his material needs from you - he also found in you a perfect Source of Narcissistic Supply: adoring, submissive, non-critical, wide-eyed, approving, admiring, the perfect narcissistic fix.

You describe a very disturbed young man. He values intelligence above all else, he uses foul language to vent his aggression (the narcissist resents his dependence on his Sources of Supply). The narcissist knows it all and best, is judgemental (without merit), hates all people (though he calls upon them if he needs something), and is never above exploiting and manipulation. When not in need, he does not contact his "friends", not even his "girlfriend". After all, emotions ("sensitivity") are a deplorable weakness.

In the pursuit of narcissistic gratification, there is no place for hesitation or pause. You put it succinctly: he will do nothing for others, nothing matters to him if it is not in his interest. As a result, he lets people down and refrains almost religiously from keeping promises and obligations.

The narcissist is above such mundane things as obligations undertaken. They counter his conviction that he is above the law - social or other - and this threatens his grandiosity.

The narcissist, being above reproach (who is qualified to judge him, to teach him, to advise him?), inevitably reverts to blaming others for his misdeeds: they should have warned/reminded/alerted him. For instance: they should have waked him up if they desired his precious company and wanted him to keep a date.

The narcissist is above normal people and their daily chores: he doesn't think that he needs to attend classes that others attend. They should go to school because they are inferior (stupid). This is the natural order of things - read Nietzsche. Most narcissists are predictable and, therefore, boring.

To love a narcissist is to love a reflection, not a real person. Donovan is the most basic, primitive type: the somatic (or anal) narcissist, whose disorder is centred on his body, his skin, his hair, his dress, his food, his health. Some of these preoccupations border on the phobic ("freaky with germs") and that is a bad sign.

Hypochondriasis could be the next mental step. But Donovan is in great danger. He should seek help immediately. His narcissism - as is usually the case - has been and is still being compounded by other, more serious disorders. He is led down a path of no return. Donovan is constantly depressed. Maybe he has had few major depressive episodes but he is distinctly dysphoric (sad) and anhedonic (hates the world and finds pleasure in nothing). He alternates between hypersomnia (sleeping too much) and insomnia (not sleeping for two days). This is one of the surest signs of depression.

Narcissists suffer, by their nature, from an undulating sense of self-worth and from all-pervasive feelings of guilt and recrimination. They punish themselves: they dress in ragged clothes contrary to their primary predilections and they direct their pent up aggression at themselves. The result is depression.

Donovan also seems to suffer from a schizoid personality. Such people prefer staying and working in their rooms, in solitary confinement, chained to their computers and books, to any social encounter or diversion. They rarely trust others and they lack the requisite emotional baggage to develop stable interpersonal relationships. They are miserable failures at communicating with people and confine their interactions to first degree relatives.

The total picture is that of a young person suffering from a Borderline Personality Disorder with strong narcissistic and schizoid traits. His reckless and self-destructive spending and his eating irregularities point in this direction. So does the inappropriate affect (for instance, smiling while pretending to shoot people). Donovan is a menace above all to himself.

Borderline patients have suicidal ideation (contemplate suicide) and tend finally to act upon these ruminations. Donovan might direct this aggression elsewhere with catastrophic consequences. But, at best, Donovan will continue to make people around him miserable and ill-at-ease.

Treatment is not very effective. My advice to you is to immediately stop your "unconditional love". Narcissists sense blood where others see only love and altruism. If, for masochistic reasons, you still wish to engage this young person, my advice to you is to condition your love. Sign a contract with him: You want my adoration, admiration, approval, and warmth, you want access to my home and money? If you do – these are my conditions. And if he says that he doesn't want to have anything to do with you anymore – count your blessings and let go.

Return

# A Dream Interpreted

## Background

This dream was related to me by a male, 46 years old, who claims to be in the throes of a major personal transformation. Whether he is a narcissist (as he believes himself to be) or not is quite irrelevant. Narcissism is a language. A person can choose to express himself in it, even if he is not possessed by the disorder. The dreamer made this choice.

Henceforth, I will treat him as a narcissist, though insufficient information renders a "real" diagnosis impossible. Moreover, the subject feels that he is confronting his disorder and that this could be a significant turning point on his way to being healed. It is in this context that this dream should be interpreted. Evidently, if he chose to write to me, he is very preoccupied with his internal processes. There is every reason to believe that such conscious content invaded his dream.

## The Dream

*"I was in a run-down restaurant/bar with two friends sitting at a table in a large open area with a few other tables and a bar. I did not like the music or the smoky atmosphere or other customers or greasy food, but we were travelling and were hungry and it was open and the only place we could find.*

*There was a woman with other people at a table about 10 feet in front of me that I found attractive, and noticed she was noticing me as well. There was also another woman with other people at a table about 30 feet to my right, old with heavy makeup and poorly dyed hair, loud, obnoxious, drunk, who noticed me. She started saying negative things to me, and I tried to ignore her. She just got louder and more derogatory, with horrible rude and jabbing comments. I tried to ignore her, but my other friends looked at me with raised eyebrows, as if to ask: 'How much more are you going to take before you stand up for yourself?' I felt sick to my stomach, and did not want to confront* her, but everyone in the place was now noticing her confrontation of me, and she was almost screaming at me. I couldn't believe no one was telling her to stop it, to be civil, to be nice.

I finally looked over at her and raised my voice and told her to shut up. She looked at me and seemed to get even angrier, and then looked at her plate and picked up a piece of food and threw it at me! I couldn't believe it. I told her I wasn't going to take one more thing, and to stop it now or I would call the police. She got up, walked towards me, picking up a plate of popcorn from another table, and upended it flat upon the top of my head. I stood up and said: 'That's it! That's assault! You're going to jail!' and went to the cash register area by the door and called the police.

The police instantly appeared and took her away, with her resisting arrest the whole time. I sat down and someone at the table next to me said: 'Now you can open up the dam gate.' I said: 'What?', and he explained how the woman was actually pretty powerful and owned a dam and had shut the gate down years ago, but that now she was locked up we could go open it up.

We piled into a truck and I was led into a cavernous room and shown a small room with a glass wall in it and a big wheel, a control valve. I was told that I could turn it whenever I wanted. So I started to turn it and the water started flowing. I could easily see it through the glass, and the level on the glass rose higher the more I turned the wheel. Soon there was a torrent, and it was thrilling. I had never seen such an incredible roar of water. It was like the Niagara Falls flowing through the huge room. I got frightened along with being thrilled, but discovered I could lessen the water with the valve if it got to be too much. It went on for a long time, and we whooped and laughed and felt so excited. Finally, the water grew less no matter how wide I opened the valve, and it reached a steady flow.

I noticed the pretty woman from the grill way across the huge area, and she seemed to be looking for someone. I hoped it was me. I opened the door, and went out to go meet her. On the way out, I got grease on my hand, and picked up a rag on the table to wipe it off. The rag had even more grease on it, and so now my hands were completely covered in grease. I picked up another rag on top of a box, and there were wet spark plugs stuck with globs of grease to the underside of the rag, lined up in order as if they used to be in an engine and someone stuck them in this order on purpose, and some of it got on my clothes. The guys with me *laughed and I laughed with them, but I left without going to meet the woman, and we went back to the grill.*

*I found myself in a tiny room with a table in it and a picture window looking out into the area where everyone was sitting and eating. The door was open into a back hallway. I started to go out, but a man was coming into the room. For some reason he frightened me, and I backed up. However, he was robot-like, and walked to the window and looked out to the dining area, making no indication that he even noticed me, and stared blandly at the people having fun. I left and went out into the dining area. I noticed everyone staring at me in an unfriendly way. I started for the exit, but one of the policemen who had arrested the woman from the night before was off-duty in plain clothes and grabbed my arm and twisted me around and shoved me face down on a table. He told me that what I did to the woman was wrong, and that no one liked me because of it. He said that just because I had the law on my side and was in the right didn't mean anyone would like me. He said if I was smart I would leave town. Others were around me and spit on me.*

*He let me go, and I left. I was driving in a car alone out of town. I didn't know what became of the friends I was with. I felt both elated and ashamed at the same time, crying and laughing at the same time, and had no idea where to go and what I was doing."*

## The Interpretation

As the dream unfolds, the subject finds himself with two friends. These friends vanish towards the end of the dream and he doesn't seem to find this worrisome. *"I didn't know what became of the friends I was with."* This is a strange way to treat one's friends. It seems that we are dealing not with three dimensional, full-blown, flesh and blood friends but with FRIENDLY MENTAL FUNCTIONS. Indeed, they are the ones who encourage the subject to react to the old woman's antics. *"How much more are you going to take before you stand up for yourself?"*, they ask him, cunningly. All the other people present at the bar-restaurant do not even bother to tell the woman *"to stop, to be civil, to be nice"*. This eerie silence contributes to the subject's reaction of disbelief that mushrooms throughout this nightmare. At first, he tries to emulate their behaviour and to ignore the woman himself. She says negative things about him, grows louder and more derogatory, horribly rude and jabbing and he still tries to ignore her. When his friends push him to react: *"I felt sick to my stomach and did not want to confront her."* He finally does confront her because *"everyone was noticing"* as she was almost screaming at him.

The subject emerges as the plaything of others. A woman screams at him and debases him, friends prod him to react, and motivated by *"everyone"* he does react. His actions and reactions are determined by input from the outside. He expects others to do for him the things that he finds unpleasant to do by himself (to tell the woman to stop, for instance). His feeling of entitlement (*"I deserve this special treatment, others should take care of my affairs"*) and his magical thinking (*"If I want something to happen, it surely will"*) are so strong that he is stunned when people do not do his (silent) bidding. This dependence on others is multi-faceted. They mirror the subject. He modifies his behaviour, forms expectations, gets disbelievingly disappointed, punishes and rewards himself and takes behavioural cues from them (*"The guys with me laughed and I laughed with them"*). When confronted with someone who does not notice him, he describes him as robot-like and is frightened by him. The word *"look"* disproportionately recurs throughout the text. In one of the main scenes, his confrontation with the rude, ugly woman, both parties do not do anything without first *"looking"* at each other. He looks at her before he raises his voice and tells her to shut up. She looks at him and gets angrier.

The dream opens in a *"run down"* restaurant/bar with the wrong kind of music and of customers, a smoky atmosphere and greasy food. The subject and his friends were travelling and hungry and the restaurant was the only open place. The subject takes great pains to justify his (lack of) choice. He does not want us to believe that he is the type of person to willingly patronize such an establishment. What we think of him is very important to him. Our look still tends to define him. Throughout the text, he goes on to explain, justify, excuse, reason and persuade us. Then, he suddenly stops. This is a crucial turning point.

It is reasonable to assume that the subject is relating to his personal Odyssey. At the end of his dream, he continues his travels, goes on with his life *"ashamed and elated at the same time"*. We are ashamed when our sense of propriety is offended and we are elated when it is reaffirmed. How can these contradictory feelings coexist? This is what the dream is all about: the battle between, on the one hand, what the dreamer had been taught to regard as true and proper, the "shoulds" and the "oughts" of his life, usually the result of overly strict upbringing - and, on the other hand, what he feels is good for him. These two do not overlap and they foster in the subject a sense of escalating conflict, enacted before us. The first domain (the "shoulds" and the "oughts") is embedded in his Superego (to borrow Freud's quasi-literary metaphor). Critical voices constantly resound in his mind, an uproarious opprobrium, sadistic criticism, destructive chastising, uneven and unfair comparisons to unattainable ideals and goals. But the powers of life are also reawakening in him with the ripening and maturation of his personality. He vaguely realizes what he missed and misses, he regrets it, and he wants out of his virtual prison. In response, his disorder feels threatened and flexes its tormenting muscles, a giant awakened, Atlas shrugged. The subject wants to be less rigid, more spontaneous, more vivacious, less sad, less defined by the gaze of others, and more hopeful. His disorder dictates rigidity, emotional absence, automatism, fear and loathing, self-flagellation, dependence on Narcissistic Supply, a False Self. The subject does not like his current locus in life: it is dingy, it is downtrodden, it is shabby, and inhabited by vulgar, ugly people, the music is wrong, it is fogged by smoke, polluted. Yet, even while there, he knows that there are alternatives, that there is hope: a young, attractive lady, mutual signalling. And she is closer to him (10 feet) than the old, ugly woman of his past (30 feet). His dream will not bring them together, but he feels no sorrow. He leaves, laughing with the guys, to revisit his previous haunt. He owes it to himself. Then he goes on with his life.

He finds himself, in the middle of the road of life, in the ugly place that is his soul. The young woman is only a promise. There is another woman *"old, with heavy makeup, poorly dyed hair, loud, obnoxious, drunk"*. This is his mental disorder. It can scarcely sustain the deception. Its makeup is heavy, its hair dyed poorly, its mood a result of intoxication. It could well be the False Self or the Superego, but I rather think it is the whole sick personality. She notices him, she berates him with derogatory remarks, she screams at him. The subject realizes that his disorder is not friendly, that it seeks to humiliate him, it is out to degrade and destroy him. It gets violent, it hurls food at him, it buries him under a dish of popcorn (cinema theatre metaphor?). The war is out in the open. The fake coalition, which glued the shaky structures of the fragile personality together, exists no longer. Notice that the subject does not recall what insults and pejorative remarks were directed at him. He deletes all the expletives because they really do not matter. The enemy is vile and ignoble and will make use and excuse of any weakness, mistake and doubt to crack the defence set up by the subject's budding healthier mental structures (the young woman). The end justifies all means and it is the subject's end that is sought. There is no self-hate more insidious and pernicious than the narcissist's.

But, to fight his illness, the subject still resorts to old solutions, to old habits and to old behaviour patterns. He calls the police because they represent the Law and What Is Right. It is through the rigid, unflinching, framework of a legal system that he hopes to suppress what he regards as the unruly behaviour of his disorder. Only at the end of his dream he comes to realize his mistake: *"He said that just because I had the law on my side and I was in the right didn't mean that anyone would like me."* The Police (who appear instantly because they were always present) arrest the woman, but their sympathy is with her. His true aides can be found only among the customers of the restaurant/bar, whom he initially found not to his liking *("I did not like ... the other customers...")*. It is someone in the next table who tells him about the dam. The way to health is through enemy territory, information about healing can be gotten only from the sickness itself. The subject must leverage his own disorder to disown it.

The dam is a potent symbol in this dream. It represents all the repressed emotions, the now forgotten traumas, the suppressed drives and wishes, fears and hopes. These are natural elements, primordial and powerful. And they are dammed by the disorder (the vulgar, now-imprisoned, lady). It is up to him to open the dam. No one will do it for him: *"Now YOU can open the dam gate."* The powerful woman is no more, she owned the dam and guarded its gates for many years. This is a sad passage about the subject's inability to communicate with himself, to experience his feelings unmediated, to let go. When he does finally encounter the water (his emotions), they are safely contained behind glass, visible but described in a kind of scientific manner *("the level on the glass rose higher the more I turned the wheel")* and absolutely regulated by the subject (using a valve). The language chosen is detached and cold, protective. The subject must have been emotionally overwhelmed but his sentences are borrowed from the texts of laboratory reports and travel guides *("Niagara Falls")*. The very existence of the dam comes as a surprise to him. *"I said: What?, and he explained."*

Still, this is nothing short of a revolution. It is the first time that the subject acknowledges that there is something hidden behind a dam in his brain *("cavernous room")* and that it is entirely up to him to release it *("I was told that I could turn it whenever I wanted")*. Instead of turning around and running in panic, the subject turns the wheel (it is a control valve, he hurries to explain to us, the dream must be seen to obey the rules of logic and of nature). He describes the result of his first encounter with his long repressed emotions as "thrilling", "incredible" "roar(ing)", "torrent(ial)". It did frighten him but he wisely learned to make use of the valve and to calibrate the flow of his emotions to accord with his emotional capacity. And what were his reactions? "Whooped", "laughed", "excited". Finally, the flow became steady and independent of the valve. There was no need to regulate the water anymore. There was no threat. The subject learned to live with his emotions. He even diverted his attention to the attractive, young woman, who reappeared and seemed to be looking for someone (he hoped it was for him).

But, the woman belonged to another time, to another place and there was no turning back. The subject had yet to learn this final lesson. His past was dead, the old defence mechanisms unable to provide him with the comfort and illusory protection that he hitherto enjoyed. He had to move on, to another plane of existence. But it is hard to bid farewell to part of you, to metamorphose, to disappear in one sense and reappear in another. A break in one's consciousness and existence is traumatic no matter how well controlled, well intentioned and beneficial.

So, our hero goes back to visit his former self. He is warned not to. Moreover, it is not with clean hands that he proceeds. They get greasier the more he tries to clean them. Even his clothes are affected. Rags, wet (useless) spark plugs, the ephemeral images of a former engine all star in this episode. Those are passages worth quoting (in parentheses my comments):

*"I noticed the pretty woman from the grill* (from my past) *way across the huge area* (my brain)*, and she seemed to be looking for someone. I hoped it was me. I opened the door, and went out to go meet her* (back to my past)*. On the way out, I got grease on my hand* (dirt, warning)*, and picked up a rag on the table to wipe it off. The rag had even more grease on it* (no way to disguise the wrong move, the potentially disastrous decision)*, and so now my hands were completely covered in grease* (dire warning)*. I picked up another rag on top of a box, and there were wet* (dead) *spark plugs stuck with globs of grease to the underside of the rag, lined up in order as if they used to be in an engine* (an image of something long gone) *and someone stuck them in this order on purpose, and some of it got on my clothes. The guys with me laughed and I laughed with them* (he laughed because of peer pressure, not because he really felt like it)*, but I left without*

*going to meet the woman, and we went back to the grill* (to the scene of his battle with his mental disorder)."

But, he goes on to the grill, where it all started, this undefined and untitled chain of events that changed his life. This time, he is not allowed to enter, only to observe from a tiny room. Actually, he does not exist there anymore. The man who enters his observation post, does not even see him or notice him. There are grounds to believe that this man is the previous, sick version of the subject himself. The subject was frightened and backed up. The robot-like person (?) looked through the window, stared blandly at people having fun. The subject then proceeded to commit the error of revisiting his past, the restaurant. Inevitably, the very people that he debunked and deserted (the elements of his mental disorder, the diseased occupants of his mind) were hostile. The policeman, this time off duty (not representing the Law), assaults him and advises him to leave. Others spit on him. This is reminiscent of a religious ritual of ex-communication. The philosopher Baruch Spinoza was spat on in a synagogue, judged to have committed heresy. This reveals the religious (or ideological) dimension of mental disorders. Not unlike religion, they have their own catechism, compulsive rituals, set of rigid beliefs and "adherents" (mental constructs) motivated by fear and prejudice. Mental disorders are like churches. They employ institutions of inquisition and punish heretical views with a severity befitting the darkest ages.

But these people, this setting, exert no more power over him. He is free to go. There is no turning back now, all bridges burnt, all doors shut firmly, he is a persona non grata in his former disordered psyche. The traveller resumes his travels, not knowing where to go and what he is doing. But he is laughing and crying and ashamed and elated. In other words, he, finally, after many years, experiences emotions. On his way to the horizon, the dream leaves the subject with a promise, veiled as a threat *"If you were smart you would leave town."* If you know what is good for you, you will get healthy. And the subject seems to be doing just that.

Return

# The Pathological Charmer

The narcissist is confident that people find him irresistible. His unfailing charm is part of his self-imputed omnipotence. This inane conviction is what makes the narcissist a "pathological charmer".

The somatic narcissist and the histrionic flaunt their sex appeal, virility or femininity, sexual prowess, musculature, physique, training, or athletic achievements. The cerebral narcissist seeks to enchant and entrance his audience with intellectual pyrotechnics. Many narcissists brag about their wealth, health, possessions, collections, spouses, children, personal history, family tree – in short: anything that garners them attention and renders them alluring.

Both types of narcissists firmly believe that, being unique, they are entitled to special treatment by others. They deploy their "charm offensives" to manipulate their nearest and dearest (or even complete strangers) and use them as instruments of gratification. Exerting personal magnetism and charisma become ways of asserting control and obviating other people's personal boundaries.

The pathological charmer feels superior to the person he captivates and fascinates. To him, charming someone means having power over her, controlling her, or even subjugating her. It is all a mind game intertwined with a power play. The person to be thus enthralled is an object, a mere prop, and of dehumanized utility.

In some cases, pathological charm involves more than a grain of sadism. Inflicting the "pain" of subjugation on his beguiled victims who "cannot help" but be enchanted sexually arouses the narcissist. Conversely, the pathological charmer engages in infantile magical thinking. He uses charm to help maintain object constancy and fend off abandonment – in other words, to ensure that the person he "bewitched" won't disappear on him.

Pathological charmers react with rage and aggression when their intended targets prove to be impervious and resistant to their lure. This kind of narcissistic injury - being spurned and rebuffed - makes them feel threatened, rejected, and denuded. Being ignored amounts to a challenge to their uniqueness, entitlement, control, and superiority. Narcissists wither without constant Narcissistic Supply. When their charm fails to elicit it, they feel annulled, non-existent, and "dead".

Expectedly, they go to great lengths to secure said supply. It is only when their efforts are frustrated that the mask of civility and congeniality drops and reveals the true face of the narcissist: a predator on the prowl.

Return

# The Narcissistic Personality Disorder (NPD) Catechism

Would you feel that this fits a narcissistic/misogynistic personality?

*"My husband and I got married a year ago. It is his 1st marriage at 39 years of age. In the two years we have been together, he has without warning physically and emotionally abandoned me six times, anywhere from overnight to more than two months. He says he aches he craves me so much, yet he abandons me repeatedly.*

*He says all women have 'thrown him to the curb with the garbage' when they are done with him. He says I am too good to be true, he's just waiting 'for the axe to fall'. He says he leaves before he gets kicked out. He kisses and nuzzles me in the morning, and then abandons me at the end of the work day.*

*He swings from overly sweet to verbally so angry it is shocking. He is the drama king, everything and everyone is stressful or frustrating."*

This behaviour is typical of many personality disorders. It is called Approach-Avoidance Repetition Complex. By behaving unpredictably and abandoning his mate, spouse, or partner, the narcissist maintains control over the situation and avoids emotional hurt and narcissistic injuries ("I abandoned her, not the other way around").

The abuser acts unpredictably, capriciously, inconsistently and irrationally. This serves to render others helpless and dependent upon the next twist and turn of the abuser, his next inexplicable whim, upon his next outburst, denial, or smile.

The abuser makes sure that HE is the only reliable element in the lives of his nearest and dearest – by shattering the rest of their world through his seemingly insane behaviour. He perpetuates his stable presence in their lives – by destabilizing their own.

Also read:

*"He has humiliated me in public, reaching in my shirt to my breasts in a mall food court, lifting my skirt while crossing on a main street intersection."*

The narcissist regards other people as objects, instruments of gratification, Sources of Narcissistic Supply.

People have a need to believe in the empathic skills and basic good-heartedness of others. By dehumanizing and objectifying people – the abuser attacks the very foundations of human interaction. This is the "alien" aspect of abusers – they may be excellent imitations of fully formed adults but they are emotionally absent and immature.

Abuse is so horrid, so repulsive, so phantasmagoric – that people recoil in terror. It is then, with their defences absolutely down, that they are the most susceptible and vulnerable to the abuser's control. Physical, psychological, verbal and sexual abuse are all forms of dehumanization and objectification.

Also read:

*"He seems to be overly sexed, at one point three times a night, constantly stating how important it is for him to know that I am available sexually."*

Broadly speaking, there are two types of narcissists loosely corresponding to the two categories mentioned in the question. Sex for the narcissist is an instrument designed to increase the number of Sources of Narcissistic Supply. If it happens to be the most efficient weapon in the narcissist's arsenal – he makes profligate use of it. In other words: if the narcissist cannot obtain adoration, admiration, approval, applause, or any other kind of attention by other means (e.g., intellectually) – he resorts to sex. He then become a satyr (or a nymphomaniac): indiscriminately engages in sex with multiple partners. His sex partners are considered by him to be objects not of desire – but of Narcissistic Supply. It is through the processes of successful seduction and sexual conquest that the narcissist derives his badly needed narcissistic "fix". The narcissist is likely to perfect his techniques of courting and regard his sexual exploits as a form of art. He usually exposes this side of him – in great detail – to others, to an audience, expecting to win their approval and admiration. Because the Narcissistic Supply in his case resides in the act of conquest and (what he perceives to be) subordination – the narcissist is forced to move on and to switch and bewitch partners very often.

Also read:

Narcissists, Sex and Fidelity

Dr. Jackal and Mr. Hide

*"He constantly states his self-importance: 'I'm so kind', 'I'm so generous', 'I'm so ethical', 'My work is so good', 'I'm a well known public figure' type of comments. He constantly is begging for compliments, to a point where it is a turn off, almost childlike. He is emotionally immature and insecure."*

- The narcissist feels grandiose and self-important (e.g., exaggerates accomplishments, talents, *skills, contacts, and personality traits to the point of lying, demands* to be recognized as superior without commensurate achievements);
- Is *obsessed* with fantasies of unlimited success, *fame, fearsome* power or *omnipotence, unequalled* brilliance (*the cerebral narcissist*), *bodily* beauty *or sexual performance (the somatic narcissist*), or ideal, *everlasting, all-conquering* love *or passion*;
- Firmly convinced that he or she is unique and, being special, can only be understood by, *should only be treated by*, or associate with, other special or unique, or high-status people (or institutions);
- Requires excessive admiration, *adulation, attention and affirmation – or, failing that, wishes to be feared and to be notorious (Narcissistic Supply)*;
- Feels entitled. *Demands automatic and full compliance* with his or her unreasonable expectations for special and *favourable priority* treatment;

- Is "interpersonally exploitative", i.e., *uses* others to achieve his or her own ends;
- *Devoid* of empathy. Is *unable* or unwilling to identify with, *acknowledge, or accept* the feelings, needs, *preferences, priorities, and choices* of others;
- Constantly envious of others *and seeks to hurt or destroy the objects of his or her frustration. Suffers from persecutory (paranoid) delusions as he or she* believes that they feel the same about him or her *and are likely to act similarly*;
- Behaves arrogantly and haughtily. *Feels superior, omnipotent, omniscient, invincible, immune, "above the law", and omnipresent (magical thinking). Rages when frustrated, contradicted, or confronted* by people he or she considers inferior to him or her and unworthy.

Also read:

Grandiose Fantasies
Addiction to Fame and Celebrity
Self Love and Narcissism
Deficient Narcissistic Supply
Multiple Grandiosity
False Modesty
Narcissism by Proxy
Grandiosity Deconstructed
A Great Admiration
Grandiosity Hangover and Narcissistic Baiting
Grandiosity and Intimacy - The Roots of Paranoia
The Narcissist's Reality Substitutes
The Narcissist's Confabulated Life

*"Through his abandonment he has destroyed his relationship with my 13 year old son. My son is an honour student, but still a teenager with typical teenage comments and behaviours. My husband blames my son as the reason he left me."*

When confronted with (younger) siblings or with his own children, the narcissist is likely to go through three phases:

At first, he perceives his offspring or siblings as a threat to his Narcissistic Supply, such as the attention of his spouse, or mother, as the case may be. They intrude on his turf and invade the Pathological Narcissistic Space. The narcissist does his best to belittle them, hurt (even physically) and humiliate them and then, when these reactions prove ineffective or counter productive, he retreats into an imaginary world of omnipotence. A period of emotional absence and detachment ensues.

His aggression having failed to elicit Narcissistic Supply, the narcissist proceeds to indulge himself in daydreaming, delusions of grandeur, planning of future coups, nostalgia and hurt (the Lost Paradise Syndrome). The narcissist reacts this way to the birth of his children or to the introduction of new foci of attention to the family cell (even to a new pet!).

Whomever the narcissist perceives to be in competition for scarce Narcissistic Supply is relegated to the role of the enemy. Where the uninhibited expression of the aggression and hostility aroused by this predicament is illegitimate or impossible – the narcissist prefers to stay away. Rather than attack his offspring or siblings, he sometimes immediately disconnects, detaches himself emotionally, becomes cold and uninterested, or directs transformed anger at his mate or at his parents (the more "legitimate" targets).

Other narcissists see the opportunity in the "mishap". They seek to manipulate their parents (or their mate) by "taking over" the newcomer. Such narcissists monopolize their siblings or their newborn children. This way, indirectly, they benefit from the attention directed at the infants. The sibling or offspring become vicarious Sources of Narcissistic Supply and proxies for the narcissist.

An example: by being closely identified with his offspring, a narcissistic father secures the grateful admiration of the mother ("What an outstanding father/brother he is."). He also assumes part of or all the credit for baby's/sibling's achievements. This is a process of annexation and assimilation of the other, a strategy that the narcissist makes use of in most of his relationships.

As siblings or progeny grow older, the narcissist begins to see their potential to be edifying, reliable and satisfactory Sources of Narcissistic Supply. His attitude, then, is completely transformed. The former threats have now become promising potentials. He cultivates those whom he trusts to be the most rewarding. He encourages them to idolize him, to adore him, to be awed by him, to admire his deeds and capabilities, to learn to blindly trust and obey him, in short to surrender to his charisma and to become submerged in his folie-de-grandeur.

It is at this stage that the risk of child abuse – up to and including outright incest – is heightened. The narcissist is auto-erotic. He is the preferred object of his own sexual attraction. His siblings and his children share his genetic material. Molesting or having intercourse with them is as close as the narcissist gets to having sex with himself.

Moreover, the narcissist perceives sex in terms of annexation. The partner is "assimilated" and becomes an extension of the narcissist, a fully controlled and manipulated object. Sex, to the narcissist, is the ultimate act of depersonalization and objectification of the other. He actually masturbates with other people's bodies.

Minors pose little danger of criticizing the narcissist or confronting him. They are perfect, malleable and abundant Sources of Narcissistic Supply. The narcissist derives gratification from having coital relations with adulating, physically and mentally inferior, inexperienced and dependent "bodies".

These roles – allocated to them explicitly and demandingly or implicitly and perniciously by the narcissist – are best fulfilled by ones whose mind is not yet fully formed and independent. The older the siblings or offspring, the more they become critical, even judgemental, of the narcissist. They are better able to put into context and perspective his actions, to question his motives, to anticipate his moves. As they mature, they often refuse to continue to play the mindless pawns in his chess game. They hold grudges against him for what he has done to them in the past, when they were less capable of resistance. They can gauge his true stature, talents and achievements – which, usually, lag far behind the claims that he makes.

This brings the narcissist a full cycle back to the first phase. Again, he perceives his siblings or sons/daughters as threats. He quickly becomes disillusioned and devaluing. He loses all interest, becomes emotionally remote, absent and cold, rejects any effort to communicate with him, citing life pressures and the preciousness and scarceness of his time.

He feels burdened, cornered, besieged, suffocated, and claustrophobic. He wants to get away, to abandon his commitments to people who have become totally useless (or even damaging) to him. He does not understand why he has to support them, or to suffer their company and he believes himself to have been deliberately and ruthlessly trapped.

He rebels either passively-aggressively (by refusing to act or by intentionally sabotaging the relationships) or actively (by being overly critical, aggressive, unpleasant, verbally and psychologically abusive and so on). Slowly – to justify his acts to himself – he gets immersed in conspiracy theories with clear paranoid hues. To his mind, the members of the family conspire against him, seek to belittle or humiliate or subordinate him, do not understand him, or stymie his growth. The narcissist usually finally gets what he wants and the family that he has created disintegrates to his great sorrow (due to the loss of the Narcissistic Space) – but also to his great relief and surprise (how could they have let go someone as unique as he?).

This is the cycle: the narcissist feels threatened by arrival of new family members – he tries to assimilate or annex of siblings or offspring – he obtains Narcissistic Supply from them – he overvalues and idealizes these newfound sources – as sources grow older and independent, they adopt anti narcissistic behaviours – the narcissist devalues them – the narcissist feels stifled and trapped – the narcissist becomes paranoid – the narcissist rebels and the family disintegrates.

This cycle characterizes not only the family life of the narcissist. It is to be found in other realms of his life (his career, for instance). At work, the narcissist, initially, feels threatened (no one knows him, he is a nobody). Then, he develops a circle of admirers, cronies and friends which he "nurtures and cultivates" in order to obtain Narcissistic Supply from them. He overvalues them (to him, they are the brightest, the most loyal, with the biggest chances to climb the corporate ladder and other superlatives).

But following some anti-narcissistic behaviours on their part (a critical remark, a disagreement, a refusal, however polite) – the narcissist devalues all these previously idealized individuals. Now that they have dared oppose him – they are judged by him to be stupid, cowardly, lacking in ambition, skills and talents, common (the worst expletive in the narcissist's vocabulary), with an unspectacular career ahead of them.

The narcissist feels that he is misallocating his scarce and invaluable resources (for instance, his time). He feels besieged and suffocated. He rebels and erupts in a serious of self-defeating and self-destructive behaviours, which lead to the disintegration of his life.

Doomed to build and ruin, attach and detach, appreciate and depreciate, the narcissist is predictable in his "death wish". What sets him apart from other suicidal types is that his wish is granted to him in small, tormenting doses throughout his anguished life.

### Custody and Visitation

A parent diagnosed with full-fledged Narcissistic Personality Disorder (NPD) should be denied custody and be granted only restricted rights of visitation under supervision.

Narcissists accord the same treatment to children and adults. They regard both as Sources of Narcissistic Supply, mere instruments of gratification – idealize them at first and then devalue them in favour of alternative, safer and more subservient, sources. Such treatment is traumatic and can have long-lasting emotional effects.

The narcissist's inability to acknowledge and abide by the personal boundaries set by others puts the child at heightened risk of abuse – verbal, emotional, physical, and, often, sexual. His possessiveness and panoply of indiscriminate negative emotions – transformations of aggression, such as rage and envy – hinder his ability to act as a "good enough" parent. His propensities for reckless behaviour, substance abuse, and sexual deviance endanger the child's welfare, or even his or her life.

Also read:

Beware the Children
Leveraging the Children
Narcissistic Parents
How Can I Save My Child from His Father's Narcissism?

*"He is angry if I don't work and make money, he is angry if I do work and am not instantly available for his phone calls. He is financially controlling, there is no joint account or credit cards, no co-mingled funds. The money he does contribute to household expenses, he makes me account for as if I am a child. He either calls me 5 times a day, or 'punishes' by not calling at all."*

Your husband is a classic abuser. Controlling you and your money is only part of it.

Perhaps the first telltale sign is the abuser's alloplastic defences – his tendency to blame every mistake of his, every failure, or mishap on others, or on the world at large. Be tuned: does he assume personal responsibility? Does he admit his faults and miscalculations? Or does he keep blaming you, the cab driver, the waiter, the weather, the government, or fortune for his predicament?

Is he hypersensitive, picks up fights, feels constantly slighted, injured, and insulted? Does he rant incessantly? Does he treat animals and children impatiently or cruelly and does he express negative and aggressive emotions towards the weak, the poor, the needy, the sentimental, and the disabled? Does he confess to having a history of battering or violent offences or behaviour? Is his language vile and infused with expletives, threats, and hostility?

Next thing: is he too eager? Does he push you to marry him having dated you only twice? Is he planning on having children on your first date? Does he immediately cast you in the role of the love of his life? Is he pressing you for exclusivity, instant intimacy, almost rapes you and acts jealous when you as much as cast a glance at another male? Does he inform you that, once you get hitched, you should abandon your studies or resign your job (forgo your personal autonomy)?

Does he respect your boundaries and privacy? Does he ignore your wishes (for instance, by choosing from the menu or selecting a movie without as much as consulting you)? Does he disrespect your boundaries and treats you as an object or an instrument of gratification (materializes on your doorstep unexpectedly or calls you often prior to your date)? Does he go through your personal belongings while waiting for you to get ready?

Does he control the situation and you compulsively? Does he insist to ride in his car, holds on to the car keys, the money, the theatre tickets, and even your bag? Does he disapprove if you are away for too long (for instance when you go to the powder room)? Does he interrogate you when you return ("Have you seen anyone interesting?") – or make lewd "jokes" and remarks? Does he hint that, in future, you would need his permission to do things – even as innocuous as meeting a friend or visiting with your family?

Does he act in a patronizing and condescending manner and criticizes you often? Does he emphasize your minutest faults (devalues you) even as he exaggerates your talents, traits, and skills (idealizes you)? Is he wildly unrealistic in his expectations from you, from himself, from the budding relationship, and from life in general?

Does he tell you constantly that you "make him feel" good? Don't be impressed. Next thing, he may tell you that you "make" him feel bad, or that you make him feel violent, or that you "provoke" him. "Look what you made me do!" is an abuser's ubiquitous catchphrase.

Does he find sadistic sex exciting? Does he have fantasies of rape or paedophilia? Is he too forceful with you in and out of the sexual intercourse? Does he like hurting you physically or finds it amusing? Does he abuse you verbally – does he curse you, demeans you, calls you ugly or inappropriately diminutive names, or persistently criticizes you? Does he then switch to being saccharine and "loving", apologizes profusely and buys you gifts?

If you have answered "yes" to ANY of the above – stay away! He is an abuser.

Also read:

The Tocsins of Abuse - How to Spot an Abuser on Your First Date
The Silver Pieces of the Narcissist

*"He has no long-term friends or any real social circle. Calls people friends, and then says 'I didn't realize they've had two children...'"*

Narcissists have no friends – only Sources of Narcissistic Supply and people they can exploit and abuse.

I compared Narcissistic Supply to drugs because of the almost involuntary and always-unrestrained nature of the pursuit involved in securing it. The narcissist is no better or worse (morally speaking) than others. But he lacks the ability to empathize precisely because he is obsessed with the maintenance of his delicate inner balance through the (ever-increasing) consumption of Narcissistic Supply.

The narcissist rates people around him according to whether they can provide him with Narcissistic Supply or not. As far as the narcissist is concerned, those who fail this simple test do not exist. They are two-dimensional cartoon figures. Their feelings, needs and fears are of no interest or importance.

Potential Sources of Supply are then subjected to a meticulous examination and probing of the volume and quality of the Narcissistic Supply that they are likely to provide. The narcissist nurtures and cultivates these people. He caters to their needs, desires, and wishes. He considers their emotions. He encourages those aspects of their personality that are likely to enhance their ability to provide him with his much needed supply. In this very restricted sense, he regards and treats them as "human". This is be his way of "maintaining and servicing" his Supply Sources. Needless to say that he loses any and all interest in them and in their needs once he decides that they are no longer able to supply him with what he needs: an audience, adoration, witnessing (memory). The same reaction is provoked by any behaviour judged by the narcissist to be narcissistically injurious.

The narcissist coldly evaluates tragic circumstances. Will they allow him to extract Narcissistic Supply from people affected by the tragedy?

A narcissist, for instance, will give a helping hand, console, guide, share grief, encourage another hurting person only if that person is important, powerful, has access to other important or powerful people, or to the media, has a following, etc.

The same applies if helping, consoling, guiding, or encouraging that person is likely to win the narcissist applause, approval, adoration, a following, or some other kind of Narcissistic Supply from on-lookers and witnesses to the interaction. The act of helping another person must be documented and thus transformed into narcissistic nourishment.

Otherwise the narcissist is not concerned or interested. The narcissist has no time or energy for anything, except the next narcissistic fix, no matter what the price is and who is trampled upon.

Also read:

Exploitation by a Narcissist
A Case Study
A Letter about Trust
The Guilt of Others
The Narcissist and His Family
The Victims of the Narcissist
Narcissism by Proxy
Narcissists in Positions of Authority
Responsibility and Other Matters
Is the Narcissist Ever Sorry?
Narcissistic Confinement
Narcissistic Immunity
Narcissists and Social Institutions
Crime and Punishment
The Ubiquitous Narcissist
The Narcissist in Court
The Narcissist in the Workplace

*"His family is a mess. His sister in therapy for 30 years, himself for more than 10 years. He says he could care less if his mother was dead or alive, then he goes to great extreme to show involvement in unreasonable errands for her. He says his mother 'emotionally' abandoned him at age 7-8. He says he went the longest distance to college to get away from her. He says his mother let his older brother beat him, and then blamed him."*

Narcissists often hail from dysfunctional families.

Parents (Primary Objects) and, more specifically, mothers are the first agents of socialization. It is through his mother that the child explores the answers to the most important existential questions, which shape his entire life. How loved one is, how loveable, how independent can one become, how guilty one should feel for wanting to become autonomous, how predictable is the world, how much abuse should one expect in life and so on. To the infant, the mother, is not only an object of dependence (survival is at stake), love and adoration. It is a representation of the "universe" itself. It is through her that the child first exercises his senses: the tactile, the olfactory, and the visual. Later on, she is the subject of his nascent sexual cravings (if a male) – a diffuse sense of wanting to merge, physically, as well as spiritually. This object of love is idealized and internalized and becomes part of our conscience (Superego). For better or for worse, it is the yardstick, the benchmark. One forever compares oneself, one's identity, one's actions and omissions, one's achievements, one's fears and hopes and aspirations to this mythical figure.

Growing up (and, later, attaining maturity and adulthood) entails the gradual detachment from the mother. At first, the child begins to shape a more realistic view of her and incorporates the mother's shortcomings and disadvantages in this modified version. The more ideal, less realistic and earlier picture of the mother is stored and becomes part of the child's psyche. The later, less cheerful, more realistic view enables the infant to define his own identity and gender identity and to "go out to the world". Partly abandoning mother is the key to an independent exploration of the world, to personal autonomy and to a strong sense of self. Resolving the sexual complex and the resulting conflict of being attracted to a forbidden figure – is the second, determining, step. The (male) child must realize that his mother is "off-limits" to him sexually (and emotionally, or psychosexually) and that she "belongs" to his father (or to other males). He must thereafter choose to imitate his father in order to win, in the future, someone like his mother. This is an oversimplified description of the very intricate psychodynamic processes involved – but this, still, is the gist of it all. The third (and final) stage of letting go of the mother is reached during the delicate period of adolescence. One then seriously ventures out and, finally, builds and secures one's own world, replete with a new "mother-lover". If any of these phases is thwarted – the process of differentiation is not be successfully completed, no autonomy or coherent self are achieved and dependence and "infantilism" characterize the unlucky person.

What determines the success or failure of these developments in one's personal history? Mostly, one's mother. If the mother does not "let go" - the child does not go. If the mother herself is the dependent, narcissistic type – the growth prospects of the child are, indeed, dim.

There are numerous mechanisms, which mothers use to ensure the continued presence and emotional dependence of their offspring (of both sexes).

The mother can cast herself in the role of the eternal victim, a sacrificial figure, who dedicated her life to the child (with the implicit or explicit proviso of reciprocity: that the child dedicate his life to her). Another strategy is to treat the child as an extension of the mother or, conversely, to treat herself as an extension of the child. Yet another tactic is to create a situation of "folie-a-deux" (the mother and child united against external threats), or an atmosphere suffused with sexual and erotic insinuations, leading to an illicit psychosexual bonding between mother and child. In the latter case, the adult's ability to interact with members of the opposite sex is gravely impaired and the mother is perceived as envious of any feminine influence other than hers. The mother criticizes the women in her offspring's life pretending to do so in order to protect him from dangerous liaisons or from ones which are "beneath him" ("You deserve more."). Other mothers exaggerate their neediness: they emphasize their financial dependence and lack of resources, their health problems, their emotional barrenness without the soothing presence of the child, their need to be protected against this or that (mostly imaginary) enemy. Guilt is a prime mover in the perverted relationships of such mothers and their children.

The death of the mother is, therefore, both a devastating shock and a deliverance. The reactions are ambiguous, to say the least. The typical adult who mourns his dead mother usually is exposed to such emotional duality. This ambiguity is the source of our guilt feelings. With a person who is abnormally attached to his mother, the situation is more complicated. He feels that he has a part in her death, that he is partly to blame, responsible, did not behave right and to the utmost of his ability. He is glad to be liberated and feels guilty and punishable because of it. He feels sad and elated, naked and powerful, exposed to dangers and omnipotent, about to disintegrate and to be newly integrated. These, precisely, are the emotional reactions to a successful therapy. The process of healing is, thus, started.

Also read:
The Development of the Narcissist
Narcissism - The Psychopathological Default
The Narcissist's Mother
The Inverted Narcissist
Narcissists, Inverted Narcissists and Schizoids

*"He hid his religion from me, then later claimed it was so important that it was one of the reasons he left."*

God is everything the narcissist ever wants to be: omnipotent, omniscient, omnipresent, admired, much discussed, and awe inspiring. God is the narcissist's wet dream, his ultimate grandiose fantasy. But God comes handy in other ways as well.

The narcissist alternately idealizes and devalues figures of authority.

In the idealization phase, he strives to emulate them, he admires them, imitate them (often ludicrously), and defends them. They cannot go wrong, or be wrong. The narcissist regards them as bigger than life, infallible, perfect, whole, and brilliant. But as the narcissist's unrealistic and inflated expectations are inevitably frustrated, he begins to devalue his former idols.

Now they are "human" (to the narcissist, a derogatory term). They are small, fragile, error-prone, pusillanimous, mean, dumb, and mediocre. The narcissist goes through the same cycle in his relationship with God, the quintessential authority figure.

But often, even when disillusionment and iconoclastic despair have set in – the narcissist continues to pretend to love God and follow Him. The narcissist maintains this deception because his continued proximity to God confers on him authority. Priests, leaders of the congregation, preachers, evangelists, cultists, politicians, intellectuals – all derive authority from their allegedly privileged relationship with God.

Religious authority allows the narcissist to indulge his sadistic urges and to exercise his misogynism freely and openly. Such a narcissist is likely to taunt and torment his followers, hector and chastise them, humiliate and berate them, abuse them spiritually, or even sexually. The narcissist whose source of authority is religious is looking for obedient and unquestioning slaves upon whom to exercise his capricious and wicked mastery. The narcissist transforms even the most innocuous and pure religious sentiments into a cultish ritual and a virulent hierarchy. He prays on the gullible. His flock become his hostages.

Religious authority also secures the narcissist's Narcissistic Supply. His coreligionists, members of his congregation, his parish, his constituency, his audience – are transformed into loyal and stable Sources of Narcissistic Supply. They obey his commands, heed his admonitions, follow his creed, admire his personality, applaud his personal traits, satisfy his needs (sometimes even his carnal desires), revere and idolize him.

Moreover, being a part of a "bigger thing" is very gratifying narcissistically. Being a particle of God, being immersed in His grandeur, experiencing His power and blessings first hand, communing with him – are all Sources of unending Narcissistic Supply. The narcissist becomes God by observing His commandments, following His instructions, loving Him, obeying Him, succumbing to Him, merging with Him, communicating with Him – or even by defying him (the bigger the narcissist's enemy – the more grandiosely important the narcissist feels).

Like everything else in the narcissist's life, he mutates God into a kind of inverted narcissist. God becomes his dominant Source of Supply. He forms a personal relationship with this overwhelming and overpowering entity – in order to overwhelm and overpower others. He becomes God vicariously, by the proxy of his relationship with Him. He idealizes God, then devalues Him, then abuses him. This is the classic narcissistic pattern and even God himself cannot escape it.

Also read:

It is My World, Who are You?
I Cannot Forgive
For the Love of God
Narcissists in Positions of Authority

*"He lies, even the smallest things."*

Confabulations are an important part of life. They serve to heal emotional wounds or to prevent ones from being inflicted in the first place. They prop-up the confabulator's self-esteem, regulate his (or her) sense of self-worth, and buttress his (or her) self-image. They serve as organizing principles in social interactions.

Father's wartime heroism, mother's youthful good looks, one's oft-recounted exploits, erstwhile alleged brilliance, and past purported sexual irresistibility – are typical examples of white, fuzzy, heart-warming lies wrapped around a shrivelled kernel of truth.

But the distinction between reality and fantasy is rarely completely lost. Deep inside, the healthy confabulator knows where facts end and wishful thinking takes over. Father acknowledges he was no war hero, though he did his share of fighting. Mother understands she was no ravishing beauty, though she may have been attractive. The confabulator realizes that his recounted exploits are overblown, his brilliance exaggerated, and his sexual irresistibility a myth.

Such distinctions never rise to the surface because everyone – the confabulator and his audience alike – have a common interest to maintain the confabulation. To challenge the integrity of the confabulator or the veracity of his confabulations is to threaten the very fabric of family and society. Human intercourse is built around such entertaining deviations from the truth.

This is where the narcissist differs from others (from "normal" people).

His very self is a piece of fiction concocted to fend off hurt and to nurture the narcissist's grandiosity. He fails in his "reality test" – the ability to distinguish the actual from the imagined. The narcissist fervently believes in his own infallibility, brilliance, omnipotence, heroism, and perfection. He doesn't dare confront the truth and admit it even to himself.

Moreover, he imposes his personal mythology on his nearest and dearest. Spouse, children, colleagues, friends, neighbours – sometimes even perfect strangers – must abide by the narcissist's narrative or face his wrath. The narcissist countenances no disagreement, alternative points of view, or criticism. To him, confabulation IS reality.

The coherence of the narcissist's dysfunctional and precariously-balanced personality depends on the plausibility of his stories and on their acceptance by his Sources of Narcissistic Supply. The narcissist invests an inordinate time in substantiating his tales, collecting "evidence", defending his version of events, and in re-interpreting reality to fit his scenario. As a result, most narcissists are self-delusional, obstinate, opinionated, and argumentative.

The narcissist's lies are not goal-orientated. This is what makes his constant dishonesty both disconcerting and incomprehensible. The narcissist lies at the drop of a hat, needlessly, and almost ceaselessly. He lies in order to avoid the Grandiosity Gap – when the abyss between fact and (narcissistic) fiction becomes too gaping to ignore.

The narcissist lies in order to preserve appearances, uphold fantasies, support the tall (and impossible) tales of his False Self and extract Narcissistic Supply from unsuspecting sources, who are not yet on to him. To the narcissist, confabulation is not merely a way of life – but life itself.

We are all conditioned to let other indulge in pet delusions and get away with white, not too egregious, lies. The narcissist makes use of our socialization. We dare not confront or expose him, despite the outlandishness of his claims, the improbability of his stories, the implausibility of his alleged accomplishments and conquests. We simply turn the other cheek, or meekly avert our eyes, often embarrassed.

Moreover, the narcissist makes clear, from the very beginning, that it is his way or the highway. His aggression – even violent streak – are close to the surface. He may be charming in a first encounter – but even then there are telltale signs of pent-up abuse. His interlocutors sense this impending threat and avoid conflict by acquiescing with the narcissist's fairy tales. Thus he imposes his private universe and virtual reality on his milieu – sometimes with disastrous consequences.

Also read:

Pseudologica Fantastica

The Narcissist's Reality Substitutes

The Narcissist's Confabulated Life

The Discontinuous Narcissist

The Weapon of Language

Ideas of Reference

The Delusional Way Out

*"His male kung fu teacher seems to be strangely overly important to him."*

Narcissists often try to imitate and emulate "narcissistic role models". They adopt their hero's mannerisms, speech patterns, dress code, gestures, and even biography.

Being in a position of authority secures the Sources of Narcissistic Supply. Fed by the awe, fear, subordination, admiration, adoration and obedience of his underlings, parish, or patients – the narcissist thrives in such circumstances. The narcissist aspires to acquire authority by any means available to him. He may achieve this by making use of some outstanding traits or skills such as his intelligence, or through an asymmetry built into a relationship. The narcissistic medical doctor or mental health professional and his patients, the narcissistic guide, teacher, or mentor and his students, the narcissistic leader, guru, pundit, or psychic and his followers or admirers, or the narcissistic business tycoon, boss, or employer and his subordinates – all are instances of such asymmetries. The rich, powerful, more knowledgeable narcissist occupy a Pathological Narcissistic Space.

These types of relationships – based on the unidirectional and unilateral flow of Narcissistic Supply – border on abuse. The narcissist, in pursuit of an ever-increasing supply, of an ever-larger dose of adoration, and an ever-bigger fix of attention – gradually loses his moral constraints. With time, it gets harder to obtain Narcissistic Supply. The sources of such supply are human and they become weary, rebellious, tired, bored, disgusted, repelled, or plainly amused by the narcissist's incessant dependence, his childish craving for attention, his exaggerated or even paranoid fears which lead to obsessive-compulsive behaviours. To secure their continued collaboration in the procurement of his much-needed supply – the narcissist might resort to emotional extortion, straight blackmail, abuse, or misuse of his authority.

The temptation to do so, though, is universal. No doctor is immune to the charms of certain female patients, nor are university professors a sexual. What prevent them from immorally, cynically, callously and consistently abusing their position are ethical imperatives embedded in them through socialization and empathy. They learned the difference between right and wrong and, having internalized it, they choose right when they face a moral dilemma. They empathize with other human beings, "putting themselves in their shoes", and refrain from doing unto others what they do not wish to be done to them.

It is in these two crucial points that narcissists differ from other humans.

Their socialization process – usually the product of problematic early relationships with Primary Objects (parents, or caregivers) – is often perturbed and results in social dysfunctioning. And they are incapable of empathizing: humans are there only to supply them with Narcissistic Supply. Those unfortunate humans who do not comply with this overriding dictum must be made to alter their ways and if even this fails, the narcissist loses interest in them and they are classified as "sub-human, animals, service-providers, functions, symbols" and worse. Hence the abrupt shifts from over-valuation to devaluation of others. While bearing the gifts of Narcissistic Supply – the "other" is idealized by the narcissist. The narcissist shifts to the opposite pole (devaluation) when Narcissistic Supply dries up or when he estimates that it is about to.

As far as the narcissist is concerned, there is no moral dimension to abusing others – only a pragmatic one: will he be punished for doing so? The narcissist is atavistically responsive to fear and lacks any in-depth understanding of what it is to be a human being. Trapped in his pathology, the narcissist resembles an alien on drugs, a junkie of Narcissistic Supply devoid of the kind of language, which renders human emotions intelligible.

Also read:

Narcissistic Leaders
Narcissism in the Boardroom
Narcissists in Positions of Authority
A Great Admiration
The Green Eyed Narcissist

*"He has a huge need to be humorous, often making up his own jokes (that are not funny) then when people don't laugh, he blames them for not getting it."*

A narcissist rarely engages in self-directed, self-deprecating humour. If he does, he expects to be contradicted, rebuked and rebuffed by his listeners ("Come on, you are actually quite handsome!"), or to be commended or admired for his courage or for his wit and intellectual acerbity ("I envy your ability to laugh at yourself!"). As everything else in a narcissist's life, his sense of humour is deployed in the interminable pursuit of Narcissistic Supply.

The absence of Narcissistic Supply (or the impending threat of such an absence) is, indeed, a serious matter. It is the narcissistic equivalent of mental death. If prolonged and unmitigated, such absence can lead to the real thing: physical death, a result of suicide, or of a psychosomatic deterioration of the narcissist's health. Yet, to obtain Narcissistic Supply, one must be taken seriously and to be taken seriously one must be the first to take oneself seriously. Hence the gravity with which the narcissist contemplates his life. This lack of levity and of perspective and proportion characterize the narcissist and set him apart.

The narcissist firmly believes that he is unique and that he is thus endowed because he has a mission to fulfil, a destiny, a meaning to his life. The narcissist's life is a part of history, of a cosmic plot and it constantly tends to thicken. Such a life deserves only the most serious attention. Moreover, every particle of such an existence, every action or inaction, every utterance, creation, or composition, indeed every thought, are bathed in this cosmic meaningfulness. They all lead down the paths of glory, of achievement, of perfection, of ideals, of brilliance. They are all part of a design, a pattern, a plot, which inexorably and unstoppably lead the narcissist on to the fulfilment of his task. The narcissist may subscribe to a religion, to a belief, or to an ideology in his effort to understand the source of this strong feeling of uniqueness. He may attribute his sense of direction to God, to history, to society, to culture, to a calling, to his profession, to a value system. But he always does so with a straight face, with a firm conviction and with deadly seriousness.

And because, to the narcissist, the part is a holographic reflection of the whole – he tends to generalize, to resort to stereotypes, to induct (to learn about the whole from the detail), to exaggerate, finally to pathologically lie to himself and to others. This tendency of his, this self-importance, this belief in a grand design, in an all embracing and all-pervasive pattern – make him an easy prey to all manner of logical fallacies and con artistry. Despite his avowed and proudly expressed rationality the narcissist is besieged by superstition and prejudice. Above all, he is a captive of the false belief that his uniqueness destines him to carry a mission of cosmic significance.

All these make the narcissist a volatile person. Not merely mercurial – but fluctuating, histrionic, unreliable, and disproportional. That which has cosmic implications calls for cosmic reactions. The person with an inflated sense of self-import, will react in an inflated manner to threats, greatly inflated by his imagination and by the application to them of his personal myth. On a cosmic scale, the daily vagaries of life, the mundane, the routine are not important, even damagingly distracting. This is the source of his feelings of exceptional entitlement. Surely, engaged as he is in securing the well being of humanity by the exercise of his unique faculties – the narcissist deserves special treatment! This is the source of his violent swings between opposite behaviour patterns and between devaluation and idealization of others. To the narcissist, every minor development is nothing less than a new stage in his life, every adversity, a conspiracy to upset his progress, every setback an apocalyptic calamity, every irritation the cause for outlandish outbursts of rage. He is a man of the extremes and only of the extremes. He may learn to efficiently suppress or hide his feelings or reactions – but never for long. In the most inappropriate and inopportune moment, you can count on the narcissist to explode, like a wrongly wound time bomb. And in between eruptions, the narcissistic volcano daydreams, indulges in delusions, plans his victories over an increasingly hostile and alienated environment. Gradually, the narcissist becomes more paranoid – or more aloof, detached and dissociative.

In such a setting, you must admit, there is not much room for a sense of humour.

Also read:

*"He used the term 'narcissistic personality' and defined it to me, apparently after one of his counselling sessions."*

Narcissists have little introspection, never admit to faults, and perceive any suggestion of n incipient pathology as a threat. Many of them are actually PROUD of their illness. They feel that it makes them unique.

Sometimes the narcissist does gain awareness and knowledge of his predicament - typically in the wake of a life crisis (divorce, bankruptcy, incarceration, near death experience, death in the family). But, in the absence of an emotional correlate, of feelings, such merely cognitive awakening is useless. It does not yield insight. The dry facts do not bring about a transformation, let alone healing.

The introspection of the narcissist is emotionless, akin to the listing of an inventory of his "good" and "bad" sides and without any commitment to change. It does not enhance his ability to empathize, nor does it inhibit his propensity to exploit others and discard them when their usefulness is over. It does not tamper his overpowering and raging sense of entitlement, nor does it deflate his grandiose fantasies.

The narcissist's introspection is a futile and arid exercise at bookkeeping, a soulless bureaucracy of the psyche and, in its own way, even more chilling that the alternative: a narcissist blissfully unaware of his own disorder.

Also read:

Return

# THE AUTHOR

## Shmuel (Sam) Vaknin

## Curriculum Vitae

Born in 1961 in Qiryat-Yam, Israel.

Served in the Israeli Defence Force (1979-1982) in training and education units.

## Education

1970-1978: Completed nine semesters in the Technion – Israel Institute of Technology, Haifa.

1982-3: Ph.D. in Philosophy (dissertation: "Time Asymmetry Revisited") – Pacific Western University, **California**, USA.

1982-5: Graduate of numerous courses in Finance Theory and International Trading in the UK and USA.

Certified E-Commerce Concepts Analyst by Brainbench.

Certified in Psychological Counselling Techniques by Brainbench.

Certified Financial Analyst by Brainbench.

Full proficiency in Hebrew and in English.

## Business Experience

*1980 to 1983*

Founder and co-owner of a chain of computerised information kiosks in Tel-Aviv, Israel.

*1982 to 1985*

Senior positions with the Nessim D. Gaon Group of Companies in Geneva, Paris and New-York (NOGA and APROFIM SA):

– Chief Analyst of Edible Commodities in the Group's Headquarters in Switzerland
– Manager of the Research and Analysis Division
– Manager of the Data Processing Division
– Project Manager of the Nigerian Computerised Census
– Vice President in charge of RND and Advanced Technologies
– Vice President in charge of Sovereign Debt Financing

*1985 to 1986*

Represented Canadian Venture Capital Funds in Israel.

## 1986 to 1987

General Manager of IPE Ltd. in London. The firm financed international multi-lateral countertrade and leasing transactions.

## 1988 to 1990

Co-founder and Director of "Mikbats-Tesuah", a portfolio management firm based in Tel-Aviv. Activities included large-scale portfolio management, underwriting, forex trading and general financial advisory services.

## 1990 to Present

Freelance consultant to many of Israel's Blue-Chip firms, mainly on issues related to the capital markets in Israel, Canada, the UK and the USA.

Consultant to foreign RND ventures and to Governments on macro-economic matters.

Freelance journalist in various media in the United States.

## 1990 to 1995

President of the Israel chapter of the Professors World Peace Academy (PWPA) and (briefly) Israel representative of the "Washington Times".

*1993 to 1994*

Co-owner and Director of many business enterprises:

– The Omega and Energy Air-Conditioning Concern
– AVP Financial Consultants
– Handiman Legal Services
  Total annual turnover of the group: 10 million USD.

Co-owner, Director and Finance Manager of COSTI
Ltd. – Israel's largest computerised information vendor
and developer. Raised funds through a series of private
placements locally in the USA, Canada and London.

*1993 to 1996*

Publisher and Editor of a Capital Markets Newsletter
distributed by subscription only to dozens of subscribers
countrywide.

In a legal precedent in 1995 – studied in business
schools and law faculties across Israel – was tried for
his role in an attempted takeover of Israel's Agriculture
Bank.

Was interned in the State School of Prison Wardens.

Managed the Central School Library, wrote, published
and lectured on various occasions.

Managed the Internet and International News
Department of an Israeli mass media group, "Ha-
Tikshoret and Namer".

Assistant in the Law Faculty in Tel-Aviv University (to Prof. S.G. Shoham).

## 1996 to 1999

Financial consultant to leading businesses in Macedonia, Russia and the Czech Republic.

Economic commentator in "Nova Makedonija", "Dnevnik", "Makedonija Denes", "Izvestia", "Argumenti i Fakti", "The Middle East Times", "The New Presence", "Central Europe Review", and other periodicals, and in the economic programs on various channels of Macedonian Television.

Chief Lecturer in courses in Macedonia organised by the Agency of Privatization, by the Stock Exchange, and by the Ministry of Trade.

## 1999 to 2002

Economic Advisor to the Government of the Republic of Macedonia and to the Ministry of Finance.

## 2001 to 2003

Senior Business Correspondent for United Press International (UPI).

## 2007 -

Associate Editor, Global Politician

Founding Analyst, The Analyst Network

Contributing Writer, The American Chronicle Media Group

Expert, Self-growth.com

*2007-2008*

Columnist and analyst in "Nova Makedonija", "Fokus", and "Kapital" (Macedonian papers and newsweeklies).

*2008-*

Member of the Steering Committee for the Advancement of Healthcare in the Republic of Macedonia

Advisor to the Minister of Health of Macedonia

Seminars and lectures on economic issues in various forums in Macedonia.

## Web and Journalistic Activities

Author of extensive Web sites in:

– Psychology ("Malignant Self Love") - An Open Directory Cool Site for 8 years.

– Philosophy ("Philosophical Musings"),

– Economics and Geopolitics ("World in Conflict and Transition").

Owner of the Narcissistic Abuse Study Lists and the Abusive Relationships Newsletter (more than 6,000 members).

Owner of the Economies in Conflict and Transition Study List , the Toxic Relationships Study List, and the Links and Factoid Study List.

Editor of mental health disorders and Central and Eastern Europe categories in various Web directories (Open Directory, Search Europe, Mentalhelp.net).

Editor of the Personality Disorders, Narcissistic Personality Disorder, the Verbal and Emotional Abuse, and the Spousal (Domestic) Abuse and Violence topics on Suite 101 and Bellaonline.

Columnist and commentator in "The New Presence", United Press International (UPI), InternetContent, eBookWeb, PopMatters, Global Politician, The Analyst Network, Conservative Voice, The American Chronicle Media Group, eBookNet.org, and "Central Europe Review".

## Publications and Awards

"Managing Investment Portfolios in States of Uncertainty", Limon Publishers, Tel-Aviv, 1988

"The Gambling Industry", Limon Publishers, Tel-Aviv, 1990

"Requesting My Loved One – Short Stories", Yedioth Aharonot, Tel-Aviv, 1997

"The Suffering of Being Kafka" (electronic book of Hebrew and English Short Fiction), Prague, 1998-2004

"The Macedonian Economy at a Crossroads – On the Way to a Healthier Economy" (dialogues with Nikola Gruevski), Skopje, 1998

"The Exporters' Pocketbook", Ministry of Trade, Republic of Macedonia, Skopje, 1999

"Malignant Self Love – Narcissism Revisited", Narcissus Publications, Prague, 1999-2007 (Read excerpts - click here)

The Narcissism, Psychopathy, and Abuse in Relationships Series
(E-books regarding relationships with abusive narcissists and psychopaths), Prague, 1999-2010

Personality Disorders Revisited (e-book about personality disorders), Prague, 2007

"After the Rain – How the West Lost the East", Narcissus Publications in association with Central Europe Review/CEENMI, Prague and Skopje, 2000

Winner of numerous awards, among them Israel's Council of Culture and Art Prize for Maiden Prose (1997), The Rotary Club Award for Social Studies (1976), and the Bilateral Relations Studies Award of the American Embassy in Israel (1978).

Hundreds of professional articles in all fields of finance and economics, and numerous articles dealing with geopolitical and political economic issues published in both print and Web periodicals in many countries.

Many appearances in the electronic media on subjects in philosophy and the sciences, and concerning economic matters.

**Write to Me:**
palma@unet.com.mk
narcissisticabuse-owner@yahoogroups.com

**My Web Sites:**

*Economy/Politics:*
http://ceeandbalkan.tripod.com/

*Psychology:*
http://www.narcissistic-abuse.com/

*Philosophy:*
http://philosophos.tripod.com/

*Poetry:*
http://samvak.tripod.com/contents.html

*Fiction:*
http://samvak.tripod.com/sipurim.html

Return

*Abused? Stalked? Harassed? Bullied? Victimized?*
*Afraid? Confused? Need HELP? DO SOMETHING ABOUT IT!*

Had a Narcissistic Parent?
Married to a Narcissist – or Divorcing One?
Afraid your children will turn out the same?
Want to cope with this pernicious, baffling condition?
OR
Are You a Narcissist – or suspect that You are one...
This book will teach you how to...
Cope, Survive, and Protect Your Loved Ones!
You should read...

## "Malignant Self Love - Narcissism Revisited"
The EIGHTH, REVISED PRINTING (January 2007) is now available!

**Nine additional e-books, All NEW Editions, JUST RELEASED!!!**
Malignant Self Love, Toxic Relationships,
Pathological Narcissism, Coping with Divorce,
The Narcissist and Psychopath in the Workplace – and MORE!!!

**Click on this link to purchase the PRINT BOOK and/or
the NINE E-BOOKS**
http://www.narcissistic-abuse.com/thebook.html

Sam Vaknin published the EIGHTH, REVISED IMPRESSION of his book about relationships with abusive narcissists, **"Malignant Self Love - Narcissism Revisited"**.

The book deals with the Narcissistic Personality Disorder and its effects on the narcissist and his nearest and dearest – in 102 frequently asked questions and two essays – a total of 600 pages!

## Print Edition from BARNES AND NOBLE and AMAZON

**Barnes and Noble** – "Malignant Self Love – Narcissism Revisited" EIGHTH, Revised, Impression (January 2007)

ON SALE starting at $40.45 !!!

INSTEAD OF the publisher's list price of $54.95 (including shipping and handling)!!!

That's more than $14 off the publisher's list price!!!!

Click on this link to purchase the paper edition:

http://search.barnesandnoble.com/bookSearch/isbnInquiry.asp?r=1&ISBN=9788023833843

And from **Amazon.com** – Click on this link:

http://www.amazon.com/exec/obidos/tg/detail/-/8023833847/

## Print Edition from the PUBLISHER

The previous revised impression of Sam Vaknin's "Malignant Self – Love - Narcissism Revisited".

Comes with an exclusive BONUS PACK (not available through Barnes and Noble or Amazon).

Contains the entire text: essays, frequently asked questions and appendices regarding pathological narcissism and the Narcissistic Personality Disorder (NPD).

The publisher charges the full list price – but throws into the bargain a bonus pack with hundreds of additional pages and seven free e-books.

Click on this link:

http://www.ccnow.com/cgi-local/cart.cgi?vaksam_MSL

Free excerpts from the EIGHTH, Revised Impression of **"Malignant Self Love – Narcissism Revisited"** are available as well as a free NEW EDITION of the Narcissism Book of Quotes

Click on this link to download the files:

http://www.narcissistic-abuse.com/freebooks.html

**"After the Rain – How the West Lost the East"**

The history, cultures, societies, and economies of countries in transition in the Balkans.

Click on this link to purchase this print book:

http://www.ccnow.com/cgi-local/cart.cgi?vaksam_ATR

## Electronic Books (e-books) from the Publisher

An *electronic book* is a computer file, sent to you as an attachment to an e-mail message. Just save it to your hard disk and click on the file to open, read, and learn!

1. **"Malignant Self Love – Narcissism Revisited"**
   Eighth, Revised Edition (January 2007)

The e-book version of Sam Vaknin's "Malignant Self – Love – Narcissism Revisited". Contains the entire text: essays, frequently asked questions (FAQs) and appendices regarding pathological narcissism and the Narcissistic Personality Disorder (NPD).

Click on this link to purchase the e-book:

http://www.ccnow.com/cgi-local/cart.cgi?vaksam_MSL-EBOOK

2. **"The Narcissism, Psychopathy, and Abuse in Relationships Series"** Eighth, Revised Edition (July 2010)

NINE e-books (more than 3000 pages), including the full text of "Malignant Self Love – Narcissism Revisited", regarding Pathological Narcissism, relationships with abusive narcissists and psychopaths, and the Narcissistic Personality Disorder (NPD).

Click on this link to purchase the EIGHT e-books:

http://www.ccnow.com/cgi-local/cart.cgi?vaksam_SERIES

3. **"Toxic Relationships – Abuse and its Aftermath"**
   Fourth Edition (February 2006)

How to identify abuse, cope with it, survive it, and deal with your abuser and with the system in divorce and custody issues.

Click on this link to purchase the e-book:

http://www.ccnow.com/cgi-local/cart.cgi?vaksam_ABUSE

4. **"The Narcissist and Psychopath in the Workplace"**
   (September 2006)

Identify abusers, bullies, and stalkers in the workplace (bosses, colleagues, suppliers, and authority figures) and learn how to cope with them effectively.

Click on this link to purchase the e-book:

http://www.ccnow.com/cgi-local/cart.cgi?vaksam_WORKPLACE

5. **"Abusive Relationships Workbook"** (February 2006)

Self-assessment questionnaires, tips, and tests for victims of abusers, batterers, and stalkers in various types of relationships.

Click on this link to purchase the e-book:

http://www.ccnow.com/cgi-local/cart.cgi?vaksam_WORKBOOK

6. **"Pathological Narcissism FAQs"**
   Eighth, Revised Edition (January 2007)

Dozens of Frequently Asked Questions regarding Pathological Narcissism, relationships with abusive narcissists, and the Narcissistic Personality Disorder.

Click on this link to purchase the e-book:

http://www.ccnow.com/cgi-local/cart.cgi?vaksam_FAQS

7. **"The World of the Narcissist"**
   Eighth, Revised Edition (January 2007)

A book-length psychodynamic study of pathological narcissism, relationships with abusive narcissists, and the Narcissistic Personality Disorder, using a new vocabulary.

Click on this link to purchase the e-book:

http://www.ccnow.com/cgi-local/cart.cgi?vaksam_ESSAY

## 8. "Excerpts from the Archives of the Narcissism List"

Hundreds of excerpts from the archives of the Narcissistic Abuse Study List regarding Pathological Narcissism, relationships with abusive narcissists, and the Narcissistic Personality Disorder (NPD).

Click on this link to purchase the e-book:

http://www.ccnow.com/cgi-local/cart.cgi?vaksam_EXCERPTS

## 9. "Diary of a Narcissist" (November 2005)

The anatomy of one man's mental illness – its origins, its unfolding, its outcomes.

Click on this link to purchase the e-book:

http://www.ccnow.com/cgi-local/cart.cgi?vaksam_JOURNAL

## 10. *"The Narcissist and Psychopath in Therapy"*

Can narcissists and psychopaths be cured? Can their behaviour be modified? How are these mental health disorders diagnosed?

Buy it from the publisher - click on this link:

http://www.ccnow.com/cgi-local/cart.cgi?vaksam_THERAPY

## 11. "After the Rain – How the West Lost the East"

The history, cultures, societies, and economies of countries in transition in the Balkans.

Click on this link to purchase the e-book:

http://www.ccnow.com/cgi-local/cart.cgi?vaksam_ATR-EBOOK

## Download Free Electronic Books

Click on this link:

http://www.narcissistic-abuse.com/freebooks.html

## More about the Books and Additional Resources

The Eighth, Revised Impression (January 2007) of the Print Edition of **"Malignant Self Love – Narcissism Revisited"** includes:

• The full text of "Malignant Self Love – Narcissism Revisited"

• The full text of 102 Frequently Asked Questions and Answers

- Covering all the dimensions of Pathological Narcissism and Abuse in Relationships
- An Essay – The Narcissist's point of view
- Bibliography
- 600 printed pages in a quality paper book
- Digital Bonus Pack! (available only when you purchase the previous edition from the Publisher) – Bibliography, three e-books, additional FAQs, appendices and more – hundreds of additional pages!

**Testimonials and Additional Resources**

You can read Readers' Reviews at the Barnes and Noble Web page dedicated to "Malignant Self Love" – HERE:

http://search.barnesandnoble.com/bookSearch/isbnInquiry.asp?r=1&ISBN=9788023833843

**Dozens of Links and Resources**

Click on these links:

The Narcissistic Abuse Study List

http://groups.yahoo.com/group/narcissisticabuse

The Toxic Relationships Study List

http://groups.yahoo.com/group/toxicrelationships

Abusive Relationships Newsletter

http://groups.google.com/group/narcissisticabuse

**Participate in Discussions about Abusive Relationships** - click on these links:

http://narcissisticabuse.ning.com/

http://www.runboard.com/bnarcissisticabuserecovery

http://thepsychopath.freeforums.org/

The Narcissistic Abuse Study List

http://health.groups.yahoo.com/group/narcissisticabuse/

The Toxic Relationships Study List

http://groups.yahoo.com/group/toxicrelationships

Abusive Relationships Newsletter

http://groups.google.com/group/narcissisticabuse/

Archived discussion threads - click on these links:

http://personalitydisorders.suite101.com/discussions.cfm

http://www.suite101.com/discussions.cfm/verbal_emotional_abuse

http://www.suite101.com/discussuions.cfm/spousal_domestic_abuse

**Links to Therapist Directories, Psychological Tests, NPD Resources, Support Groups for Narcissists and Their Victims, and Tutorials**

http://health.groups.yahoo.com/group/narcissisticabuse/message/5458

**Support Groups for Victims of Narcissists and Narcissists**

http://dmoz.org/Health/Mental_Health/Disorders/Personality/Narcissistic

*BE WELL, SAFE AND WARM WHEREVER YOU ARE!*

Sam Vaknin

Made in the USA
Monee, IL
16 January 2023

25340015R00229